Shallow Equality and Symbolic Jurisprudence in Multilingual Legal Orders

OXFORD STUDIES IN LANGUAGE AND LAW

Oxford Studies in Language and Law includes scholarly analyses and descriptions of language evidence in civil and criminal law cases as well as language issues arising in the area of statutes, statutory interpretation, courtroom discourse, jury instructions, and historical changes in legal language.

The Legal Language of Scottish Burghs: Standardization and Lexical Bundles (1380–1560)
Joanna Kopaczyk

"I'm Sorry for What I've Done": The Language of Courtroom Apologies
M. Catherine Gruber

Dueling Discourses: The Construction of Reality in Closing Arguments
Laura Felton Rosulek

Entextualizing Domestic Violence: Language Ideology and Violence Against Women in the Anglo-American Hearsay Principle
Jennifer Andrus

Speak English or What?: Codeswitching and Interpreter Use in New York City Small Claims Court
Philipp Sebastian Angermeyer

Law at Work: Studies in Legal Ethnomethods
Edited by Baudouin Dupret, Michael Lynch, and Tim Berard

Speaking of Language and Law: Conversations on the Work of Peter Tiersma
Edited by Lawrence M. Solan, Janet Ainsworth, and Roger W. Shuy

Confronting the Death Penalty: How Language Influences Jurors in Capital Cases
Robin Conley

Discursive Constructions of Consent in the Legal Process
Edited by Susan Ehrlich, Diana Eades, and Janet Ainsworth

From Truth to Technique at Trial: A Discursive History of Advocacy Advice Texts
Philip Gaines

Discourse, Identity, and Social Change in the Marriage Equality Debates
Karen Tracy

Translating the Social World for Law: Linguistic Tools for a New Legal Realism
Edited by Elizabeth Mertz, William K. Ford, and Gregory Matoesian

Conceptions in the Code: How Metaphors Explain Legal Challenges in Digital Times
Stefan Larsson

Deceptive Ambiguity by Police and Prosecutors
Roger W. Shuy

Legal Integration and Language Diversity: Rethinking Translation in EU Lawmaking
C. J. W. Baaij

Legal Translation Outsourced
Juliette R. Scott

Shallow Equality and Symbolic Jurisprudence in Multilingual Legal Orders
Janny H. C. Leung

Shallow Equality and Symbolic Jurisprudence in Multilingual Legal Orders

Janny H. C. Leung

OXFORD
UNIVERSITY PRESS

OXFORD
UNIVERSITY PRESS

Oxford University Press is a department of the University of Oxford. It furthers the University's objective of excellence in research, scholarship, and education by publishing worldwide. Oxford is a registered trade mark of Oxford University Press in the UK and certain other countries.

Published in the United States of America by Oxford University Press
198 Madison Avenue, New York, NY 10016, United States of America.

Library of Congress Cataloging-in-Publication Data
Names: Leung, Janny H. C., author.
Title: Shallow equality and symbolic jurisprudence in multilingual legal orders / Janny H. C. Leung.
Description: New York : Oxford University Press, 2019. |
Series: Oxford studies in language and law | Includes bibliographical references and index.
Identifiers: LCCN 2018031469 (print) | LCCN 2018041224 (ebook) |
ISBN 9780190210342 (updf) | ISBN 9780190210359 (online content) |
ISBN 9780190930608 (epub) | ISBN 9780190210335 (hardback)
Subjects: LCSH: Linguistic rights. | Multilingualism. | Linguistic minorities—Legal status, laws, etc. | Law—Language. | Discrimination in language. | Language policy. | BISAC: LANGUAGE ARTS & DISCIPLINES / Linguistics / Sociolinguistics. | LANGUAGE ARTS & DISCIPLINES / Linguistics / Historical & Comparative.
Classification: LCC K3259 (ebook) | LCC K3259 .L48 2019 (print) |
DDC 340/.14—dc23
LC record available at https://lccn.loc.gov/2018031469

9 8 7 6 5 4 3 2 1

Printed by Sheridan Books, Inc., United States of America

For the struggle against disciplinary boundaries.

CONTENTS

PART II Consequences

ACKNOWLEDGMENTS

This book would not exist if my colleague Christopher Hutton did not infect me with the idea that studying law is "fun." Two post-doctoral degrees later, my exploration in language and law continues. His thirst for knowledge, characteristic humility, caring for humanity, and endless patience have been a constant source of inspiration.

I am indebted to Alan Durant, a long-term collaborator whom I have learnt a great deal from. I have not met a more conscientious academic and a more detail-minded thinker, writer, and reader.

I am also grateful to Janet Ainsworth, Lawrence Solan, Peter Goodrich, and William Alford for their unfailing support, continuous encouragement, and professional guidance at different stages of my intellectual pursuit.

The manuscript has benefited from my discussions with Daniel Markovits and Michael Reisman from Yale Law School; constructive feedback I have received from Brook Bolander, Christopher Hutton, and other colleagues from the School of English and Faculty of Law at the University of Hong Kong; as well as editorial support from Hallie Stebbins and Hannah Doyle at Oxford University Press.

My gratitude extends to Jennifer Allison (librarian from the Harvard Law School Library), and my research assistants Brian Chan, Zena Prodromou, Patrick Jiang, and Matthew Yeung.

The time and resources required for the undertaking of this project were made possible by the generous support from a Hong Kong government grant (HKU 747812H of General Research Fund), a visiting scholarship from the Harvard Yenching Institute in 2013–2014, and a Universitas 21 fellowship that supported my stay at McGill Law School during the revision period of the book.

Last but not least, I would like to thank my parents, Leung Yung Fuk and Ng Man Yin, for their love and trust through the years, and Joseph Yang for always challenging me to think deeper and harder.

SYNOPSIS

Given that one can find linguistic diversity in any society, why have some states, but not others, decided to give official recognition to multiple languages? How has official multilingualism mushroomed, both nationally and internationally? What legal meaning is attached to such terms as *official language* and *national language*, and what consequences follow from such designations? Is linguistic equality an unqualified social good? To answer these questions, the two parts of this book respectively dissect the sociopolitical and ideological forces that create official multilingualism, and evaluate how official multilingualism affects public institutions and legal processes.

There are apparent strong tides against official multilingualism. Underlying the formation of modern states is the Romantic notion of nationalism, which calls for people who share the same cultural roots and speak the same language to come together and form a political unit. Linguistic nationalism idealizes linguistic homogeneity, which has been seen as vital to both democratic and economic development, for it is presumed to facilitate the creation of a shared public discourse and to enhance efficiency and productivity. Throughout most of modern history, minority communities have been expected to assimilate through learning and speaking the national language, which has a superior status over other languages. The rise of bilingual and multilingual polities raises the questions of whether this norm has been challenged, and whether there has been a shift in popular ideology in relation to language and sovereignty. Does the transition from linguistic supremacy toward linguistic equality mark the triumph of liberal multiculturalism and minority rights? Or is it better seen as the result of a political compromise necessitated by social realities, and strategic tolerance that is used to extract instrumental benefits? Part I of this book shows three things: first, the contemporary practice of official multilingualism distinguishes itself from historical approaches in linguistic management, including the monolingual model that emerged along with the modern nation-state. Second, the phenomenon is widespread and has penetrated polities at sub-state, state, and international levels. Its prevalence in post-colonial polities shows its perceived value as a conflict-avoidance strategy and as a means of mitigating colonial influence in nation-building. Adopting a national language policy for economic integration and trade, on the other hand, reflects increased acceptance of the commodification of national symbols under late capitalism. Third, official multilingualism is driven primarily by pragmatic concerns, rather than normative forces: the granting of official status to two or more languages can be used to achieve such goals as balancing rival powers, establishing political legitimacy, making a sovereignty claim, and pursuing economic interests. Such divergent functions may be performed because official language law works chiefly as a discursive resource, showcasing what I call a *symbolic jurisprudence*.

Part II of the book examines the practical impact of official multilingualism on public institutions and legal processes, and investigates how linguistic equality is applied on the ground. The study raises questions about the nature of official language rights and linguistic equality, the value of which is often taken for granted, thanks to, at least in part, the positive connotations that the terms *rights* and *equality* carry. The investigation shows that if linguistic equality – implicitly or explicitly provided by parallel multilingualism – is taken seriously, it calls for elaborate administrative effort in public institutions and carries a potential to clash with existing legal practices (from legal drafting and interpretation, to language rights in trial proceedings). However, such changes hardly ever disrupt the status quo. Moreover, formal adoption of multilingualism in sovereign states always falls short of full-fledged implementation and languages that receive equal official status are never really treated equally. Not only is there an issue of political goodwill and commitment, but linguistic equality habitually fails to compete with other priorities for resources, and in many practical domains it is not clear at all how linguistic equality is achievable without compromising other legal values and social good. But perhaps it is a good thing that linguistic equality has to compete with other social values and legal norms, because, as I argue, linguistic equality as claimed and practiced today is shallow in character, and *shallow equality* needs to be distinguished from popular conceptions of equality which form the foundation of liberal politics and have clear emancipatory potential. The book concludes that both symbolic jurisprudence and shallow equality are components of a policy of strategic pluralism that underlies official multilingualism. Although official multilingualism is not necessarily morally superior to official monolingualism, it can be legitimately used to pursue collective goals, but with the underlying risks that formal equality may disguise socioeconomic inequalities, and that over-investment in a multilingual regime may displace efforts that can bring about more progressive social change.

Introduction

LANGUAGE AND LAW IN THE WHIRLPOOL OF POLITICS

The day after former Ukrainian president Viktor Yanukovych was ousted, the first act in power by the new interim government was to revoke a controversial law. The targeted legislation, called *On the Principles of the State Language Policy*, makes any minority language an additional official language of a region if 10% or more of its population speaks it as a first language. Ukraine only has one state language (Ukrainian) but this law—seemingly politically neutral because its application is based purely on linguistic demographics—has the practical effect of making Russian a second official language in 13 out of 27 regions of the country, and was widely seen as a move to strengthen Yanukovych's Russian-speaking political base in the parliamentary election.[1] It was adopted in 2012 amid fistfights in the parliament, sparking violent riots and drawing concerns that it would threaten the sovereignty of the country.[2] The nationalist administration that took over power in 2014 vowed to restore Ukrainian to its position as the sole official language of the whole state. This would include the Autonomous Republic of Crimea, which had a majority Russian population and had a constitution[3] that guaranteed the official use of Russian and Crimean Tatar[4] along with Ukrainian. The move to repeal the

---

[1] In 2011, 42.8% of the population spoke the Ukrainian language as their first language, and 38.7% spoke Russian.

[2] Miriam Elder, "Ukrainians Protest against Russian Language Law," *The Guardian*, July 4, 2012, sec. World news, https://www.theguardian.com/world/2012/jul/04/ukrainians-protest-russian-language-law; David Stern, "Ukrainians Polarised over Language Law," *BBC News*, July 5, 2012, sec. Europe, http://www.bbc.com/news/world-europe-18725849.

[3] The 1998 Constitution of the Autonomous Republic of Crimea, which was in effect until it was replaced by the Constitution of the Republic of Crimea on April 11, 2014.

[4] A quarter of a million people identify themselves as Crimean Tatars. They are descended from a Turkic vassal state of the Ottoman Empire, known as the Crimean Khanate, between the 15th and 18th C.

law[5] catalyzed pro-Russian protests all around the country. It might have been the tipping point, as some analysts called it, that provided an opportunity for the Russian annexation of Crimea shortly thereafter.[6]

Crimea has a Russian-speaking majority (58.5%) but also a significant minority population who speak Ukrainian (24.4%) and Crimean Tatar (12.1%). These minorities are generally opposed to the Russian occupation. After the annexation, the Crimean-Tatar language has been promoted to a *state language*, alongside Ukrainian and Russian, on the peninsula. This formal elevation of legal status (from *official* to *state*) and assertion of linguistic equality, however, was accompanied by the Russian Supreme Court's decision to declare the self-governing body of the Crimean Tatars (known as the Mejlis) an extremist organization and to ban all its activities,[7] as well as United Nations reports of human rights abuses against pro-Ukrainian minorities, the tightening of political control (for example, seven popular Crimean Tatar media outlets were denied license to operate[8]), and dwindling minority linguistic rights[9] in the region.

The language politics in Ukraine is particularly intriguing in view of the complexities of its language situation. Census data provide a grossly simplified picture.[10] First, the boundary between Ukrainian and Russian is far from clearly drawn, both in terms of the languages and the ethnic identity of their speakers. The Ukrainian language is heavily Russified (in addition to having Polish influence), after five hundred years of foreign rule (especially under Russian decrees) in Ukraine. Bilingualism in Ukrainian and Russian is part of everyday life in major Ukrainian cities. A significant population of Ukrainians speak *surzhyk*, a sort of mixed language between Ukrainian and Russian.[11] Furthermore, the language that people identify with may not be their main language of communication or their first language. Survey data show that Ukrainians who claim that Ukrainian is their native language may nevertheless prefer to use Russian

---

[5] At the time of writing, a replacement bill—Draft Law on the State Language—is being tabled. In the meantime, other legislation has been passed to restrict the use of Russian in national television and education.

[6] Robert Hunter Wade, "The Ukraine Crisis Is Not What It Seems," *Le Monde Diplomatique (English Edition)*, 2015, https://mondediplo.com/outsidein/the-ukraine-crisis-is-not-what-it-seems.

[7] In September 2016. Office of the United Nations High Commissioner for Human Rights, "Report on the Human Rights Situation in Ukraine 16 August to 15 November 2016," n.d.

[8] Office of the United Nations High Commissioner for Human Rights, "Report on the Human Rights Situation in Ukraine 16 February to 15 May 2015," n.d.

[9] Directorate-General for External Policies, Policy Department, "The Situation of National Minorities in Crimea Following Its Annexation by Russia" (European Parliament, 2016).

[10] Census data rely on self-report and tend to be organized into mutually exclusive categories that bear little resemblance to reality.

[11] See Laada Bilaniuk, "A Typology of Surzhyk: Mixed Ukrainian-Russian Language," *International Journal of Bilingualism* 8, no. 4 (December 1, 2004): 409–25, https://doi.org/10.1177/13670069040080040101, for a typology of language use that the term has come to stand for.

in communication, that only just over half of Ukraine's residents who claim Russian as their native language declare themselves as ethnically Russian, and that some respondents reported mixed ethnic identities.[12] Finally, language ideologies about Ukrainian and Russian are multifaceted, due to the transition of what has been largely a class distinction (corresponding with education level and the urban vs. rural divide) into an ethnic one. Although the Russian language represented a dominating power in the Ukrainian history, the language is associated positively with prestige, modernity, and economic opportunities.[13] On the other hand, Ukrainian is viewed more as a peasant language, but at the same time it also indexes an ethnocultural and national identity.

Ukraine provides a dramatic example of how deeply language cuts into identity politics, illustrating that the power of language rests not only in its function as a communication tool, but also in its capacity for indexing identity.[14] Even where the change of an official language status does not impede communication in the public domain, the symbolic significance of such status alone can affirm some citizens' sense of self and offend others. It is not a coincidence that the enactment or amendment of official language law invariably happens at critical political junctures, when a shift of power takes place or threatens to take place.

The case of Ukraine also raises questions about the meaning of official language law and the nature of linguistic equality implied or proclaimed in such law. Both the inclusion of Russian as a second official language and its threatened expulsion later on were seen as extremely provocative. Status recognition or non-recognition may express deep political meaning—but it may also be taken only as political theater. For example, status equality among Russian, Ukrainian, and Crimean-Tatar conferred in the Crimean constitution after the Russian annexation is seen as a political act done only for show, creating a rhetoric of equality that exists only on paper. The actual linguistic freedom enjoyed by the Crimean Tatars appears to be diminishing, disclosing a disjuncture between legal recognition of official language status and political reality. The astonishing semiotic flexibility of official language status makes one wonder what purposes official language law is meant to serve.

For all the blood and sweat that have been shed over it, official language status is surprisingly void of legal meaning. Although the status label may be

---

[12] Volodymyr Kulyk, "Language Identity, Linguistic Diversity and Political Cleavages: Evidence from Ukraine," *Nations and Nationalism* 17, no. 3 (2011): 627–48; Volodymyr Kulyk, "Language Policy in Ukraine: What People Want the State to Do," *East European Politics and Societies* 27, no. 2 (May 1, 2013): 280–307, https://doi.org/10.1177/0888325412474684.

[13] Aneta Pavlenko, "Multilingualism in Post-Soviet Successor States," *Language and Linguistics Compass* 7, no. 4 (April 1, 2013): 262–71, https://doi.org/10.1111/lnc3.12024.

[14] Michael Silverstein, "Language Structure and Linguistic Ideology," in *The Elements: A Parasession on Linguistic Units and Levels*, ed. Paul R. Clyne, William F. Hanks, and Carol L. Hofbauer (Chicago: Chicago Linguistic Society, 1979), 193–247.

socially meaningful and may create all sorts of expectations, such as greater political rights, career advantage, respect, and access to public resources for speakers of an official language, its vagueness in legal meaning opens up possibilities for political use that is tangential to these expectations.

Making Sense of Multilingual Legal Orders

The Ukrainian case also exemplifies how societal multilingualism and law,[15] the former an ubiquitous condition and the latter a default governing regime of modern societies,[16] at times have a treacherous relationship. Such a relationship has not entirely escaped research attention, but systematic effort to study it has been circumscribed by disciplinary biases and boundaries. This book builds upon fragmented studies from various related disciplines (including but not limited to linguistics, law, sociology, anthropology, and political science) and tackles important questions that existing studies (see next section of this Introduction) have not confronted in depth.

Today more than 7,000 languages (according to ethnologue.com; estimates vary[17]) exist in fewer than 200 countries (193 of which are members of the United Nations since 2011). Societal multilingualism confronts almost every modern state—hardly any state governs a population that speaks only one language.[18] How do states deal with the gap between the ideal of one nation, one language, and the reality of their multilingual population? Why do some states become officially multilingual but not others? How do international organizations cope with linguistic diversity among their member states? In fact, since societal multilingualism has perpetuated throughout human civilization, why has official multilingualism become more prevalent today than ever before? Not all language policies have to acquire legal force, and not all legal intervention of

---

[15] Although the boundary of law has been increasingly challenged by legal anthropologists and sociolegal scholarship, for the purpose of this book I will restrict my discussion of legal multilingualism to official law (including state law, and codified practices in international organizations, regional unions, and international agreements), while acknowledging that official legal systems may be formalized to various degrees (consider, for example, customary law that may operate in parallel with a modernized legal system within the same polity). Sally Falk Moore, "Law and Anthropology," *Biennial Review of Anthropology* 6 (1969): 252–300; Sally Engle Merry, "Legal Pluralism," *Law and Society Review* 22, no. 5 (1988): 869–96.

[16] Philip R. Wood, *The Fall of the Priests and the Rise of the Lawyers* (Oxford; Portland, OR: Hart, 2016).

[17] No "accurate" estimate is possible, given the fuzzy boundary between languages. The delineation of languages in a dialectal spectrum is notoriously arbitrary.

[18] Iceland, Korea, and Japan are often cited as rare examples of monolingual states, not taking into account immigrants and visitors. The issue is debatable. For example, in Japan, Ainu and arguably Okinawan are distinct languages from Japanese, and in Korea, the Jeju language is recognized as a distinct local language. Although there used to be Gaelic- and Danish-speaking minorities in Iceland, it may be the closest thing to a monolingual state today.

language has to be done through conferring official status, so why law, why official status, and why multiplicity of official status? What role does law play in managing societal multilingualism, and why is official status often recognized constitutionally, by the supreme law of the land? In practical terms, what changes does such high-level legal recognition have the potential to create in public institutions, including legislature and judiciary? More specifically, how often do language rights flow from official status? What does effort, or sometimes the lack of effort, in translating official status into legally enforceable legislation say about official language law? Do language rights necessarily have emancipatory power, and is linguistic equality necessarily socially valuable?

Part I of the book, consisting of three chapters, focuses on forces that create official multilingualism. The first chapter historicizes the phenomenon. It discusses the various solutions that polities have used in the past to deal with linguistic diversity, and what social and political climates prompt the adoption of these different solutions. I highlight why some earlier solutions are unattractive or impractical in many modern states, and outline the distinctiveness of official multilingualism in the contemporary world. In order to give a sense of scale, the second chapter surveys officially bilingual or multilingual jurisdictions in the world today. The data lend empirical support to the historical analysis of the preceding chapter, and reveal patterns and trends in the global adoption of official multilingualism. Analysis of the data suggests that official multilingualism has become a core element of many national narratives as told through their constitutions. Contributing to the political stability of transitional states, official multilingualism is also very much a post-colonial legacy. Building from observations made in the preceding chapters, Chapter 3 assesses why official status is granted to multiple languages in some jurisdictions but not others, and offers a theory of how official multilingual law works. In my account of symbolic jurisprudence, official language law is usually vaguely drafted and provides the rhetorical resource to satisfy the demands of multiple audiences. The symbolic capital it raises can then be turned into political and economic capital. In international organizations, for example, equal recognition of dominant languages is used to balance centers of political power. For sovereign states, official multilingualism has become a popular strategy to subdue potential threats to territorial integrity, make assertions about sovereignty, and legitimize a political regime. There is also a growing trend to use state language law as a commodity in transnational economics, exemplifying capitalist logic in what is traditionally a terrain used to mark national pride and identity. Adoption of a global language into domestic law is used to trade for access to regional or global markets.

Part II of the book, consisting of four chapters, focuses on forces that may be created by official multilingualism. Chapters 4 to 7 are devoted to the practical dimensions of official multilingualism, illustrating the kind and degree of accommodation that has been made to implement linguistic equality, and what ripples and ruptures have been created in public institutions and legal processes. By focusing on different areas of legal implementation, these chapters offer a range of perspectives about why linguistic equality is a seemingly unachievable goal, and why official multilingualism does not tend to disrupt the status quo. These chapters are not meant to be encyclopedic, to detail the full range of impacts that official multilingualism may bring; nor do they investigate what impact is most typically observed among all bilingual and multilingual jurisdictions. If anything, the primary examples chosen are among jurisdictions that are most radically multilingual: either in terms of number of official languages, or in terms of their long history, elaborate institutional effort, and evident commitment to the cause. This approach allows us to gauge what the possible impacts of official multilingualism are, as it develops and matures. Chapter 4 compares efforts made by different jurisdictions in institutionalizing official multilingualism, such as turning constitutional aspirations into enforceable legislation and setting up administrative structures to ensure compliance. Significant legal weight is often conferred to official language law, but the strength of the law tends to dramatically weaken during implementation. This may have to do with the fact that although elaborate institutional structures have sometimes been developed, they are non-representational and bureaucratic in character. Chapter 5 deals with challenges in creating the texts of multilingual law, through translation, innovation in drafting practices, and linguistic and ideological engineering. Despite the formal equality offered to official languages in some jurisdictions, existent power hierarchies still seep through translation and drafting practices. Formal equality provided by the law cannot easily alter socially constructed ideologies about languages. Chapter 6 discusses inherent dilemmas in interpreting multilingual law. Since multilingual texts of the law are capable of having more than one literal meaning, multilingual jurisdictions that uphold the equal authenticity principle tend to move away from a textualist approach to legal interpretation. I argue that judicial discretion is widened in multilingual interpretation, and that emphasis on the equality of texts may paradoxically come into conflict with linguistic access to law. Given that official status creates the expectation of legal protection and rights, Chapter 7 investigates how language status may be translated into enforceable rights in legal proceedings. In states where official status serves a purely symbolic function, no language rights at all flow from it. Where language rights have been derived from official status, some of these rights, such as the right to a bilingual jury, threaten to challenge existing legal practices, raising questions about how linguistic equality should be valued against legal principles that come into conflict with it.

The final chapter, Chapter 8, takes stock of the insights developed in the preceding chapters and examines the nature of linguistic equality that is often proclaimed in multilingual jurisdictions. It critiques the shallow character of linguistic equality as posited and practiced in multilingual legal order today, and cautions against excessive optimism about the emancipatory potential of official language rights. Both shallow equality and symbolic jurisprudence are components of strategic pluralism, which prioritizes the interests of the polity before those of language communities.

The scope of issues that this book deals with does not fit neatly into a single academic discipline. Such is the nature of real world problems. In order to form a holistic picture, I have drawn concepts and ideas from not only from law and linguistics (including its subfields such as language policy and language politics), but also from anthropology, sociology, political theory, and history, and have attempted to converge cross-disciplinary knowledge wherever possible. I can, of course, in no way claim expertise in all of these fields. As such, errors and omissions are unavoidable, and I must acknowledge the limitations of my reach. Moreover, the multidimensionality of the subject matter defies a singular research method. I have used the best available sources of data that I have access to, which include constitutional and legislative documents, governmental publications and records, official communications and brochures, legal cases, news reports, official websites, speeches, and academic work. Most of the book comprises data-driven comparative study, and both quantitative and qualitative analyses have been performed wherever appropriate. Although the book makes reference to some ethnographic work done by others and myself, one obvious shortcoming is that it does not offer extensive, original fieldwork done on the ground (e.g., interviews and site observations). This is inevitable given the macroscopic focus and global coverage of the project. My analysis of the consequences of official multilingualism is also limited to public institutions (where the most direct impact of official multilingualism is supposed to take place), and does not extend to how these forces affect people's private lives, group identity, or inter-group relationships. Neither does it directly probe into people's subjective experiences of the law. In terms of theoretical contribution, I have no desire to propose a grand theory of official multilingualism, but I am eager to connect the dots and have endeavored to do enough theorizing to make sense of the phenomena that I have observed and reported. I encourage interested readers to supplement, refine, or challenge the account made in this book based on their work in different geographical locations.

My hope, despite all the potential imperfections and inherent risks of the project, is that this book lays the groundwork for mapping and dissecting a global phenomenon that has been under-documented, under-analyzed and under-theorized. Some of the references, even if incomplete, can give the reader a pointer in his or her explorations.

A Search for Meaning at a Multidisciplinary Crossroads

Linguistic diversity is a human condition. It is a task for social scientists, especially linguists, to describe and analyze the dynamics of a multilingual world, both at an individual and societal level. *Individual multilingualism*[19] refers to the acquisition by an individual of two or more languages, as a child or as an adult, concurrently or sequentially. Psycholinguists have looked into questions such as how these languages are represented in the brain, what factors affect their acquisition, and how proficiency may depend on task and situation of use. Educational sociolinguists have asked what encourages or discourages someone to learn a second language, and how interactions between teachers and students affect motivation. *Societal multilingualism*, on the other hand, describes societies where two or more languages are used. Societal multilingualism does not always go hand in hand with individual multilingualism. In fact, some linguistically diverse states offer multilingual services in order to serve its monolingual citizens. Discourse analysts have described how speakers switch among languages and have analyzed social forces that drive observable patterns of code-switching. Sociolinguists have studied how languages influence one another when they come into contact, how maintenance and shift of language is influenced by migration, social structure, and forces of assimilation, and how a language spreads.

There are linguists who resist the notion of *multilingualism* altogether, because this term assumes that "languages" can be counted, but in reality they have no clear boundaries. Some contemporary sociolinguists believe that given what we now know about linguistic variation and the situatedness of language use, common terms such as *language, English, multilingualism*, and *speakers of language X* are all derived from idealized notions of language and are thus fundamentally flawed.[20] While their account of the complexities of language use informs my discussion, this book will not shy away from using these idealized terms, for they clearly remain socially and legally relevant. We cannot afford to ignore the social reality created by social constructs. In fact, just about any

---

[19] A note on terminology: the terms *multilingualism* and *plurilingualism* are often used interchangeably, in everyday language and various academic disciplines. Council of Europe differentiates the terms by using *multilingualism* to refer to the presence of more than one language in a society, and *plurilingualism* to refer to the speaking of more than one language by an individual. Thus monolingual and plurilingual individuals may live in multilingual societies, and several monolingual groups may also form a multilingual society. This distinction will not be followed in this book. Due to the limited currency of the term *plurilingualism* (one indication being that it is flagged by my word processor as a non-word), I will stick to the terms *bilingualism* and *multilingualism* to describe both individuals and societies. In the interest of space, when I describe individuals and societies with two or more languages in this book, the term *multilingualism* will be used as a cover term for both bilingualism and multilingualism.

[20] Jan Blommaert, "Situating Language Rights: English and Swahili in Tanzania Revisited," *Journal of Sociolinguistics* 9, no. 3 (2005): 390–417.

social construct (with race and gender being prime examples) that is a source of identity politics and social division requires strategic essentialism.[21] For as long as these constructs remain pertinent, social progress cannot be made without public discussion about them.

Formal linguistics continues to treat its object of inquiry as an apolitical subject. Even in applied linguistics, few linguists see their research interest as having much to do with the law. However, not only is law a linguistic enterprise, it also both affects and responds to language phenomena that linguists are interested in. The intellectual neglect has been corrected to some extent by the emergent interdisciplinary field of language and law,[22] where researchers have attended to questions such as how linguistic evidence may be analyzed in criminal investigations,[23] what sources of miscommunication may become a barrier to justice,[24] and how language contributes to indeterminacy in legal texts.[25] Some of these interdisciplinary scholars tackle the way law handles individual and societal multilingualism, by for example pointing out the invisible power that court interpreters wield in influencing the outcome of a trial[26], or unveiling how failure to recognize cross-cultural differences in communication leads to miscarriage of justice.[27] Although incredibly informative and valuable work has

---

[21] Referring to the provisional acceptance of essentialist foundations for identity categories as a strategy for collective representation in order to pursue chosen political ends. Gayatri Chakravorty Spivak, *The Post-Colonial Critic: Interviews, Strategies, Dialogues* (London; New York: Routledge, 1990); Gayatri Chakravorty Spivak, "Subaltern Studies: Deconstructing Historiography," in *The Spivak Reader: Selected Works of Gayatri Chakravorty Spivak*, ed. D. Landry and G. MacLean (London and New York: Routledge, 1996), 203–36.

[22] Sometimes this field is identified as "forensic linguistics." I resist this term because I find the term *forensic* too narrow to capture the scope of work that is covered in the field. See Alan Durant and Janny H. C. Leung, *Language and Law: A Resource Book for Students* (Milton Park, Abingdon, Oxon; New York: Routledge, 2016).

[23] Malcolm Coulthard and Alison Johnson, eds., *The Routledge Handbook of Forensic Linguistics*, reprint ed. (London; New York: Routledge, 2013); Malcolm Coulthard, Alison Johnson, and David Wright, *An Introduction to Forensic Linguistics: Language in Evidence*, 2nd ed. (Abingdon, Oxon; New York: Routledge, 2016); John Gibbons, *Forensic Linguistics: An Introduction to Language in the Justice System* (Malden, MA: Wiley-Blackwell, 2008).

[24] Chris Heffer, Frances Rock, and John Conley, *Legal-Lay Communication: Textual Travels in the Law* (New York: Oxford University Press, 2013).

[25] Christopher Hutton, *Language, Meaning and the Law*, 1st ed. (Edinburgh: Edinburgh University Press, 2009); Christopher Hutton, *Word Meaning and Legal Interpretation: An Introductory Guide* (Houndmills, Basingstoke, UK; New York,: Palgrave, 2014); Lawrence M. Solan, "The Interpretation of Multilingual Statutes by the European Court of Justice," *Brooklyn Journal of International Law* 34 (2009): 277; Lawrence M. Solan, "Multilingualism and Morality in Statutory Interpretation," *Language and Law / Linguagem e Direito* 1, no. 1 (2014): 5–21. See also Timothy A. O. Endicott, "Linguistic Indeterminacy," *Oxford Journal of Legal Studies* 16, no. 4 (1996): 667–97.

[26] Susan Berk-Seligson, *The Bilingual Courtroom: Court Interpreters in the Judicial Process*, 1st ed. (Chicago: University of Chicago Press, 2002).

[27] One notable series of research into this question has been conducted by Australian sociolinguist Diana Eades, whose work details how Aboriginal English speakers are often misunderstood when they communicated with law enforcers. Australian aboriginals are 15 times more likely to be incarcerated than non-aboriginal people. Diana Eades, "Legal Recognition of Cultural Differences

been done, two tendencies in the field limit its potential impact. First, just like most modern linguistic studies, the main bulk of work done has a microscopic focus, with minimal recognizable effort to connect findings in a specific legal case or legal site to wider legal development or social processes. Second, such work is largely linguistics applied in a legal context rather than truly interdisciplinary, often positioning the linguist as a warrior of justice while ignoring constraints and concerns of law, as well as the political structures that law is situated in.

One specific intersection between multilingualism and law concerns assertions of language-related rights as a universal human right. Various international instruments, although without binding force, have recognized the right to "mother-tongue" education.[28] Native peoples who have been subjugated and marginalized may see preserving their language as a major battle of resistance and key to their cultural survival.[29] The potential of law to intervene in language use has captured the attention of researchers (sometimes known as ecolinguists or linguistic ecologists) who have become deeply alarmed by the unprecedented rate at which linguistic diversity is diminishing in recent decades. They describe the decrease in linguistic diversity with terms such as *linguicide, linguistic genocide*, and *language death*.[30]. They advocate for a kind of *linguistic human rights*,[31] and urge states to take positive actions to prevent or slow down language loss by subsidizing education in minority languages and conferring official status to minority languages. Their activism is sometimes dismissed as linguistic sentimentalism[32] and a revival of linguistic prescriptivism. What such kind of activism fails to acknowledge is that not all causes of language loss are morally suspect. It is one thing to condemn forced assimilation, it is

in Communication: The Case of Robyn Kina," *Language & Communication: Language, Society and the Law*, 16, no. 3 (July 1, 1996): 215–27, https://doi.org/10.1016/0271-5309(96)00011-0. See also Janet Ainsworth, "Law and the Grammar of Judgment," in *Meaning and Power in the Language of Law*, ed. Janny H. C. Leung and Alan Durant (Cambridge: Cambridge University Press, 2018).

[28] Such as Declaration on the Rights of Persons Belonging to National or Ethnic, Religious and Linguistic Minorities (1992) and United Nations Declaration on the Rights of Indigenous Peoples (2007).

[29] Reinstantiation of suppressed minority languages in public domains may be considered a correction of historical injustice. Stephen May, "Contesting Hegemonic and Monolithic Constructions of Language Rights 'Discourse,'" *Journal of Multicultural Discourses* 7, no. 1 (March 1, 2012): 21–27, https://doi.org/10.1080/17447143.2012.660944.

[30] See Douglas A. Kibbee, "Language Policy and Linguistic Theory," in *Languages in a Globalising World*, ed. Jacques Maurais and Michael A. Morris (Cambridge, UK: Cambridge University Press, 2003), 47–57, for a critique of the ecolinguistic perspective.

[31] Language rights advocates see states as the greatest threat to language survival, and so by positing a kind of linguistic human rights, they aspire to use international human rights regimes to impose obligations on states to protect languages. See review in Janny H. C. Leung, "Language Rights," in *Handbook of Communication in the Legal Sphere*, ed. Jacqueline Visconti (Boston; Berlin: DeGruyter, 2018), 54–82.

[32] Abram De Swaan, "Endangered Languages, Sociolinguistics, and Linguistic Sentimentalism," *European Review* 12, no. 4 (October 2004): 567–80, https://doi.org/10.1017/S1062798704000481.

another to intervene when speakers choose to abandon a language, or when a language disappears after all its speakers pass away. Where the state does try suppress the use of certain languages, in the modern world this is frequently done through soft power, and it is doubtful whether legal protection can mitigate it. Moreover, some contributors to the loss of linguistic diversity, such as the development of written language, spread of literacy, and urbanization, arguably have social value.[33] Some advocates seem to care more about the survival of "endangered" languages as a human heritage and cultural artifact than the livelihood or agency of the people who speak those languages. Underlying the language rights paradigm is the ideology of law as a protector of language, which sometimes entails an overestimation of state power in contemporary global politics and a somewhat naïve understanding of legal realities at both domestic and international levels. As Critical Legal scholars[34] have argued, the value of rights cannot be taken for granted; in fact, rights discourse may even impede progressive social movements. This is a discussion we will return to later in the book.

Another cluster of researchers who are interested in the relationship between law and multilingualism work in the field of language policy and planning (LPP), which generally refers to targeted efforts to change the learning, distribution, and use of a language in society. The field started in the age of nationalism with the orientation of using LPP to contribute to nation-building.[35] In LPP studies, the conferral of official status to a language is known as *status planning*. This term is not adopted in what follows because it connotes design effort and active management, and presumes that officialization is a stage of a larger process in language planning (consisting of not only status, but also corpus and acquisition planning), none of which I believe can be accepted without question. LPP studies also tend to assume that the goal of language planning is to influence language or language behavior,[36] an assumption I will diverge from in my study of official multilingualism.

In legal scholarship concerned with language rights and linguistic equality, the language issue is usually subsumed in the discourse of minority rights (especially in international law), which has received considerable attention after the world wars. Although linguistic inequalities may be treated as a proxy to

---

[33] Alan Patten and Will Kymlicka, "Introduction: Language Rights and Political Theory: Context, Issues, and Approaches," in *Language Rights and Political Theory*, ed. Will Kymlicka and Alan Patten (repr., Oxford: Oxford University Press, 2007).

[34] Mark Tushnet, "An Essay on Rights," *Texas Law Review* 62, no. 8 (1984): 1363–1403; Duncan Kennedy, "The Critique of Rights in Critical Legal Studies," in *Left Legalism/Left Critique*, ed. Janet Halley and Wendy Brown (Durham, NC: Duke University Press, 2002), 178–228.

[35] Sue Wright, *Language Policy and Language Planning: From Nationalism to Globalisation* (New York: Springer, 2016).

[36] Moshe Nahir, "Language Planning Goals: A Classification," *Language Problems and Language Planning* 8, no. 3 (January 1, 1984): 294–327, https://doi.org/10.1075/lplp.8.3.03nah.

social inequalities arising from race, class, and gender, the fact that law on language often receives the highest level of legal protection in many national constitutions suggests that there is something special about language that begs for analysis.

Political scientists have debated the philosophical justifications for minority languages rights, and the normative question of what makes a just language policy when it is practically impossible for states to be completely neutral in their choice of medium of communication.[37] They are concerned more with what should happen in an ideal world, or what stance liberal political theory should take on the issue of minority language rights and the global dominance of English, than with the descriptive and analytical question of what is going on right now and how to make sense of it. I will address the normative question in the last chapter of this book.

Some attempts have been made to study multilingual practices in international and supranational law. The most thorough historical overview of language use in international relations and international law is offered in an ambitious 963-page two-volume set of books entitled *Language, Law, and Diplomacy* by Alexander Ostrower.[38] Published in a similar period of time was an essay by Hardy on the interpretation of multilingual treaties, covering cases where authentic[39] versions of a treaty are found to be divergent in meaning.[40] A slightly more updated account that focused on how multilingual law is drafted and interpreted in modern international law may be found in Tabory.[41] In her seminal book, Tabory reviews the highly controversial codification process of legal provisions governing multilingual treaties (resulting in the 1969 Vienna Convention on the Law of Treaties, or VCLT) and offers one of the first comprehensive analyses on challenges in interpreting multilingual law. Since the VCLT articles on multilingual interpretation were drafted conservatively and included only less disputed broad principles, her account reminds us of the ample interpretive space that VCLT leaves open in the interpretation of multilingual treaties. As I have explained in an earlier essay, principles in the interpretation of multilingual treaties have become an influential model for the interpretation of other multilingual legal texts, including multilingual state

---

[37] For example, see a collection of essays in Will Kymlicka and Alan Patten, eds., *Language Rights and Political Theory* (repr., Oxford: Oxford University Press, 2007).

[38] Alexander Ostrower, *Language, Law, and Diplomacy: A Study of Linguistic Diversity in Official International Relations and International Law* (Philadelphia: University of Pennsylvania Press, 1965).

[39] "Authenticity" here refers to a legal status, describing a text as carrying the authority of an original. A translation may be authenticated such that it is legally treated as reliable and authoritative as the original.

[40] Jean Hardy, "The Interpretation of Plurilingual Treaties by International Courts and Tribunals," *British Year Book of International Law* 37 (1961): 72–155.

[41] Mala Tabory, *Multilingualism in International Law and Institutions* (Alphen aan den Rijn, the Netherlands; Rockville, MD: Sijthoff & Noordhoff, 1980).

law.[42] Although multilingual practices have been developed in the drafting and interpretation of international agreements, it is in international and regional intergovernmental organizations (IGOs) that they become institutionalized. Both Ostrower and Tabory discussed in length the multilingual regime in the United Nations and some other IGOs. The regional IGO that has generated the most attention is the European Union, which is also a supranational polity. Its elaborate multilingual regime has drawn much research interest. Existing works have explored issues in legal drafting, legal translation, the sustainability of its linguistic regime,[43] the harmonization and interpretation of multilingual law,[44] and relationships between linguistic diversity and European democracy.[45]

At the national level, the largest body of research has focused on the bilingual and bijural legal system of Canada, including notable works by Rémi Michael Beaupré[46] and former Justice of the Supreme Court of Canada Michel Bastarache[47] on statutory interpretation. Beaupré's *Interpreting Bilingual Legislation* (1986) was the first monograph to deal systematically

---

[42] Janny H. C. Leung, "Cross-Jurisdiction Appropriation of the Equal Authenticity Principle," *The Journal of Legal Pluralism and Unofficial Law* 45, no. 2 (July 2013): 209–26, https://doi.org/10.1080/07329113.2013.772463.

[43] Lucja Biel, "Translation of Multilingual EU Legislation as a Sub-Genre of Legal Translation," in *Court Interpreting and Legal Translation in Enlarged Europe 2006*, ed. D. Kierzkowska (Warszawa: Translegis, 2007), 144–63; Lucja Biel, *Lost in the Eurofog: The Textual Fit of Translated Law* (Bern: Peter Lang, 2014); Karen McAuliffe, "Enlargement at the European Court of Justice: Law, Language and Translation," *European Law Journal* 14, no. 6 (November 1, 2008): 806–18, https://doi.org/10.1111/j.1468-0386.2008.00442.x; Karen McAuliffe, "Language and Law in the European Union: The Multilingual Jurisprudence of the ECJ," in *The Oxford Handbook of Language and Law*, ed. Peter M. Tiersma and Lawrence M. Solan (Oxford: Oxford University Press, 2012), 200–216; Susan Šarčević, *New Approach to Legal Translation* (Dordrecht: Kluwer Law International, 1997); Susan Šarčević, *Language and Culture in EU Law: Multidisciplinary Perspectives* (London: Routledge, 2015); Arturo Tosi, ed., *Crossing Barriers and Bridging Cultures: The Challenges of Multilingual Translation for the European Union* (Buffalo, NY: Multilingual Matters, 2003).

[44] Cornelis J. W. Baaij, "Fifty Years of Multilingual Interpretation in the European Union," in *The Oxford Handbook of Language and Law*, ed. Peter M. Tiersma and Lawrence M. Solan (New York: Oxford University Press, 2012), 217–31; Mattias Derlén, *Multilingual Interpretation of European Union Law* (Dordrecht: Kluwer Law International, 2009); Antonio Gambaro, "Interpretation of Multilingual Legislative Texts," *Electronic Journal of Comparative Law* 11, no. 3 (2007): 1–20; Tadas Klimas and Jurate Vaiciukaite, "Interpretation of European Union Multilingual Law," *International Journal of Baltic Law* 3 (June 1, 2005): 1–13; Elina Paunio, *Legal Certainty in Multilingual EU Law: Language, Discourse and Reasoning at the European Court of Justice* (Burlington, VT: Ashgate Publishing, 2013); Barbara Pozzo and Valentina Jacometti, eds., *Multilingualism and the Harmonisation of European Law* (Dordrecht: Kluwer Law International, 2006); Dinah Shelton, "Reconcilable Differences: The Interpretation of Multilingual Treaties," *Hastings International and Comparative Law Review* 20 (1997): 611–38; Solan, "The Interpretation of Multilingual Statutes by the European Court of Justice."

[45] Anne Lise Kjær and Silvia Adamo, eds., *Linguistic Diversity and European Democracy* (Surrey, England; Burlington, VT: Ashgate, 2011).

[46] Rémi Michael Beaupré, *Construing Bilingual Legislation in Canada* (Toronto: Butterworths, 1981); Rémi Michael Beaupré, *Interpreting Bilingual Legislation* (Toronto: Carswell, 1986).

[47] Michel Bastarache et al., *The Law of Bilingual Interpretation* (Markham, ON: LexisNexis Canada, 2008); Michel Bastarache, "Bilingual Interpretation Rules as a Component of Language

with problems of interpreting equally authentic Canadian bilingual statutes. Bastarache et al.'s *The Law of Bilingual Interpretation* (2008) built upon the research begun by Beaupré and extended his discussion by probing the legal tradition and legislative thinking behind the interpretation of bilingual laws in Canada. Yet other relevant book-length publications in Canada focus on language politics and language rights,[48] where opinions diverge as to whether official bilingualism in Canada has not done enough[49] or has gone too far.[50] In a 1997 journal article, a rare attempt was made by former McGill law professor Roderick A. MacDonald to theorize the significance of official bilingualism for a legal system, and bring lessons of legal bilingualism back to the world of monolingual legal order.[51]

A number of academic and policy research studies compared multilingual legal practices across jurisdictions, such as approaches to multilingual interpretation.[52] Such comparative studies remain few and small in scale, usually focusing on two or three localities,[53] but they can be invaluable in revealing complex and interconnected forces that are almost invisible when looking at single sites. Effort in the comparative study of official multilingualism has also come from governments. Canada, South Africa, Wales, Ireland, and the European Union have all commissioned and published relevant research reports, indicating a real desire to survey and contrast practices at the frontline. As far as I am aware, the current volume is the first book-length attempt to map and make sense of official multilingualism on a global scale.

Rights in Canada," in *The Oxford Handbook of Language an Law*, ed. Peter M. Tiersma and Lawrence M. Solan (New York: Oxford University Press, 2012), 159–74.

[48] Pierre A. Coulombe, *Language Rights in French Canada* (New York: P. Lang, 1995); Scott Reid, *Lament for a Notion: The Life and Death of Canada's Bilingual Dream* (Vancouver: Arsenal Pulp Press, 1993); Michel Bastarache, ed., *Language Rights in Canada* (Montréal, Que: Les Editions Yvon Blais, 1987).

[49] Coulombe, *Language Rights in French Canada*.

[50] Reid, *Lament for a Notion*.

[51] Roderick A. Macdonald, "Legal Bilingualism," *McGill Law Journal* 42 (1997): 119.

[52] Deborah Cao, *Translating Law* (Buffalo, NY: Multilingual Matters, 2016); Janny H. C. Leung, "Statutory Interpretation in Multilingual Jurisdictions: Typology and Trends," *Journal of Multilingual and Multicultural Development* 33, no. 5 (August 1, 2012): 481–95, https://doi.org/10.1080/01434632.2012.680462.

[53] With the notable exception of Fernand de Varennes, "International and Comparative Perspectives in the Use of Official Languages: Models and Approaches for South Africa" (South Africa: South African Language Council Afrikaanse Taalraad, 2012).

PART I

Causes

Chapter 1

Tracing Linguistic Management through Time

LAW AS A LENS

> (T)he history of the language of the law . . . cannot be satisfactorily treated as a mere "digression" from the history of the law. . . .
>
> —David Mellinkoff[1]

This chapter offers a historical account of how polities have operated in a linguistically diverse society. Although societal multilingualism has been commonplace throughout human civilization, *official* multilingualism is clearly a modern phenomenon, for the defining, classifying, and "officializing" of entities, spaces, and procedures are part of the processes of modernization, and the politicization of language is tied to the rise of national identities.[2] However, whether the use of a language is mandated by policy or law, or is a matter of convention, polities have always had to deal with linguistic diversity. Therefore, instead of comparing the language(s) that receive official recognition, I will use law as a site to examine the internal language practice of a polity in different historical periods. My account shows that official multilingualism today, encapsulating contemporary ethics and politics, has characteristics that distinguish it from treaded paths of linguistic management.

This chapter will therefore be exploring monolingual and multilingual practices in legal texts and processes. It may be helpful here to explain the interrelationships between *official multilingualism* and *legal multilingualism.*[3] I use *official multilingualism* to refer to the situation where two or more languages are legally recognized as the language of a polity, an organization, or an agreement. These languages usually acquire labels such as *official languages* and *national languages. Legal multilingualism* refers to the situation where legal

---

[1] David Mellinkoff, *The Language of the Law* (Eugene, OR: Wipf & Stock, 1963), 33.

[2] Peter A. Kraus, *A Union of Diversity: Language, Identity and Polity-Building in Europe* (Cambridge: Cambridge University Press, 2008).

[3] I adopt the term *legal multilingualism* based on MacDonald's work. MacDonald, "Legal Bilingualism."

systems function in two or more languages. Legal multilingualism may be taken as a formal marker of official multilingualism. On the other hand, the legal designation of official languages does not guarantee their use in the legislature or judiciary, so in that way official multilingualism and legal multilingualism are separable—but often overlapping—phenomena.

Functional Multilingualism in Medieval Class Society

Let us begin with the formative period of the Western legal tradition—the Middle Ages (ca. 5th–15th C). This is commonly dated from the fall of the Western Roman Empire (476 AD), which marked the end of the ancient world. The medieval period saw the popularization of literacy and widespread functional multilingualism in aristocratic societies organized by distinct social classes. The feudal ruling class often had a multilingual repertoire, while the peasant spoke a vernacular. In most areas of medieval Western Europe, prestige languages such as Latin and French were used in religion, science, law, and high culture, while vernaculars were spoken locally in everyday life.[4] Such hierarchically ordered languages may be distinguished as High versus Low varieties[5] (or H vs. L), the former typically a standardized variety performing prestigious functions and the latter spoken informally at home and on the street.[6] Ferguson calls the situation where two or more varieties of the same language coexist but perform differential functions *diglossia*;[7] the term has later been expanded to include the hierarchical relationship between two language varieties (whether they may be considered the same language or not).

---

[4] Prestigious languages were also spoken as an everyday language by elites. See Ad Putter and Keith Busby, "Introduction: Medieval Francophonia," in *Medieval Multilingualism: The Francophone World and Its Neighbours*, ed. Christopher Kleinhenz and Keith Busby (Turnhout: Brepols, 2010), https://doi.org/10.1484/M.TCNE-EB.6.09070802050003050208030703.

[5] In Ferguson's original conception, such varieties referred to varieties within a language, such as High German and Low German. But subsequently the concept has been extended to refer to varieties with any degree of linguistic difference. The reference to H and L varieties has been criticized for being too coarse to capture the nuances and instability of discursive practices, but for the purposes of the current discussion it suffices to highlight the functional differentiation of languages.

[6] C. A. Ferguson, "Diglossia," *Word* 15 (1959): 325–40; Joshua Fishman, "Bilingualism with and without Diglossia; Diglossia with and without Bilingualism," *The Journal of Social Issues* 23, no. 2 (1967): 29–38.

[7] Since language choice is highly context dependent, the idea of diglossia and the linguistic landscape I offer here can only be a generalization. For example, a historical study of letters in the 16th C shows that Latin, German, Italian, French, and Romansch were used in correspondence within a Swiss family. Choice of language depended on gender, social relations and hierarchy, topic, and language ideologies in relation to identity, individuality, autonomy, etc. Randolph C. Head, "A Plurilingual Family in the Sixteenth Century: Language Use and Linguistic Consciousness in the Salis Family Correspondence, 1580–1610," *The Sixteenth Century Journal* 26, no. 3 (1995): 577–93, https://doi.org/10.2307/2543140.

The first half of the Middle Ages, sometimes referred to as the Dark Ages, is characterized by intellectual depression and a return to oral culture. Relatively little is known about the period due to the scarcity of available written records. During the Migration Period, between Late Antiquity and the Early Middle Ages, numerous Germanic tribes (e.g., the Angles, Bavarians, Franks, Lombards, and Saxons) settled on the western territories of the former Roman Empire. Since these tribes had a weak written culture, law was primarily folk law that was transmitted verbally in the form of ritual oaths. The law codes (known as *leges barbarorum*, or laws of the barbarians) of these tribes that survived from the Early Middle Ages were written in Latin (such as *Lex Salica*) and Anglo-Saxon (the earliest compilation on record being Laws of Ethelbert from the 7th C). The linguistic landscape of medieval Europe may be described as a dialectal continuum, where neighboring peasant communities could understand each other, and comprehensibility is in reverse proportion to distance. This continuum was not truncated by political borders as it is in modern states today, where more effort is made to control linguistic variation through codification, standardization, and centralized education.[8] In parallel to the localized, agricultural economy, law was not a centralized affair. Every tribe had its own laws, which might overlap with larger, territorial-based legal units. Legal professionals, law schools, and legal scholarship had yet to appear. The overlapping administration of law and religion reinforced the perception that law was sacred and made it seem natural that the language of the law was alienated from the populace.

During the second half of the medieval period, the use of Latin as a lingua franca had considerably facilitated the development of Western legal scholarship. Concepts from Roman law served as a common foundation, through which educated minorities across Europe were able to form a cultural unit. The Western legal system took shape in the twelfth century when the first universities were created (most notably in Bologna) and law began to be studied as a discipline.[9] These universities were transnational, educating people coming from all over Europe. The first legal materials that became an object of their study were reproductions of Roman law issued by the Eastern Roman Emperor Justinian I (ca. 482–565 AD) from over five centuries earlier, a manuscript that provided a basic legal vocabulary and laid the foundation of modern law across Europe. The profession of jurists that emerged fulfilled the social need to reconcile conflicts between and within secular and ecclesiastical authorities.[10] Roman law not only formed the foundation of law in Europe, but also influenced English common law, and has spread to many non-European countries.

---

[8] Wright, *Language Policy and Language Planning*.

[9] Harold J. Berman, "The Origins of Western Legal Science," *Harvard Law Review* 90, no. 5 (1977): 894–943.

[10] Berman, "The Origins of Western Legal Science."

During the development of both the civil and the common law traditions, the diglossic (or sometimes even triglossic or tetraglossic) situation was commonplace in medieval Europe. As courts became formalized around the twelfth to thirteenth centuries[11] and the written record in judicial activities was increasingly emphasized, H varieties naturally dominated trial processes with their developed written forms. Language may be used as a dividing tool in a class society where elites have more opportunities to master the H variety. The functional differentiation among languages is maintained through gatekeeping institutions such as courts and schools.[12] Latin, as the legacy of the Roman Empire and also the language of law, religion, government, and military, was the dominant H variety, spoken as a second language across medieval Europe. Territorial-based vernaculars were used for daily communication, feudal, customary and merchant law, and spoken communication in other courts of law. Two or more languages might be used in court but for different functions: typically, cases might be heard in a vernacular, but court judgments were handed down in Latin.[13] This kind of linguistic division of labor may be called *functional multilingualism*. The assignment of legal functions to different languages is evident for example in Galizia, a small medieval kingdom in the border area of present-day Poland and Ukraine, which had a trilingual legal practice: Polish was used in rural and municipal courts, Latin in courts for some businesses and aristocracy, and German in appellate and specialized courts.[14]

In England, after the 1066 Conquest, legal trilingualism was practiced in the emergent common law system. Norman French, as the language of the rulers, was the H variety for spoken communication, spoken and written extensively between the twelfth and the fifteenth centuries. English was the L variety for daily communication and the first language of the subjugated people; it was also used in local courts. Before the Conquest, both English and Latin were used to write legal documents, but during the first two hundred years after the Normans arrived, Latin became the default written language of law, only to be replaced by French as the statutory language in 1310.[15] The use of Latin during the infancy of the common law system means that many common law terms were originally formulated in Latin. By the second half of the thirteenth century, proceedings in royal courts were conducted in French (with code-switching to English during interactions with lay people[16]), but Latin

---

[11] Following the emergence of Ständestaat, or the polity of the Estates, as a form of political arrangement. This arrangement would last until its replacement by sovereign states in the 17th C. Rodolfo Stavenhagen, *The Ethnic Question: Conflicts, Development, and Human Rights* (Tokyo: United Nations University Press, 1990).

[12] Douglas A. Kibbee, *Language and the Law* (Cambridge: Cambridge University Press, 2016).

[13] Heikki E. S. Mattila, *Comparative Legal Linguistics: Language of Law, Latin and Modern Lingua Francas* (Farnham, UK: Ashgate, 2013).

[14] Grodziski (1971), cited in Mattila, *Comparative Legal Linguistics*, 167.

[15] Peter M. Tiersma, *Legal Language* (Chicago: University of Chicago Press, 1999).

[16] Tiersma, *Legal Language*.

was still used in some legal documents. In essence, these three languages in the English courtroom rarely duplicated in function. The Statute of Pleading in 1362 condemned the fact that most people could not understand trial proceedings in Law French and required that all pleas be made in English; this statute, ironically written in French as was the norm at the time, had limited effect.[17] The move away from Latin in the Church and in courts of law started with the Reformation (1517), which decentralized power from the Church and played a significant part in strengthening national identity. Due to the "linguistic conservatism of the legal profession,"[18] the transition from Latin and Law French to English in law took a few centuries to complete.

It should be noted that even though languages were conveniently referred to in the preceding discussion as separable entities, contact-induced language change is pervasive in diglossic situations: features of H are frequently incorporated into the vernacular and vice versa. Such language change is the most visible form of heteroglossia that Bakhtin describes—the condition where a seemingly unitary language expresses a multiplicity of voices and worldviews.[19] Language contact provides a centrifugal force that stratifies a language, putting its internal elements in a dialogical relation[20] with one another. Legal language is no exception to the heteroglot character of language. Law Latin in England frequently employed English terms and also borrowed words from French.[21] Conversely, most of the technical vocabulary of legal English stems from Latin roots via Norman French,[22] even though some Anglo-Saxon remnants also survived. Take the Holy Roman Empire (962–1806), which used both Latin and German for official purposes throughout its entire existence,[23] as a further example. German overtook Latin as the language of the law in the thirteenth century, only to be taken over again by Latin following renewed interest in Roman law at the end of the Middle Ages.[24] Legal German remained in use but was partly Latinized, having absorbed loan words from legal Latin. German judgments and legislation contained many Latin quotations and references.

---

17 Tiersma, *Legal Language*.

18 Tiersma, *Legal Language*, 28.

19 Mikhail M. Bakhtin, "Discourse in the Novel," in *The Dialogic Imagination: Four Essays*, ed. Michael Holquist, trans. Caryl Emerson and Michael Holquist (Austin and London: University of Texas Press, 1981), 259–422.

20 A dialogue may yet be unfolded, but the potential for meanings to interact with each other is created. Bakhtin, "Discourse in the Novel."

21 Tiersma, *Legal Language*.

22 Harold J. Berman, *Law and Language: Effective Symbols of Community*, ed. John Witte Jr., rev. ed. (New York: Cambridge University Press, 2013).

23 Mattila, *Comparative Legal Linguistics*.

24 The adoption of Roman law not only affected the judicial language but also the professionalization of judges and lawyers; judges now required a theoretical training in law in order to adjudicate. Mattila, *Comparative Legal Linguistics*, 206.

Legal German also borrowed extensively from French later on in the seventeenth and eighteenth centuries.

Colonial Diglossia in European Imperialism

As legal anthropologist Sally Engle Merry observes, "(t)he law of contemporary societies was forged in the colonial era."[25] Not only did European imperialists spread their legal systems to the rest of the world through colonization, they also brought their language with them. Colonial diglossia, with the imperial language being the H variety and local vernaculars as the L variety, was a common condition in colonies.

European colonization (late 15th–early 19th C), which began with Christopher Columbus's (1451–1506) exploration in 1492, is seen by some as an early stage of globalization. Colonizers were diffusionists who saw imperial conquests as the spread of civilization from "progressive" Europe to the "backward" non-European world.[26] Such diffusion was bidirectional: as European colonizers provided their colonies with the "gift of civilization,"[27] they extracted wealth and material goods from the colonies as "compensation," which in turn supported the development of Europe and consolidated the power of European monarchies. Not only was colonial law imposed on native peoples, law was used as a rhetoric to legitimize colonization, as native peoples were deemed not to have the concept of property and therefore could not possess territorial rights.[28] European domination was most extensive and lasting in the settler colonies of the Americas and Australasia; it was widespread but less enduring in African and Asian exploitation colonies.

Linguistic assimilation was used to a varying extent by colonizers as a means of social control. This strategy was made explicit in the writing of Elio Antonio de Nebrija (1441–1522), who published *Gramática Castellana* (1492), the first grammar book of Castilian Spanish, 15 days after Columbus set sail from Castile. Nebrija created this grammar by synthesizing speech forms that he came across every day in Spain, and presented it to Queen Isabella.[29] He convinced the queen to replace the untutored speech of the people with his standardized artificial Castilian by arguing that language is a pillar of political power:

---

[25] Sally Engle Merry, "Colonial and Postcolonial Law," in *The Blackwell Companion to Law and Society*, ed. Austin Sarat (London: Blackwell, 2004), 569.

[26] J. M. Blaut, *The Colonizer's Model of the World: Geographical Diffusionism and Eurocentric History* (New York: Guilford Press, 1993).

[27] Blaut, *The Colonizer's Model of the World*, 16.

[28] Blaut, *The Colonizer's Model of the World*, 25.

[29] Ivan Illich, *Shadow Work* (London; New York: Marion Boyars, 1981).

> This our language followed our soldiers whom we sent abroad to rule. It spread to Aragon, to Navarra, even to Italy . . . the scattered bits and pieces of Spain were thus gathered and joined into one single kingdom.[30]

Apart from attaching different values and functions to their colonies, colonizers also tended to follow different priorities in their ruling style, which affected their colonial language policy. By way of example, the Spanish colonial enterprise in the Americas had both political-economic and religious goals.[31] These were reflected in the configuration of Spanish settlement in the region, which consisted of the Crown administration and the Church. During the early period of colonization, native languages and Spanish coexisted in Latin America. The Castilianization process, which started in the mid-seventeenth century, gained full force in 1768 when Charles III imposed the policy to Spain as well as its colonies. By the eighteenth century, Castilian Spanish became the dominant linguistic variety throughout the colonies and was the default language of public life. Elites were monolingual in Spanish, and a large population was functionally bilingual. English and Dutch colonizers, by contrast, used bilingual elites as intermediaries and were not particularly concerned about spreading their languages.

Modernization also affected the way imperial powers governed their colonies, which may have the effect of shaking the local linguistic hierarchy. Compared with the early modern period, when imperialists conquered and ruled their colonies through the might of the monarchy, modern nation-states governed with bureaucratic institutions. The public education system that modern governments instated in some non-settler colonies was responsible for purging classical languages that originally occupied the position of H varieties in the local society and replacing them with colonial languages. Vernaculars may be retained as L varieties for the practical purpose of efficiently communicating with and educating the masses.[32]

Take India as an example. Prior to the passing of the English Education Act in 1835, education in India was dominated by a classical curriculum, with Arabic, Persian, and Sanskrit being the languages of learning. Persian was also the language of court and official communication, Sanskrit the language of Hindu law, and Arabic the language of Muslim law. Exemplifying the ideology that European languages are a source of knowledge but non-European languages are not, Hindu advocate of English-language instruction Ram Mohun Roy wrote, "What we spend on Arabic and Sanscrit Colleges is not merely a

---

[30] Nebrija (1492), translated and cited in Illich, *Shadow Work*, 8.

[31] Clare Mar-Molinero, *The Politics of Language in the Spanish-Speaking World: From Colonisation to Globalisation* (London; New York: Routledge, 2000).

[32] Pennycook calls this "pragmatic vernacularism." See Alastair Pennycook, *English and the Discourses of Colonialism* (London: Routledge, 2002).

dead loss to the cause of truth. It is bounty money paid to raise up champions of error."[33] Famously, President of Committee of Public Instruction Thomas Babington Macaulay asserts in his Minute on Education[34] (dated February 2, 1835) the superiority of a Western education:

> It is impossible for us, with our limited means, to attempt to educate the body of the people. We must at present do our best to form a class who may be interpreters between us and the millions whom we govern; a class of persons, Indian in blood and colour, but English in taste, in opinions, in morals and in intellect. To that class we may leave it to refine the vernacular dialects of the country, to enrich those dialects with terms of science borrowed from Western nomenclature, and to render them by degrees fit vehicles for conveying knowledge to the great mass of the population.

Despite Macaulay's distaste of non-European languages, he still saw a role for the vernaculars in mass education. In the 1840s, Urdu and Hindi were introduced in village schools.[35] Support for classical learning was withdrawn, and students were paid to study Urdu and Hindi. The decline of the classical languages was also accelerated by changing market demands. The making of English as the official language of the British government of India closed off employment opportunities for graduates of Hindu and Muslim institutions and ensured the ascendency of English as the new H variety.

Apart from public education, colonial legal systems also created an opportunity for imperial languages to penetrate local life. Using the Indian example again, during the early modern period the East India Company secured political control following the path of least resistance, by incorporating a systematized and translated version of Hindu and Muslim codes into a colonial legal system that followed British procedures and principles of adjudication.[36] In the nineteenth century, under the influence of the modern ideology that the same law should be applied to everyone, a unified criminal code was adopted, and laws of British origin largely supplanted indigenous codes. In many non-settler colonies, colonial legal systems were a mix of imposed colonial laws and customary laws (which govern private affairs such as family and marriage); thus both colonial and native languages may be used for law but in different domains. In other words, colonial law was often legally plural,[37]

---

[33] Cited in Elmer H. Cutts, "The Background of Macaulay's Minute," *The American Historical Review* 58, no. 4 (1953): 824–53, https://doi.org/10.2307/1842459.

[34] Thomas B. Macaulay, "Minute on Education in India [1835]," in *Politics and Empire in Victorian Britain: A Reader*, ed. Antoinette Burton (New York: Palgrave, 2001), 18–20.

[35] Tariq Rahman, "Urdu as the Language of Education in British India," *Pakistan Journal of History and Culture* 32, no. 2 (2011): 1–40.

[36] Bernard S. Cohn, *Colonialism and Its Forms of Knowledge: The British in India* (Princeton, NJ: Princeton University Press, 1996).

[37] Merry, "Legal Pluralism."

functionally multilingual, and always dialogic in character. Colonialism dramatically widens and deepens the heteroglossia of both the colonial and native languages, enlarging the worldviews that are embedded in them.[38]

Colonial languages have an even more pervasive influence in settler colonies. English settlers brought with them their conception of the English legal system to North America, for example, and along with it, legal English—and all its Anglo-Saxon, French, and Latin features. Even after independence, Americans retained the English common law and continued to cite English case law extensively in the early years.[39]

Many colonized territories happened to be some of the most linguistically diverse places on Earth. The impact of colonization on endogenous languages depended on the colonial style and local factors. Colonizers generally saw endogenous languages as backward and inadequate, and sometimes suppressed or even penalized their use (notable penalties were soap in the mouth or corporal punishment in schools[40]). Such suppression was, at least at some point, common in British, French, Spanish, and Portuguese colonial policies in Africa and Latin America. That said, Pennycook notes that the British colonial government had also used vernacular education as a pacifying strategy in places such as Hong Kong, Malaya, and India.[41] Diglossia has continued to thrive in these places even after the departure of the British. Sometimes the impact on endogenous languages was not a result of policy and planning, but of other incidental events, such as warfare and the spread of infectious disease. In the Americas, over 90% of the indigenous population was estimated to have died from diseases that European colonizers brought with them, taking with them their native languages.[42] According to Mufwene,[43] European colonizers had endangered endogenous languages more often in settlement colonies than in exploitation or trade colonies. This may be seen in the Americas, Australia, and New Zealand. However, it is not always the colonized languages that died out. In a few cases, such as Norman French in England, the Tutsi in Rwanda and

---

[38] This is of course not to say that each language conveys a singular worldview. Bakhtin, "Discourse in the Novel."

[39] Tiersma, *Legal Language*; Peter M. Tiersma, "A History of the Languages of the Law," in *The Oxford Handbook of Language and Law*, ed. Peter M. Tiersma and Lawrence M. Solan (Oxford: Oxford University Press, 2012), 13–26.

[40] David Crystal, *Language Death* (Cambridge: Cambridge University Press, 2000), 84–86. See also Chapter 5 of Tove Skutnabb-Kangas, *Linguistic Genocide in Education—or Worldwide Diversity and Human Rights?* (New York: Routledge, 2000).

[41] Alastair Pennycook, "Language, Ideology and Hindsight: Lessons from Colonial Language Policies," in *Ideology, Politics, and Language Policies: Focus on English*, ed. Thomas Ricento (Amsterdam: John Benjamins, 2000), 49–65.

[42] Crystal, *Language Death*.

[43] Salikoko S. Mufwene, "Colonization, Globalization, and the Future of Languages in the Twenty-First Century," *International Journal on Multicultural Societies* 4, no. 2 (2002): 162–93.

Burundi, or Peranakan Chinese in Malacca, the colonizer's language was lost.[44] These are, however, by far the exceptions rather than the norm.

Linguistic Nationalism and the Birth of Monolingual Modern States

Following the Age of Discovery, the Romantic era saw the expansion of a nationalist ideology, which holds that each nation that shares a common historical, cultural, and linguistic root have the right to self-determination and should form a political unit.[45] In the language of Herder, a nationality—or *Volk*—is characterized by its unique spirit. But the defining ethnocultural qualities of a nation are notoriously fuzzy. In the majority of cases, homogeneity in language, culture, and customs is fostered or invented after sovereignty is attained. The belief that a state[46] should have a common language still forms the backbone of the monolingual policies of many modern states today, regardless of the fit of their linguistic landscape with the ideal prototype of nation-states.[47]

The idea of a nation and its linkage to a sovereign people and statehood was developed during the Age of Revolution, a period starting in the late eighteenth century that saw the absolutist state giving way to a constitutional state, and subjects being promoted to citizens.[48] A constitutional state is "an independent state with a written constitution, ruled in the name of a nation of equal citizens."[49] It is founded on a

---

[44] Mufwene, "Colonization."

[45] Ernest Gellner, *Nations and Nationalism* (Ithaca, NY: Cornell University Press, 1983).

[46] The concept of the sovereign state, which forms the basis of international law and world legal order today, was formulated in the Treaty of Westphalia in 1648, a peace treaty signed at the end of the Thirty Years War. The Treaty drew political boundaries between signatory states, and established the sovereignty of each state over its land and people and the principle of non-interference in domestic affairs.

[47] Nation-states fuse a political organization with a seemingly homogenous community that shares one cultural, ethnic, and linguistic root. Not all nations become sovereign states; the former is often said to be a sociological collectivity, and the latter a political institution. Stavenhagen (1990) estimates that there are somewhere between 5,000 and 8,000 different ethnic groups or nations. Many nations exist within or across states (e.g., Wales in the United Kingdom, Catalan in Spain, Corsica in France, or Kurdistan across Iran, Iraq, Turkey, and Syria); and states can exist within a state (e.g., American states in the federal government of the United States of America). Most modern states are not truly nation-states, despite the popularity of the term.

[48] The reconceptualization from subjects to citizens was dramatically captured in a draft of the Declaration of Independence, where Thomas Jefferson originally wrote the phrase "our fellow subjects," wiped off the word "subjects" when the ink was still wet, and wrote "citizens" over it. Marc Kaufman, "Jefferson Changed 'Subjects' to 'Citizens' in Declaration of Independence," *The Washington Post*, July 3, 2010, sec. Nation, http://www.washingtonpost.com/wp-dyn/content/article/2010/07/02/AR2010070205525.html.

[49] Andreas Wimmer and Yuval Feinstein, "The Rise of the Nation-State across the World, 1816 to 2001," *American Sociological Review* 75, no. 5 (October 1, 2010): 764–90, https://doi.org/10.1177/0003122410382639.

republican[50] form of government, where the legitimacy of the ruling state is no longer derived from divinity or private ownership but the will of the people. The idea that people rule, also known as popular sovereignty, is a principle of democracy. The citizens of a republic have the capacity of self-government and collectively have the power to amend the structure of government as laid down in the constitution. The modern English word *republic* is derived from the Latin phrase *res publica*, which literally means "the public affair." Compared with an absolutist state where orders may be passed down through intermediaries from a ruler to its subjects, in a democratic republic citizens need to have public dialogue in order to form consensus, and this is believed to be facilitated by a national language. Language thus became not only a marker of national identity, but also "the most important single defining characteristic of nationality" in the Western world.[51] Even today, knowledge of a national language is a prerequisite to citizenship for migrants to many states. However, in the two founding examples of a constitutional state, neither America nor France was linguistically homogenous when the revolutions that led to the formation of the modern state broke out.

When America became independent from the British in 1776, the country was led mostly by descendants of Anglophone colonial settlers, and the significance of English was never challenged.[52] Immigrant languages continued to flourish for generations until after the Civil War (1864), when English was prioritized as the language of law and education in order to promote national unity.[53] Even though there is no explicit legal recognition at the federal level,[54] English has been the de facto official language of the United States. Given the instrumental value of English, assimilation presents itself as a route to empowerment in "the melting pot." Recent immigrants usually switch from monolingual foreign language to monolingual English within three generations, with bilingualism being an intermediary stage.[55]

---

[50] Akhil Reed Amar, "The Central Meaning of a Republican Government: Popular Sovereignty, Majority Rule, and the Denominator Problem," *University of Colorado Law Review* 65 (1993): 749–86.

[51] Ronald Inglehart F. and Margaret Woodward, "Language Conflicts and Political Community," *Comparative Studies in Society and History* 10, no. 1 (1967): 27.

[52] Benedict Anderson, *Imagined Communities: Reflections on the Origin and Spread of Nationalism* (repr., London; New York: Verso, 1992).

[53] A letter written by President Theodore Roosevelt on January 3, 1919, to the president of the American Defense Society contains this excerpt: "We have room for but one language here, and that is the English language, for we intend to see that the crucible turns our people out as Americans, of American nationality, and not as dwellers in a polyglot boarding-house; and we have room for but one soul [*sic*] loyalty, and that is loyalty to the American people."

[54] More than half of US states have some form of official English legislation.

[55] Joshua A. Fishman, "The Status and Prospects of Bilingualism in the United States," *The Modern Language Journal* 49, no. 3 (March 1965): 143, https://doi.org/10.2307/322757.

When the French Revolution erupted in 1789, less than half of the population of France spoke French,[56] despite the dominance French had had over other languages for centuries. The Ordinance of Villers-Cotterêt of 1539, which pronounced French as the only official court language, was directed against both Latin and provincial languages, ending the use of Picard, Champenois, Provencal, and Tolozan in regional courts.[57] The French pursuit of linguistic homogeneity, intertwined with its obsession with linguistic purity (a language is kept "pure" by avoiding influences from other languages), was important in its revolutionary discourse, which claims that societal monolingualism is necessary for democracy, equality, and freedom, as exemplified by Barère (1755–1841):

> Federalism and superstition speak low-Breton; emigration and hate for the Republic speak German; counter-revolution speaks Italian and fanaticism speak Basque. Let us break these instruments of domination and error. . . . The monarchy had reasons to resemble the Tower of Babel; in democracy, allowing the citizens to be ignorant of the national language, incapable of controlling the power, that is to betray the homeland. . . . Being the language of the people, French will become the universal language. . . . It must become the language of all the French. Among a free people language must be one and the same for all.[58]

Nationalist movement spreads ideologies about specific languages by linking some of them with oppression and deficiency and others with progress and modernity. Learning the national language became a civil duty and refusing to speak it is unpatriotic. Such ideologies were internalized not only by the elites, but also by the linguistic minorities that such ideologies count against. The myth that French was of unmatched clarity and sophistication gradually led to the decline of other languages spoken in France.

The ideology underlying the French Revolution quickly spread to neighboring countries. Philosopher Johann Gottlieb Fichte[59] (1762–1814), a founding father of German nationalism, began his speech at the Academy of Berlin during the French occupation with the idea that linguistic boundary makes a natural political boundary:

> The first, original, and truly natural boundaries of states are beyond doubt their internal boundaries. Those who speak the same language are joined

---

[56] Only 3 million out of 25 million of the French population spoke French as a first language, and a further 3 million had some competence in French. Wright, *Language Policy and Language Planning*.

[57] Tony Judt and Denis Lacorne, eds., *Language, Nation, and State: Identity Politics in a Multilingual Age* (London: Palgrave Macmillan, 2004).

[58] Barère 1794, cited in Judt and Lacorne, 7.

[59] His work was later criticized as being xenophobic for placing the German language and culture above others. This serves as a reminder that linguistic nationalism is sometimes used to justify racial nationalism.

> to each other by a multitude of invisible bonds by nature herself, long before any human art begins; they understand each other and have the power of continuing to make themselves understood more and more clearly; they belong together and are by nature one and an inseparable whole.
>
> (Thirteenth Address in *Addresses to the German Nation*, 1808/1922)

Compared with imperialists who impose their language on their conquered populations by sheer force, just as the Assyrian king Sargon II did to the people he defeated,[60] linguistic nationalism induces language change through the seductive ideology of *one state, one nation, one language*, regardless of whether the populations of a so-called national group are polyethnic and multilingual.[61] The yearning for a glorious common root can only be satisfied through fictional creation, including the invention of "languages" by drawing arbitrary boundaries on the dialectal continuum and converging speech varieties through standardization.[62] That a nation is an imagined community has been convincingly argued by Anderson.[63] Irvine and Gal point out further that the homogeneity of language is as much an imagination as is community.[64] Linguistic nationalism is thus much less a project of uniting speakers of a language than one of asserting the supremacy of a variety of language and coercing language shift for speakers of other varieties. The existence of a common language has not been a *prerequisite* for nationhood; instead, language has been used as a *tool* for national unification and identity construction. Linguistic standardization and institutionalization were thus crucial to central governance. The Romantic nationalist idea had evolved into this: "the nation exists, therefore it must be given a language."[65] As Bourdieu notes, promotion of a dominant language variety is a means for the ruling elites to defend their privileges and shape the market to maximize the utility of their own linguistic capital.[66] In the French Revolution, for example, linguistic nationalism enabled French-speaking upper classes to monopolize political power. Importantly, the choice of official language not only affects government institutions, but also trickles down to education policy and the structure of the labor market, allowing linguistic capital to translate into cultural and economic capital. The challenge for

---

[60] A cylinder inscription of the king says, "Populations of the four quarters of the world with strange tongues and incompatible speech . . . whom I had taken as booty at the Command of Ashur my Lord by the might of my sceptre, I caused to accept a single voice."

[61] Stavenhagen, *The Ethnic Question*.

[62] Michael Billig, *Banal Nationalism* (Los Angeles: Sage, 1995).

[63] Anderson, *Imagined Communities*.

[64] Judith T. Irvine and Susan Gal, "Language Ideology and Linguistic Differentiation," in *Regimes of Language: Ideologies, Polities, and Identities*, ed. Paul V. Kroskrity (Santa Fe, NM: School for Advanced Research Press, 2000), 35–84.

[65] Judt and Lacorne, *Language, Nation, and State*, 4.

[66] Pierre Bourdieu, *Language and Symbolic Power*, ed. John Thompson, trans. Gino Raymond and Matthew Adamson (Cambridge: Polity Press, 1991).

the ruling class is to balance between the desire to retain class differentiation and the need to ensure political stability by allowing some degree of social mobility through assimilation. The latter goal may require the dominant group to recast its ethnic identity in new national terms.[67]

Linguistic nationalism contributed to the dissolution of multilingual empires, most notably the Ottoman Empire (1299–1922), the Russian Empire (1721–1917), and the Austro-Hungarian Empire (1867–1918). Ottoman Turkish, a high variety of Turkish with heavy influence from Arabic and Persian, was the language of government of the Ottoman Empire. After the 1453 Conquest of Constantinople, many speakers of Greek, Jewish, Armenian, and other languages migrated to the Empire. The Islamic Empire was tolerant of not only religious but also linguistic diversity; multilingual education flourished. Ethnic relations went downhill when the Empire fell in the hands of successors to Suleyman, who were much less committed to a pluralistic society.[68] In the nineteenth century, linguistic nationalism spreading from the west encouraged ethnolinguistic groups to revolt against the Empire and led to the independence of Greece, Serbia, and Bulgaria. Compared to the Ottoman Empire, Imperial Russia had a stronger agenda in cultural assimilation. Non-Russians, such as Poles, Ukrainians, Germans, Finns, Tatars, and Jews, were all required to learn Russian. During the First World War, under the slogan of national self-determination, Finland, Estonia, Latvia, and Lithuania achieved independence from the Empire. The Austro-Hungarian Empire had a linguistically very diverse population with no dominant majority.[69] In the Dual Monarchy of Cisleithania[70] (on the Austrian side) and Transleithania[71] (on the Hungarian side), there were laws that provided for the equal rights of every race and equality of all customary languages. This legal equality did not prevent linguistic conflicts, and nationalistic ethnolinguistic groups still competed

---

[67] "And so we have Americans, not WASPS; Ottomans not Turks; British not English; Spaniards not Castilians." Roman Szporluk, "The Imperial Legacy and the Soviet Nationalities," in *The Nationalities Factor in Soviet Politics and Society*, ed. Lubomyr Hajda and Mark R. Beissinger (Boulder, CO: Westview Press, 1990), 17.

[68] Amy Chua, *Day of Empire: How Hyperpowers Rise to Global Dominance—and Why They Fall*, reprint ed. (New York: Anchor, 2009).

[69] According to 1911 census, 23% of its population speak German, 20% Hungarian, 13% Czech, 10% Polish, 9% Croatian, 8% Ukrainian, 6% Romanian, 4% Slovak, 2% Slovene, 2% Italian, etc.

[70] Article 19 of the 1867 Basic State Act for Cisleithania says: "All races of the empire have equal rights, and every race has an inviolable right to the preservation and use of its own nationality and language. The equality of all customary languages in school, office and public life, is recognized by the state. In those territories in which several races dwell, the public and educational institutions are to be so arranged that, without applying compulsion to learn a second country language, each of the races receives the necessary means of education in its own language."

[71] The 1868 Hungarian Law on the Equality of Nationalities also provides for the equality of right with respect to the official use of "various languages of the country."

for dominance in different regions and sought independence.[72] At the conclusion of the First World War, all three empires fragmented into modern states, and the violent fallout continues to this day.

Linguistic nationalism remains a powerful ideology in the modern world. In fact, a radicalized form of linguistic nationalism, focused on an essentialized connection between mother-tongue and identity, was a driving force behind the Second World War. Hitler opened his book *Mein Kampf* with depictions of the German struggle to protect their language and culture. Central to the Nazi ideology was what Hutton calls "mother-tongue fascism": an understanding of language as primal bonding that was laid down before a child can speak, and an attempt to overcome the horror of assimilation by seeking to use political power to protect this quasi-natural endowment through generations. Mother tongue was a nexus to the *Volk*, which was understood to be the Germans and more globally as the Aryans during the Nationalist Socialist period.[73] In the world of nation-states, the surest way of ensuring the survival of the mother tongue is through drawing the political boundaries of the fatherland, and possibly expanding them.

Linguistic Rivalry during Decolonization

Linguistic nationalism has spread to other continents and has taken on varied meanings in different localities. American independence inspired a wave of anti-colonial nationalist movements in the Americas between 1770 and 1830. Creole nationalism spread among settler colonies, starting in the North and then sprawling over South and Central Americas. Post-colonial states in the Americas were mostly "creole states" formed by people who shared the same language and descent with those they revolted against.[74] The fact that Spanish could not be said to be a common characteristic to all the people in Latin America did not become an obstacle to state formation. In fact, some Indian languages died out only after the end of colonization, when Castilianization was stepped up in Latin America to enhance national unity. The status of Spanish was readily enshrined in constitutions and statutes in newly formed states and the language was recast as "a national identity marker," "a passport to citizenship," and a prerequisite for political participation.[75] Spanish-language education was a means of national integration. Indigenous resistance against

---

[72] László Marácz, "Multilingualism in the Transleithanian Part of the Austro-Hungarian Empire (1867–1918): Policy and Practice," *Jezikoslovlje* 13, no. 2 (2012): 269–298.

[73] Christopher M. Hutton, *Linguistics and the Third Reich: Mother-Tongue Fascism, Race and the Science of Language* (London; New York: Routledge, 1999).

[74] Anderson, *Imagined Communities*, 47.

[75] Mar-Molinero, *The Politics of Language in the Spanish-Speaking World*, 32.

continuous colonization has been largely unsuccessful; these communities tend to remain poor, underprivileged, and marginalized.[76]

The twentieth century saw the "last wave" of nationalist movements,[77] and political boundaries in Europe were redrawn according to the principle of nationality.[78] Most of this last wave occurred in exploitation colonies in Africa and Asia, after European imperialist powers were effectively annihilated by the world wars. In fact, the majority of modern states today were formed after the conclusion of the two world wars. The territorial boundaries of these newly independent states were drawn as a result of power struggles between colonial powers and had very little to do with the demographics of the people who were affected by this boundary-drawing. This means that a given speech community was likely to be split across political borders, and that the newly formed states tended to have an ethnically and linguistically diverse population. Under the influence of nationalist ideology, some leaders of these post-colonial states saw monolingualism as crucial to the building of a unified state.[79] These include Gandhi, who subscribed to the ideology of linguistic nationalism and believed that it was necessary to establish Hindi as the national language of India.[80]

But linguistic nationalism, a European invention, clashed readily with the political realities and linguistic demographics in much of the post-colonial world. Given that people's construction of identity is frequently tied to their first language, the "explosive potential" of the language issue is enormous in linguistically diverse states.[81] To avoid multiethnic rivalry, if a state language had to be chosen in post-colonial Africa, this language "invariably was the language of the departing colonial power."[82] Instead of calling it a *national* language, which does not seem politically appropriate, the colonial language is usually called an *official* language. Fishman describes that the language choice of many new states that were formed in the twentieth century was driven by considerations of political integration, which he calls *nationism*, or the very operational integrity of the nation. He writes, "(n)ationism—as distinguished from nationalism—is primarily concerned not with ethnic authenticity but with

---

[76] Mar-Molinero, *The Politics of Language*, 53.

[77] Anderson, *Imagined Communities*, 113.

[78] E. J. Hobsbawm, *Nations and Nationalism Since 1780: Programme, Myth, Reality* (Cambridge: Cambridge University Press, 1990).

[79] Such a process is often called "nation-building." However, it has been pointed out that "nation-building" in post-colonial states is really state-building that requires destruction of "nations"; see Stavenhagen, *The Ethnic Question*.

[80] Florian Coulmas, "What Are National Languages Good For?," in *With Forked Tongues: What Are National Languages Good For?*, ed. Florian Coulmas (Ann Arbor, MI: Karoma, 1988), 15. The irony is that Gandhi wrote in English, the language that he was seeking to banish.

[81] Coulmas, 13.

[82] Beban Sammy Chumbow, "Towards a Legal Framework for Language Charters in Africa," in *Law, Language and the Multilingual State*, ed. Claudine Brohy et al. (Bloemfontein: SUN MeDIA, 2012), 1–26.

operational efficiency."[83] To ensure stability, many decolonizing states have retained the colonial legal system, which is entrenched in a colonial language. The colonial linguistic legacy is generally difficult to remove, as is the ideology that colonial languages are more progressive or sophisticated than endogenous languages. Such legacy and ideology are reinforced by the fact that major imperial languages have remained powerful world languages. On the other hand, decolonizing states feel the need to end the oppression of their endogenous languages, to revive their use, and to assert a new national identity. Many endogenous languages have gained recognition as national languages—and sometimes also as official languages, alongside colonial languages. Unlike in Latin America, some post-colonial countries in Asia and Africa do not see the continued use of a colonial language as a long-term strategy. As the data in the next chapter will show, the confluence of the lingering power of the colonial language and the rising importance of endogenous languages has significantly contributed to the phenomenon of parallel multilingualism in modern states, where multiple languages may be used in parallel for the same function (in contrast with functional multilingualism).

Parallel Multilingualism in International Legal Order

Let us turn for a moment from official communication between a government and its people to communication between governments. Throughout most of human history, civilizations communicated with one another through diplomatic languages, or lingua francas. In the world of Antiquity known to us, examples of the earliest languages used in official communication between civilizations (i.e., equivalent to international relations and international law today) were Sumerian, Akkadian, Assyrian, Persian, Aramaic, Latin, Chinese, and Greek.[84] Archaeological evidence includes a treaty of peace between the city-states of Lagash and Umma inscribed in Sumerian on a stone pillar dated around 2600 BC, which was arbitrated before Mesilim, the Semitic ruler of Kish.[85] The prominence of Sumerian was superseded by Akkadian (Babylonian), which became the universal language found on stones and clay tablets across west Asia, including codes of law, treaties, and diplomatic messages between kingdoms (such as Egypt and the Hittites).

Throughout the medieval period, classical and liturgical languages became the medium of international legal encounters. Greek, Latin, and Arabic were

---

[83] Joshua A. Fishman, "National Languages and Languages of Wider Communication in the Developing Nations," in *Language in Sociocultural Change* (Stanford, CA: Stanford University Press, 1972), 194.

[84] Ostrower, *Language, Law, and Diplomacy*.

[85] Ostrower, *Language, Law, and Diplomacy*.

some of the dominant diplomatic languages. Latin was the primary language of international treaties until it was ousted in the seventeenth century by the linguistic ascendency of national languages such as French and Castilian Spanish. For example, in the Final Act of the Congress of Vienna in 1815, which was signed by all the major powers in Europe at the time, French was the only treaty language. French was used even in treaties to which France was not a party.

Linguistic nationalism brought on the decline of diplomatic languages,[86] injecting a sense of pride into national languages, which would contend for dominance and supremacy on the international stage. As modern states emerged, they have sought to use their own language in the treaties they become a party to. In the eighteenth and nineteenth centuries, it was common for two or more treaty languages to be recognized as official, but the tendency was for one version to be binding.[87]

Scattered attempts to overcome linguistic diversity in international law started as early as the seventeenth century, consisting of efforts to create a universal language that would be simple, easy to learn as a second language, and have the benefit of being politically neutral.[88] But there was no artificial language that managed to gain some currency until 1885, when Volapük became popular in German-speaking countries. In 1887, Dr. Lazarus (Ludovic Lazarus Zamenhof, 1859–1917) published a book on Esperanto, which went on to become the most successful artificial language known. Although it never became an auxiliary international language, its potential applicability had been considered with interest by the League of Nations and UNESCO. The prospect of a possible artificially constructed international language lingered into the early twentieth century. In the 1930s, English linguist Charles Ogden (1889–1957) attempted to advance Basic English, a simplified subset of regular English with a vocabulary size reduced to 850, as a global lingua franca, but the plan had limited success. Sentiment for an artificial international language subsided after the Second World War.

The development of an international legal order has consolidated parallel multilingualism as a norm. After the First World War, it became a common practice for treaties to be drawn in two or more languages that are seen as equally authentic, in order to acknowledge the equality and sovereignty of the states that are parties to the agreement (known as the doctrine of equality of states), and to ensure the genuine consent of all parties. In some cases, a "neutral language" that is not the primary language of any contracting party is agreed upon. It will be the decisive version in case of discrepancies. This practice is particularly common in tax treaties, where the neutral language tends to

---

[86] Hardy, "The Interpretation of Plurilingual Treaties by International Courts and Tribunals."
[87] Ostrower, *Language, Law, and Diplomacy*.
[88] Ostrower, *Language, Law, and Diplomacy*.

be English or French.[89] In other cases, all treaty languages are equally authentic, and discrepancies among language versions need to be reconciled, without assuming that one language is superior to another. This kind of parallel multilingualism is now a standard feature of international organizations, including the United Nations and its many auspices.

Characterizing Contemporary Legal Multilingualism

We have seen that throughout the history of Western legal traditions, there are two major ways for legal systems to cope with linguistic diversity. The first is official monolingualism: the adoption of one language for official use—a lingua franca, a diplomatic language, an imperial language, or language of the ruling class, be it in a tribe, kingdom, colony, empire, modern state, or an international legal encounter. The second is functional multilingualism or diglossia, where socially stratified languages serve different purposes (e.g., law, religion, literature, and everyday life) in the same polity, which loosely correspond to the perceived value of these languages and the power structures they represent. Both options entail *linguistic supremacy*: the placing of one language above others for official functions.

It is challenging to reconcile linguistic supremacy with contemporary politics where the linguistic plurality of multiple power groups needs to be accommodated for, and with modern, universalist ethics where a liberal polity is expected to be neutral to cultural and social norms. Parallel multilingualism, as it emerged in the twentieth century, became the norm in international law and saw a rapid expansion in national law. Similar to its adoption in international law based on equality of states, parallel multilingualism has become a popular method of managing linguistic diversity in modern states. Compared with official monolingualism, functional multilingualism, or diglossia characterized by a well-established hierarchy, which is still practiced in many modern states today, parallel multilingualism implies or emphasizes *linguistic equality*. Instead of using different languages for different jobs based on their perceived value, some multilingual states today perform the same act in two or more languages.

The political need to give official recognition to multiple languages and to treat them equally is a product of the politics of recognition, famously discussed by Charles Taylor. In a pre-modern class society, people were born either with or without honor; today every person is believed to have dignity. This gives rise to *a politics of universalism*. Since identity is no longer pre-assigned, an individual or a group—searching for their unique authentic self (a.k.a. what

[89] "Studies on Translation and Multilingualism," Language and Translation in International Law and EU Law (European Commission, 2012).

is *not* universally shared)—has to negotiate their identity through dialogue with others. The quest for identity in the modern world gives rise to *a politics of difference*. According to Taylor, the politics of equal recognition has come to mean both a politics of universalism and a politics of difference. This need for recognition became an important driving force behind nationalist movements. Consistent with the republican ideal of equal citizenship, equal recognition has become an essential quality of democratic culture.[90]

Official multilingualism arises from the politics of recognition. For many, an important marker of identity is the first language they learn to speak. On the one hand, there is a universalist basis for minority groups to demand equal recognition for their language with the language of the dominant group. If the language of one national group should have official status, then it seems fair that the same status is extended to that of another national group within the same state. Such politics of universalism has a moral nucleus: deprivation of status appears to be immoral, if such status recognition can be successfully argued to be a core element of human dignity. On the other hand, their desire to be recognized as a nation simultaneously grew from a politics of difference. In the nationalist context, status recognition is not offered to individuals, but rather to individuals who come together and identify themselves as a political unit. This recognition is not universally granted to every political group, but is often assigned and justified based on historical connection to the territory. Multiplicity of official language status thus embodies an internal conflict where it needs to be inclusive enough to address the universalist concern, and exclusive enough so that it satisfies the politics of difference. Since official language status originates from a politics of difference, official recognition becomes meaningless when everyone has it. The currency of official status is diluted by the multiplicity of status holders, but it cannot be so diluted that it loses a sense of prestige altogether. Linguistic equality is the pragmatic balance between these driving forces of official language policy.

When it comes to post-colonial polities, the granting of official status to endogenous languages has been claimed as a moral right and has been presented as a righteous response to historical injustice. Regardless of whether such recognition leads to changes in official language practice, the symbolic value of such elevated status is undeniable. The desire to recognize endogenous languages stems from a politics of difference—the need to reaffirm local identities and construct a unique and authentic nation, and the politics of universalism—the need to restore a national dignity and put it on equal footing with others after colonial deprivation.

---

[90] Charles Taylor, *Multiculturalism and the "Politics of Recognition"* (Princeton, NJ: Princeton University Press, 1992).

But discussion of such politics of recognition does not explain clearly why some states have adopted parallel multilingualism but others have not, nor does it predict how the tension between the politics of universalism and the politics of difference will pan out in specific contexts. To more closely inspect global patterns of official multilingualism, we will turn to some empirical data in the next chapter.

Chapter 2

Mapping a Global Phenomenon

THE SPECTACLE OF OFFICIAL MULTILINGUALISM

> The die is cast in Canada: there are two main ethnic and linguistic groups; each is too strong and too deeply rooted in the past, too firmly bound to a mother-culture, to be able to engulf the other. But if the two will collaborate at the hub of a truly pluralistic state, Canada could become the envied seat of a form of federalism that belongs to tomorrow's world. Better than the American melting-pot, Canada would offer an example to all those new Asian and African states . . . who must discover how to govern their polyethnic populations with proper regard for justice and liberty.
>
> —Pierre Elliot Trudeau[1]

> Total Hindi dominance, achieved at the expense of other languages, would evoke festering resentment in the non-Hindi regions and would thus be self-defeating; total triumph of the regional languages would minimize India's intellectual and political communion; total decline of English would sever India from meaningful contact with western technology.
>
> —Selig S. Harrison[2]

Having explored how official multilingualism has emerged as a product of historical and sociopolitical development, this chapter moves on to survey the extent of the phenomenon in the contemporary world. The data set offers a panoramic view of jurisdictions around the world that are officially bilingual or multilingual. Although there is not enough room to provide a detailed history

[1] Pierre Elliott Trudeau, "The New Treason of the Intellectuals," in *Federalism and the French Canadians* (Toronto: Macmillan, 1968), 151–81. Originally published in *Cité Libre* in April 1962 as "La nouvelle trahison deds clercs."

[2] Selig Harrison, "Leadership and Language Policy in India.," in *Leadership and Political Institutions in India*, ed. Richard Park and Irene Tinker (Princeton, NJ: Princeton University Press, 1959), 152.

of any particular jurisdiction, the chapter annotates the data and makes a number of generalized observations.

Although every effort is made to ensure the accuracy of the data, it is unlikely that this mammoth undertaking will end up error free. Omissions are inevitable. As a matter of fact, the data are as volatile as politics itself. During the time of writing this book, a new country was almost formed, existing language laws were revoked, and new ones came into place. Having said this, the global data provide a sense of scale that speaks for itself and allows us to observe patterns and trends that help us make sense of the phenomenon.

Some Precursors

Attempts to quantify bilingual and multilingual jurisdictions on a global scale have been scarce, with somewhat divergent results depending on the inclusion criteria.

A list compiled by the Office of the Commissioner of Official Languages contains 45 bilingual states (Table 2.1).[3] The list is entitled "Officially Bilingual Sovereign States"; thus it does not include bilingual non-sovereign territories such as Hong Kong and Macau, supranational jurisdictions such as the African Union and the European Union, and international organizations (such as the United Nations and the World Trade Organization) that have judicial powers. The website on which this information is hosted does not indicate when the list was last updated. It seems to have left out some bilingual/multilingual sovereign states (such as Bolivia and Zimbabwe). The list, in alphabetical order, is reproduced in Table 2.1.

Another attempt was made by de Varennes in a research report he produced in 2012 for Die Afrikaanse Taalraad (Afrikaans Language Council) when South Africa considered its official languages bill (Table 2.2).[4] He has included countries that have a bilingual or multilingual policy at a sub-state level. Following this criterion, countries that are generally perceived as monolingual, such as China, Italy, the United Kingdom, and the United States, have made it to the list. De Varennes's list has 71 entries, which amount to more than a third of the world's countries.

Both lists have helpfully demonstrated the prevalence of official multilingualism, but both seem to be incomplete, and little data exploration has been done to analyze the phenomenon that they were trying to capture.

---

[3] The list is available at http://www.ocol-clo.gc.ca/newsletter_cyberbulletin/etats_bil_stat_e.htm
[4] de Varennes, "International and Comparative Perspectives in the Use of Official Languages."

TABLE 2.1

List of Bilingual Sovereign States Compiled by the Office of the Commissioner of Official Languages

Afghanistan	Chad	Israel	Nauru	Singapore
Belarus	Comoros	Kenya	New Zealand	South Africa
Belgium	Djibouti	Kiribati	Norway	Sri Lanka
Bosnia-Herzegovina	East Timor	Kyrgyzstan	Pakistan	Swaziland
Burundi	Eritrea	Lesotho	Palau	Switzerland
Cameroon	Finland	Madagascar	Philippines	Tanzania
Canada	Haiti	Malta	Rwanda	Tonga
Cape Verde	India	Mauritania	Samoa	Tuvalu
Central African Republic	Ireland	Namibia	Seychelles	Vanuatu

TABLE 2.2

List of Countries with Two or More Official Languages at the Provincial, State, or Regional Levels, According to de Varennes

Afghanistan	Denmark	Kazakhstan	Norway	Spain
Algeria	Djibouti	Kosovo	Pakistan	Sri Lanka
Austria	East Timor	Kyrgyzstan	Palau	Swaziland
Belgium	Equatorial Guinea	Lesotho	Paraguay	Switzerland
Belarus	Ethiopia	Luxembourg	Peru	Tanzania
Bolivia	Fiji	Macedonia	Philippines	Ukraine
Bosnia	Finland	Madagascar	Portugal	United Kingdom
Burundi	Georgia	Malta	Russia	United States
Cameroon	Germany	Marshall Islands	Rwanda	Vanuatu
Canada	Guatemala	Micronesia	Serbia	Vatican
Chad	Haiti	Moldova	Seychelles	Zimbabwe
China	India	Morocco	Singapore	
Central African Republic	Iraq	Netherlands	Slovenia	
Comoros	Ireland	New Zealand	South Africa	
Cyprus	Italy	Nicaragua	South Sudan	

Inclusion Criteria

There is no correct way of compiling such a list—the data are too complex to fit into neat categories. For example, since only a few US states and territories have more than one official language, to call the country a bilingual or multilingual jurisdiction does not seem to be an entirely accurate portrayal. Similarly,

China has special administrative regions that have different legal systems from the one used in the mainland, with their own language policies. In my data coding, I have therefore chosen to list separately multilingual practice at the state and sub-state level.

The purpose of my data collection is less about quantification of the phenomenon than critical analysis of macro-level factors that might have led to the emergence of official multilingualism. Such an analysis provides empirical support for the insight developed from the historical analysis in Chapter 1. For example, this data set allows me to gauge the extent to which official multilingualism reflects a decolonization struggle. To facilitate such kind of analysis, I have opted for a detail-oriented approach to data presentation and, wherever practicable, I have surveyed not only sovereign states, but also political units that are smaller or bigger than states, thus including sub-state, state, and inter-state legal orders. Given that legal systems are my chief concern, I have decided to include any political entity that has juridical power and is capable of having its own language law. To help the reader appreciate the variables in such language practice, I have organized my data into separate lists, although unavoidably, marginal members exist for each list. I consider my criteria generous and inclusive, allowing the possibility for the data to be recomposed later by future researchers who are interested in exploring alternative variables.

An important inclusion criterion is whether an official multilingual policy is entrenched in law or otherwise clearly articulated by the government. This does not at all deny the relevance of de facto legal multilingual practices, but is a pragmatic decision to impose some boundary to an otherwise infinitely expandable discussion. This decision allows us to gauge the role of law in jurisdictions that do entrench its linguistic practice in the law. It also follows that jurisdictions that are not on my list may not be strictly monolingual. As de Varennes has pointed out, even officially monolingual countries inevitably engage in some official use of more than one language. Many have no official language law whatsoever or allow for flexible linguistic practice. In some cases, not enough data are publicly available for my accurate assessment. Toward the end of the chapter, I have included some data on political units that have a de facto bilingual or multilingual policy for illustrative purposes, but the list is far from exhaustive. By definition, the key quality of a de facto practice is its lack of a clearly stated rule, which poses a great challenge for data collection.

In this chapter I will not concern myself with the specific status label (e.g., state/official/national/working language) given to a language, as long as it has some kind of official or legal recognition. Recognition as a minority or indigenous language will be excluded, as its legal origins and ramifications tend to be different; such recognition does not come to characterize a polity, but is applied to a language or its speakers. Moreover, an official or national language status can be applied to dominant, minority, and indigenous languages, and rights flowing from such status are not minority or indigenous rights. Variation in status labels and their significance will be dealt with in the next chapter.

My data are primarily drawn from electronic and printed materials from published law, official government publications, newspaper archives, journal articles, and academic references. Despite likely imperfections, this data set provides the possibility for a systematic evaluation of the bilingual and multilingual situation in global jurisdictions today. Before I present the data, I would like to address some contestable issues.

Contestable Issues

Any attempt to draw any boundary to the data or put them in boxes will be subject to challenges. The categories adopted in the following are laden with contested concepts such as *language, jurisdiction*, and *colonization*. Instead of avoiding them, I will take the opportunity to problematize them, in the hope of clarifying the sources of conceptual uncertainties in the current context.

WHAT IS A LANGUAGE?

According to Billig, the concept of a language may be a historical construct of nationalism. If this is true, then "language does not create nationalism, so much as nationalism creates language."[5] Even in the aftermath of such a historical invention, contemporary sociolinguistic analysis shows that language is not a countable, static, discrete, and finite thing. Gal and Woolard call *languages, dialects*, and *speech communities* "cultural categories of communication" that are constructed from "the messy variability of spoken interaction."[6]

Just as nations are imagined communities, national languages also must be imagined.[7] Linguistic difference has been constructed or maintained to mark social difference and sustain different senses of identity. Consider the official languages of Bosnia-Herzegovina: Bosnian, Croatian, and Serbian have minimal linguistic differences and are often considered variants of the same "language." They are mutually intelligible and share essentially the same grammar and phonology. It may therefore be argued that there is only one official language in Bosnia-Herzegovina, but that this language carries three different names. The different names are of crucial political importance, for they represent the identity of three constituent nations and ethnic groups in

---

[5] Billig, *Banal Nationalism*, 15.

[6] Susan Gal and Kathryn A Woolard, "Constructing Languages and Publics: Authority and Representation," *Pragmatics* 5, no. 2 (1995): 129.

[7] Billig, *Banal Nationalism*.

the country. Norway presents a similar case. Norwegian law recognizes two official forms of written Norwegian: Bokmål and Nynorsk. Bokmål was adapted from Danish and is associated with elitism, and Nynorsk is the lesser-used, folk, purist Norwegian alternative. Supporters of these two written varieties of the Norwegian language are politically divided. Other examples of closely related language varieties that have separately received formal recognition include Czech and Slovak, Kven and Finnish, Dutch and Afrikaans.

The converse problem is that mutually unintelligible varieties may be treated as the same language for political reasons. Language varieties in China have different tonal systems and orthography, for example, but they are considered dialects rather than languages because their speakers live within the state borders of China.[8]

Another source of convolution comes from language change: the same "language" may develop distinctive properties in different territories. English, French, and German are an official language in different territories, but the varieties used in these territories may be rather different (thus the popularization of the term "Englishes" rather than English[9]). Pidgins and creoles that developed during colonial encounters (such as Tok Pisin in Papua New Guinea, which is an English Creole[10]) may become official languages in their own right. Language change may occur organically, may be triggered by language contact, or may be engineered top-down. More fundamentally, languages are inherently heteroglot, encompassing diachronically and synchronically diverse points of view and intersecting with one another in different ways.[11]

Much as countries have seemingly no difficulty in conferring official status to languages, we will not have problems referring to and counting languages based on conventional wisdom in the rest of the book. But the slipperiness of the concept of language remains an important insight, especially in discussing its malleability in identity politics. Although clichéd, the comment "a language is a dialect with an army and navy" (a statement credited to Yiddish linguist Max Weinreich[12]) still captures well the recognition that it is power that distinguishes a language from a dialect.

---

[8] Interestingly, Mandarin, the standard dialect of Chinese in China, is recognized as an official *language* in Singapore.

[9] See the works of Kachru, such as Barj B. Kachru, "World Englishes: Approaches, Issues and Resources," *Language Teaching* 25, no. 1 (January 1992): 1–14.

[10] Though biases against pidgins and creoles persist. See critique by Michel DeGraff, "Against Creole Exceptionalism," *Language* 79, no. 2 (June 2003): 391–410.

[11] Bakhtin, "Discourse in the Novel."

[12] Max Weinreich, "Der YIVO Un Die Problemen Fun Undzer Zayt [The Yiddish Scientific Institute and the Problems of Our Time]," *Yivo-Bleter* 25 (1945): 13.

WHAT IS A JURISDICTION?

Jurisdiction, derived from the Latin equivalent of "law's speech/saying," refers to the authority to exercise legislative and judicial power, or the geographical or subject area where such authority applies. I have chosen to use jurisdiction as a unit of analysis, because many bilingual and multilingual jurisdictions in the world today exist within a state (e.g., Hong Kong) or beyond state boundaries (e.g., the EU). Jurisdictions may not be sovereign, autonomous, or independent; they may overlap with one another.

The sub-state legal orders discussed here enjoy some devolved authority from the state to practice their own language law. To avoid running into the problem, as faced by studies of legal pluralism, of having to identify the legal from what is not, I have decided not to include customs or other informal law operating independently of official law. In practice, many jurisdictions have a mixed legal system, and if taking, say, customary and religious (such as Sharia) courts into account, the number of bilingual and multilingual jurisdictions will be higher than what is summarized in the following.

Since I have chosen to use jurisdiction as a unit of analysis in this chapter, my survey does not include non-institutionalized forms of international law practice, such as treaty making, which also contribute to the multilingual legal order.

WHAT IS COLONIZATION?

In my data set in the following, I consider whether one or more official languages in each bilingual or multilingual jurisdiction are inherited from a former colonizer. A categorical problem is thus the question of what *colonization* means. The term typically refers to political and economic domination of one population by another, traditionally achieved through military means. The colonized land may be used for settlement or exploited for economic benefits.

As Moore has put it, "It is no doubt true that there is, on this planet, not a single square meter of inhabited land that has not been, at one time or another, colonized and then post-colonial."[13] Nevertheless, the literature on colonization is dominated by discussions of the Western European hegemony. Similarly, the term *post-colonial* tends to be applied to territories that had been colonized between 1492 (which marks the beginning of the Age of Discovery) to the nineteenth century but not earlier.

While many bilingual and multilingual jurisdictions in my data set have been subjugated by Western imperialists, there are other forms of dominations that do not involve the prototypical European colonizer. The most notable

[13] David Chioni Moore, "Is the Post- in Postcolonial the Post- in Post-Soviet? Toward a Global Postcolonial Critique," *PMLA* 116, no. 1 (2001): 111–28.

examples are the United States,[14] China,[15] Japan, the Ottoman Empire, and Russia.[16] Whether Soviet expansion was a form of colonization is disputed, in part due to Russia's denial of its colonial past and its effort to whitewash the relevant history. Unlike European colonizers that conquered overseas territories, the Soviet Union expanded outward through a series of accretion, military annexation, and—at least somewhat involuntary—political and economic integration. Such expansion was projected in a positive light and was described as the development of "friendship" and as protection from other conquerors at the time.[17] Notwithstanding the distinctive propaganda, I will treat Russia as a communist variant of a colonizer. In my classification I have included European and non-European colonization that started or was still ongoing post-1492, and have excluded those that took place earlier, such as Arabization that followed extensive Muslim conquests in Central and South Asia, Middle East, and parts of Africa and Europe between the seventh and eleventh centuries.

The status of protectorates is less clear and deserves a remark. Protectorate is a relationship established by treaty where a stronger state offers protection of and has decisive control over a weaker state, which retains formal sovereignty over internal affairs. It was a common and relatively affordable technique for colonial empires to expand their territorial control in the late nineteenth century, which allows them to benefit economically from weaker states without assuming an administrative burden. It has been suggested that the distinction between external and internal sovereignty is an artificial one, for the protecting power has paramount authority to redefine its scope of control. In any event, Anghie argues that the distinction between protectorates and colonies "gradually eroded" over time.[18] For example, the British gradually assumed political control over most of the territories that were initially its protectorates in order to ensure economic stability. Territories that were protectorates, and those that were subjected to variant treatment such as administration or trusteeship, are therefore included and annotated in the data.

There are also ongoing forms of colonization, such as that of native peoples in Australia, Canada, New Zealand, and the United States, Gilgit people

---

[14] Alyosha Goldstein, ed., *Formations of United States Colonialism* (Durham, NC: Duke University Press Books, 2014).

[15] The Qing Empire expanded into the heart of Central Eurasia (including Turkistan and Mongolia) in the 17th and 18th C. Peter C. Perdue, *China Marches West: The Qing Conquest of Central Eurasia*, reprint ed. (Cambridge, MA; London: Belknap Press, 2010).

[16] The Soviet Russian Red Army occupied and Sovietized Chechnya, Armenia, Azerbaijan, and Georgia in 1920–1921.

[17] Solomon M. Schwarz, "Revising the History of Russian Colonialism," *Foreign Affairs* 30, no. 3 (1952): 488–93.

[18] Antony Anghie, *Imperialism, Sovereignty and the Making of International Law* (2004; reprint, Cambridge: Cambridge University Press, 2007), 89.

in the Northern Areas of Pakistan,[19] and arguably Tibetans and Xinjiang Uyghurs in China. A few disputed cases involve the British Empire—whether Ireland was in some sense an English colony and whether Wales and Scotland are English colonies. The cases of Ireland and Scotland seem particularly contentious. These are annotated wherever relevant.

GAP BETWEEN POLICY AND PRACTICE

One challenge to identifying bilingual and multilingual jurisdictions is the gap between policy and practice. In a way, this resembles the general mismatch between law on paper and the everyday lived experience of law, but with its own share of complexities.

The granting of de jure status to a language creates the expectation that it will be used for official purposes, but does not guarantee so. Sometimes the recognition seems to be merely symbolic, based on historical relevance; in these cases, the difference between policy and practice is not a performative gap. Others aspire to become bilingual or multilingual but have yet to reach the stage of implementation. Languages that have the same official status may not be used symmetrically, as status labels and actual usage may be incongruent. For instance, Irish is the first official language of Ireland but its use is still more limited than the second official language. Some nations have made status-planning decisions without following up with policy implementation, for one reason or another—some may be restrained by the availability of resources and a functioning government; some lack motivation; some others are preoccupied with managing more urgent crises.

Many jurisdictions—monolingual, bilingual, or multilingual—have never assigned any official status to language, but their choice of language in public domains has been established by practice and may be thought of as de facto official languages. For example, English is the default language with no official status at the federal level in Australia, the United Kingdom, and the United States. One may also be surprised to learn that French acquired official status through a constitutional amendment only in 1992, and Italian only became an official language of Italy in 2007. Many nations (such as Argentina, Liberia, and Mexico) also have legislation that grants linguistic rights to minority groups without conferring any official status to their languages.

Having chosen one or more official languages does not necessarily exclude the use of other languages in official communication. Many jurisdictions, including monolingual ones, tolerate the use of non-official and non-standard vernaculars in regional courts, tribunals, family courts, and traditional courts

---

[19] Martin Sökefeld, "From Colonialism to Postcolonial Colonialism: Changing Modes of Domination in the Northern Areas of Pakistan," *The Journal of Asian Studies* 64, no. 4 (2005): 939–73.

that practice customary law, and thus practice a form of de facto multilingualism in these courts. For example, in the officially monolingual but linguistically diverse country of Namibia, English is the only official language, but Afrikaans is the lingua franca of the country.[20] While English is generally the language of the court, it is up to a community court to use any language, including sign language, in any proceedings (s15 of Community Courts Act 2003, Namibia).

Even for polities that have implemented a bilingual or multilingual policy, legal systems tend to be more resistant to language change than executive branches of government. In other words, adoption of a language policy in the legal system may lag behind that in other public domains. This was the case in Hong Kong, where Chinese acquired an official status in 1974 but it was to be used in all public domains except law; the use of Chinese extended to the legal domain only in the late 1980s. On the other hand, there are those that practise bilingualism or multilingualism in law but have no statewide bilingual or multilingual language policy, especially mixed jurisdictions (e.g., English common law and Shariah law in the officially bilingual country of Brunei).

There is also the issue of unbalanced bilingualism and multilingualism. Languages may share the same status or are held to be equal, but are not treated as though they are equal. Just as bilingual and multilingual individuals do not usually have equal command of all their languages, bilingual and multilingual jurisdictions may in practice show overt or covert preference to using one or more languages over others (see examples in Chapter 6).

All in all, it is safe to say that there is often a huge gap between policy and practice in official multilingualism. Pool's conceptual framework might be helpful here in helping us make sense of some of the divergence. He defines a language regime as a set of official languages and a set of rules governing their use.[21] Therefore, language status alone does not dictate a language regime; rules that govern usage may be written rather differently across jurisdictions. Conferring status to a language and adopting a language into an institution are separable processes.[22] In this chapter I endeavor to include all jurisdictions that have embraced multilingualism officially, and will deal with the question of practice in the second half of the book.

---

[20] http://www.gov.na/languages-spoken.

[21] Jonathan Pool, "Optimal Language Regimes for the European Union," *International Journal of the Sociology of Language* 121 (1996): 159–79.

[22] Stephen May, *Language and Minority Rights: Ethnicity, Nationalism and the Politics of Language* (New York: Routledge, 2012).

Bilingual and Multilingual Sovereign States

A total of 74 bilingual and multilingual sovereign states have been identified; the findings are summarized in Table 2.3. Taking an inclusive approach to data collection, the table features Abkhazia, Kosovo, South Ossetia, and Sahrawi Arab Democratic Republic, which have a disputed sovereign status.

The next section will offer brief commentaries on observable patterns and trends in the adoption of official multilingualism in each continent.

AFRICA

Thirty-five African nations[23] are included in the list, making up approximately 64% of all African states, or 47% of all bilingual and multilingual sovereign states. All bilingual and multilingual sovereign states in Africa had been colonized by European powers (predominantly British and French). The great majority of them, apart from Algeria (former French colony), Mauritania (former French colony), Morocco (former French and Spanish protectorate) and Somalia (former part-British, part-Italian colony), have retained one or more languages (English, French, Spanish, or Portuguese) of a former colonizer (Belgian, British, French, Spanish, or Portuguese) as an official language. This means that 89% (or 31) of the bilingual and multilingual sovereign states in Africa have become bilingual and multilingual in part due to the legacy of colonial rule.

Thirteen of the listed states are bilingual with official status given to a colonial language and an endogenous language.[24] Fifteen African states are multilingual with official status given to at least one colonial language and an endogenous language.[25] Among these, seven states have five or more official or national languages: Democratic Republic of Congo (5), Mali (14), Niger (13), Senegal (7), South Africa (11), Zambia (8), and Zimbabwe (16). These figures do not include Cameroon, which has an unspecified number of national languages (Part 1, Article 1(3) of the 1996 Constitution), a term which in context is used to refer to its indigenous languages. Estimates vary, but there are somewhere between 200 and 300 indigenous languages in the country of 21 million

---

[23] Algeria, Botswana, Burundi, Cameroon, Cape Verde, Central African Republic, Chad, Comoros, Democratic Republic of Congo, Djibouti, Equatorial Guinea, Kenya, Lesotho, Madagascar, Malawi, Mali, Mauritania, Morocco, Niger, Nigeria, Republic of the Congo, Republic of Guinea, Rwanda, Sahrawi Arab Democratic Republic, Senegal, Seychelles, Somalia, South Africa, South Sudan, Sudan, Swaziland, Tanzania, Uganda, Zambia, and Zimbabwe.

[24] These include Botswana, Cape Verde, Central African Republic, Chad, Djibouti, Kenya, Lesotho, Madagascar, Malawi, Sahrawi Arab Democratic Republic, Sudan, Swaziland, and Tanzania.

[25] These include Burundi, Comoros, Democratic Republic of Congo, Mali, Niger, Nigeria, Republic of Congo, Republic of Guinea, Rwanda, Senegal, Seychelles, South Africa, South Sudan, Zambia, and Zimbabwe.

TABLE 2.3

Bilingual and Multilingual Sovereign States in the World

Jurisdiction	Official (O) / National (N) Languages	Former Colonial Language as Exoglossic Language[a]
Abkhazia[b]	Abkhaz (O), Russian ("Language of State")[c]	Yes (Russian, 1801–1991[d])
Afghanistan	Pashto (O & N), Dari[e] (O)[f]	No (modern state from 18C)
Algeria	Arabic (O & N), Tamazight (a standard dialect of Berber) (O & N)[g]	No[h] (independence from France in 1962)
Belgium	French (O), Dutch (O), German (O)[i]	No (modern state from early 19th C)
Belarus	Belarusian (O), Russian (O)[j]	Yes (Russian, ca. 1795–1991)
Bolivia	Spanish (O) and 36 indigenous languages[k] (total 37[l]).	Yes (Spanish, ca. 1524–1825)
Bosnia and Herzegovina	Bosnian (O), Croatian (O), Serbian (O)[m]	No (modern state from 1992)
Botswana	English (O), Setswana (N)[n]	Yes (British protectorate, 1885–1966)
Brunei	Malay (O), English (O)[o]	Yes (British protectorate, 1888–1984)
Burundi	English (O)[p], French (O), Kirundi (O, N)[q]	Yes (Belgian, 1916–1962)
Cameroon	English (O), French (O), an unspecified number of indigenous languages are known as national languages[r]	Yes (British & French,[s] 1919–1960)
Canada	English (O), French (O)[t]	Yes (British & French, early 16th C–1982)
Cape Verde	Portuguese (O), Crioulo (O)[u]	Yes (Portuguese, 15th C–1975)
Central African Republic	French (O), Sango (O)[v]	Yes (French, 1911–1960)
Chad	French (O), Arabic (O)[w]	Yes (French, 1900–1960)
Comoros	French (O), Arabic (O), Comorian/ Shikomor (O, N)[x]	Yes (French, 1886–1975)
Cyprus	Greek (O), Turkish (O)[y]	Yes (Ottoman Empire, late 16C–1960)
Democratic Republic of the Congo[z]	French (O), Kituba (called "Kikongo" in the Constitution) (N), Lingala (N), Swahili (N), Tshiluba (N)[aa]	Yes (as Belgian Congo 1908–1960)
Djibouti	French (O), Arabic (O)[bb]	Yes (French, 1894–1977)
Equatorial Guinea	French (O), Spanish (O), Portuguese (O)[cc]	Yes (Spanish & Portuguese, 1474–independence from Spain 1968)
Fiji	English (O), Fijian (O), Fiji Hindi/ Hindustani (O)[dd]	Yes (British, 1874–1970)
Finland	Finnish (N), Swedish (N)[ee]	Yes (Swedish, ca. 1250–1809)
Haiti	French (O), Haitian Creole (O)[ff]	Yes (French 1664–1804, recognized 1825)
India	Hindi (O); English (semi-O, used for official purposes)[gg]	Yes (British, 1757–1947)
Iraq	Arabic (O), Kurdish (O)[hh]	Yes (Ottoman, 1534–1918; also former British colony)
Ireland	Irish Gaelic (N & 1st O), English (2nd O)[ii]	Disputed (British, late 12th C–1922)

TABLE 2.3 CONTINUED

Jurisdiction	Official (O) / National (N) Languages	Former Colonial Language as Exoglossic Language[a]
Kazakhstan	Kazakh (O & S)[ll] and Russian (O)[mm]	Yes (Russian, 1813–1991)
Kenya	Swahili (O & N), English (O)[nn]	Yes (British, 1888–1963)
Kiribati	English (O), Kiribati/Gilbertese (O)[oo]	Yes (British, 1892–1979)
Kosovo[pp]	Albanian (O), Serbian (O)[qq]	Yes (Ottoman, 1455–1912; Serbia/ Yugoslavia 1912–2008?; declared independence in 2008)
Kyrgyzstan	Kyrgyz (O), Russian (O)[rr]	Yes (Russian, 1876–1991)
Lesotho	English (O), Sesotho (O)[ss]	Yes (British protectorate 1868–1966)
Luxembourg	French (O), German (O), Luxembourgish (O & N)[tt]	Yes (French & German; independence 1867)
Madagascar	Malagasy (O), French (O)[uu]	Yes (French, 1895–1960)
Malawi	Chichewa (O[vv]), English (O)	Yes (British, 1891–1964)
Malaysia	Bahasa Malay[ww] (O & N); English (O)[xx]	Yes (British, 1824–1957)
Mali	French (O), Bambara (N), Bomu (N), Tieyaxo Bozo (N), Toro So Dogon (N), Maasina Fulfulde (N), Hasanya Arabic (N), Mamara Senoufo (N), Kita Maninkakan (N), Soninke (N), Koyraboro Senni Songhay (N), Syenara Senoufo (N), Tamasheq (N), Xaasongaxango (N)	Yes (French, late 19th C–1960)
Malta	English (O), Maltese (O, N),[yy] Maltese Sign Language (O)[zz]	Yes (British, 1800–1964)
Marshall Islands	Marshallese (O), English (O)[aaa]	Yes (US administration, 1947–1986; currently in "free association" with the US)
Mauritania	Arabic (O, N), Poular (N), Soninké (N), Wolof (N)[bbb]	No[ccc]
Mexico	Spanish (N), Mexican Sign Language (N), and 68 indigenous languages (N)[ddd]	Yes (Spanish, 1519–1821)
Morocco	Arabic (O), Tamazight[eee] (O)	No (modern state from 1956)
New Zealand	English[fff] (O), Māori (O), New Zealand Sign Language (O)[ggg]	Yes (British, 1840–1947[hhh])
Niger	French (O), Hausa (N), Songhai-Zarma (N), Tamajeq (N), Fulfulde (N), Kanuri (N), Arabic (N), Gurma (N), Toubou (N), Buduma (N), Tassawaq (N)[iii]	Yes (French, 1900–1958)
Nigeria	English (O), Hausa (M[jjj]), Yoruba (M), Igbo (M)	Yes (British, 1885–1960[kkk])
Norway	Two forms of Norwegian: Nynorsk (O), Bokmål (O)[lll]	Disputed[mmm] (modern state from 1905)
Pakistan	Urdu (O, N), English (semi-O)[nnn]	Yes (British, 1843–1947)
Palau	English (O), Palauan (O), Palauan traditional languages (N)[ooo]	Yes (US administration 1947–1978)
Paraguay	Guaraní (O & N), Castilian Spanish (O & N)[ppp]	Yes (Spanish; early 16th C–1811)

(continued)

TABLE 2.3 CONTINUED

Jurisdiction	Official (O) / National (N) Languages	Former Colonial Language as Exoglossic Language[a]
Philippines	English (O), Filipino (O)[qqq]	Yes (USA, 1901–1946[rrr])
Republic of the Congo[sss]	French (O), Kituba (N), Lingala (N)[ttt]	Yes (French, 1880–1960)
Republic of Guinea (Guinea-Conakry)	French (O), Susu (N), Peul (N), Maninka (N), Kissi (N), Toma (N), Bassari (N), Guerzé (N), Koniagui (N)[uuu]	Yes (French, 19th C–1958)
Rwanda	French (O), English (O), Kinyarwanda (O & N)[vvv]	Yes (Belgian, 1922–1961)
Sahrawi Arab Democratic Republic[www]	Arabic (O, N), Spanish as "second language"[xxx]	Yes (Spain, 1884–1976)
Samoa[yyy]	English (O), Samoan (O)[zzz]	Yes (New Zealand administration 1914–1962)
Senegal	French (O, N), Jola (N), Malinké (N), Pulaar (N), Sereer (N), Soninké (N), and Wolof (N)[aaaa]	Yes (French, 1850s–1960)
Seychelles	French (O), English (O), Seselwa Creole French Language (O)[bbbb]	Yes (British & French, 1756–1976)
Singapore	English (O), Malay (O & N), Chinese (O), Tamil (O)[cccc]	Yes (British from 1819; independence from Malaysia 1965)
Somalia	Somali (O), Arabic (O)[dddd]	No (modern state from 1960)
South Africa	Afrikaans (O), English (O), Ndebele (O), Northern Sotho (O), Sotho (O), Swazi (O), Tswana (O), Tsonga (O), Venda (O), Xhosa (O) and Zulu (O)[eeee]	Yes (Dutch, 1652–1795; British, 1795–1960; note Dutch influence on Afrikaans)
South Ossetia[ffff]	Ossetian (O), Russian (O)[gggg]	Yes (Russian, 1801–1991; declared independence from Georgia in 1990)
South Sudan	English (OW ["official working language"]), "all indigenous languages" (N)[hhhh]	Yes (as part of Sudan; British with Egypt 1858–final independence 1956; independence from Sudan in 2011
Sri Lanka	Sinhala (O, N), Tamil (O, N), English ("link language")[iiii]	No, except for "link language" (former Portuguese, Dutch and British colony 1796–1948)
Sudan	Arabic (O, N), English (O)[jjjj]	Yes (British with Egypt 1858–final independence 1956)
Swaziland	English (O), Swati (O)[kkkk]	Yes (British, 1903–1968)
Switzerland	French (O, N), German (O, N), Italian (O, N), Romansh (semi-O, N)[llll]	No (modern state since 1848)
Tanzania	Swahili (N), English (O?)[mmmm]	Yes (British, 1919–1961)
Timor-Leste (East Timor)	Portuguese (O), Tetum (O, N), Indonesian (W), English (W)[nnnn]	Yes (Portuguese, 1702–1975, until Indonesian invasion)
Tonga	English (O), Tongan (O)[oooo]	Yes (British Protectorate, 1900–1970)
Tuvalu	English (O), Tuvaluan (O)[pppp]	Yes (British, 1892–1978)
Uganda	English (O), Swahili (O)[qqqq]	Yes (British, 1894–1962)

TABLE 2.3 CONTINUED

Jurisdiction	Official (O) / National (N) Languages	Former Colonial Language as Exoglossic Language[a]
Vanuatu	French (O), English (O), Bislama (O, N)[rrrr]	Yes (British & French; independence 1980)
Zambia	English (O), Bemba (N), Nyanja (N), Tonga (N), Lozi (N), Lunda (N), Kaonde (N), Luvale (N)[ssss]	Yes (British, 1911–1964)
Zimbabwe	Chewa (O), Chibarwe (O), English (O), Kalanga (O), Koisan (O), Nambya (O), Ndau (O), Ndebele (O), Shangani (O), Shona (O), sign language (O), Sotho (O), Tonga (O), Tswana (O), Venda (O) and Xhosa (O)[tttt]	Yes (British, 1888–1965)

[a] Referring to an exogenous language being used in an official capacity. Colonization history that is not directly related to the ascendency of such languages do not receive annotation here. Period of colonial occupation, if any, is indicated in brackets.

[b] Sovereign status disputed (Georgia); not recognized by the UN.

[c] Article 6 of the 1994 Constitution.

[d] Russia annexed Georgia in 1801; Georgia became independent in 1991 and Abkhazia declared independence from Georgia in 1992.

[e] Also known as Farsi or Afghan Persian.

[f] Official languages first declared in Article 3 of 1964 Constitution; now in Article 16 of 2004 Constitution.

[g] Tamazight became an additional national language through a 2002 constitutional amendment, and further acquired official status in 2016.

[h] The country experienced Ottoman and French colonization. Despite government effect to Arabicize the country and remove the colonial legacy, French remains the lingua franca of Algeria. Documents prepared by Algeria to UN forums also tend to be written in French. French is arguably a de facto working language of the country.

[i] Official languages are organized based on a territorial principle; this is enshrined in Article 4 of the Constitution. Article 30 adds that "[t]he use of languages spoken in Belgium is optional; only the law can rule on this matter, and only for acts of the public authorities and for judicial affairs." Language legislation first appeared in 1873, and equality of Dutch and French was conferred in the Coremans–De Vriendt law of 1898.

[j] Belarusian was the only official language in the 1994 Constitution. Russian was added as another official language in the 1996 Constitution, Article 17: "The Belarusian and Russian languages shall be the official languages of the Republic of Belarus."

[k] Some of the indigenous official languages, such as Canichana, Cayubaba, Guarasuawe, and Puquina are already extinct.

[l] Recognition granted in Article 5.I. of the 2009 Constitution: "The official languages of the State are Spanish and all the languages of the rural native indigenous nations and peoples, which are Aymara, Araona, Baure, Bésiro, Canichana, Cavineño, Cayubaba, Chácobo, Chimán, Ese Ejja, Guaraní, Guarasu'we, Guarayu, Itonama, Leco, Machajuyai-kallawaya, Machineri, Maropa, Mojeñotrinitario, Mojeño-ignaciano, Moré, Mosetén, Movima, Pacawara, Puquina, Quechua, Sirionó, Tacana, Tapiete, Toromona, Uruchipaya, Weenhayek, Yaminawa, Yuki, Yuracaré and Zamuco."

[m] Equality of the three official languages was affirmed by the Constitutional Court in 2000.

[n] The constitution does not specify official languages; but the ability to speak and read English is a prerequisite of membership to the House of Chiefs and the National Assembly. Setswana may be used in the Parliament from 1998 onwards. Trials are conducted in English in High Courts and Magistrates' courts; customary courts operate in indigenous languages. Elma Thekiso, "A Sociolinguistic Study of Communication Processes in a Court of Law in Gaborone, Botswana" (PhD thesis, University of Warwick, 2001).

[o] Although Article 82 of the 1959 Constitution only calls Malay an official language, it provides that all official documents are bilingual in Malay and English, and the official English text of law is authentic. Article 5A of the Language of the Supreme Court provides that all Supreme Court proceedings to be in the English language. Hjh Masmahirah Hj Mohd Tali, "Courtroom Discourse: A Case Study of the Linguistic Strategies in Brunei Courtrooms," in *The Use and Status of Language in Brunei Darussalam: A Kingdom of Unexpected Linguistic Diversity*, ed. Noor Azam Haji-Othman, James McLellan, and David Deterding (Springer, 2016).

[p] Since August 28, 2014. "English Is Now Official Language of Burundi," *IWACU English News*, September 17, 2014, http://www.iwacu-burundi.org/englishnews/english-is-now-official-language-of-burundi/.

(*continued*)

TABLE 2.3 CONTINUED

[q] National language status enshrined in Article 5 of the 2005 Constitution. The same Article also provides that the "official languages are Kirundi and all other languages determined by the law." The same provision is also found in Article 8 of the 1992 Constitution.

[r] Article 1, Part 1(3) of the 1996 Constitution.

[s] British and French jointly administered Cameroon before partitioning it into an English sector and a French sector.

[t] Official languages first enshrined in Constitution Act, 1867, s133; then Official Languages Act, 1969.

[u] Also known as Cape Verdean Creole. Its official status is ambiguous. Although there is no explicit conferral of official language status to the creole, Article 9 of the 2010 Constitution promotes its "officialization" and states that it is the duty of every citizen to know the official languages (note the use of plural).

[v] Article 18 of the 2004 Constitution.

[w] Official languages first enshrined in Article 1 of the 1982 Constitution; now Article 9 of the 1996 Constitution.

[x] Article 1 of the 1978/2001 Constitution.

[y] Currently in Article 3 of the 2013 Constitution; recognized in the 1960 Constitution since independence.

[z] Not to be confused with the Republic of the Congo.

[aa] Recognition in the Constitution dated back from at least 1993. The latter four all as provincial language in different regions under Article 1(8) of the Constitution; see http://www.ethnologue.com/country/CD/languages

[bb] Official bilingualism since the 1992 Constitution.

[cc] Status of official languages enshrined in Article 4 of the Constitution. "Equatorial Guinea Adds Portuguese as the Country's Third Official Language," *PR Newswire*, October 14, 2011, http://www.prnewswire.com/news-releases/equatorial-guinea-adds-portuguese-as-the-countrys-third-official-language-131882808.html. See also http://www.guineaecuatorialpress.com/noticia.php?id=703&lang=en.

[dd] Official languages were recognized in the 1997 Constitution. Such status has neither been revoked nor mentioned in the 2013 Constitution.

[ee] Official languages provision has been present in the 1919 Constitution since its inception. Official minority languages are also recognized: Sami, Romani, Finnish Sign Language, and Karelian.

[ff] Official languages enshrined in the 1983 Constitution. French was the sole official language in the previous Constitution of 1964.

[gg] Also see discussion in this chapter on regional multilingual policy. Article 343 of the 1949 Constitution provides for the use of English in official purposes.

[hh] Official languages recognized since the 1970 interim Constitution.

[ii] Official languages recognized since the Constitution of the Irish Free State, 1922.

[ll] Known as the "state" language in Article 7 of the 1995 Constitution.

[mm] Official languages recognized in the 1995 Constitution.

[nn] Official bilingualism was added as amendment (Article 53, as amended by Act 1 of 1975, s. 3, and Act 1 of 1979, s. 3) to the 1963 Constitution. It is now in Article 7 of the 2010 Constitution.

[oo] Official status not explicitly provided in Constitution, but Article 127 reads: "127. The provisions of this Constitution shall be published in a Kiribati language text as well as this English text, but in the event of any inconsistency between the 2 texts this English text shall prevail." Official status of English and Kiribati are mentioned in the national report submitted to the UN General Assembly. "National Report Submitted in Accordance with Paragraph 15 (a) of the Annex to Human Rights Council Resolution 5/1: Kiribati" (UN General Assembly, 2010).

[pp] Sovereign status disputed.

[qq] Official languages recognized in Article 5 of the 2008 Constitution. Turkish, Bosnian, and Roma also have official status at the municipal level.

[rr] Official languages recognized in the 1993 Constitution (amended in 1998).

[ss] Recognized since the 1966 Constitution.

[tt] Official languages recognized in the Language Law of February 24, 1984.

[uu] Official languages recognized since its first Constitution (1959).

[vv] According to the Malawi Government Official Website (www.malawi.gov.mw), English is the official language and Chichewa is the "Common Language"; according to the Malawi High Commission (United Kingdom), both Chichewa and English are official languages (see www.malawihighcommission.co.uk/Languages.php). No mention of official languages in Constitution.

[ww] Also known as "Bahasa Malaysia" or "Malay language."

[xx] Article 152 of the 1957 Constitution recognizes Malay as the national language; it also allows for the use of English for official purposes. National Language Acts, 1963/1967, provide that English may be used for official purposes and is used extensively in law. The country has a dual justice system.

[yy] Official languages recognized since the 1964 Constitution. Article 74 of the Constitution states that Maltese should prevail if there is any conflict between Maltese and English texts of any law.

TABLE 2.3 CONTINUED

[zz] The Maltese Sign Language does not have constitutional recognition but is declared official through the Maltese Sign Language Recognition Act of 2016.

[aaa] No official languages named in the Constitution; Section 5 of Article XIV says that that the Marshallese and English texts of the Constitution are equally authentic. The US Embassy of Marshall Islands website (http://www.rmiembassyus.org) refers to both Marshallese and English as official languages.

[bbb] Article 6 of the 1991 Constitution with amendments through 2012.

[ccc] French, a colonial language, was an official language of Mauritania until 1991.

[ddd] Status conferred in a 1992 amendment to the Constitution and in General Law on the Linguistic Rights of Indigenous Cultures, 2003; the Act also provides that indigenous languages have the same validity as Spanish in territories where they are spoken, and indigenous language speakers should have full access to public services in their language. Spanish is also the de facto official language of Mexico.

[eee] Also known as Amazigh or Berber. Article 5 of the 2011 Constitution.

[fff] English is only a de facto official language in that its status has not been declared in law. However, the New Zealand government refers to all three languages as official.

[ggg] Maori recognized in Maori Language Act, 1987; NZ Sign Language recognized in New Zealand Sign Language Act, 2006.

[hhh] Exact date disputed. See research paper by New Zealand Parliament, "New Zealand Sovereignty: 1857, 1907, 1947, or 1987?" (Parliamentary Library, August 28, 2007).

[iii] See Article 2 of Law No. 2001-037. "Combined Periodic Report of the Republic of Niger 2003–2014 on the Implementation of the African Charter on Human and Peoples' Rights" (Republic of Niger, July 2014), http://www.achpr.org/files/sessions/16th-eo/state-reports/2-2003-2014/periodic_report_2003_2014_eng.pdf.

[jjj] The term "national language" is avoided in Nigeria; three languages are recognized as "majority languages." Article 55 of the 1999 Constitution provides for the National Assembly to be conducted in English, and in Hausa, Ibo, and Yoruba "when adequate arrangements have been made therefore."

[kkk] Colony and Protectorate (Protectorate 1901–1960).

[lll] Also Sami (O) and Kven (O) for some municipalities. There are two equal versions of the Norwegian Constitution: one in Bokmål and another in Nynorsk. The official status of the two varieties was recognized through a parliamentary resolution in 1885, and provisions for their official use were further strengthened through Law on Language Use in the Official Service (1980).

[mmm] Norway was in a union with Denmark for about 300 years until 1814; some argue that it was virtually a Danish colony.

[nnn] As in the case of India, Article 251 of the Pakistan Constitution of 1973 provides that "English may be used for official purposes" until it is replaced by Urdu. A Supreme Court judgment in 2015 calls for the replacement of English with Urdu to satisfy constitutional requirement (of making Urdu a language for official and all other purposes within 15 years). M. Ilyas Khan, "Uncommon Tongue: Pakistan's Confusing Move to Urdu," *BBC News*, September 12, 2015, sec. Asia, http://www.bbc.com/news/world-asia-34215293.

[ooo] Official languages recognized in the 1979 Constitution. English is official in all 16 states of Palau. In three states, languages other than Palauan are second official languages. Sonsorolese is the official language in Sonsoral, as are Anguar and Japanese in Anguar, and Tobi language in the state of Tobi. Colin Baker and Sylvia Prys Jones, *Encyclopedia of Bilingualism and Bilingual Education* (Buffalo, NY: Multilingual Matters, 1998).

[ppp] Status enshrined in Article 5 of the 1967 constitution; Article 140 of the 1992 Constitution (with amendments through 2011).

[qqq] English is official until otherwise provided by law. Section 7 of the 1987 Constitution.

[rrr] Thompson calls the American occupation of the Philippines "humanitarian imperialism." Roger M. Thompson, *Filipino English and Taglish: Language Switching from Multiple Perspectives* (Amsterdam/Philadelphia: John Benjamins, 2003).

[sss] Not to be confused with the Democratic Republic of the Congo.

[ttt] Article 3 of the 1992 Constitution; Article 6 of the 2002 Constitution.

[uuu] Official status of French is in Article 1 of the 2010 Constitution. National languages not named but acknowledged in Article 25.

[vvv] The 1962 Constitution has French and Kinyarwanda only; the 2003 Constitution added English as official. At the time of writing, Rwanda is in the process of making Swahili its fourth official language.

[www] Partially recognized state.

[xxx] Sahrawi Arab Democratic Republic, "Periodic Report of the Sahrawi Arab Democratic Republic to the African Commission on Human and Peoples Rights Containing All the Outstanding Reports in Accordance with Article 62 of the Charter," 2011, http://www.achpr.org/files/sessions/55th/state-reports/2nd-2002-2012/periodic_report_sahrawi_eng.pdf.

[yyy] Note that Samoa includes the island American Samoa, which is an "Unincorporated territory of the United States" discussed later in the chapter.

(*continued*)

TABLE 2.3 CONTINUED

[zzz] The Constitution does not explicitly provide for "official languages," but states in Article 54 that "All debates and discussions in the Legislative Assembly shall be conducted in the Samoan language and the English language" and that "(2) The Minutes and the debates of the Legislative Assembly, every bill introduced therein, every paper presented thereto and all minutes of proceedings, minutes of evidence, and reports of committees of the Assembly shall be in the Samoan language and the English language." Thus the country is officially bilingual at least for legal purposes.

[aaaa] Article 1 of the 1963 Constitution; now Article 1 of the 2001 Constitution. National languages were introduced in 1978 amendment. Additional national languages may be recognized provided that these languages are codified.

[bbbb] Official languages recognized since its first Constitution in 1979.

[cccc] Article 7 of the Republic of Singapore Independence Act; Article 153A of the Constitution of the Republic of Singapore.

[dddd] Official languages recognized in Article 3 of the 1979 Constitution. Somalia was under Italian and British administration from the late 19th C to the md-20th C. Both Italian and English were considered as potential official languages at one point; see discussion in David D. Laitin, *Politics, Language, and Thought: The Somali Experience* (Chicago: University of Chicago Press, 1977).

[eeee] Afrikaans and English recognized as official languages in Article 32 of the 1961 Constitution; Article 89(1) of 1983 Constitution. Article 3(1) of the 1993 Constitution extended official status to 11 languages; Article 6 of the 1996 Constitution.

[ffff] Partially recognized state.

[gggg] Official languages decided based on a referendum that was held on November 13, 2011; 84% of the voters said "yes" to official bilingualism.

[hhhh] Article 6(1) of the 2011 Transitional Constitution.

[iiii] The "link language" status is enshrined in the Constitution (Article 18(3)). Tamil "also" official, along with Sinhala, since 1987 amendment to the Constitution.

[jjjj] English first recognized in the Interim Constitution of 2005 (current), Article 8. Art 8(1) also provides, "All indigenous languages of the Sudan are national languages and shall be respected, developed and promoted."

[kkkk] Official languages recognized in the 2005 Constitution.

[llll] Article 4 and 70 of the 1999 Constitution. German, French, and Italian recognized as national languages since 1848 Constitution.

[mmmm] Official status not conferred in current constitution. English is the de facto language of the judiciary. At the time of writing, a referendum on a draft constitution is scheduled to be held; Article 4 of the draft constitution provides for Swahili as the national language and English as an official language.

[nnnn] Indonesian and English are working languages; Section 13 and 159 of the 2002 Constitution.

[oooo] Law is bilingual in Tongan and English. Law Revision (Miscellaneous Amendments) Act 2009 provides that the Tongan version takes precedence where the Tongan and English versions of the law differ in meaning.

[pppp] Both English and Tuvaluan are official languages, according to a national report submitted to the UNESCO World Education Forum.

[qqqq] English has been an official language since Uganda's independence in 1962. The official status of English is enshrined in the 1995 Constitution. Swahili became a second official language through the Constitution (Amendment) Act of 2005. The primacy of English seems to be unchallenged. The 2005 Act specifies that Swahili is "to be used in such circumstances as Parliament may by law prescribe."

[rrrr] Official languages recognized in the 1980 Constitution (as amended in 1983).

[ssss] Only English is recognized as the official language in the constitution. Seven national languages have also been identified. L. Marten and N.C. Kula, "Zambia: One Zambia, One Nation, Many Languages," in *Language and National Identity in Africa*, ed. A. Simpson (Oxford: Oxford University Press, 2007), 291–313.

[tttt] The official status of these languages is enshrined in the 2013 constitution.

people. Despite their plethora, national languages play no real role in official administration in Cameroon.[26] Its official languages are English and French, both of colonial heritage. Such heritage is fully reflected in the country's legal

[26] Eric A. Anchimbe, "Functional Seclusion and the Future of Indigenous Languages in Africa: The Case of Cameroon," in *Selected Proceedings of the 35th Annual Conference on African Linguistics*, ed. John Mugane (Somerville, MA: Cascadilla Proceedings Project, 2006), 94–103.

system, which is both bilingual and bijural. The status asymmetry between the colonial and indigenous languages is also clearly manifested in Botswana, Cape Verde, Democratic Republic of Congo, Mali, Mauritania, Niger, Nigeria, Republic of Congo, and Senegal.

Currently in many African states[27] the only official language is a colonial language. In Uganda, both official languages are exogenous: English was a colonial import, and Swahili is an East African lingua franca that became official as a result of the country's membership in the East African Community. Endogenous languages, such as Luganda—the language of the largest ethnic group Baganda—do not enjoy official status in Uganda. Even where endogenous languages have gained some official status, their importance and use rarely surpass that of colonial languages. In Nigeria, English is the language of law courts at both the state and federal level (but not in Alkali, Sharia, and customary courts)[28]. Similarly, law is written in English and proceedings in High Courts and Magistrates Courts take place in English[29] in Botswana, despite the fact that about 80% of the population speak Setswana.[30] South Africa, a former Dutch (1652–1795) and British (1795–1934) colony, has one of the most advanced multilingual jurisdictions in the region, offering extensive legal protection of language rights. It was formerly officially bilingual in English and Afrikaans (a language largely derived from Dutch). To empower indigenous African languages in the state, Section 6 of the 1996 Constitution of the Republic of South Africa expanded the number of official languages to 11, which now cover the home languages of approximately 98% of the population. The revised constitution requires all official languages to enjoy parity of esteem and to be treated equitably. It also gives recognition to 14 other languages commonly spoken in South Africa. Despite so, it is obvious that Afrikaans and English routinely occupy higher functions, while other official African languages are still in a developmental phase.[31]

The figure of official multilingualism in Africa is projected to be on the rise. Although post-colonial African governments, ruled by elites who benefit from maintaining the status quo, generally seem to be lacking in political will

---

[27] Such as Angola, Benin, Burkina Faso, Gabon, Gambia, Ghana, Guinea, Guinea-Bissau, Ivory Coast, Liberia, Mozambique, Namibia, Sierra Leone, and Togo.

[28] Tunde Olusola Opeibi, "Investing the Language Situation in Africa," in *The Oxford Handbook of Language and Law*, ed. Peter M. Tiersma and Lawrence M. Solan (Oxford: Oxford University Press, 2012), 272–84.

[29] Customary courts take place in indigenous languages.

[30] Thekiso, "A Sociolinguistic Study of Communication Processes in a Court of Law in Gaborone, Botswana."

[31] de Varennes, "International and Comparative Perspectives in the Use of Official Languages."

to end the dominance of colonial languages,[32] there is some sign of change. The African Academy of Languages was founded in 2001 under the auspices of the African Union to promote the vitality of African languages and to advocate for multilingualism, especially in education. An increasing number of African states are offering bilingual education that includes at least one indigenous language. The African Union's Language Plan of Action for Africa, adopted in 2006,[33] requires its member states to formulate language policies that promote the use of African languages in conjunction with partner languages (i.e., colonial languages).[34] In particular, legislation to confer official status to African languages is encouraged among its 54 member states (i.e., all African states except for Morocco). Although uptake of the policy has been slow, the Language Plan expresses the vision of pan-African leaders to raise the status of endogenous African languages.

In northern Africa there has been a turn toward Arabic, a symbol of independence and liberation from colonial influences. Morocco, a former French colony, dropped French in favor of Arabic. Libya, a former Italian colony, adopted Arabic as its only official language (although there are movements that call for the adoption of Tamazight, a Berber language brutally suppressed by Gaddafi, as an additional official language, especially after the recent uprisings[35]). Arabic is also an official language in Algeria.

Apart from colonialization, economic incentives seem to be another driver of language policy in Africa. Endogenous languages do not have official status in Equatorial Guinea, but the former Spanish colony is interesting not only because it is officially multilingual in three European languages only, but also because some of these languages were introduced post-independence. Spanish has been an official language of Equatorial Guinea since 1844, and remains the language of education and administration. Being the only Spanish speaking country in Africa and one of the smallest nations on the continent, Equatorial Guinea has adopted French and Portuguese strategically as additional official languages to strengthen regional ties, decades after it became an independent country. French became the second official language in 1997 as a means of fostering economic integration with other Central African states. In 2011, the country—which was a Portuguese colony from the fifteenth to eighteenth centuries—introduced Portuguese as the third official language in 2011

---

[32] Neville Alexander, "The Potential Role of Translation as Social Practice for the Intellectualization of African Languages," 2005, Keynote address delivered at the XVII World Congress of the International Federation of Translators held at Tampere, Finland, August 4–7, 2005.

[33] This is the second Language Plan of Action for Africa. The first one was adopted by the Organization of African Unity (OAU), predecessor of the African Union, in 1986.

[34] Chumbow, "Towards a Legal Framework for Language Charters in Africa."

[35] Edwin Lane, "After Gaddafi, Libya's Amazigh Demand Recognition," *BBC News*, December 23, 2011, sec. Africa, http://www.bbc.com/news/world-africa-16289543.

to enhance relations with Portuguese-speaking countries.[36] In 2014, the country was successfully admitted into the Community of Portuguese Language Countries (CPLP) as a member and gained access to cooperation opportunities with other Lusophone member states.

On the African continent, there is also strong gravitation toward English as a global language. English was adopted by the linguistically diverse country of South Sudan as its sole official language (in addition to languages assigned national status) upon its independence in 2011, even though it was never a British colony.[37] In Rwanda, almost everyone speaks Kinyarwanda, so an exogenous language is not needed as a lingua franca. However, in addition to having French as a second official language, the country introduced English as its third official language in 2008, almost half a century after becoming an independent country, in order to join the East African Community and the Commonwealth, and to improve its trading with its English-speaking neighbors, including Uganda, Kenya, and Tanzania.[38] At the time of writing, Rwanda is in the process of making Swahili its fourth official language to fulfill its obligation to the East African Community and to boost economic integration.[39] The former German and Belgian colony now publishes laws in three official languages, namely French, English, and Kinyarwanda. As stipulated in the Constitution, these languages have equal value.[40] Its judicial system, which follows the civil law tradition, went through major reforms from 2003 onward, with the result of replacing many of the earlier colonial (Belgian) codes and procedures and introducing some common law principles. English was also introduced in Burundi as an additional official language in 2014. During Belgian colonization, official bilingualism was practiced in French and Dutch. Upon independence in 1962, the Belgian legal system was largely retained, but Kirundi (the

---

[36] "Equatorial Guinea Adds Portuguese as the Country's Third Official Language," *PR Newswire*, October 14, 2011, http://www.prnewswire.com/news-releases/equatorial-guinea-adds-portuguese-as-thse-countrys-third-official-language-131882808.html.

[37] Quote of Edward Mokole, Ministry of Higher Education. Rosie Goldsmith, "BBC News - South Sudan Adopts the Language of Shakespeare," October 8, 2011, http://www.bbc.co.uk/news/magazine-15216524.

[38] Another reason for moving away from French to English, less cited in official political rhetoric, concerns the role of French in the genocide. Chris McGreal, "Why Rwanda Said Adieu to French," *The Guardian*, January 16, 2009, sec. Education, http://www.theguardian.com/education/2009/jan/16/rwanda-english-genocide.

[39] "Rwanda Moves to Make Swahili Its Fourth Official Language," Africanews, February 10, 2017, http://www.africanews.com/2017/02/10/rwanda-moves-to-make-swahili-its-fourth-official-language/.

[40] Article 93 of the Rwandan Constitution states that in case of conflict between the three official languages, the prevailing language shall be the language in which the law was adopted. The law may be prepared in any of the official languages. In practice, most laws are drafted in Kinyarwanda. Raymond Gateraruke, "Overview of Rwandan Legislative Process," *The Loophole: Journal of the Commonwealth Association of Legislative Counsel*, no. 1 (2012): 35–41; Vastina Nzanze, "Challenges of Drafting Laws in One Language and Translating Them: Rwanda's Experience," *The Loophole: Journal of the Commonwealth Association of Legislative Counsel*, no. 1 (2012): 42–53.

first language of the great majority of Burundi nationals) replaced Dutch as an official language and a new diglossic system has been adopted.[41] Even though French is spoken by only 3% of the population, it is still commonly used in Burundi courts and government services today. With the addition of English, the country is now officially trilingual in Kirundi, French, and English.

ASIA

While Africa has some of the most linguistically diverse nations in the world, Asia is home to more living languages than any other continent.[42] There are 14 bilingual and multilingual sovereign states[43] in Asia, making up 28% of all Asian states and accounting for 19% of the worldwide figure. Apart from Afghanistan[44] these Asian states had been colonized by Russia or by European forces.[45] Twelve of these 13 states, with Sri Lanka[46] being the exception, have retained one or more languages from a former colonizer as an official language.

Among the Asian territories that had been colonized during the Age of Discovery, many that have retained a colonial language as an official language are former British colonies.[47] These former colonies tend to also retain the English common law system, sometimes in parallel with other local legal traditions or customs. In most cases, English remains dominant over endogenous languages, arguably due to its bridging function with the common law world, its political neutrality as perceived in relation to other language varieties that are seen as belonging to a particular ethnic group, and the economic value of English as an emergent global lingua franca.

Singapore is a good example. English, one of the four official languages, is the only working language of administration and law, and has clearly superior status. In Singapore, "mother tongue" is officially assigned by the government; children of mixed marriages are assigned the father's ethnicity.[48] English is deemed an ethnically neutral language and cannot be considered a "mother tongue" (notwithstanding the fact that it is the first language of many young Singaporeans). The country has a bilingual education policy that encourages

---

[41] Jean-Baptist Bigirimana, "Translation as a Dynamic Model in the Development of the Burundi Constitution(S)," in *Translation Issues in Language and Law*, ed. F. Oslen, A. Lorz, and D. Stein (London: Palgrave Macmillan, 2009), 193–212.

[42] See ethnologue.com.

[43] Abkhazia, Afghanistan, Brunei, India, Iraq, Kazakhstan, Kyrgyzstan, Malaysia, Pakistan, Philippines, Singapore, South Ossetia, Sri Lanka, and Timor-Leste.

[44] Both the British and the Soviet Union invaded Afghanistan without success.

[45] Iraq fell into the hands of both the Ottoman Empire and the British.

[46] Where English *is* officially recognized as a link language.

[47] For example, Hong Kong (not in Table 2.3 because it is not a sovereign state), India, Malaysia, Pakistan, and Singapore (a British colony before it became an independent country).

[48] Antonio L. Rappa and Lionel Hock An Wee, *Language Policy and Modernity in Southeast Asia: Malaysia, the Philippines, Singapore, and Thailand* (New York: Springer, 2006).

citizens to be proficient in both English and their respective "mother tongue" (Mandarin, Malay, or Tamil[49]). Although only spoken by a minority, Malay has the additional status of a national language. It is used in the national anthem, coat of arms, and military commands, performing a ceremonial function marking the original inhabitants of the Singapore island.

Similarly, in India, English serves as a politically neutral language where no endogenous language can work as a viable lingua franca. India is bilingual in English and Hindi at the federal level, but Indian states are given the power to devise their own official language policy, which has given rise to more than 20 other official languages. There have been attempts to make Hindi the sole official language of the country, but resistance is strong, given that more than half of the population does not speak it as a first language[50] and fear that they would be relegated as "second-class citizens."[51]

Both Brunei and Malaysia have retained English for official use, but they have explicitly demoted the language to a second place by prioritizing Malay. Brunei law does not label English as an *official language*, but its constitution states that English can be used for all official purposes. English is still of clear significance, given that Brunei has retained the English common law system. Although the Malay language is the official language, official documents are written bilingually. The case of Malaysia is similar, where Malay has the official and national language status, but the law (National Language Acts 1963/1967) also explicitly provides for the use of English for official purposes. Both English and Malay texts of the law are authoritative. In both Brunei and Malaysia, such official bilingualism was envisioned as a temporary stage of decolonization, a transitional phase for consolidating the position of the native language and developing its vocabulary and formal register, with the vision that the native language will ultimately be employed exclusively. However, the significance of English has not faded as quickly as planned.

Vietnam, Cambodia, Laos,[52] Indonesia,[53] Myanmar,[54] and Sri Lanka are some of the few post-colonial polities in Asia that have officially removed the former colonial language(s) from its public institutions, even though they have largely retained a colonial legal system. In Sri Lanka, after the official withdrawal of English, linguistic rivalry and ethnic conflict between Sinhala and

---

[49] This policy thus ignores those who speak other first languages, such as English, other dialects of Chinese, or other Asian languages and dialects.

[50] Eastern and southern states tend to either use English or a local language.

[51] Aditya Kalra and Shyamantha Asokan, "Indian PM's Push for Hindi Struggles to Translate in Some States," *Chicago Tribune*, June 19, 2014, http://articles.chicagotribune.com/2014-06-19/news/sns-rt-us-india-language-20140619_1_hindi-indian-pm-language.

[52] Vietnam, Cambodia, and Laos were part of the former French Indochina.

[53] The Indonesian legal system, a fusion of Roman Dutch law, customary (*adat*), and Sharia law, functions in the Indonesian language.

[54] Although English may still be used in courts, Burmese is the only official language of Myanmar.

Tamil ensued. The Sri Lankan legal system has a complex structure embracing English common law, Roman-Dutch civil law, and customary law. During 152 years of British rule (1796–1948), English was the language of administration and of the courts (except for Rural Courts). Following independence, the country was determined to function in its native languages (known as *Swabasha*, or the "mother tongue"), although English is still officially recognized as a *link language* (Article 18(3) of the constitution). Although in a 1944 language resolution the State Council decided that Sinhala and Tamil should both become official languages,[55] the tide was turned in 1956 when Parliament passed the Sinhala Only Act, making Sinhala the only official language, replacing English. This decision prevented minority Tamils from obtaining public service employment and became a trigger for decades of civil war in the country.[56] A more conciliatory language policy started in the late 1970s, when the 1978 Constitution made Tamil a national language, but it was not until a constitutional amendment in 1987 that Tamil became an official language.[57]

Choice of official languages also reflects the perceived relationship between a post-colonial polity and its former colonizer. After Timor-Leste became independent in 2002, the government chose not to adopt Bahasa Indonesia as an official language (it, however, has the status of a working language) because of its negative association as the language of an invader who occupied the nation for 24 years.[58] Instead, it reinstated Portuguese, the language of the preceding colonizer, as its official language, along with the mostly widely spoken local language, Tetum. Portuguese, after over 450 years of colonial presence, is viewed more favorably by locals, for it had become a language of resistance in the country's struggle for independence from Indonesia.[59]

As discussed earlier, not all colonizers were from Western Europe. For example, the Philippines was conquered by not only Spain but also the United States. Its official languages are English and Filipino,[60] but regional languages have also been accorded the status of "auxiliary official languages in the regions" in the current constitution (Article 14, 1987). Iraq, once ruled by the Ottoman Empire, is officially bilingual in both Arabic and Kurdish, with a few other minority languages sharing official status in dominant regions. In

---

[55] Robert B. Kaplan, *Language Planning in the Asia Pacific: Hong Kong, Timor-Leste and Sri Lanka* (New York: Routledge, 2013).

[56] L. J. Mark Cooray, *Changing the Language of the Law: The Sri Lanka Experience* (Québec: Presses de l'Université Laval, 1986).

[57] Kaplan, *Language Planning in the Asia Pacific*.

[58] Kerry Taylor-Leech, "Language and Identity in East Timor," *Language Problems & Language Planning* 32, no. 2 (June 1, 2008): 153–80, https://doi.org/10.1075/lplp.32.1.04tay.

[59] John Macalister, "Language Policies, Language Planning and Linguistic Landscapes in Timor-Leste," *Language Problems and Language Planning* 36, no. 1 (January 1, 2012): 25–45, https://doi.org/10.1075/lplp.36.1.02mac.

[60] See further discussion of the evolution of Filipino as an official language in Chapter 5.

practice, Arabic is used predominantly in official communications, except in the Kurdistan region, where both Arabic and Kurdish are used.

Table 2.3 also includes some ex-Soviet territories in Central Asia—Abkhazia, Kazakhstan, Kyrgyzstan, South Ossetia—that have adopted Russian along with endogenous languages as official languages. Their official language policy reflects the political alignment of these territories. Unlike Uzbekistan, Turkmenistan, and Tajikistan, which have oriented toward Muslim countries, Kazakhstan and Kyrgyzstan have remained allies with Russia in post-Soviet times.[61] Russia has supported the independence of Abkhazia and South Ossetia from Georgia. Many post-Soviet states are trying to undo the effect of Russification, often seeing a bilingual policy as a pragmatic transitional stage with the ultimate aim of removing Russian's influence and becoming a monolingual nation-state.[62] Tajikistan has recently dropped Russian as a second official language, despite the fact that the country's economy is heavily dependent on remittance from its migrant workers to Russia. Only Armenia and Lithuania transitioned to monolingualism smoothly and rapidly.[63] In the former Soviet Union, from the 1930s onward, Russian was promoted as the language of socialist expression (an H variety), with the anticipation that national languages (L varieties) would eventually die out.[64] The Soviet government also linguistically interfered with local languages by making them orthographically, morphologically, and syntactically more similar to Russian,[65] for example by publishing vocabulary lists that replaced native language terms with words that are more similar to their Russian equivalents. "Bilingualism" had become a mask for Russification.[66] Language policies, contact, and pressure on local language speakers to speak Russian resulted in language mixing and blending between Russian and local languages; post-independence states often seek not only to restore the status of their local languages, but also to reconstruct these languages.[67] Beauvois describes the lingering influence of the Russian language in post-independent Soviet countries as "clearly a colonial legacy."[68] Despite its association with a colonial past, the popularity of Russian in post-Soviet states

---

[61] Aneta Pavlenko, "Multilingualism in Post-Soviet Countries: Language Revival, Language Removal, and Sociolinguistic Theory," *International Journal of Bilingual Education and Bilingualism* 11, no. 3–4 (2008): 275–314.

[62] Pavlenko, "Multilingualism in Post-Soviet Successor States."

[63] Pavlenko "Multilingualism in Post-Soviet Successor States."

[64] Ostrower, *Language, Law, and Diplomacy*.

[65] Laada Bilaniuk, *Contested Tongues: Language Politics and Cultural Correction in Ukraine* (Ithaca, NY: Cornell University Press, 2005).

[66] Bilaniuk, *Contested Tongues*.

[67] Daniel Beauvois, "Linguistic Acculturations and Reconstructions in the ULB Group (Ukraine, Lithuania, and Belarus)," in *Language, Nation, and State: Identity Politics in a Multilingual Age*, ed. Tony Judt and Denis Lacorne (London: Palgrave Macmillan, 2004), 201–13.

[68] Beauvois, "Linguistic Acculturations and Reconstructions," 202.

has not ceded due to its instrumental value as a regional lingua franca and as a gateway to geopolitical and economic power.[69]

EUROPE

Eleven sovereign states[70] in Europe are officially bilingual or multilingual, including the disputed state of Kosovo. This amounts to about 22% of all European states and about 15% of the bilingual and multilingual states documented in Table 2.3. Among these states, eight[71] have adopted an official language brought by a former colonizer. The exceptions are Belgium, Bosnia-Herzegovina, and Switzerland.

Belarus is a former Soviet state that has adopted Belarusian and Russian as official languages. Despite growing interest in reviving Belarusian, especially after the Ukrainian crisis, such effort is an uphill battle given that more than 70% of the population now speak Russian.[72] Some other ex-Soviet states try to minimize Russian influence through promoting official monolingualism. A referendum to include Russian as a second official language was rejected recently in Latvia.[73]

Kosovo is an unusual case because its language provisions were adopted under the recommendation and monitoring of the United Nations, after NATO intervention in its interethnic war in 1998–1999. Kosovo does not include Russian as one of its official languages. Its Law on the Use of Languages provides for the equal status of Albanian and Serbian.

A few bilingual and multilingual states in Europe did not directly arise as a result of colonization, although in the case of Bosnia-Herzegovina, the long-term effects of the collapse of the Austro-Hungarian and Ottoman empires and the Cold War may still be felt. Following the dissolution of Yugoslavia, the newly formed states sought to establish their own linguistic identity, and the Serbo-Croatian language thus disintegrated, with Croatian becoming an official language of Croatia and Serbian in Serbia. Three official languages—Bosnian, Croatian, and Serbian—are adopted in Bosnia-Herzegovina, corresponding to the constituent peoples of the country—Bosniaks, Croats, and

---

[69] Pavlenko, "Multilingualism in Post-Soviet Successor States."

[70] Belgium, Belarus, Bosnia-Herzegovina, Cyprus, Finland, Ireland, Kosovo, Luxembourg, Malta, Norway, and Switzerland. It is debatable whether England colonized Ireland and whether Denmark colonized Norway.

[71] Belarus, Cyprus, Finland, Ireland, Kosovo, Luxembourg, Malta, and Norway.

[72] Katerina Barushka, "After Decades of Russian Dominance, Belarus Begins to Reclaim Its Language," *The Guardian*, January 28, 2015, sec. World news, https://www.theguardian.com/world/2015/jan/28/-sp-russian-belarus-reclaims-language-belarusian.

[73] Associated Press, "Latvians Reject Russian as Official Language," *The Guardian*, February 19, 2012, sec. World news, https://www.theguardian.com/world/2012/feb/19/latvians-reject-russian-official-language.

Serbs. The three languages are closely related varieties, often said to be of the same "language."

Belgium and Switzerland arose from alliances among multilingual constituent groups. The Swiss Confederation started, in 1291, as military alliances across three German-speaking cantons. As the Confederation expanded to French-, Italian-, and Romansh-speaking regions, their local autonomy and linguistic diversity were maintained.[74] It now consists of 26 cantons, 17 of which are German speaking, 4 French speaking, one Italian speaking, and 4 of which are bilingual or multilingual.[75] It is believed that the high degree of autonomy enjoyed by its mostly monolingual cantons has contributed to the stability of the confederation and its resistance from linguistic nationalism during its heyday.[76] The earliest legal marker of official multilingualism could be found during the short-lived Helvetic Republic (1798–1803), in a 1798 decree that provided for laws to be published in the three major Swiss languages. Although the trilingualism policy was interrupted briefly from 1815, in 1848 the new Constitution declared German, French, and Italian the national languages of Switzerland. A 1938 constitutional amendment added Romansh as a fourth national language, but also declared German, French, and Italian to be the only three official languages, providing for a cultural recognition but adding little instrumental value to Romansh. It has been argued that "language frictions have been minimal throughout Swiss history."[77] The country has monolingual courts at the cantonal level. Appeal cases are heard in the language they were initiated in. Romansh became a semi-official[78] language in 1996 and can be used as a medium of communication by Romansh speakers with the federal government and in law courts in Graubünden and at the federal level. Given its high immigration rate, the Swiss government offices use many more languages than what is officially designated.[79]

When Belgium as a modern state was founded in 1830, French was the only official language and was the language of aristocracy and bourgeoisie. Dutch gained equal status as an official language through the Law on Equality in 1898.

---

[74] Kenneth Douglas McRae, *Conflict and Compromise in Multilingual Societies: Switzerland* (Waterloo, ON: Wilfrid Laurier University Press, 1983).

[75] Thomas Fleiner, "Recent Developments of Swiss Federalism," *Publius* 32, no. 2 (2002): 97–123; Dagmar Richter, "The Model Character of Swiss Language Law," in *Linguistic Diversity and European Democracy*, ed. Anne Lise Kjær and Silvia Adamo (Surrey, England; Burlington, VT: Ashgate, 2011), 189–205.

[76] Wright, *Language Policy and Language Planning*.

[77] McRae, *Conflict and Compromise in Multilingual Societies*, 46.

[78] Section 1, Article 70 of the Swiss constitution: The official languages of the Confederation are German, French, and Italian. Romansh shall be an official language for communicating with persons of Romansh language.

[79] Andreas Lötscher, "Multilingual Law Drafting in Switzerland," in *Formal Linguistics and the Law*, ed. G. Grewendorf and M. Rathert (Berlin; New York: Mouton deGruyter, 2009), 371–400.

Multilingualism in Belgium is based on *the territoriality principle*,[80] whereby language rights varied according to the partitioned geographies occupied by the two major communities (Dutch-speaking Flemish and French-speaking Walloon), which have had persistent but non-violent conflict. In 2010–2011, Belgium set a world record of taking 541 days to form a new government, in part due to language tensions between the Flemish and the Walloons. The federal state of Belgium is organized roughly along the lines of linguistic demographics: Flemish-[81] (a variant of Dutch), French-, and German-speaking areas, except for the officially bilingual (Dutch and French) capital of Brussels (where the medium of public services depends on the user rather than the territory, known as *the personality principle*).

PACIFIC

Nine sovereign states[82] in the Pacific are officially bilingual or multilingual, which is roughly 64% of all Pacific states and 12% of all the bilingual and multilingual states in Table 2.3. All of these states had been colonized and have adopted a language of a former colonizer (Britain, United States, New Zealand, Australia, and France) as an official language, alongside an endogenous language. The former colonial languages and pidgins derived from them often serve as lingua francas in linguistically diverse places such as Fiji. These states all have two to three official languages in total. Due to colonization by English speakers, English is an official language in all of these states.

Some of the official local languages were pidgins and creoles developed from colonial languages. This is the case for Bislama in Vanuatu, which is an English Creole. In addition to Bislama, Vanuatu has adopted two former colonial languages as official languages because it had been ruled jointly by the British and the French. Bislama has the additional status as the national language, but the principal languages of education are English and French. Court proceedings may be conducted in any of the three official languages.

New Zealand was populated by Maori when European explorers arrived. British settlers quickly outgrew the indigenous population, and New Zealand became part of the British Empire from 1840. Creole nationalism[83] was developed in both New Zealand and the neighboring Australia. Post-independence, Maori and New Zealand Sign languages gained official status through the Maori Language Act of 1987 and the New Zealand Sign Language Bill of

---

[80] The territoriality principle refers to the situation where language privileges are assigned based on geographical location. It is contrasted with the personality principle, where language rights are enjoyed by its speakers within a polity regardless of where they are.

[81] Flemish has the highest number of speakers in the country.

[82] Fiji, Kiribati, New Zealand, Marshall Islands, Palau, Samoa, Tonga, Tuvalu, and Vanuatu.

[83] Anderson, *Imagined Communities*.

2006, although common law ideas have been translated and adopted into the Maori language since the early nineteenth century.[84] One can choose to use these languages in court with interpreters. New Zealand is one of the few countries in the world that have conferred official status to a national sign language. Although without statutory reinforcement, English is a de facto official language and is widely acknowledged as one of three official languages of New Zealand by government departments (such as the official website of the New Zealand government [beehive.govt.nz], Statistics New Zealand Tatauranga Aotearoa, Human Rights Commission, etc.).

THE AMERICAS

There are only five sovereign states[85] in the Americas that are officially bilingual or multilingual. This accounts for about 14% of all states in Americas and 7% of bilingual and multilingual states in the world. All these states had been colonized and have adopted one or more colonial languages as an official language.

It is noticeable that few indigenous languages have acquired official status in the Americas, and where they do the effect is mostly symbolic. Despite the vast linguistic diversity in the region, there are many officially monolingual states where the only official language is a former colonial language. For example, Spanish remains the only de jure or de facto official language in Argentina, Chile, Columbia, Costa Rica, Cuba, Dominican Republic, Ecuador, El Salvador, Guatemala, Honduras, Nicaragua, Panama, Uruguay, and Venezuela; English in Antigua and Barbuda, Bahamas, Belize, Barbados, Dominica, Grenada, Guyana, Jamaica, Saint Kitts and Nevis, Saint Lucia, Saint Vincent and the Grenadines, Trinidad and Tobago; French in French Guiana; Portuguese in Brazil, and Dutch in Suriname.

The relative scarcity in bilingual and multilingual states in the Americas is remarkable, and may be attributable to the fact that many post-colonial states in the region were creole states,[86] that the Castilianization process persisted after wars of independence in Spanish Americas (prompted by both nationalist and racist ideologies[87]), and that the mestizo population (people of mixed European and American Indian ancestry) also continued to increase. In the United States, Canada, Argentina, Brazil, Uruguay and other Latin American

---

[84] Mamari Stephens and M. Boyce, "The Struggle for Civic Space between a Minority Legal Language and a Dominant Legal Language: The Case of Māori and English," in *Legal Lexicography: A Comparative Perspective*, ed. Máirtín Mac Aodha (Surrey, England; Burlington, VT: Ashgate, 2014), 289–319.

[85] Bolivia, Canada, Haiti, Mexico, and Paraguay.

[86] Anderson, *Imagined Communities*.

[87] Stavenhagen, *The Ethnic Question*.

countries, the native population was almost exterminated; in Mexico, Peru, Guatemala, and Bolivia, there was substantial mixing between the colonial rulers and the native populations, even though ethnic stratification remains.[88] Colonial languages have become so engrained that their use has arguably been dissociated from the colonial context.[89] Although integration and homogeneity as a fundamental policy orientation remain deeply entrenched, from the beginning of the twentieth century some Latin American states have begun to offer symbolic recognition to minority languages, legal protection to minority rights, and some degree of autonomy to indigenous communities.[90]

Bolivia, a former Spanish colony, has one of the greatest numbers of official languages in the world, according to its 2009 constitution. Some of the indigenous languages designated as official languages have long been extinct. Most Bolivians today speak Spanish, but more than a third of the population can speak an endogenous language. Among the indigenous languages, Quechua and Aymara are most widely spoken,[91] followed by Guaraní, which is spoken by about 1% of the population. Indigenous languages have been legitimized, but their use has not been fully institutionalized.[92] Government departments are required to operate in at least two languages, one of which must be Spanish.

Mexico has the highest level of linguistic diversity in the Americas. It is notable in that Spanish, a colonial language, is not only a de facto official language but also became a national language. At the end of the colonial period, indigenous languages still dominated everyday communication. As in many other Latin American countries, it was during the independence process that there was a dramatic shift to the colonial language.[93]

When compared with the marginalized status of many aboriginal languages in the rest of Latin America, the aboriginal language Guaraní is the only aboriginal language that is used on a daily basis by the majority of the population in the former Spanish colony of Paraguay.[94] Guaraní became a co-national language in 1967 (National Constitution of the Republic of Paraguay), and was made co-official with Spanish in 1992 (Article 140, New

---

88 Stavenhagen, *The Ethnic Question*, 13.

89 Hiroshi Ito, "With Spanish, Guaraní Lives: A Sociolinguistic Analysis of Bilingual Education in Paraguay," *Multilingual Education* 2, no. 6 (2012): 1–11.

90 Mar-Molinero, *The Politics of Language in the Spanish-Speaking World.*

91 2001 census data show that 27.6% of Bolivians speak Quechua, and 18.5% of them speak Aymara. The figures have been falling over the years.

92 Ito, "With Spanish, Guaraní Lives: A Sociolinguistic Analysis of Bilingual Education in Paraguay."

93 M. Hidalgo, ed., *Mexican Indigenous Languages at the Dawn of the Twenty-First Century* (Berlin: Mouton de Gruyter, 2006).

94 See historical reasons detailed in Ito, "With Spanish, Guaraní Lives: A Sociolinguistic Analysis of Bilingual Education in Paraguay"; Robert Andrew Nickson, "Governance and the Revitalisation of the Guaraní Language in Paraguay," *Latin American Research Review* 44, no. 3 (2009): 3–26; Joan Rubin, *National Bilingualism in Paraguay* (The Hague: Mouton, 1968).

National Constitution). Although bilingualism is widespread, the language situation remains diglossic, where Spanish, being the H variety, is dominant in official domains, and Guaraní, being the L variety, is used informally.[95] Despite the fact that over 80% of Paraguayans speak Guaraní, the language is not used in court proceedings, and witness statements are not permitted in Guaraní.[96]

Canada was a settler colony of France and Britain, where settlers quickly outnumbered its indigenous populations. The country was created by both English-speaking and French-speaking creoles. Today the country has one of the most advanced bilingual legal systems in the world. Its founding constitution (1867) provides for the use of English and French in the courts. Laws are published in English and French at the federal level, and also in some provinces and territories (Quebec, Manitoba, New Brunswick, Ontario, Yukon, Northwest Territories, and Nunavut). Aboriginal languages have official status in some territories (e.g., Northwest Territories), but such status seems to be largely symbolic.[97] One motivation for an elaborate bilingual policy is to contain the separatist movements in Quebec.

Bilingual and Multilingual Non-State Jurisdictions

AT THE SUB-STATE LEVEL

Some regionally spoken languages have received official status not across the state, but within a particular locality. In many cases, these are languages spoken by endogenous communities that have been colonized or otherwise absorbed into a wider country, and the recognition of regional official languages may be accompanied by some devolution of powers to the region. Although situated within independent sovereign polities, some of these communities still consider themselves as being subjugated and colonized today, notwithstanding the fact that most have—willingly or unwillingly—integrated into the rest of the state and enjoy equal citizen rights with the majority. For them, linguistic autonomy is a step toward decolonization. These territorial-based bilingual or multilingual jurisdictions are treated as the exceptions rather than the norm in the state; their linguistic autonomy is especially granted by the state. In Ecuador, for example, the 2008 constitution provides that "ancestral languages are in official use by indigenous peoples in the areas where they live."

---

[95] Ito, "With Spanish, Guaraní Lives: A Sociolinguistic Analysis of Bilingual Education in Paraguay"; Nickson, "Governance and the Revitalisation of the Guaraní Language in Paraguay."

[96] Nickson, "Governance and the Revitalisation of the Guaraní Language in Paraguay."

[97] See discussion in Mark Fettes, "Life on the Edge: Canada's Aboriginal Languages under Official Bilingualism," in *Language and Politics in the United States and Canada*, ed. Thomas Ricento and Barbara Burnaby (Mahwah, NJ: Lawrence Erlbaum Associates, 1998), 117–49.

Some states have a top-down language policy simply based on linguistic demographics, such that official bilingualism or multilingualism is practiced "where numbers warrant." As discussed in the Ukrainian example at the beginning of the book, this seemingly political neutral policy can be easily deployed for political purposes.

Table 2.4 is by no means an exhaustive list. It offers only a taste of bilingual and multilingual jurisdictions at the sub-state level. When it comes to whether one or more official language in these territories is adopted from a former or current colonizer, the answers are often far from straightforward, and depend largely on how historical narratives are constructed. Some communities living in these territories are still in a state of internal colonialism; others have been a minority population in a larger polity for time immemorial.

Although the central governance in states such as China, the United Kingdom, and the United States is primarily monolingual, officially bilingual and multilingual jurisdictions exist within these states.

Hong Kong and Macau are distinctive post-colonial jurisdictions in that the end of colonization did not result in independence, but a transfer of sovereignty to China. They are currently special administrative regions of China that have retained the colonial legal systems (English common law in Hong Kong, and Portuguese civil law in Macau), as well as the language of their former colonial masters as an official language (English and Portuguese, respectively), along with Chinese as another official language.

Official bilingualism is developing with great momentum within the sovereign state of the United Kingdom. In the country of Wales, Welsh and English enjoy equal status. Historically, the use of Welsh had been suppressed.[98] Although everyone in Wales speaks English, in 2011, 19% of the population of Wales could also speak Welsh (i.e., 562,000 out of 3.1 million). The devolution of powers to Wales[99] means that Wales has a dual legal system—legislative powers are partially devolved to the National Assembly for Wales and partially retained by Westminster. Both legislatures have enacted acts concerning the use of Welsh (the Welsh Language Measure of 2011 and the Welsh Language Act of 1993, respectively) and the overlapping jurisdiction may be a source of confusion.[100] Acts of the Westminster Parliament are enacted in English for England and Wales, while The National Assembly for Wales enacts legislation bilingually, with both English and Welsh texts of the law having equal standing.

Gaelic is also en route to becoming an official language of Scotland. That Gaelic will command equal respect with English is the goal of the Gaelic Language (Scotland) Act of 2005, which contains strategies that increase the

---

[98] E.g., "Welsh Not" in late 19th and early 20th C.

[99] Through Government of Wales Act, 1998 and 2006; Wales Act, 2014.

[100] Catrin Fflur Huws, "(Language + Law)2 = ?," in *Current Legal Issues*, Volume 15: *Law and Language*, ed. Michael Freeman and Fiona Smith (Oxford: Oxford University Press, 2013), 400–416.

TABLE 2.4

Examples of Sub-State-Level Bilingual and Multilingual Jurisdictions

Sovereign States	Regional Official Languages	Sub-State Territory with Official Multilingualism
Afghanistan	Uzbeki (O), Turkmani (O), Pachaie (O), Nuristani (O), Baluchi (O), or Pamiri (O) as third official language, in addition to Pashto (O) and Farsi (O)[a]	Where it is spoken by the majority of people
Argentina	Spanish (O),[b] Guaraní (O)	Corrientes Province[c]
	Spanish (O),[d] Kom (O), Moqoit (O), Wichí (O)[e]	Chaco Province[f]
Australia	English (O),[g] Norfuk (O)[h]	Norfolk Island
Austria	German (O), Slovene (O)	Carinthia
	German (O), Croatian (O), Hungarian (O)	Burgenland
Canada	English (O), French (O), Inuktitut (O), Inuinnaqtun (O)[i]	Nunavut
	Chipewyan (O), Cree (O), English (O), French (O), Gwich'in (O), Inuinnaqtun (O), Inuktitut (O), Inuvialuktun (O), North Slavey (O), South Slavey (O), Tłįchǫ (O)[j]	Northwest Territories
China	English (O), Chinese (O)[k]	Hong Kong[l]
	Portuguese (O), Chinese (O)[m]	Macau[n]
Columbia[o]	Spanish (O), English (O)[p]	San Andrés, Providencia and Santa Catalina Islands
Croatia[q]	Czech (O), Hungarian (O), Slovak (O), Serbian (O), Italian (O), Pannonian Rusyn (O)	Where numbers warrant
Finland	Finnish (N), Swedish (N), Sami (O)[r]	Enontekiö, Inari, Sodankylä and Utsjoki
India	23 official languages	Decided by states
Iraq	Arabic (O), Assyrian (O), Kurdish (O), Turkmen (O), Syriac (O)[s]	Iraqi Kurdistan
Italy	German (O), Italian (O) and Ladin (O)[t]	South Tyrol
	French (O), Italian (O)[u]	Aosta Valley
Kosovo	Turkish (O), Bosnian (O) and Roma (O)	Municipal level[v]
New Zealand	English (O), Cook Islands Māori (O)[w]	Cook Islands
	English (O), Niuean (O)[x]	Niue[y]
	English (O), Tokelauan (O)	Tokelau[z]
Nicaragua	'languages of the Communities'[aa]	The Atlantic Coast
Norway	Norwegian (O), Sami (O)[bb]	Some municipalities in the counties of Troms and Finnmark
Pakistan	Sindhi (O), Urdu (O), English (O)	Province of Sindh
Peru[cc]	Spanish (O), Quechua (O), Aymara (O)	Wherever they are prominent,[dd] such as Puno
Portugal	Mirandese (O), Portuguese (O)[ee]	Municipalities of Miranda do Douro, Mogadouro, and Vimioso
Spain[ff]	Spanish (O), Catalan (O), Aranese (O), Catalan Sign Language (O)[gg]	Catalonia

(*continued*)

TABLE 2.4 CONTINUED

Sovereign States	Regional Official Languages	Sub-State Territory with Official Multilingualism
	Spanish (O), Catalan (O)	The Balearic Islands
	Spanish (O), Basque (O)	Basque Country and northern Navarre
	Spanish (O), Valencian (O)[hh]	The Valencian Country
	Spanish (O), Galician (O)	Galicia
The Netherlands	Dutch (O), Frisian (O)[ii]	Friesland
	Dutch (O), Papiamento (O)[jj]	Aruba
	Dutch (O), Papiamento[kk] (O), English (O)	Curaçao
	Dutch (O), English (O)[ll]	Sint Maarten
The United Kingdom	Scottish Gaelic (to-be-O),[mm] English (O)	Scotland
	Welsh (O), English (O)[nn]	Wales[oo]
	English (O), French (O)[pp]	Jersey[qq]
	English (O), Manx Gaelic[rr] (O)	Isle of Man[ss]
The United States	Inupiaq (O), Siberian Yupik (O), Central Alaskan Yup'ik (O), Alutiiq (O), Unanga (O), Dena'ina (O), Deg Xinag (O), Holikachuk (O), Koyukon (O), Upper Kuskokwim (O), Gwich'in (O), Tanana (O), Upper Tanana (O), Tanacross (O), Hän (O), Ahtna (O), Eyak (O), Tlingit (O), Haida (O), Tsimshian languages (O)[tt]	Alaska[uu]
	English (O), Samoan (O)	American Samoa[vv]
	English (O), Chamorro (O)[ww]	Guam[xx]
	English (O), Hawaiian (O)[yy]	Hawaii[zz]
	English (O), Chamorro (O), Carolinian (O)[aaa]	Northern Mariana Islands[bbb]
	English (O), Spanish (O)[ccc]	Puerto Rico[ddd]

[a] Article 16 of the 2004 Constitution: "In areas where the majority of the people speak in any one of Uzbeki, Turkmani, Pachaie, Nuristani, Baluchi or Pamiri languages, any of the aforementioned language, in addition to Pashto and Dari, shall be the third official language, the usage of which shall be regulated by law."

[b] Note that at the federal level, Argentina does not have an official language.

[c] September 28, 2004, Provincial Law No. 5598.

[d] Ditto.

[e] The three indigenous languages were declared official in the Chaco Province in 2008.

[f] Starting 2010.

[g] Note that the Federation of Australia does not have an official language.

[h] Norfolk Island Language (Norf'k) Act 2004, s 5(1): "The Norfolk Island Language may be used in all forms of communication between persons of Norfolk Island (but need not be) but when used in official communications must always be accompanied by an accurate translation in the English language."

[i] Inuit Language Protection Act (2008) and Official Languages Act (2008) of Nunavut.

[j] Provided by The Northwest Territories' Official Languages Act.

[k] Since the enactment of the Official Languages Ordinance in 1974.

[l] Former British colony (1841–1997).

[m] Since 1991.

[n] Former Portuguese colony (1887–1999).

[o] Spanish is the official language of Colombia (Article 10 of 1991 Constitution).

[p] Article 42 of Law 47 of 1993.

TABLE 2.4 CONTINUED

[q] Its constitutional law provides that where a minority community comprises over half of the population of a municipality, their language and script can be used officially, along with the Croatian language and Latin script. See Article 7 of Constitutional Law of Human Rights and Freedoms and the Rights of National and Ethnic Communities or Minorities in the Croatia (as amended in May 2000).

[r] Sami Language Act of 1991.

[s] Article 4 of 2005 Constitution allows for additional regional official languages. Law on official local languages passed in 2014.

[t] Ladin is the third official language in Ladin-speaking areas only. Ladins are a minority within a minority. Jens Woelk, Francesco Palermo, and Joseph Marko, *Tolerance through Law: Self Governance and Group Rights in South Tyrol* (Boston: Martinus Nijhoff, 2008).

[u] Le Statut spécial de la Vallée d'Aoste, Article 38, Title VI.

[v] Article 5.2 of the 2008 Constitution.

[w] Te Reo Maori Act 2003; see http://www.paclii.org/ck/legis/num_act/trma2003130/

[x] http://www.paclii.org/ck/legis/num_act/trma2003130/.

[y] "Niue is not a member of the United Nations, but its status as a freely-associated state has been accepted by UN organizations as equivalent to independence for international law purposes." http://www.justice.govt.nz/publications/publications-archived/2000/pacific-peoples-constitution-report-september-2000/documents/Bibliography.doc.

[z] The United Nations General Assembly designates Tokelau a Non-Self-Governing Territory.

[aa] Provided in Article 11 of the 1987 Constitution (with Amendments through 2005); Article 5 of Statute on Autonomy for the Regions of the Atlantic Coast of Nicaragua of 1987.

[bb] Article 110a of 1988 Constitution; Sami Language Act 1992.

[cc] Former Spanish colony (early 16th C–1824, recognized 1879).

[dd] Regional language policy enshrined in current Constitution (1993).

[ee] Official bilingualism recognized since Law No. 7-99 of January 29, 1999.

[ff] Section 3 of the 1978 constitution provides that Castilian is the official Spanish language of the state, but the other Spanish languages should also be official in their respective self-governing communities.

[gg] Regional policy enshrined in 1978 Constitution. Section 3(2): The other Spanish languages shall also be official in the respective Self-governing Communities in accordance with their Statutes.

[hh] Considered by many as a a dialect of Catalan.

[ii] Bilingual since 1956.

[jj] Bilingual since 2003.

[kk] Papiamentu became official language in 2007, along with Dutch and English. Simon Romero, "A Language Thrives in Its Caribbean Home," *The New York Times*, July 4, 2010, http://www.nytimes.com/2010/07/05/world/americas/05curacao.html.

[ll] Enshrined in the 2010 Constitution.

[mm] Gaelic Language (Scotland) Act 2005: "An Act of the Scottish Parliament to establish a body having functions exercizable with a view to securing the status of the Gaelic language as an official language of Scotland commanding equal respect to the English language."

[nn] Welsh Language (Wales) Measure 2011.

[oo] Wales is a country but not a jurisdiction (it is within the supranational jurisdiction of England and Wales); talk of devolution underway. The country does have a bilingual policy that affects the judicial system within its geographical boundaries.

[pp] The possibility of making the indigenous language Jèrriais an "official minority language status" was raised in 2005. "Development of a Cultural Strategy for the Island" (Education, Sport and Culture Committee, July 19, 2005).

[qq] A crown dependency; it is not part of the United Kingdom but not independent from the United Kingdom.

[rr] Manx Gaelic has official status since 1985. The language was pronounced extinct by UNESCO, but it has been successfully revived in recent years.

[ss] A crown dependency; it is not part of the United Kingdom but not independent from the United Kingdom.

[tt] Official status since 2014.

[uu] Alaska was bought from Russia on August 1, 1867; attained statehood in 1959.

[vv] Occupation by US began ca. 1900; protectorate status since 1911.

[ww] Officially bilingual since 1974. The predominance of English is stipulated in Section 706 ("English and Chamorro are the official languages of Guam, provided, however, that the Chamorro language shall not be required for official recording of public acts and transactions") and Section 707 ("Wherever there is found to exist a material difference between the English version and Chamorro version of any law or public document, the English version shall be held to be binding") of Guam Code Annotated.

(*continued*)

TABLE 2.4 CONTINUED

[xx] Guam was ceded by Spain to US, based on the Treaty of Paris, 1898.

[yy] Bilingual since 1978, Hawaii Constitution s.4. Hawaiian Pidgin English is also recognized by the US Census as a third official language. Alia Wong, "De-Stigmatizing Hawaii's Creole Language," *The Atlantic*, November 20, 2015, https://www.theatlantic.com/education/archive/2015/11/hawaiian-pidgin-recognized/416883/.

[zz] Annexed by US in 1898.

[aaa] Trilingual since 1978, Constitution Article 22(3).

[bbb] US administration since 1947, pursuant to UN Security Council Resolution 21.

[ccc] Official Languages Act of 1993. A bill was passed in 2015 to make Spanish the first official language of Puerto Rico, relegating English to the second. "P. Rico Senate Declares Spanish over English as First Official Language," *Agencia EFE*, September 4, 2015, http://www.efe.com/efe/english/life/p-rico-senate-declares-spanish-over-english-as-first-official-language/50000263-2704154.

[ddd] Colony of Spain 1508–1898; ceded to US since 1898 under Treaty of Paris.

use of Gaelic and promote its status. It requires the government to set up a Gaelic Language Plan, which gave rise to the National Gaelic Language Plan of 2012–2017.

In Northern Ireland, a proposed Irish Language Act is being drafted and the official status of Irish is being planned,[101] although no relevant language legislation has come into force yet at the time of writing, and political opposition to their implementation is expected.[102] Although the significance of the Irish language for Northern Ireland was affirmed in the Belfast Agreement of 1998, and it is recognized as a minority language in the United Kingdom under the European Charter for Regional or Minority Languages (ECRML), the language currently enjoys limited usage in public domains. In 2010, the Northern Ireland Court of Appeal dismissed a request to apply for an occasional liquor license in the Irish language (*Caoimhin MAC Giolla Cathain v. The Northern Ireland Court Service*[103]), arguing that differential treatment to English and non-English speakers is "manifestly necessary and proportionate in a democratic society" given that English is the language of the overwhelming majority of the population.

The United States, which does not have an official language policy at the federal level, does have a varied language policy in its different states and territories. French has special status in Louisiana, and so does Spanish in New Mexico. In addition to English, Hawaiian is also an official language in Hawaii. Alaska recognizes 20 native languages as official languages, along with English; this recognition has symbolic value, even though the relevant bill makes clear that it does not impose any obligation on the government to conduct any

[101] Adrian Rutherford, "Irish Language Act: Stormont Business Would Be Translated and Courts Heard in Irish," *Belfast Telegraph*, February 10, 2015, http://www.belfasttelegraph.co.uk/news/politics/irish-language-act-stormont-business-would-be-translated-and-courts-heard-in-irish-30980190.html.

[102] Verona Ni Dhrisceoil, "Language Conflict in Northern Ireland: Revisiting the Irish Language Rights Debate," *Public Law* 4 (October 2013): 693–701.

[103] *Caoimhin MAC Giolla Cathain v. The Northern Ireland Court Service* [2010] NICA 24; 2010 WL 5126438.

activities in any language other than English. The country also has overseas territories that have adopted a local language as an official language along with English.

AT THE INTERNATIONAL AND SUPRANATIONAL LEVEL

From the League of Nations (1920–1946) to the United Nations (1945–present), intergovernmental organizations (IGOs) established after the wars have created a new norm in the language practice of inter-state agreements and alliances. These IGOs designate a number of official languages, emphasizing their equal authenticity. For administrative necessity, they often also distinguish working languages, which provide the primary means of communication. Prior to the popularization of equal authenticity by these organizations, even though treaties were commonly drafted in two or more languages, one version of the text would usually be considered binding in case of discrepancy. The binding version is frequently written in English or French, even where no English- or French-speaking party is involved. The French text prevailed, for example, in the 1905 Portsmouth Treaty between Japan and Russia, and in treaties between China and the Netherlands of 1863, and between China and Spain of 1864.[104] Since the rise of nationalism and the emergence of the modern international legal order,[105] multiple authenticity became the prevailing practice.

Both official and working languages adopted by international IGOs represent dominant world powers. Most primary languages spoken in member states do not become official. The United Nations and the World Trade Organization are prime examples of an IGO. Although the United Nations has 193 member states, it has only six official languages: Arabic, Chinese, English, French, Russian, and Spanish. Originally, only French and English were to be the working languages; the other languages were later also added as working languages. The World Trade Organization has three official languages: English, French, and Spanish. Similarly, multiple authenticity among official languages is also commonly adopted among IGOs established regionally, such as in the African Union[106] (official languages: Arabic, French, English, and Portuguese), North Atlantic Treaty Organization (official languages: English and French), and Council of Europe (official languages: English and French).

Many IGOs have their own judicial organs, which generally share the same official languages as the wider organization. Thus French and English are the official languages of the European Court of Human Rights, even though the

---

[104] Ostrower, *Language, Law, and Diplomacy*.

[105] Referring to the development of modern international law and its institutions between and after the world wars.

[106] Formerly the Organization of the African Unity (1963–2002), which was also set up as a multilingual supranational body.

Court also accepts submissions and correspondence in any official language of a member state of the Council of Europe.[107] The African Court on Human and People's Rights uses Arabic, English, French, Portuguese, and any other African languages.[108] The Appellate Body of the World Trade Organization operates in English, French, and Spanish. Courts established by the United Nations and its subsidiaries do not necessary adopt all its six official languages. English and French still dominate the linguistic landscape of international courts. The primary judicial branch of the United Nations, the International Court of Justice, operates in French and English. The International Criminal Court recognizes all six official languages of the United Nations, but French and English are its working languages. Similarly, French and English are the official languages of the International Tribunal for the Law of the Sea.[109]

The European Union is unusual as a regional IGO for its strong emphasis on linguistic inclusivity and equality. Official languages of member states do not automatically become official languages of the Union.[110] Applications are considered by the Council, and unanimous agreement is required before official status is conferred to a language. At the time of writing, the European Union has 28 member states and 24 official languages,[111] but not all 24 languages are used all the time in all seven EU institutions.[112] These institutions have different internal language practice. For example, the day-to-day business of the European Commission is conducted in three *working languages*: English, French, and German. Policy documents are only translated into other official languages in the final phases of development.[113] By contrast, the European Parliament is more fully multilingual. All Parliamentary documents are drawn up in all official languages. All official languages may be used in all formal meetings. The primary judicial body that interprets EU law, the Court of Justice

---

[107] http://www.echr.coe.int/Pages/home.aspx?p=languagedocs.

[108] Article 11 of the Protocol on Amendments to the Constitutive Act of the African Union will add Spanish and Swahili to the list, but has not come into force yet at the time of writing.

[109] https://www.itlos.org/en/general-information/.

[110] Agnieszka Doczekalska, "Drafting and Interpretation of EU Law: Paradoxes of Legal Multilingualism," in *Formal Linguistics and Law*, ed. Günther Grewendorf and Monika Rathert (Berlin; New York: Mouton deGruyter, 2009), 339–70.

[111] Bulgarian, Croatian, Czech, Danish, Dutch, English, Estonian, Finnish, French, German, Greek, Hungarian, Irish, Italian, Latvian, Lithuanian, Maltese, Polish, Portuguese, Romanian, Slovak, Slovenian, Spanish, and Swedish. The process of making Turkish its 25th official language has started. "EU Parliament Recommends Making Turkish 25th Official Language," *France 24*, April 19, 2016, http://www.france24.com/en/20160419-eu-parliament-turkish-25th-official-language-cyprus-anastasiades.

[112] Namely, the European Parliament, the European Council, the Council of the European Union (often referred simply as "the Council"), the European Commission, the Court of Justice of the European Union, the European Central Bank, and the Court of Auditors.

[113] Barbara Pozzo, "Multilingualism, Legal Terminology and the Problems of Harmonising European Private Law," in *Multilingualism and the Harmonisation of European Law*, ed. Barbara Pozzo and Valentina Jacometti (Dordrecht: Kluwer Law International, 2006), 3–19.

of the European Union, is composed of judges from each member state. It recognizes all 24 official languages, but its internal working language is French.

Many scholars have warned that as the European Union continues to enlarge, its current commitment to linguistic equality can be self-destructive, as the financial costs and time required to maintain full multilingualism would become unsustainable. It is predicted that some limits will inevitably be made on the principle of linguistic equality.[114] There are campaigns[115] for adopting a single official language as the working language of the Union. Contenders include English, Latin, or an artificial language (such as Esperanto or Glosa). Alternatively, some have suggested adopting one or a few core languages (the popular contestants being English, French, and German) in some meetings and documents, but still making available Community law in the languages of all member states.[116]. There are, however, concerns that limitation of multilingualism might impair equality of rights, equality of political representatives, and democratic participation.[117]

Jurisdictions with De Facto Bilingual or Multilingual Law

Even officially monolingual jurisdictions tolerate or welcome bilingual and multilingual practices when their public servants deal with immigrants and tourists, especially in cosmopolitan cities. Linguistic accommodation for minorities in official settings may be considered a requirement of due process and an emergent international norm. Such accommodation may become so entrenched that certain languages are considered de facto official languages.

There are many jurisdictions that routinely practice law in two or more languages in official settings without legal entrenchment of the practice. In some cases, the multilingual practice is so well established that there is no need to spell it out. In some other cases, language conflicts and politics make it too politically sensitive to codify an existing practice as law.

Some examples of de facto bilingual and multilingual jurisdictions are offered here for illustrative purpose:

---

[114] Susan Šarčević, "Multilingualism: The Challenge of Enlargement," *Perspectives* 9, no. 4 (January 1, 2001): 313–24, https://doi.org/10.1080/0907676X.2001.9961427.

[115] For six other possible models, see Michele Gazzola, "Managing Multilingualism in the European Union: Language Policy Evaluation for the European Parliament," *Language Policy* 5 (November 1, 2006): 393–417, https://doi.org/10.1007/s10993-006-9032-5.

[116] "The principle of legal certainty requires that Community legislation must allow those concerned to acquaint themselves with the precise extent of the obligations it imposes upon them, which may be guaranteed only by the proper publication of that legislation in the official language of those to whom it applies." *Skoma-Lux sro v. Celní ředitelství Olomouc*, Case C-161/06, para 38.

[117] For an overview of the pros and cons of full multilingualism in the EU, see ibid.

- Apart from Hong Kong and Macau, there are reasons to think that the Chinese legal system is more multilingual than it seems. Chinese court proceedings take place in a multitude of languages and dialects, especially in rural areas. This practice is also officially endorsed in the Chinese Constitution Article 134, although the Law on the Standard Spoken and Written Chinese Language, which was adopted in 2000 and came into force in 2001, recognizes Putonghua as the only official language.
- Eritrea was under British administration between 1941 and 1950, and was federated with Ethiopia until it became independent in 1993. The country has not designated any official language, but its Constitution (Article 3(3)) states that all Eritrean languages are equal. In practice, Tigrinya, Arabic, and English are de facto official languages.
- Mauritius has no official language but is practically bilingual and bijural, having been colonized by Britain (1810–1968) and France (1710–1810) and having adopted both English common law and French civil law.
- The former British colony (1920–1968) of Nauru is de facto bilingual in English and Nauruan.
- Similarly, Papua New Guinea, which was under British and Australian administration between 1884 and 1975, is trilingual in English, Tok Pisin, and Hiri Mot.
- Pitcairn Islands (British Overseas Territories since 1838) is bilingual in English and Pitkern (a creole language derived from English and Tahitian). English tends to be used for formal occasions and Pitkern in social settings.
- In the former French colonies of Algeria and Morocco, even though both countries are eager to Arabicize and have adopted Arabic and Berber as official languages, French remains a de facto official language and a lingua franca.

De facto multilingual practice may be considered a routinized and institutionalized form of linguistic accommodation. It does not offer symbolic recognition of the linguistic communities concerned.

Observations

The data presented in the preceding present an overview of official bilingualism and multilingualism around the world today. I will draw some generalizable observations based on the data.

PREVALENCE

The first and broadest insight is the prevalence of the phenomenon. More than a third of sovereign states have two or more official languages. If we also take into account its manifestation at the sub-state, supranational, and international levels, as well as de facto multilingual practices, it will not be far-fetched to say that multilingualism in law has become a norm. The phenomenon of official multilingualism alone does not suggest that the ideology of "one nation, one language" is defeated, given that many states still officially function in one language, and that many post-colonial states see official multilingualism as a transitory strategy. That said, a great number of states have embraced linguistic pluralism as part of their national identity, and this leads to the second point.

LEGAL SUPREMACY

The legal meaning of an official language status should be determined in the context of where it is located. It is significant that in the great majority of bilingual and multilingual states, the status of official languages is conferred constitutionally, as annotations to Table 2.3 have shown. Constitution, historically an instrument of liberal democracy that came into being during the Age of Revolution, is fundamental law that outlines the basic principles of the way a people live together. An effective constitution circumscribes government powers and offers strong protection of individual liberties. Although often written by elites, a constitution is presumed to represent the will of the people, and—in democratic societies—is counter-majoritarian by design, being amendable only by a supermajority. It trumps statute law that is in conflict with it, and is relatively resistant to change of government,[118] partisan politics, and tyranny of the majority in democratic societies. Even where language status is conferred through legislation, such statutes are arguably quasi-constitutional (see further discussion of this in Chapter 4), and should be distinguished from minority-language legislation.

There may be a historical reason why official multilingualism is often recognized constitutionally. As mentioned in the previous chapter, linguistic nationalism was a popular ideology when the constitutional state emerged. A national language forms part of the narrative in nation-building, and its status is enshrined in national constitutions. Even where national languages multiplied or where its conception mutated (leading to variant labels such as *official* or *working languages*), language is still a pillar of the constitutional epic, in Cover's terms.[119] That is to say, the connection between language and national identity has not faded.

---

[118] Though the frequency of radical constitutional changes is high in some places, notably Latin America.

[119] Robert M. Cover, "Foreword: Nomos and Narrative," *Harvard Law Review* 97 (1983): 4–68.

Given that many states that are bilingual and multilingual are developing states, their official language law may be considered a constitutional arrangement that facilitates political transition: from colonial to post-colonial or from authoritarian to democratic.[120] Official multilingualism is therefore a strategy in transitional constitutionalism. At the same time, transitional polities are also prone to experience sham constitutionalism[121] where constitution on paper has no bearing on reality.

POST-COLONIAL LEGACY

The third observation is that legal bilingualism and multilingualism are almost exclusively a post-colonial phenomenon that picked up steam in the twentieth century. Among the 74 bilingual and multilingual states in Table 2.3, 63 of them (or 85%) had retained one or more colonial languages as an official language. The great majority of these states were formed after the two world wars. Most other bilingual and multilingual states result from the union of multilingual communities during state formation. In a few recent cases, including in Equatorial Guinea and Rwanda, an international language is introduced as an additional official language for perceived economic benefits.

The data presented in this chapter provide texture to the general observation that former imperial powers still dominate the world linguistically.[122] Few post-colonial jurisdictions have managed to eliminate the influence of colonial languages.[123] However, the linguistic landscape of post-colonial polities is affected by not only the fact that they had been colonized, but also the manner and type of colonization that these states experienced,[124] as well as by the

---

[120] Michel Rosenfeld, "Constitution-Making, Identity Building, and Peaceful Transition to Democracy: Theoretical Reflections Inspired by the Spanish Example," *Cardozo Law Review* 19 (1998): 1891.

[121] David S. Law and Mila Versteeg, "Sham Constitutions," *California Law Review* 101, no. 4 (August 2013): 863–952.

[122] English is an official language in over 70 countries; see David Crystal, *English as a Global Language* (Cambridge: Cambridge University Press, 1997); French in 30 states, and Spanish in 20; see Michael Krauss, "The World's Languages in Crisis," *Language* 68, no. 1 (1992): 4–10. It has been reported before that among the 54 Commonwealth countries, 19 of them (approx 35 %) have more than one official languages, and the majority of these 19 countries publish their laws in two or more languages; see Marie-Claude Guay, "The Yin and the Yang of Drafting in Two Languages: From Finesse to Faux Pas: A Canadian Perspective," *The Loophole: Journal of the Commonwealth Association of Legislative Counsel*, no. 1 (2012): 7–20.

[123] For example, Gambia, which gained independence from Britain in 1965, has announced that it will drop English as an official language because it is a "colonial relic"; but there is no timetable yet as to when this will happen. "Gambia to Drop English as 'Colonial Relic,'" *Al Jazeera*, March 14, 2014, http://www.aljazeera.com/news/africa/2014/03/gambia-drop-english-as-colonial-relic-2014313141814734996.html.

[124] Apart from style of colonization, institutional implantations play a significant role in post-colonial development; see James Mahoney, *Colonialism and Postcolonial Development: Spanish America*

sociopolitical conditions of the post-colonial state, such as the extent to which the new political structure is dominated by local elites who have been socialized in the colonial culture and language. States that experienced exploitation colonialism, as in the case of many African states[125] where a small number of colonial administrators governed a large population of colonial subjects and exploited them for economic benefits, are more likely to see their bilingual and multilingual policy as a transition stage of the decolonization process. In some of these cases, their bilingual and multilingual policy is not part of a long-term plan in nation building, but a pragmatic response to the sociopolitical situations they find themselves in. On the other hand, former settler colonies such as Canada and New Zealand see bilingualism and multilingualism as a means for structuring the coexistence of different linguistic groups in the nation and a long-term goal, where settlers and their descendants have secured domination in the post-independent state. It has been argued that settler colonies are particularly resistant to decolonization,[126] and this is manifested linguistically.

As reviewed in Chapter 1, in some Asian colonies the colonial diglossia was created by purging non-Western classical languages. The endogenous varieties that remain in use are vernaculars that may not have a standardized written form. This adds to the difficulty of their promotion as official or national languages and perpetuates the dominance of colonial languages.

SUB-STATE NATIONALISM

Some regional or state-wide multilingual practice arises from the coexistence of multiple national groups that live within a state. Prominent examples include Quebec, Scotland, and Catalonia. Some sub-state nationalism is created by colonial and post-colonial conditions, when a national group is incorporated into a bigger polity. The fact that the language of some of these national groups becomes official state-wide, but others are only recognized regionally or not recognized at all, speaks volumes about the way these groups are related to the rest of the polity. Some sub-state national groups are indigenous communities that live in a state of internal colonialism.

Sub-state nationalism is not a stable condition. Not all people who belong to a national group seek political independence, but nationalist sentiments tend to fluctuate with political climate and economic conditions.

---

in Comparative Perspective, Cambridge Studies in Comparative Politics (New York: Cambridge University Press, 2010).

[125] There are also settler colonies in Africa, such as Algeria and Kenya.

[126] Lorenzo Veracini, "Settler Colonialism and Decolonisation," *Borderlands* 6, no. 2 (2007), http://ro.uow.edu.au/lhapapers/1337/.

LINGUISTIC DEMOGRAPHICS

As earlier stated, there is hardly any state that has a monolingual population; thus linguistic demographics alone cannot explain the patterns of official multilingualism observed. Linguistic demographics, however, remains relevant to our discussion, especially in relation to colonization. Regions that were subjected to exploitation colonization, in Africa, the Pacific, and parts of Asia, also happen to have some of the highest levels of linguistic diversity in the world. In many of these post-colonial polities, colonial languages became a lingua franca whose perceived political neutrality makes them a source of stability in the building of ethnically diverse nations, especially because many of these states are formed with newly drawn political borders.

Linguistic demographics seem to be a sufficient driver for sub-state official multilingualism in some states, where official status is granted to whichever language spoken by a certain minimum number of speakers in a region. The decision is likely to aim at facilitating administrative efficiency in managing territorially concentrated speech communities. However, it is also likely that such a policy has taken into account which languages are likely to receive official status, and the political impact of such status recognition (consider again the Ukrainian example at the beginning of the book).

RECOGNITION OF NON-VERBAL LANGUAGES

Malta, Mexico, and New Zealand have all recently (in 2005, 2015, and 2006, respectively) given national or official status to sign languages. The European Parliament Resolution on Sign Languages of 1988 also calls for its member states to give official recognition to their national sign languages.

Official recognition of sign languages indicates a commitment to remove obstacles to the use of sign languages by deaf communities in the public domain. This involves, for example, the provision of sign language interpreters in legal proceedings. In the New Zealand Sign Language Act of 2006, other than the right to use New Zealand Sign Language in legal proceedings (as provided in Section 7), Section 8 of the Act explicitly limits the implications of the Act by stating that the official status granted "does not create any legally enforceable rights."

Official status of sign language is usually conferred by statutes and is conceived more as a measure of non-discrimination and a gesture of goodwill than as part of a nationalistic discourse.

LINGUISTIC EQUALITY

Linguistic equality emerged as a contemporary norm in inter-state communication. It is also increasingly widespread in the domestic law of sovereign states.

Some states explicitly provide for the supremacy of some official language over others, either in terms of a hierarchy of authority (such that one text prevails over another in case of discrepancy), or in terms of usage (such that one language is used more widely or in more important settings than others). In contrast, other states explicitly proclaim equality among their official languages. Most of the time, however, law on official language simply does not mention equality. Where the same status is conferred to two or more languages, these languages are prima facie equal, and thus equality may be asserted even where it is not explicitly proclaimed. As Chapter 4 shows, linguistic equality in Canada was a judicial invention based on the coexistence of two languages used in official texts. In fact, this logic is consistent with treaty interpretation in international law: where a treaty is silent on equal authenticity but is drawn up in the languages of the contracting parties, the texts are presumed to be equal.

It is important to note not only what languages are made equal, but also what languages are left out. This leaves crucial clues as to why official status is granted to some languages, to be explored further in the next chapter.

NATIONALISM, NEO-NATIONALISM, OR POST-NATIONALISM?

The one-language-one-nation ideology still certainly has its stronghold, as exemplified in states that have a clearly articulated state language, and in the current global surge in right-wing nationalism, such as the resurgence of the xenophobic English-Only Movement in the United States. Even among officially multilingual states, some of their constitutional provisions provide that multilingualism is only a temporary solution until an endogenous language is ready to take over as the only official language. In fact, in many places nationalism is the raison d'être of official multilingualism—consider, for example, the drive to revive Gaelic and Welsh as a struggle against the dominance of English. However, it may be argued that there is now an alternative way of imagining a nation, which does not require it to be linguistically homogenous. Since the ideology of linguistic nationalism applies just as well to minorities as to dominant ethnolinguistic groups, it has more potential to divide than unite in a linguistically diverse state, especially those undergoing or those that have recently undergone political transition. To place one language above all others inevitably creates factions and threatens the identity of other language communities. With colonialism still a living memory today, the forceful imposition of one's language and culture on others can easily be considered fascist. Whether it is motivated by conflict-avoidance or liberal democratic ideologies, linguistic pluralism is now taken by some states as a defining component of their national identity. Although there is speculation that globalization has blazed a path to post-nationalism,[127] the end of linguistic hegemony (even if it happens) does not put an end to nationalistic discourse.[128] When Justin Trudeau called Canada the first post-national state,[129] he is likely to have meant that the Canadian national identity is not monolithic. Nationalism has found a way of adapting to pluralism without compromising its core. Even though the global linguistic market has influenced national language policies, such policies are still designed with national interests in mind, and therefore it is too early to consider our time a post-nationalist era.

Constitutional recognition of linguistic plurality within a state may be read, in polities where sub-state nationalism (also known as neo-nationalism) thrives, as a political acknowledgment that the state is not only multicultural but multinational. Constitutional accommodation of sub-state national groups thus redefines the state.

LANGUAGE POLICY UNDER LATE CAPITALISM

With the rise of English as a global lingua franca, English is spoken in any major city today regardless of its official language policy, used not only in the private sector (such as business transactions) but sometimes also as medium of instruction in publicly funded schools and universities (such as undergraduate programs in the Netherlands and Israel), and as an accepted medium of communication when police stations and public hospitals deal with foreigners. Such kind of linguistic accommodation, driven by market forces, pragmatism, and social norms, may operate outside of national language policies.

The data set shows that linguistic accommodation for globalization may penetrate into national language policies. This is surprising because national language policy and its legal entrenchment are not usually the kind of things that we think of in economic terms. The phenomenon seems to be part of a late capitalist trend where concepts and goods traditionally associated with culture and nationhood have become commodities. In the words of Duchêne and Heller, discourses about national *pride* have gradually shifted toward a neoliberal discourse where *pride* and *profit*[130] are co-constructed. Although many post-colonial states envision the day when they could retire the colonial language, a strong counter force to linguistic decolonization is the instrumental value of colonial languages in the globalized world today, most notably

---

[127] Monica Heller, *Paths to Post-Nationalism: A Critical Ethnography of Language and Identity* (New York: Oxford University Press, 2011).

[128] In fact, as discussed earlier, in most "nation-states," linguistic homogeneity never existed.

[129] Guy Lawson, "Trudeau's Canada, Again," *The New York Times*, December 8, 2015, https://www.nytimes.com/2015/12/13/magazine/trudeaus-canada-again.html.

[130] Alexandre Duchêne and Monica Heller, eds., *Language in Late Capitalism: Pride and Profit* (New York: Routledge, 2012).

English. Many languages of former imperial regimes are still a resource for regional or international alignment, especially for smaller nations. The external pressure exerted by the rise of English as a global language is enormous, and this is seen even in places that have never been colonized by the British Empire. South Sudan has chosen English as its official language, using it as a tool for development. Rwanda added English as official language in 2008 and joined the Commonwealth since 2009. Georgia is replacing Russian with English as its second official language.[131] The former French colony of Gabon changed its official language from French to English, in order to "diversify" the country's "partnerships."[132] A Swiss national research program has suggested that Switzerland adopt English as a semi-official language in order to "bring Switzerland an advantage in international fields where English is the dominant language."[133] There were also proposals to add English as a second official language in Japan,[134] South Korea,[135] Taiwan,[136] and Thailand.[137] These trends underscore the importance of language skills in the knowledge-based economy, and the role that language policy plays in altering the conditions of the linguistic market.[138] Although there is no evidence that English is replacing local languages in these countries, such trends provide an argument for a kind of global linguistic imperialism[139] or recolonization, as well as the penetration of late capitalism in state language policy.

---

[131] "Georgia Begins Universal English Classes - Al Jazeera English," *Al Jazeera*, September 26, 2010, http://www.aljazeera.com/video/europe/2010/09/201092614516312607.html.

[132] A government representative explains the change of official language policy this way: "When you leave the French-speaking space, if you don't know English, you are almost handicapped. It's a question of diversifying our partnerships, ensuring that the people of Gabon are armed and better armed." Palash Ghosh, "Sacre Bleu! After More Than 120 Years of French Domination, Gabon Adopts English as Official Language," *International Business Times*, October 12, 2012, http://www.ibtimes.com/sacre-bleu-after-more-120-years-french-domination-gabon-adopts-english-official-language-845629.

[133] Jessica Dacey, "Make English an Official Language, Study Urges," *SWI Swissinfo. Ch*, February 18, 2009, http://www.swissinfo.ch/eng/make-english-an-official-language--study-urges/7224750.

[134] Kathryn Tolbert, "English Could Become Japan's Official Second Language," *The Guardian*, February 23, 2000, sec. Education, https://www.theguardian.com/education/2000/feb/23/tefl1.

[135] Jae Jung Song, "English as an Official Language in South Korea: Global English or Social Malady?" *Language Problems and Language Planning* 35, no. 1 (2011): 35–55, https://doi.org/10.1075/lplp.35.1.03son.

[136] Jennifer Creery, "Taiwan to Make English an Official Language Next Year, Says Official," *Hong Kong Free Press*, August 31, 2018, https://www.hongkongfp.com/2018/08/31/taiwan-make-english-official-language-next-year-says-official/.

[137] Sirikul Bunnag, "English Skills Receive Boost," *Bangkok Post*, July 6, 2010, sec. News, http://www.bangkokpost.com/learning/news/185082/english-skills-receive-boost.

[138] Monica Heller, "The Commodification of Language," *Annual Review of Anthropology* 39, no. 1 (2010): 101–14, https://doi.org/10.1146/annurev.anthro.012809.104951.

[139] Robert Phillipson, *Linguistic Imperialism* (Oxford: Oxford University Press, 1992).

Chapter 3

How Official Multilingualism Works

A SYMBOLIC JURISPRUDENCE

> Law is a resource in signification that enables us to submit, rejoice, struggle, pervert, mock, disgrace, humiliate, or dignify.
>
> —Robert Cover[1]

Synthesizing the observations made in the preceding chapters, this chapter spells out major sociopolitical forces that have contributed to the widespread adoption of official multilingualism, and offers an explanation of how official multilingualism works through law. Jurisdictions that adopt multilingual law are primarily driven by pragmatic rather than normative forces. This observation resonates with an instrumental view of law, as articulated by notable legal theorists including Rudolph von Jhering, Roscoe Pound, Oliver Wendell Holmes, and Karl Llewellyn, who see law as a means and not an end.[2] Official language law can perform a plethora of instrumental functions because such law works chiefly through its symbolic power. This discursive reading of law is contrary to the dominant, positivist view of law as command of a sovereign backed by force. Although symbolism is sometimes defined in opposition to what is real or substantive, law that works through symbolism is not necessarily empty in content or limited in impact. In fact, its semiotic flexibility allows for interpretive potential that may stretch beyond what is envisioned by the lawmakers.

It is only when motivations are understood that predictions of behavior can be made. The motivations identified in this chapter can therefore help anticipate and explain some of the implementation patterns reported in the second half of this book. Analysis of motivations behind law or policymaking,

---

[1] Cover, "Foreword," 8.

[2] Roscoe Pound, "The Need of a Sociological Jurisprudence," *The Green Bag* 19, no. 10 (1907): 607–15; Rudolf von Jhering, *Law as a Means to an End* (Boston: Boston Book, 1913); Karl N. Llewellyn, "Some Realism about Realism: Responding to Dean Pound," *Harvard Law Review* 44, no. 8 (1931): 1222–64, https://doi.org/10.2307/1332182; Oliver Wendell Holmes, Jr., "The Path of the Law," *Harvard Law Review* 10, no. 8 (1897): 457–78.

however, runs into the same kind of difficulty as encountered when one tries to identify legislative intention in legal interpretation. When a legislature works as a collective, with negotiations and trades taking place behind the scene,[3] any claim of unitary intention has a fictive taste to it. Is it possible to talk about motivation or intention behind law-making, when whatever agreement reached is likely to be a political compromise, as captured by the text of the agreement but no more? Although political compromise is part and parcel of law-making processes, the widespread adoption of official multilingualism in some jurisdictions but not others, in contemporary times but not earlier, suggests that there may be system-wide factors at work. It is therefore necessary to look at not only the text of the law, but also the sociopolitical realities of multilingual jurisdictions, in order to assess what these factors may be.

The Legal and Political Meaning of Status Labels

Language is a marker of jurisdiction. The Latin roots of the term *jurisdiction* (*juris* for law and *dictio* for speech) corroborate the argument that the scope and force of law is founded and enacted through its language,[4] which has the power to bring into existence what it utters. Under the Westphalian system of sovereignty, many modern states have indexed their power to govern and marked the boundaries of their sovereignty through unifying the languages spoken within their territory and granting official status to one or more of them. In supranational and international organizations, languages that receive special status often represent a common denominator or dominant sources of power in the organizations.

Labels of language status provide a textual clue to what specific language law is meant to do. Status label is not only an ideological choice but may reflect different "approaches to language management."[5] In supranational and international organizations, the most commonly adopted labels are *official* and *working* languages. Choice of labels is more varied in the national context. As shown in the survey presented in the previous chapter, a range of adjectives, such as *official, national, working, authentic, link*, and *state*,[6] has been used to

[3] William N. Eskridge, Philip P. Frickey, and Elizabeth Garrett, *Legislation and Statutory Interpretation* (New York, NY: Foundation Press, 2006).

[4] See discussion in Justin B. Richland, "Jurisdiction: Grounding Law in Language," *Annual Review of Anthropology* 42, no. 1 (October 21, 2013): 209–26, https://doi.org/10.1146/annurev-anthro-092412-155526; Marianne Constable, *Our Word Is Our Bond: How Legal Speech Acts* (Stanford, CA: Stanford University Press, 2014).

[5] Lucie Lecomte, "Official Languages or National Languages? Canada's Decision," Library of Parliament: Background Papers, February 6, 2015, http://www.lop.parl.gc.ca/Content/LOP/ResearchPublications/2014-81-e.html?cat=government.

[6] And of course, their translation equivalents, which cannot be detailed here.

describe languages with special legal status. Just like any other law, the law that assigns status labels to languages is a performative utterance—the act of declaring a language as an official or national language brings such statuses into existence. While the meaning of these labels cannot be determined based on language alone, the choice of label may nevertheless provide some pointers about the intentionality behind the laws that designate them. It is thus possible to make a few general comments about their meaning and their interrelationships. Among the labels, only *official language* and *national language* have "currency as terms of art in constitutional law,"[7] and the rest of this section will focus mostly on them.

The most commonly used label is *official language*. An official language is a language of authority. At the national level, an official language has the backing of constitutional or statutory law as a language of the state. The literal meaning of the term creates the expectation that languages carrying this status will be used in official communication. As detailed in the previous chapter, the label of official language has been assigned to not only endogenous languages but also exogenous languages in some sovereign states.

According to the Compendium of Language Management in Canada (CLMC), "(w)ithout a doubt, the most prestigious status for any language is that of official language, because states or countries that grant it automatically commit to using that language in all of their operations."[8] Similarly, in *Mentzen alias Mencena v. Latvia*,[9] the European Court of Human Rights (ECHR) argues that a country that declares a specific language to be the official language undertakes to guarantee its citizens the right to use it without intervention not only in their private life, but also in communication with public authorities when sending or receiving information in that language. There are caveats to the assumptions made in these statements. First, it is not true that jurisdictions that have one or more official languages automatically commit to using them in all of their operations. States have the sovereign power to assign meaning to their official language provisions. In fact, official status has been offered to extinct languages and sometimes only has a tokenistic value. Second, although it is true that an official language is more likely to be used in state operations than a language bearing other status labels, the symbolic significance of a national language during nation-building cannot be underestimated, and the meaning of one status label needs to be interpreted in relation to other labels that are also used in the same jurisdiction (such as the presence of *working languages* and *national languages*). The label *national language* carries strong emotive content. Due to its close ties with national identity and heritage, it is

---

[7] Lecomte, "Official Languages or National Languages?"

[8] https://www.uottawa.ca/clmc/official-language-status.

[9] No. 71074/01, admissibility decision of December 7, 2004.

normally reserved for endogenous languages. A national language has less legal weight than an *official language* and may or may not be used by the government in official communication. Owing to the influence of linguistic nationalism on Western nations for centuries,[10] *national language* traditionally appears only in the singular. However, designation of multiple national languages is not uncommon today.

Sometimes languages receive official recognition without being assigned clear labels. The Welsh Language (Wales) Measure 2011, for example, falls short of declaring Welsh an *official language* but states that the Welsh language "has official status in Wales." Although neither *official status* nor *official language* convey a clear meaning or confer any specific rights or duties, advocates argue that the latter formulation provides a stronger implication that the language will be used in official dealings.[11]

Despite their frequent appearance in national constitutions, terms such as *official language* and *national language* have a remarkably elusive meaning, and thus the adoption of one term over another does not itself guarantee strong commitment to the protection or promotion of a language. In fact, one supporting argument for the Canadian adoption of the term *official language* is its legal fuzziness, so that its meaning can be determined through jurisprudence over time.[12] Similarly, policymakers did not worry that confirming the official status of Welsh would present too many difficulties because such confirmation, of itself, does not confer any specific duties or rights.[13] Where more than one label is used within a jurisdiction, the significance of a label changes and a status hierarchy is created among the named languages. For example, if a state confers *official* and *national* status to different languages, chances are that the labels differentiate between functional and ideological concerns and that national languages are hardly used in national governance. This is the case in countries such as Cameroon, Mali,[14] Mauritania, Niger, Republic of Congo, Republic of Guinea, Senegal, and Zambia. A Cameroon linguist laments that national languages in Cameroon "have no national function."[15] On the other

[10] Nancy H. Hornberger, "Multilingual Language Policies and the Continua of Biliteracy: An Ecological Approach," *Language Policy* 1, no. 1 (2002): 27–51.

[11] See Chapter 7 of Diarmait Mac Giolla Chríost, *The Welsh Language Commissioner in Context: Roles, Methods and Relationships* (Cardiff: University of Wales Press, 2016).

[12] Lecomte, "Official Languages or National Languages?"

[13] Mac Giolla Chríost, *The Welsh Language Commissioner in Context*, 160.

[14] In Mali, although governance is primarily in French and to a limited extent in Bamanankan, national languages have been introduced as medium of instruction, together with French, in schools since 1994.

[15] Anchimbe, "Functional Seclusion and the Future of Indigenous Languages in Africa: The Case of Cameroon," 95. The author further notes that the "honorary and inconsequential recognition and appellation" of indigenous languages as national languages came just after the abolishment of indigenous language teaching in the 1970s (p. 97). Assessment of literacy is based only on knowledge of English or French, not of indigenous languages. He argues that the role of indigenous languages in the national life actually diminished after these languages became national languages.

hand, where a jurisdiction has both *official* and *working* languages, a working language may displace an official language in official communication. This arrangement may be motivated by the multiplicity of official languages in some jurisdictions, where it has become impractical to operate in all official languages. With a strong procedural overtone, the term *working language* "seeks to remain above the kinds of ideological conflict and power struggle that can surround language selection by appealing explicitly to pragmatic concerns."[16]

Official Rhetoric

Closely related to status labels is the rhetoric that supports their placement. On what basis do states justify rewarding one language with a higher legal status than another? The keywords they use fall into three clusters, which will be categorized as universal principles (such as *equality* and *diversity*), lineage (such as *national identity* and *cultural heritage*), and utility (such as *economic value* and *political stability*). These three rhetorical tropes can come into tension with one another.

Universal principles are frequently invoked. Thanks to their close fit with liberal democratic values, once invoked they hardly require further justifications. However, since the celebration of equality and diversity extends only to languages that have received special status in a polity but not others, such principles cannot justify selectivity without being supplemented by a national narrative about lineage.

Equality is emphasized, for example, in Canada and South Africa. The Official Languages Act in Canada seeks to "ensure equality of status and equal rights and privileges" (Section 2) associated with English and French, which are "at the heart of our identity." Embedded in such provisions is an imagery of two communities that were critical to the formation of the nation now living harmoniously with each other. In South Africa, Nelson Mandela emphasizes equality among the country's official languages as a corrective of historical oppression:[17]

> [W]e are extremely proud that the new Constitution asserts equality among South Africa's languages, and that, for the first time, the languages particularly of the Khoi, Nama and San communities will receive the attention they deserve, after years of being trampled upon in the most humiliating and degrading manner. . . .

---

[16] Janny H. C. Leung, "Negotiating Language Status in Multilingual Jurisdictions: Rhetoric and Reality," *Semiotica* 209 (November 4, 2016): 377.

[17] Nelson Mandela, "Don't Silence Mother Tongues," *Sunday Times*, April 25, 2004, sec. Editorial.

Diversity is often emphasized where there is a multiplicity of official or national languages, such as in Switzerland, which is conceptualized as a *Willensnation* (a country united by the desire of its citizens to live together with their diversities) and in the European Union, which has "Unity in Diversity" as its motto.

Utility is the one and only reason that justifies the granting of a special legal status to an exogenous language, which is most likely to be a colonial language, or a regional or international lingua franca. Singapore, for example, has been upfront about the utilitarian value of English for its nation-building. When Singapore became independent, the dominant ethnic groups were Chinese, Malay, and Indian. Although English, Malay, Mandarin Chinese, and Tamil are all official languages, English was chosen as the working language of the country in order to strengthen connections between Singapore and the external world and to diffuse Malay nationalism and the threat of communism (associated primarily with the Chinese), considering the political neutrality of English in relation to racial conflicts that immediately preceded the country's independence.[18] The idea that a foreign language is capable of uniting a country may seem bizarre at first glance, but the pragmatically motivated policy has been regarded as a huge success and a core element of Singaporean national identity. The nation's founding father Lee Kuan Yew has stated that English is critical to the political unity of the country:

> We decided to opt for English as a common language and it was the only decision which could have held Singapore together. If we had Chinese as a common language, national language, we would have split this country wide apart, and we would be foolish to have Malay or Tamil.[19]

From his remark it is possible to infer that, although Chinese, Malay, and Tamil are the country's official languages—with Malay doubling as the national language as well—these statuses have predominately tokenistic value. Despite the fact that between 74% and 79% of the population of Singapore is ethnic Chinese,[20] Lee justified his decision not to adopt Chinese as country's lingua franca by citing extrinsic incentives: "Singapore would be economically isolated from the wider world if Chinese was chosen. And China then could not be of much help to our economic development."[21]

---

[18] Rappa and Wee, *Language Policy and Modernity in Southeast Asia*.

[19] T. P., "The Language Holding Malays, Tamils and Chinese Together," *The Economist*, January 28, 2011, http://www.economist.com/blogs/johnson/2011/01/singapore.

[20] According to the Singapore Department of Statistics.

[21] Kuan Yew Lee, "Speech given at the Launch of the English Language Institute of Singapore (ELIS)," September 6, 2011.

The Excluded Others

Every act of inclusion is an act of exclusion. It is through inclusion and exclusion that identity is negotiated and shaped. The legitimation of one or more languages tacitly delegitimizes other languages[22] and does symbolic violence to speakers of these languages, who may feel that their deserved recognition is denied. Curiously, the same rhetorical tropes that justified the granting of special legal status to some languages can be used to deny it to others. Cynics may say that since these rhetorical tropes can be deployed against one another, they can be used flexibly to justify almost any policy decision.

There is a touch of hypocrisy in the notions of equality and diversity used in the context of official multilingualism. These terms have universal appeal, but they are not applied universally. They are often not extended to, for example, indigenous communities, who have an even longer lineage to the land. In fact, even countries that glorify equality, diversity, and multiculturalism systematically marginalize non-official languages that exist within their national boundaries. In Canada, for example, it has been argued that the national preoccupation with official bilingualism has hindered the development of other languages in the country, most notably the 60 or more aboriginal languages that have quickly diminishing numbers of fluent speakers.[23] Despite the formal equality among South Africa's official languages, English and Afrikaans are used in official communication much more extensively than others. In Switzerland, the Romansh-speaking communities do not enjoy equality with other official language groups either.[24] In fact, attempts to introduce formal equality into the country's language policy have been thwarted. A draft bill, the Federal Language Act, which contained the principle that the four national languages should be treated "identically" (Section 3), was abandoned in 2004 because such a policy would be too expensive.[25] Instead, the Federal Act on National Languages and Understanding between the Linguistic Communities, which eventually came into force in 2010, is committed to the equality of only three of its four national languages, with Romansh omitted.

Not only can utility trump equality and diversity, it may also trump authenticity and heritage. The enactment of a state language is often accompanied by language standardization. It turns out that even the semi-official status granted to Romansh is of questionable value to the Romansh-speaking communities. Romansh Grischun (RG) was created in 1982 in order to provide speakers of

---

[22] Bourdieu, *Language and Symbolic Power*.

[23] Fettes, "Life on the Edge: Canada's Aboriginal Languages under Official Bilingualism."

[24] Romansh has semi-official status.

[25] Doris Lucini, "Romansh Row Inspires Strong Language," *SWI Swissinfo.Ch*, October 6, 2004, http://www.swissinfo.ch/eng/romansh-row-inspires-strong-language/4132548.

five different Romansh idioms[26] with a standard written language. Its invention is sometimes viewed as a cost-cutting measure, adopted to avoid the same material having to be translated and printed in all five idioms. The artificiality of the resulting language has been widely criticized. Until it gains wider acceptance, RG is akin to a language spoken only by an imaginary speech community. "Romansh is something which has grown and become established, you cannot replace that with another language that has been artificially constructed," says Annemieke Buob, president of an organization that promotes Romansh.[27] A local language teacher, Renata Bott, complained to a reporter that it is "ridiculous to make kids learn a language they don't understand and that no one speaks." The leader of a Pro-Idioms group Domenic Toutsch has called RG a "bastard language,"[28] pinpointing the perceived illegitimacy of the language in his use of a kinship relation term extending the semantic field triggered by "mother tongue." Official recognition and standardization may end up destructing vernacular vitality and perception of authenticity.

Excluded from official language law inevitably are not only diasporic populations such as immigrants, forced laborers, and refugees, whose linguistic presence in a state may not be stable or deep-rooted, but often also indigenous groups who have become incorporated into later formed states through conquest, annexation, or merger. Indigenous struggles in independent states that were formed from settler colonies tend to be subsumed in the discourse of multiculturalism during the promulgation of official language policies. To avoid isolation, they are under pressure to integrate, at the cost of losing their identity and heritage. Minority-language speakers need to invest time, effort, and sometimes also money in learning the dominant language, and they are at risk of communication failure in their dealing with officials. The distributive impact of a national language policy on them is rarely addressed in official rhetoric.

The omission of immigrants is particularly noteworthy in the context of population mobilization in the globalized world. Outside of well-known immigration countries such as Australia, Canada, and the United States, many European and Middle Eastern states also have a foreign-born population that is much larger in size than their indigenous peoples or traditional minority groups. The expectation is that new migrants will either assimilate to the majority or survive in enclosed communities (in the form of "ghettos" or "expatriate bubbles"). Philosophers have tried to justify the exclusion of immigrants

---

26 The term *idiom* enjoys wide usage in the Swiss language context; more commonly known as *varieties* in sociolinguistics.

27 Isobel Leybold-Johnson, "Controversy Rages over Standardised Romansh," *SWI Swissinfo.Ch*, August 6, 2006, http://www.swissinfo.ch/eng/controversy-rages-over-standardised-romansh/41074.

28 Deborah Ball, "Swiss Effort to Save a Language Opens a Rift," *Wall Street Journal*, September 1, 2011, sec. World News, http://www.wsj.com/articles/SB10001424053111903352704576540252076676760.

in state language policy based on the assumption that they have accepted the risk of losing their language and culture and have agreed to be bound by the law of a different constitutional project by moving to a new environment.[29]

Languages may be excluded simply because their speakers do not occupy dominant positions in the society. For example, the decolonization of Malaysia has focused on promoting Malay as a national language and fighting the colonial influence of English. But Malaysia is a multiethnic state, consisting of not only Malay but also sizable Chinese, Indian, and indigenous populations. The privileging of Malay over other local languages may be taken as a form of cultural imperialism, making it unpatriotic for speakers of Chinese and Tamil to advance the status of their languages. The hegemony of Malay is effectively used to maintain racial boundaries: even when non-Malays speak the national language, they are often criticized for their impure renditions of the language.[30]

One may further argue that these populations are not merely excluded. Not only does planning for one language have repercussions on another,[31] Kymlicka posits that national language policies are often *targeted* at ethnocultural minorities in state-building (emphasis added), and that minority language rights are a defensive response to such a threat.[32] States may create linguistic domination and limit the use of minority languages or dialects to private domains, and simultaneously play the role of their protector by providing some support for their vitality (such as through minority language legislation), which never truly reverses power relationships. As Safran reminds us, language policy is as much about nation-building as political control.[33]

Such political control may work by influencing language ideologies,[34] such that the dominated participate in reinforcing their own subjugation in social hierarchies. May notes that majority language has come to be lauded

---

[29] See related discussion and some counter-arguments in Heinz Kloss, "Language Rights of Immigrant Groups," *International Migration Review* 5, no. 2 (Summer 1971): 250–68, and Will Kymlicka, *Multicultural Citizenship* (Oxford; New York: Oxford University Press, 1995).

[30] Rachel Leow, *Taming Babel: Language in the Making of Malaysia* (Cambridge: Cambridge University Press, 2016).

[31] Nancy H. Hornberger, "Frameworks and Models in Language Policy and Planning," in *An Introduction to Language Policy: Theory and Method*, ed. Thomas Ricento (New York: John Wiley & Sons, 2006), 24–41.

[32] Will Kymlicka, *Politics in the Vernacular: Nationalism, Multiculturalism, and Citizenship* (Oxford; New York: Oxford University Press, 2001).

[33] William Safran, "Introduction: The Political Aspects of Language," *Nationalism and Ethnic Politics* 10, no. 1 (January 1, 2004): 1–14, https://doi.org/10.1080/13537110490450746.

[34] Language ideologies are, broadly speaking, beliefs that people have about language and about the relationship between language and society, politics, and morality. The study of language ideologies corrects long-lasting neglect of subjective ideas that people hold about language in formal studies of linguistics, and provides analytical attention to non-referential functions that language plays through these ideas. See Paul V. Kroskrity, "Regimenting Languages: Language Ideological Perspectives," in *Regimes of Language: Ideologies, Polities, and Identities*, ed. Paul V. Kroskrity (Santa Fe, NM: School for Advanced Research Press, 2000), 1–34.

for its "instrumental" value, leading to increased social mobility and economic opportunities; minority language, on the other hand, is accorded "sentimental" value.[35] This is clearly a problematic dichotomy because it assumes that such values are intrinsic properties of the languages. Given such a popular impression, minority-language groups face a vicious circle. Low status associated with their language discourages outside groups from learning it and the younger generation from using it. Its lack of use in public domains means that a language may not be standardized or has not developed a formal register, reinforcing its stigmatization as a backward language. Furthermore, majority language and dominant culture may be masked as politically neutral, and minority language as factional and thus not conducive to a liberal polity that claims to be neutral to cultural and social norms.

The Symbolic Jurisprudence of Official Language Law

Language is often said to have both instrumental and symbolic functions.[36] Given that language is constitutive of law, it should not be surprising that law is capable of performing not only instrumental but also symbolic functions, and it does. Notwithstanding the dominant positivist conceptions that see law as a set of rules or a mechanism of social control, some legal scholars have distinguished between the instrumental and symbolic dimensions of law.[37] The instrumental function of law orients toward inducing behavioral changes, and its effectiveness relies on enforcement. For example, a traffic law which says that all vehicles on the road must display a valid registration plate works through sanctions against non-compliance. The symbolic function of law, in contrast, focuses on values and attitudes. A symbolic statute makes a statement about who we are as a society and has the potential to influence social norms, which may then influence behavior. Gusfield uses the Prohibition legislation in the United States to illustrate that the significance of law may have less to do with behavioral control than with a public affirmation of one set of

---

[35] Stephen May, "Language Policy and Minority Rights," in *An Introduction to Language Policy: Theory and Method*, ed. Thomas Ricento (New York: John Wiley & Sons, 2006), 263.

[36] In the study of language, the former is sometimes also known as *communicative* and the latter as *expressive*. I have chosen the terms *instrumental* and *symbolic* intentionally for their broader semantic scope.

[37] Tushnet and Yackle have further identified a third category which—following Sunstein—they called "expressive" statutes, which sits in between the instrumental and symbolic dimensions of law. However, Sunstein himself has not clearly distinguished between "expressive" and "symbolic" functions, and thus this third category will not be discussed here. Mark Tushnet and Larry Yackle, "Symbolic Statutes and Real Laws: The Pathologies of the Antiterrorism and Effective Death Penalty Act and the Prison Litigation Reform Act," *Duke Law Journal* 47, no. 1 (1997): 1–86; Cass R. Sunstein, "On the Expressive Function of Law Special Reports," *East European Constitutional Review* 5 (1996): 66–72.

cultural values over another.[38] Whether the legislation was instrumentally effective, the fact that one culture defeated another by winning legal affirmation was what mattered. Building upon Gusfield's idea, Dwyer identifies Section 112 of the Clean Air Act in the United States as symbolic legislation, for it allows legislators to reap political benefits by pronouncing how much they care about public health, while disregarding feasibility and costs.[39] Dwyer calls symbolic legislation pathological because it is unenforceable when read literally. The burden and risk of reformulation is thus transferred from the legislature to regulatory agencies or the courts. Similarly, Tushnet and Yackle have criticized the symbolic nature of the Antiterrorism and Effective Death Penalty Act and the Prison Litigation Reform Act in the United States, arguing that leaving it to the courts to resolve the conflicts between symbolic and instrumental statutes may sometimes produce peculiar results.[40]

I am using the term *symbolic jurisprudence* in place of symbolic legislation or symbolic law, as my interest is not in singling out pieces of law that are symbolic in nature, and suggesting that they are therefore problematic in some ways. Gusfield, Dwyer, Tushnet, and Yackle all criticized the statutes that they identified as symbolic. In my account of symbolic jurisprudence, symbolic law is not an exception, an irregularity, or a disease that needs to be cured. Symbolism is an important function of lawmaking and has a more systematic and persistent presence than usually acknowledged.

Statutes are not the only type of law that may have a strong symbolic function. In fact, constitutional law is more frequently endowed with such a function, and international law is largely sustained by its discursive power. Symbolic law is applied more often in constitutional law than in statutory law because the former imposes obligations on governments rather than citizens. Constitutional law often works through its authority to define a concept, an entity, or power relations. Some of these definitions have a relatively clear meaning: for example, a constitutional provision may stipulate the composition of a legislature and the method of elections. Constitutional provisions that grant official status to languages also read like definitions (e.g., "the official/national languages of state S shall be X and Y")—the only problem is that official status is itself an undefined concept, or it is more undefined than people assume it to be. Under-specification is a common, though not exclusive, property of symbolic law. Official language law works chiefly through its symbolic power rather than coercive sanction. Symbolic law is real law; it may have rich social meaning even if its legal consequence is negligible.

---

[38] Joseph R. Gusfield, "Moral Passage: The Symbolic Process in Public Designations of Deviance," *Social Problems* 15, no. 2 (1967): 175–88, https://doi.org/10.2307/799511.

[39] John P. Dwyer, "The Pathology of Symbolic Legislation," *Ecology Law Quarterly* 17, no. 2 (1990): 233–316, https://doi.org/10.15779/Z388J9K.

[40] Tushnet and Yackle, "Symbolic Statutes and Real Laws."

It is obvious that any status recognition, socially established or legally conferred, conveys prestige or honor, and thus has symbolic significance. A symbolic jurisprudence takes this a step further and posits that the legal consequences of official language law are derived chiefly from the often underspecified symbolic value of an assigned status only during interpretation. It is open to recontextualization and reconstruction. Viewing law as a discursive practice explains both the nature and varied effects of official language law and has a few analytical consequences, as detailed in the following.

I. Semiotic Flexibility and Narrative Power

Symbolic law is often vaguely drafted.[41] Its meaning is unstable and open to negotiation. Official language status may index different meanings for different people and at different times, including meanings that may conflict with one another. Its potential to fit into the narratives of different protagonists provides the necessary ambiguity for a political compromise. Not only is there semiotic flexibility in the status labels themselves, but the parallel listing of languages that receive the same legal recognition can also project a sense of equality, which may or may not be reflected in actual practice. Despite the potential for divergent readings, since the state has a monopoly over legal meaning, legal interpretation can be used to kill off alternative meanings when necessary.[42]

It is possible for polities to draw symbolic profit from law, such as by proclaiming equality on paper, without disrupting existing power relationships. However, the symbolic power of official language law may be weakened by habitual mismatches between popular understanding of the law and reality. If, for example, a national or official language is hardly ever used by the administration, the symbolic capital of terms such as *national language* and *official language* may deplete over time.

Working as a symbolic resource, law must be interpreted in the nomos (or normative universes) in which it is situated.[43] According to Cover, law should be understood less as a set of rules and institutions or a source of power, than as a system of meaning that helps define the world we live in. The meaning of official language law must therefore be interpreted in the normative universe of a locality, with all the history that comes with it. Law itself is constitutive of how people make sense of their world. Symbolic law, working more as a political gesture than a mechanism of social control, is especially

---

[41] Bart Van Klink, "Symbolic Legislation: An Essentially Political Concept," in *Symbolic Legislation Theory and Developments in Biolaw*, ed. Bart Van Klink, Britta Van Beers, and Lonneke Poort, Legisprudence Library (Cham: Springer, 2016), 19–35.

[42] Robert M. Cover, "Violence and the Word," *Yale Law Journal* 95 (1985): 1601–29.

[43] Cover, "Foreword."

rich as a rhetorical resource. Frequently enshrined in national constitutions, language law has huge narrative potential in political discourse, bridging between reality and divergent visions. In many national contexts, languages of special legal status are a crucial piece to the national epic.

II. Indirectness of Effect and Transformational Potential

Official language law is an ongoing discursive event that is subject to reconstruction and recontextualization. Contextual factors determine the extent to which an underspecified piece of law may be translated into practice, or whether its symbolic capital can be successfully transformed into cultural, economic, political, or social capital. What is important here is that whatever consequences that flow from official language law are derived through interpretation in a facilitating context, instead of being directly created by words of the law. In other words, emancipatory effects such as enhancement of language rights are epiphenomenal. The translation from symbolic capital to substantive legal effects depends on regulatory agencies, courts, and enabling legislation.

Some find such dependence problematic. Mac Giolla Chríost argues, for example, that symbolic law is "good politics but bad law."[44] In the same vein, Sunstein posits that law that is expressive in character should only be supported when its consequences are properly evaluated and taken into account.[45] In contrast, some European scholars have adopted a much more charitable interpretation of symbolic law. Van Klink, for example, sees symbolic law as a more communicative and interactive way of law-making than instrumental law, which regulates behavior through imposing sanctions on non-compliance, based on top-down authority.[46] For Van Klink, symbolic law stimulates public discussion, raises awareness, and affirms certain social values. It provides a rhetorical resource and a guiding viewpoint that people can use to settle their differences. Through ongoing dialogue that such law triggers, one may aspire that social norms will be developed and their applications concretized over time. Between the interpretations that symbolic law is somewhat reckless or that it is liberating, the truth is likely to be a messier picture, as the case of official language law attests.

III. Hermeneutic Visibility and Social Presence

The language of office is the most basic insignia of legality as administration, providing a visible platform for the public assertion of dogma. Official languages may be displayed and paraded in public notices, wall plaques,

---

[44] Mac Giolla Chríost, *The Welsh Language Commissioner in Context*, 191.
[45] Sunstein, "On the Expressive Function of Law Special Reports."
[46] Van Klink, "Symbolic Legislation: An Essentially Political Concept."

> letterheads, and road signs, such that their symbolic significance radiates not only from the law, but also from their presence in the public sphere. Even where official status has not been translated into substantive rights, it enhances the cultural capital of the communities concerned and may serve as a foundation for social groups to negotiate with one another.
>
> It must be noted, however, that the language of office is not only linguistic. For example, courts also communicate in signs, such as emblems and legal dress, that elude language and are recognizable across speakers of different languages. These signs simultaneously assert the predominance of a certain culture over others in law and public administration, despite the conflicting message that the multiplicity of official languages may send.
>
> For the polity, the meaning and effect of the legal status granted may be less important than the act of granting those statuses, and the impact of the law may be felt stronger outside than within public institutions. The granting of formal equality symbolically negates the social hierarchy among languages and the communities they index. It communicates a sense of solidarity that may facilitate community building among minority-language speakers. Polities profit, such as in electoral politics, from this symbolic act without actually having to disrupt existing power relations, which are simultaneously negated and implicitly confirmed by the act of recognition.

The description of official language law as *symbolic capital* is, of course, Bourdieu's terminology from his seminal book *Language and Symbolic Power*. Bourdieu indeed sees official language policy as the epitome of the symbolic power of language. In his example of revolutionary France, he regards the promotion of French as a national language and the relegation of other languages as patois (which was defined by a dictionary published at the time as "corrupted and coarse speech, such as that of the common people"[47]) as a way for the dominant group to reinforce its authority. In Bourdieu's view, the status label of official or national language normalizes such dominance. Linguistic capital that dominant groups enjoy can then be transferred into other kinds of capital, such as economic capital, through the nexus between the national education system and the labor market.

The assumption that official status provides symbolic capital makes sense when a state has only one national language. However, in face of a multiplicity of status labels and of languages that may share the same status label, a more nuanced account is needed. My account of symbolic jurisprudence does not assign a certain amount of symbolic capital to a legal status; in the same vein, it does not assume that languages that share the same status label automatically

---

[47] Bourdieu, *Language and Symbolic Power*, 47.

have the same symbolic capital. A legally assigned status has the potential of increasing the competitive value of a language in a linguistic market, but the symbolic capital of a language does not only come from law. Importantly, even when the same legal status is given to two or more languages, the symbolic meaning of the status may be quite different. This is possible because the same language status can index different aspects of context, drawing a connection with, for example, communicative versus identity functions of language; that is to say, for example, one official language may be seen as serving communicative function and another official language as serving an identity function. These languages may then have differential potentials as economic capital.

In noting the rise of multilingual polities, some linguists have posited that what underlies official multilingualism in contemporary states is the increased recognition of multilingualism as a resource or asset. Hornberger observes that a homogenizing and assimilationist discourse has been transformed into discourses about diversity and emancipation.[48] To understand these "new ideologies" as underlying national language planning seems to be an optimistic and somewhat superficial reading of state behavior. Even where some states adopt official multilingualism because they see economic value in embracing regional and international languages, it is not so much diversity and emancipation that they care about most. Although it is true that many individuals see value in learning foreign languages in the globalized world, the ideology of *multilingualism as resource* largely fails to explain state behavior, especially considering the incongruence between policy planning and implementation and the high concentration of official multilingualism in post-colonial polities. The ideology is entirely irrelevant to multilingual practice in international legal order. It is not so much multilingualism per se that is seen as a resource but the *discourse* about multilingualism that is exploited as a resource. If states are chiefly motivated by multilingualism as resource, one would expect stronger implementation of official multilingualism, more investment in multilingual education, less interest in granting official status to languages that have limited instrumental value, and no reason to honor a language that is extinct. Moreover, such discourse about multilingualism often takes place as *legal* discourse. It is law that provides a platform for symbolic recognition. If there is any prevalent ideologies underlying the phenomenon of official multilingualism, it is—consistent with Cover's jurisprudence—the ideology of law as a system of meaning,[49] and the realization that legal discourse about multilingualism can be used as a symbolic resource to achieve political and economic ends.

---

[48] Hornberger, "Multilingual Language Policies and the Continua of Biliteracy."

[49] Cover, "Foreword."

SYMBOLIC JURISPRUDENCE IN INTERNATIONAL AND SUPRANATIONAL LAW

Multiple authenticity is a manifestation of the doctrine of the equality of states developed in modern international law. Equality of states, despite being largely fictional, has a few legal consequences, such as "one state, one vote" and sovereign immunity in international law. It is also manifested linguistically to some extent. Where the number of parties to a treaty is limited, such equality is normally extended to the primary languages of all contracting parties. Here linguistic equality symbolizes equal footing and mutual respect, notwithstanding actual differences in economic, military, and political power among the parties.

When a large number of states come to an agreement, as in the case of treaties administered by the United Nations, equality among the primary language of all states is no longer manageable. As shown in the preceding chapter, most international IGOs operate in much fewer official languages than the primary languages spoken in all their member states. The pragmatic expediency of giving official status to only a few dominant languages is deemed an administrative necessity. However, the choice of official languages is still an indicator of political power. Political inequality is a reality within the United Nations, evident in the veto power retained by the five permanent member states. That said, incentives for weaker states to join these organizations by far outweigh considerations of inequalities within them, linguistic or otherwise.

Some departures from multiple authenticity cannot be explained by administrative necessity. For example, the Italian Peace Treaty of 1947 was drafted in French, English, Russian, and Italian, but only the French, English, and Russian texts were legally authentic. This linguistic arrangement understandably reflects unequal power relations among the signatories of a treaty: between Italy as a defeated state and the victorious powers of the Second World War. In contrast, the international military tribunal that prosecuted German war criminals after the Second World War produced its official documents and conducted its trial proceedings in English, French, Russian, and in the language of the defendant (based on Article 25 of Constitution of the International Military Tribunal). By emphasizing the language rights of the defendant, the tribunal, which was the first of its kind, wished to project a sense of fairness and justice.[50] In other words, the choice of languages in these examples is motivated not only by communicative needs, but also by how such a choice facilitates the political narrative through which these legal events were constructed. The legal consequences of these linguistic arrangements were likely to be secondary to their symbolic significance.

---

[50] There are, of course, many criticisms of these trials as victor's justice. See review in Kirsten Sellars, "Imperfect Justice at Nuremberg and Tokyo," *European Journal of International Law* 21, no. 4 (November 1, 2010): 1085–1102.

That linguistic equality has strong political significance and rich symbolic meaning may be further observed when regular IGOs are compared with the European Union. IGOs deal with relationships among states and have minimal democratic accountability toward individual citizens. In fact, equality of states is at times in tension with equality of citizens, when for example a state of 50 million citizens has the same amount of say in voting as a state of 50 thousand citizens. Unlike most IGOs, the European Union attempts to incorporate all the primary languages of its member states as official languages and thus implement linguistic equality to a fuller extent. This can be explained by the political structure of the Union.

Even though the European Union is a regional IGO, it is distinguished by its supranational character—some sovereign power is ceded by member states to the political union. Despite frequently criticized for its democratic deficits, the European Union aims to be a democratic supranational polity that balances equality of states (as do IGOs) and equality of citizens (as do sovereign states). Although member states retain ultimate sovereignty, the union is organized like a super-state, where citizens of all member states enjoy electoral rights in the Union. Its law is supreme to the national law of member states (the primacy of EU law) and has direct effect on citizens of member states (principle of direct effect). [51] These legal foundations of the Union make it necessary that EU law is linguistically accessible to its citizens. However, linguistic accessibility for individual citizens is only a secondary concern—the EU language regime is primarily a mechanism for maintaining inter-state relations.[52] Not all languages spoken in all member states are adopted by the Union. The choice of languages that become official and working languages in the Union represent a state-centered policy. This policy is full of internal contradictions: through a system of official and working languages, the regime simultaneously asserts linguistic equality and maintains status hierarchy; linguistic pluralism also potentially conflicts with the communicative requirement of a democratic public sphere and a European Common Market.[53] Nevertheless, the Union's emphasis on equality among its official languages[54] and the corresponding elaborate multilingual regime provide rhetorical support for the legitimacy of its unique political and democratic structure.

---

[51] In *Skoma-Lux*, Case C-161/06 [2007] ECR I-10841, EU law that has not been published in the language of a new member state was precluded from imposing obligations on individuals in that state.

[52] Anne Lise Kjær and Silvia Adamo, "Linguistic Diversity and European Democracy: Introduction and Overview," in *Linguistic Diversity and European Democracy*, ed. Anne Lise Kjær and Silvia Adamo (Surrey, England; Burlington, VT: Ashgate, 2011), 1–15.

[53] Peter A. Kraus, "Neither United nor Diverse? The Language Issue and Political Legitimation in the European Union," in *Linguistic Diversity and European Democracy*, ed. Anne Lise Kjær and Silvia Adamo (Ashgate, 2011), 17–33.

[54] Their institutional use is regulated by Council Regulation No.1/58.

Official multilingualism in international and supranational law achieves its major functions through symbolism. It is an expression of state identity. States assert their status through linguistic presence, but only the most powerful states manage to do so in IGOs. Parallel multilingualism naturally supports an equality narrative, and thus such law can be taken as a formal acknowledgment and manifestation of equality of states among contracting parties of a treaty and member states of an IGO. However, the equality narrative competes with an efficiency narrative, according to which limiting the number of official languages promotes administrative expediency. If some languages have to acquire higher status, the choice of languages can be justified not through state equality, but the rationale that underlies it. The doctrine of state equality is built upon the belief that a balance of power is crucial to collective security. Therefore, when an IGO does not extend full linguistic equality to all its member states, it is the languages of great powers that receive equal treatment, for conflicts between great powers have the biggest potential to destroy international peace. The same logic underlies the most frequent justification given for the continued concentrated powers in a few states in the UN Security Council. From this perspective, the symbolic power of official multilingualism, along with the prevailing practices of multiple authenticity and linguistic equality, serves an instrumental purpose in balancing power relations and maintaining minimum order in international relations. Alternatively, the choice of languages may be justified through their supposed currency in the global linguistic market. However, linguistic demographics cannot be the whole story, for there are more Hindi and Bengali speakers than speakers of German and French, and the former languages rarely become the working languages of IGOs. The geographical reach of English and European languages may prove that these languages have a higher currency, and such reach is itself an index of power (both military might during colonial expansion and economic power in the globalized economy).

EU multilingualism works similarly. Just like the national flags that are displayed outside EU buildings, the 24 official languages form a spectacle of unity in diversity. Despite the visibility of this spectacle, the semiotic flexibility of official language law allows for simultaneous assertion of equality among *official* languages and further designation of some official languages as *working* languages. The effect of official language law is therefore indirect and can only be interpreted and developed in context. Notwithstanding the indeterminacy in effect, the equality narrative that linguistic equality supports in turn promotes the democratic foundation of the European Union as a supranational polity. In other words, the narrative potential that official multilingualism fulfills helps the Union strengthen its democratic legitimacy and maintain minimum order.

SYMBOLIC JURISPRUDENCE IN SOVEREIGN STATES

Before one may analyze state motivation in adopting official multilingualism, an important premise that needs to be discussed is whether states made the decision voluntarily. An exceptional example where post-conflict nation-building was heavily guided by international bodies is Kosovo. The constitutional framework for the provisional self-government in Kosovo, developed by the United Nations Interim Administration Mission in Kosovo (UNMIK),[55] stipulates both Albanian and Serbian as the languages of the Assembly of Kosovo. This was later followed up in the Assembly of Kosovo with the passing of legislation on the use of languages (Law No. 02/L-37) that specifically provides for the equal and official status of Albanian and Serbian in Kosovo. The Kosovo experience demonstrates that official multilingualism has become an international norm, which has particular utility in transitional states.

Although most modern states took nation-building in their own hands, since the Paris Peace Conference of 1919, a system of minority protection has been developed internationally. Newly created states that applied for membership in the League of Nations had to guarantee[56] that basic rights would be conferred to all inhabitants in their state, including the right to speak one's language and the right to teach in minority languages where the minority population was sizable. But such obligations were practically only imposed on weaker states. International law took an individualist turn when the United Nations replaced the League after the Second World War, but there has been more attention to collective rights since the 1980s. Today, weakly worded covenants of the United Nations offer a system of minority protection,[57] but still allow plenty of freedom for states to choose their official language(s) as long as basic principles (such as non-discrimination, fair trial, and freedom of expression) are observed.[58] No international declaration has asserted a right to official language status. There may also be regional pressure on the protection of minority rights, such as the conditions that the European Union imposes on states that

---

[55] After NATO intervened during the two-year war in the Federal Republic of Yugoslavia in 1998–1999, the United Nations was involved in the administration of the territory and in overseeing the institutional development of a democratic self-government.

[56] In the form of minority treaties during the life span of the League of Nations.

[57] For a summary, see Dominik Bohl, "Language Rights in the World Polity: From Non-Discrimination to Multilingualism," in *Language Rights Revisited: The Challenge of Global Migration and Communication*, ed. Dagmar Richter et al. (Oisterwijk; Berlin: Wolf Legal Publishers; Berliner Wissenschafts-Verlag, 2012), 113–28.

[58] Essential Linguistic Provisions at the Paris Peace Conference for example provides, among other things, that "[n]otwithstanding any establishment . . . of any official language, adequate facilities shall be given to . . . nationals of [other] speech for the use of their language, either orally or in writing, before the courts." See Jacqueline Mowbray, *Linguistic Justice: International Law and Language Policy* (Oxford; New York: Oxford University Press, 2012), for an overview of international law on state language policy. See also discussion on international law on language rights in Chapter 7 of this book.

want to join the Union. However, the minimal guarantee of minority language rights leaves plenty of scope for the granting of superior status to selected languages.[59] In short, while there may be some pressure on states to grant minority rights, states generally grant official status to languages at their own volition, largely based on bottom-up pressure from domestic politics and top-down pressure in global trade.

Granting official status to a language is not the only way of showing solidarity or offering protection to minority-language communities. States may instead choose to pass minority-language legislation that provides specific language rights, such as educational provision in minority languages. Nevertheless, many states have resorted to status recognition. Since the same rights and obligations can be granted in minority-language legislation, the conferral of official multilingualism must serve additional functions.

Although linguistic equality has been interpreted and applied as a legal principle in many advanced multilingual jurisdictions, the constitutional conferral of official status is essentially a political declaration. It is typically included in the opening part of a constitution that articulates the defining characters of the state, such as its name, national anthem, and emblem, before moving on to detail governmental organization and division of powers. These definitional clauses are deeply political, unmistakably depicting the state as a historical and social construction. Provisions on language and symbols may be read as part of the main commitments of the state.[60] Although a constitution is supposed to be prior to state politics, it in fact encapsulates the sociopolitical conditions of a state. According to dominant theories, a primary function of constitutional law is to limit the exercise of arbitrary power. It entrenches basic values, broad principles, and fundamental rights such that they are superior to other laws and provide stability over time. While democratic decision-making is grounded on representativeness, a constitution is legitimated by its distance from everyday politics, its provision of "the rules of the game,"[61] and its prevention of majority tyranny. Government authority and action are generally considered legitimate if they fall within the scope of constitutional power.

Constitutions generally impose obligations on government institutions but not private citizens.[62] However, it is not always clear what obligations are

---

[59] Kraus, "Neither United nor Diverse? The Language Issue and Political Legitimation in the European Union."

[60] Ruth Gavison, "What Belongs in a Constitution?" *Constitutional Political Economy* 13, no. 1 (March 1, 2002): 89–105, https://doi.org/10.1023/A:1013691208701.

[61] Gavison, 90.

[62] See Chapter 4 of this volume for examples of how constitutionally conferred official language status may indirectly impose obligations on private actors. For general discussion of how constitutional rights may also exert their effects horizontally such that private actors could not obstruct the rights enjoyed by others, see Stephen Gardbaum, "The 'Horizontal Effect' of Constitutional Rights," *Michigan Law Review* 102, no. 3 (2003): 387–459, https://doi.org/10.2307/3595366.

supposed to be created by the constitutional conferral of official status to languages—in other words, how a government may act constitutionally or unconstitutionally. Official multilingualism entrenched in a constitution may be read as a broad statement of the state's commitment to respect diversity and to ensure peaceful coexistence of national groups. However, given that linguistic diversity is a universal condition, such constitutional provisions do not explain why some states but not others have chosen to adopt official multilingualism. In fact, as critiqued by Tierney, traditional approaches to constitutionalism assumes that a people—in the singular—live within the state, taking for granted the political power of the dominant society.[63] If a state represents "we the people*s*," then constitutional narratives about political sovereignty and legal legitimacy need to be pluralized.

States use the semiotic flexibility of official language law to serve instrumental functions that respond to their social and political needs. While all constitutional provisions are in some ways a product of the social and political circumstances of a state, not all of them work through symbolism. The analysis of state behavior presented here is informed by both contemporary jurisprudential theories, as well as interest-based approaches (as opposed to norm-based approaches[64]) in constitutional theories, international relations, and international law. This analysis understands law not as a system of rules and principles, but rather as a system of meaning which is used to achieve goals that are extrinsic to the legal system, such as economic efficiency, social values, political agendas, and public policy directions that target situation-sensitive problems.[65] Applying an interest-based approach to symbolic law, one can see that the symbolic power of official language law can be used to achieve one or more of these overt or covert goals simultaneously. Symbolic jurisprudence draws special attention to the affective dimensions and promotional function of law, as contrasted with its power in commanding and sanctioning behavior. An interest-based approach to understanding states also assumes that states act rationally, according to rewards and consequences. A norm-based approach, in contrast, argues that states act according to a commitment to norms or moral ideals. My account in the following is consistent with the former approach, locating rationales for law-making in terms of how interests and values are balanced in the wider political system and social context.

---

[63] Stephen Tierney, *Constitutional Law and National Pluralism* (Oxford; New York: Oxford University Press, 2006).

[64] Integrated approaches also exist, see Oona A. Hathaway, "Between Power and Principle: An Integrated Theory of International Law," *The University of Chicago Law Review* 72 (2005): 469–536. Although these approaches are primarily used to explain state behavior in the international arena, I am borrowing them here to explain state decisions on a domestic matter.

[65] William Michael Reisman and Aaron M. Schreiber, *Jurisprudence: Understanding and Shaping Law: Cases, Readings, Commentary* (New Haven, CT: New Haven Press, 1987).

At the risk of redundancy, a baseline must be acknowledged. State interests are rarely unitary: law-making processes tend to be influenced by divergent groups with conflicting interests. The resultant political struggle can only be fully analyzed in a particular space and time. The purpose of the analysis here is to highlight major forces that have been observed across states.

In LPP research, Ager has proposed that there are seven motives for language planning and policy actions: identity, ideology, image creation, insecurity, inequality, integration with a group, and instrumental motives for advancement.[66] These motives are derived from social psychological studies on why people or groups of people are motivated to learn a language. To the extent that official language law may be considered a stage of LPP, these motives are presumed to apply. But it is difficult to see how to apply them. For one thing, these motives appear to be overlapping categories. For example, Ager cites linguistic homogenization in France as an example of LPP with an "identity" motive, but his own analysis of the example covers the ideologies associated with different languages spoken in France at the time and the instrumental goal of reducing regional power bases, so it is not at all clear why the example does not fall under "ideology," "insecurity," or "instrumental motives for advancement." Moreover, the assumption that motives for individuals to learn a language and motives for states to implement a language policy are shared or comparable is built on shaky ground. Importantly, it is doubtful that some of these motives (think, for example, of "inequality"), when acting on their own, are sufficient to drive a state to adopt official multilingualism.

A simpler way to capture what prompts states to adopt official multilingualism is presented here. State motivations will be understood in terms of political and economic capital. These motives may be summarized by Fishman's use of the term *nationism* (see related discussion in Chapter 1). By contrasting the term with *nationalism*, which is at least superficially associated with the ideals of equality and democracy at the time of its inception, Fishman argues that states are primarily concerned with their operational integrity. The political and economic motives discussed in the following may be considered instrumental to the survival of the state. They are not primarily concerned with the interests or survival of official language communities. As the interest convergence thesis[67] in Critical Race Theory suggests, minority interests are promoted only when they converge with the interests of the dominant group. Consistent with that logic, minority languages gain official recognition only if the state can reap political or economic benefits from the move.

---

[66] Dennis Ager, *Motivation in Language Planning and Language Policy* (Buffalo, NY: Multilingual Matters, 2001).

[67] Derrick A. Bell, "Brown v. Board of Education and the Interest-Convergence Dilemma," *Harvard Law Review* 93, no. 3 (1980): 518–33, https://doi.org/10.2307/1340546.

The adoption of an official multilingual policy tends to be reactive (i.e., a response to political crisis or economic need), rather than proactive (i.e., a change led by a vision of what society a state wants to create). Decision about state language law is best explained by an interest in political and economic power, rather than by normative values such as respect for traditions and cultures or the principles of equality and diversity, which dominate the rhetorical tropes that states use in promulgating their official multilingualism policy (as discussed at the beginning of this chapter). Such tropes are not, however, irrelevant to the discussion—although states may be instrumentally motivated in their decision-making, adoption of a multilingual policy can potentially lead to norm creation and the embracing of these normative values.

Political Capital

To gauge motivation behind national language law, it is much more helpful to look at events that lead up to the law, such as social context, legislative debates, and records of policy research, than officially presented rhetoric during the promulgation of the law. Consider the following quote, taken from a report prepared by The Royal Commission on Bilingualism and Biculturalism (1963–69) in Canada:

> . . . any community which is governed through the medium of a language other than its own has usually felt itself to some extent disfranchised, and that this feeling has always been a potential focus for the political agitation.[68]

The Commission was set up in response to renewed Quebecois nationalism that called for the secession of Quebec from Canada. The Commission would lead to the passage of the Official Languages Act, which ended monolingual practices (i.e., English only) in the federal government. It is evident that the Official Languages Act was taken by legislators as a possible solution to calm a threat to the country's territorial integrity by eliminating linguistic disfranchisement as ground for secessionism. By contrast, indigenous populations in Canada have not posed such a threat, and their languages have only been offered official status at a regional level. By acknowledging that English and French became official languages because these colonial languages were spoken by "people that were able to take hold and maintain their domination in Canada," Commissioner Rudnyckyj leaves no doubt that power relations form the basis of official bilingualism in Canada.[69]

---

[68] Privy Council Office, *Report of the Royal Commission on Bilingualism and Biculturalism. General Introduction*, Book 1: The Official Languages, 1967.

[69] Lecomte, "Official Languages or National Languages?"

In South Africa, the expansion of official status from two (English and Afrikaans) to 11 languages, in what is hailed as a transformative constitution, took place at the end of apartheid which saw extreme racial inequality. Given the unrest and resistance that peaked in the decade before the end of apartheid, expanding the number of official languages in the 1996 constitution was at least as much a reflection of political necessity as that of political goodwill and changing ideologies.

Official multilingualism is a strategy for increasing the political capital of a governing body, which helps to secure political stability and legitimacy. This strategy tends to be deployed during important political transitions. The most dramatic kind of political transition is state formation, and thus official multilingualism is often adopted by decolonizing states that need to make a clear gesture about the change in political regime and construct a new national identity. Promotion of endogenous[70] language(s) is necessary to establish the legitimacy of the new political power. In multiethnic transitional states, competition for power often continues after the departure of a colonial regime, and official language status may be seen as a marker of dominance. As the experience of Sri Lanka shows, promoting the language of one ethnolinguistic group at the cost of another may trigger conflict. Pluralism in state language law makes a statement that people of different ethnolinguistic groups are full citizens of a state and have legitimate existence within the state. Meanwhile, the retention of colonial languages and the simultaneous promotion of endogenous languages are a means of ensuring political stability. Official multilingualism has thus become a common strategy in transitional constitutionalism. Unlike the equality of two or more endogenous languages, the holding of formal equality between the colonial and endogenous languages does not readily form a coherent national narrative and can only be pragmatically motivated.

My view here concurs with that of Billig, who asserts that official national languages and the suppression of rivals are an achievement of national hegemony. According to Billig, "(s)ometimes when hegemony is assured, or when it is later threatened, this legal suppression of language is relaxed, either in the interests of recapturing a harmless heritage, or to ward off demands from separatist or irredentist groups."[71] Official multilingualism may be understood as a relaxation of such suppression.

More often than not, expanded linguistic inclusivity is born not out of harmony, but rather out of fear of conflict and disintegration. The political atmosphere that underlies it is agitation, not contentment. As observed by de Witte, the granting of new language rights and status tends to be a result of political mobilization instead of legal mobilization (i.e., litigation in domestic

---

[70] Or sometimes known as "autochthonous" in European human rights instruments.

[71] Billig, *Banal Nationalism*, 13.

and international courts).[72] In his study of the European impact on domestic law, he found that language rights are most likely to be extended when the move can gather additional legitimacy and where the state's constitutional identity is not threatened. Groups whose language gains recognition tend to be those that have political leverage arising from the potential for violence. The more ethnolinguistic communities congregate geographically, the higher the threat of separatism. Official multilingualism aims not at preserving the languages or language communities in question, but at preserving the state, by maintaining security and minimum order.

For many sub-state national groups, language is a symbol of resistance against assimilation. From the perspective of minority-language communities, the gaining of official status may be read as an acknowledgment of their nationhood and an affirmation of their group identity. This optimistic reading is shared by Patten and Kymlicka, who argue that the expansion of official multilingualism is a sign of increased acceptance of minority nationalism.[73] There is hope that official status may come with the devotion of public resources to minority causes such as cultural survival. Situated in localities with a history of linguistic injustice, official multilingualism may be read as a moral statement: a determination to end inequality, oppression, and marginalization. Read in light of international regimes of human rights, it may be taken to express a constitutional commitment to protect individual and minority rights. As such, official multilingualism may help ease political agitation and unrest from minority populations.

From the perspective of the government, however, an inclusive official language law may also be read as an assertion of the political representativeness and legitimacy of the government, a jurisdictional claim over linguistically diverse territories, and a means of building political reputation. Linguistic inclusivity, and the respect and dignity that it symbolizes, is offered in return for the ceding of political power to a centralized government. As Bourdieu reminds us, giving is a way of possessing.[74] Similarly, Tannen suggests that power and solidarity are in a paradoxical relationship—any show of power entails solidarity, and any show of solidarity entails power.[75] Accepting the symbolic gesture of the government also means acknowledging the legitimacy in its exercise of power.

---

[72] Bruno de Witte, "Language Rights: The Interaction between Domestic and European Development," in *Linguistic Diversity and European Democracy*, ed. Anne Lise Kjær and Silvia Adamo (Surrey, England; Burlington, VT: Ashgate, 2011), 167–88.

[73] Patten and Kymlicka, "Introduction: Language Rights and Political Theory: Context, Issues, and Approaches."

[74] Bourdieu, *Language and Symbolic Power*.

[75] Deborah Tannen, "The Relativity of Linguistic Strategies: Rethinking Power and Solidarity in Gender and Dominance," in *The New Sociolinguistics Reader*, ed. Nikolas Coupland and Adam Jaworski (Basingstoke, UK: Palgrave Macmillan, 2009), 168–86.

The semiotic flexibility of official language law thus fulfills competing narratives at the same time: the narrative that the state has sovereign claim over its diverse population, and that sub-state national groups are distinctive and deserve political autonomy. Its narrative potential thus allows it to respond to top-down pressure of nation-building and bottom-up demands for political recognition at the same time. This has conflicting implications for the sub-state national groups. On the one hand, state conferral of language status may acknowledge and strengthen the identity of these groups. On the other, a tolerant outlook on the part of the state weakens the legitimacy of separatist claims by minorities. Language has been used as an organizing principle for the drawing of political boundaries both within states and in the formation of new states. Forced assimilation infringes political freedom and incites nationalistic resistance. If a state appears to be tolerant, however, there may be less sympathy toward sovereignty claims made by sub-state national groups.

Economic Capital

Social cohesion that results from the easing of inter-ethnic conflicts through an official multilingual policy may also contribute to economic development. In other words, symbolic capital derived from official multilingualism can boost a sense of collective community, trust, and altruism, which are social capital that in turn enhances economic capital.[76]

Under the influence of globalization, some states have adopted a more direct way of harnessing the economic potential of language policy. In stark contrast with linguistic nationalism, state language law has become a means of expanding political alliances and economic partnerships. Such instrumental motivation is clearly outward rather than inward looking. For the sake of profit, some states have given official status to a language that few of its citizens speak fluently and have raised the stakes for the rest to learn it. This is the case in Gabon[77] and Rwanda.[78] Both countries adopted English as an official language, even though the vast majority of its population have limited English proficiency. Enhancing the instrumental motivation for learning a globally dominant language is a means of translating the symbolic capital of official language status into the economic capital of the state. States that have made such a choice tend to be transitional or developing states that are seeking to develop a sustainable economy and to integrate into the globalized market.

---

[76] Amy H. Liu, *Standardizing Diversity: The Political Economy of Language Regimes* (Philadelphia: University of Pennsylvania Press, 2015).

[77] More than 80% of Gabonese are estimated to have fluency in French.

[78] According to the 2012 census in Rwanda, only 6.6% of the population claims to be bilingual in Kinyarwanda and English, and 5.8% of the population claims to be trilingual in Kinyarwanda, English, and French.

It is not news that language can be exploited as commodity. In fact, colonial powers have been benefiting from the spread of their languages for a very long time. Language may be considered a hyper-collective good, in that "the more people use it, the more valuable it becomes."[79] This explains why English language teaching (ELT) is one of the largest and fastest-growing sectors in education, which is valued at US$11.6 billion globally in 2011. In the same year, the United Kingdom has made £17.5 billion (approx. US$21.5 billion) export earnings from education, of which £2.5 billion (approx. US$3 billion) came from ELT.[80] English language education is also a big earner for former settler colonies of the British Empire, such as Australia, Canada, and New Zealand. The market dominance by these countries is supported by popular language ideologies about standard language, native speaker,[81] and accent[82]—entrenched beliefs that are often linked up with race.[83]

Not only has the globalization of economic and legal order stimulated language industries such as translation, teaching, and communication, it has provided a re-legitimizing discourse for former colonial languages to maintain their influence, prestige, and value in newly independent states. This has been described as a kind of linguistic imperialism or neo-colonialism,[84] with the effect that social hierarchy established with political power now perpetuates in economic terms. A language that once represented colonial power may now be recast as a language of economic opportunity, allowing former colonial powers to acquire a market share in the economy of post-colonial states. Economic benefit may be extracted not only from the currency of a language, but also from the image that a language projects. The British Council reports that the English language brings a brand value to the United Kingdom, citing an estimate that the benefit it brings to the United Kingdom in both domestic economy and international trade is worth £405 billion (approx. US$497 billion).

As observed by Heller, both language-as-skill and language-as-identity are commodifiable.[85] This means that, corresponding with popular language ideologies, both colonial and endogenous languages are commodifiable

---

79 François Grin, "Economic Considerations in Language Policy," in *An Introduction to Language Policy: Theory and Method*, ed. Thomas Ricento (New York: John Wiley & Sons, 2006), 81.

80 Department for Business, Innovation and Skills, "International Education – Global Growth and Prosperity: An Accompanying Analytical Narrative," July 2013, www.gov.uk/bis.

81 See Ben Rampton, "Displacing the 'Native Speaker': Expertise, Affiliation and Inheritance," in *The Language, Ethnicity and Race Reader*, ed. Roxy Harris and Ben Rampton (London; New York: Routledge, 2003), 107–11.

82 Lucie Moussu and Enric Llurda, "Non-Native English-Speaking English Language Teachers: History and Research," *Language Teaching* 41, no. 3 (2008): 315–48, https://doi.org/10.1017/S0261444808005028.

83 Ryuko Kubota and Angel Lin, "Race and TESOL: Introduction to Concepts and Theories," *TESOL Quarterly* 40, no. 3 (2006): 471–93, https://doi.org/10.2307/40264540.

84 Phillipson, *Linguistic Imperialism*.

85 Heller, "The Commodification of Language."

in post-colonial polities. Knowledge of colonial languages is a resource (outsourced call centers in India, Pakistan, and the Philippines being frequently cited examples[86]) and a sign of accessibility to the foreign visitor or investor. But language is more than a tool of communication. Authenticity of endogenous languages has also become a marketable feature in the tourism industry, which generates a main source of income for many developing states. Endogenous languages may be packaged and sold in the form of printed words on magnets and T-shirts or in the form of a cultural experience, along with displayable heritage, performable traditions, and re-enacted ways of living in a ticketed zone.

The economic role of language has become more prominent in the globalized economy.[87] Given the economic value of both exogenous and endogenous languages, official multilingualism becomes a natural way of maximizing the linguistic capital of a state. Indeed, as we have seen in our earlier discussion on official rhetoric, leaders of some countries such as Singapore have been frank about the utilitarian purpose of the language policy they promulgate. Although commodification of language is not a novel observation, the commodifiability of constitutionally conferred state language law takes the relevant discussion to a new level. In essence, state language law directly participates in negotiating transnational economic relations in the globalized world and offers another example of global forces penetrating local institutions and cultures[88] and capitalist logic seeping into what is traditionally a nationalist discourse.

An instrumental view of language is not only seen in top-down policymaking. Parents are often made to choose between preserving their family heritage and maximizing their children's opportunities for upward social mobility. Linguists have documented popular demand for learning languages perceived as valuable or powerful. In Bolivia, parents have reported a desire for their children to be educated in Spanish rather than Quechua; in South Africa, Xhosa-speaking parents prefer sending their children to English-medium schools.[89]

Apart from embracing the instrumental view of language, state inclusion of colonial or global language into its national institutions may be justified through a conceptual transferral of ownership of such languages. Post-colonial states may reclaim authenticity and autonomy by detaching colonial languages or their adaptive forms from their imperial heritage (de-nationalization) and

[86] Tariq Rahman, "Language Ideology, Identity and the Commodification of Language in the Call Centers of Pakistan," *Language in Society* 38, no. 2 (April 2009): 233–58, https://doi.org/10.1017/S0047404509090344.

[87] Heller, "The Commodification of Language."

[88] Michael Peter Smith and Luis Eduardo Guarnizo, *Transnationalism from Below* (New Brunswick, NJ: Transaction Publishers, 1998).

[89] Hornberger, "Multilingual Language Policies and the Continua of Biliteracy."

reassigning transnational or national identities to them (re-nationalization), for example through asserting local varieties such as Nigerian English as types of World Englishes.[90] It certainly happens that foreign languages acquire local meaning over time, just as Portuguese came to be known as a language of resistance in Indonesian-occupied East Timor (now Timor-Leste). The recasting of foreign languages as having domestic significance is a way of controlling and limiting the narratives derivable from the open texture of official language law.

Finally, ideologies about global languages underlie decision-making in state language law. The desirability of a language is affected not only by its actual utility, but also by feelings and beliefs that people have about the languages. The Education Minister for South Sudan told the BBC that English was chosen as an official language in his country because it "will make us different and modern,"[91] notwithstanding the fact that few South Sudanese can speak it. People have in the past preferred French to English because it was believed to be more precise or more refined;[92] today many people prefer English to their local languages because it is supposed to be more precise, more refined, or more "modern." The hope here seems to be that granting official status to a global language will increase the symbolic capital of a state.

SYMBOLIC JURISPRUDENCE IN SUB-STATE POLITIES

It may be argued that administrative convenience is an instrumental reason for adopting official multilingualism at the sub-state level. Where a region is dominated by a language, governing in that language saves cost. However, in many states such convenience is well served by de facto multilingualism. The question of why official status is conferred still needs to be considered.

Official multilingualism at the sub-state level may be interpreted similarly to the state level, in that the power that official status grants to territorially concentrated languages is primarily symbolic before it acquires substantive legal meaning. Compared with official status at the state level, official status in a sub-state region has a lower degree of recognition, says less about sovereignty, and is less integrated with the national narrative. This policy simultaneously acknowledges the linguistic supremacy of nationally recognized language(s), and the higher status of a regionally recognized language over other local languages. Sub-state official multilingualism does not challenge a dominant national identity asserted across the state. Minority groups that have their

---

[90] World Englishes has developed as a subfield of sociolinguistics and linguistic typology for a few decades.

[91] Quote of Edward Mokole, Ministry of Higher Education. Goldsmith, "BBC News - South Sudan Adopts the Language of Shakespeare," October 8, 2011, https://www.bbc.co.uk/news/magazine-15216524.

[92] Tiersma, *Legal Language*.

language recognized at a regional level gain visibility and a strengthened identity, but such recognition is more limited than state-wide recognition, in that these regional groups are not regarded as national groups that are constitutive of the state.

States that grant official status to languages wherever population number warrants may do so for administrative convenience, but the approach may also be used to achieve political ends. We have seen that a blanket policy in Ukraine—granting official status to any language spoken by more than 10% of the population in a region—has the practical effect of promoting the status of Russian in the country. The law may therefore be used to gain electoral support from Russian speakers, even though the law itself does not mention any particular language group. An inclusive linguistic policy may also be used to water down the recognition enjoyed by sub-state national groups, similar to how a multiculturalist discourse that gives attention to not just national groups but also immigrants and indigenous peoples may be seen as a way of drowning sub-state nationalism (as exemplified by the tension between linguistic duality and multiculturalist policies in Canada).

Identity Formation and Norm Creation

The realist, interest-based account of official multilingualism presented in the preceding lies in theoretical opposition to norm-based accounts. For example, Bohl argues that the multilingual turn in national language policies can be explained by discursive changes in the global legal and political environment, such as the increased attention that international law pays to minority identity rights.[93] In contrast, my account suggests that norms have relatively little role to play in *motivating* official multilingualism. Post-colonial states—which constitute the great majority of multilingual states in the world—do not become officially multilingual because they are more drawn to the multiculturalist ideal, but because they need to ensure political stability. Moreover, if official multilingualism is driven by the multiculturalist ideal, one would expect officially multilingual polities to be more tolerant and respectful of their unrecognized linguistic minorities than officially monolingual polities, but there is hardly any evidence that this is the case. Linguistic communities that experience the horror of assimilation are more likely to be hostile to minorities that live among them. For example, concerned with the survival of French in Canada, Quebec has a rigid policy of assimilating its immigrants into francophones. Similarly, to promote and secure their regional language and identity, regional governments

[93] Bohl, "Language Rights in the World Polity: From Non-Discrimination to Multilingualism."

in Spain (most notably in Catalonia) have adopted defensive language policies that may feel oppressive to linguistic minorities in the region.[94]

Official multilingualism is more accurately described as a political compromise or economic strategy, rather than a reflection of the long-term vision of a pluralistic state. However, the instrumental motivations of official multilingualism do not imply that such law is devoid of social meaning, that such law fails to induce a national identity, or that norms are irrelevant to understanding the impact of such law. Once official multilingualism is entrenched in law, especially if it is enshrined constitutionally, linguistic pluralism is capable of becoming a powerful national imaginary. The point here is that normative ideas are much more likely a product of than a cause for lawmaking, as captured by Bertrand Russell words,

> Ethical notions are very seldom a cause, but almost always an effect, a means of claiming universal legislative authority for our own preference, not as we fondly imagine, the actual ground of those preferences.[95]

Once established, norms can do what law cannot do, or does at a much greater cost.[96] Given the moral weight that law has, regardless of the effectiveness of its implementation, official multilingualism makes a statement about the value of a society and may reinforce tolerance and pluralism as social norms.

The beauty and mystery of a symbolic jurisprudence are that the same law is capable of communicating different messages, allowing for divergent uptake. This property of language is what Bakhtin calls "heteroglossia," a condition that every language is rooted in, where a plurality of voices from different socio-ideological strata inhabit every utterance.[97] The language of the law bifurcates into a double voice, simultaneously expressing different intentions and meanings, creating the potential for both an internal dialogue and divergent discourses.[98] This double-voicedness draws its energy from social realities. Depending on the uptake, the law may have impact that does not directly flow from the original motivation(s) for law-making. Pragmatically made policy decisions can nevertheless contribute to the consolidation of identity and the creation of norms, even if such effects may be indirect, unintentional, or incidental. Official multilingualism may even improve linguistic access to justice or strengthen language rights for certain language groups. But these are all

---

[94] Charlotte Hoffmann, "Monolingualism, Bilingualism, Cultural Pluralism and National Identity: Twenty Years of Language Planning in Contemporary Spain," *Current Issues in Language and Society* 2, no. 1 (April 1, 1995): 59–90, https://doi.org/10.1080/13520529509615435.

[95] Cited in Oona Anne Hathaway and Harold Hongju Koh, *Foundations of International Law and Politics* (New York: Foundation Press, 2004), 29.

[96] Sunstein, "On the Expressive Function of Law Special Reports."

[97] Bakhtin, "Discourse in the Novel."

[98] See Bakhtin, "Discourse in the Novel," for discussion of double-voiced and dialogic discourse, which is commonly observed in rhetoric.

epiphenomena, flowing from context-dependent interpretation of official multilingual law. Moreover, a symbolic jurisprudence admits the potential not only for varied interpretation, but also for the evolution of interpretation: a motivation that brings a policy into being does not have to be identical to the motivation behind the continuation of the policy.

As argued earlier, the dominant ideology underlying official language law is more about law as language than about language per se: *law as a resource in signification*. As a resource in signification, official language law is able to speak to different ideologies of language. On the one hand, adding an official language for gaining access to trade echoes a clearly instrumental view of language: taking language as a communication tool, or multilingualism as a resource. This instrumental ideology of language tends to be associated with ideologies about specific languages, such as English as a language of empowerment. On the other hand, official multilingual law also views language as a proxy to identity—in fact, it is awareness of the connection between language and identity that drives the pragmatic adoption of multiple official languages as a means of keeping a country together, or, in international organizations, as an act of power balance. Official multilingual law reinforces existing ideologies about specific languages: for example, labeling a minority language a national language and then using a dominant language as official language may have the effect of validating the popular ideology that minority languages have high identity but low instrumental value.[99] Meanwhile, this ideology may be countered to some extent if a polity does decide to expand the use of a minority language in the public realm.

The craving for political and economic capital does not offer a direct explanation to some observations associated with official multilingualism. Instead, they may be better understood through norms that are potentially created or reinforced by official multilingualism. This is where behavior cannot be fully explained by an interest-based account. For example, in addition to the effect of political reputation, it is likely that equality as a norm motivates the official recognition of sign languages. It may also be norms that encourage some states to make more than minimum effort to recognize minority language rights, which give the dominant power structures of the state no apparent benefit (other than appearing to be norm-abiding, which can, again, potentially increase political legitimacy). For example, where states such as Bolivia offer official status to extinct languages, it is doubtful that political or economic reward fully justifies the decision. At the same time, one may also say that the conferral of official status does not cost anything, since no official communication will actually take place in these languages, so the normative force that drives this move does not have to be strong. Or consider the fact that settler

---

[99] May, *Language and Minority Rights*.

colonies such as Canada and New Zealand have offered some official recognition to indigenous languages. Such a decision is, at least in part, a response to emergent international norms in minority language rights.[100]

Kosovo provides an illustrative case that official multilingualism has indeed become an international norm, by offering a glimpse of what official language law may be created by an external authority that is presumably not deeply entangled with domestic interests. Although motivations behind official multilingualism diverge across jurisdictions, it has been adopted widely enough to become an international norm.

In the great majority of cases, however, norms remain secondary in their ability to shape official language law. Norms alone are generally not sufficient to drive official multilingualism at the state level, unless such law is only tokenistic, as in the case of extinct languages in Bolivia. Conformity to norms is restricted by political interests. Official status and minority language rights are granted insofar as they do not disrupt existing power structures in a society. In states that adopt more than one status label (such as national and official languages), the status differentiation created tends to preserve entrenched interests and reproduce social hierarchy. As in many other social domains, preservation of the status quo is often confounded with the maintaining of peace and order.

Even though it does not fundamentally challenge the status quo, the symbolic value of official multilingual law may still help protect national minorities or endogenous speech communities from globalizing influences and provide thrust to democratic development and political struggles. As the next chapters will show, when linguistic equality is taken seriously, official multilingualism can create ripples and ruptures in existing legal practices and public institutions. These potential changes may be wide-reaching (in terms of administrative structure and costs), but tend to be less than radical (in terms of power relationships between groups).

Part II of the book will examine the practical changes that official multilingualism may induce in public institutions and legal processes, and how equality is negotiated in official language practice. Theoretical implications and wider significance will be discussed in Chapter 8.

---

[100] On the other hand, it is the four major former settler colonies—Australia, Canada, New Zealand, and the United States—that voted against the United Nations Declaration on the Rights of Indigenous Peoples in 2007, suggesting a limited commitment to indigenous rights.

PART II

Consequences

Chapter 4

Institutionalizing Multilingualism

WATCHDOGS ON A LEASH AND THE BUREAUCRATIC TRAP

> But in all such cases, wherever the existing law is backed by interests, the new has to undergo a struggle to force its way into the world.
> —Rudolf von Jhering[1]

As observed in Chapter 2, law on official languages often enjoys constitutional or quasi-constitutional status in modern states. Official languages seem to have, at least on paper, the strongest possible legal protection a state can afford. Despite the important legal position that such law occupies, public institutions rarely live up to the expectations explicitly or implicitly communicated by the law.

This gap is a product of, among other things, the general lack of specificity in constitutional provisions. The status of official or national language does not carry a fixed legal meaning. What does a government have to do to "enforce" an official language status? What potential does official multilingualism have in improving citizens' experience of the public sphere, or the relationship between the state and its citizens in general? Polities that have granted official language status diverge in their understanding of the legal implications of such a status, their degree of commitment, and their corresponding institutional adaptation. This chapter compares some of the ways in which official multilingualism has transformed public institutions across jurisdictions, and comments on why these transformations fall short of expectations.

Negotiating the Legal Meaning of Language Status

Unlike supranational bodies that are designed to be multilingual at the outset, many national and subnational polities go through various developmental

---

[1] Rudolf von Jhering, *The Struggle for Law*, trans. John J. Lalor, 2nd ed. (Union, NJ: The Lawbook Exchange, 2006), 11.

phases toward official multilingualism that involve all branches of government. Although, as the following account shows, such development does not have to follow any particular order, generally speaking, official status enshrined constitutionally may be translated through legislation into liberty rights and claim rights[2]—the former consisting of the freedom for the right-holder to do something, and the latter an obligation on another party regarding the right-holder. Legislation on official language typically gives citizens the right to communicate with public bodies in the official language of their choice and imposes legal duty on the government to use the official languages to perform specified public functions. In addition to official communication, language rights have occasionally been expanded to cover the right to education in an official language and other related rights that support the vitality of official language communities.

CONSTITUTIONAL RECOGNITION

The great majority of officially multilingual states have conferred language status in their constitution—the supreme law of the land that is immune to changing public opinions and party politics. Constitutions outline fundamental principles about how people in a state should live together, "whose specific implications for each age must be determined in contemporary context."[3] This is why constitutional provisions tend to be vague, directive, and aspirational.

It is therefore not surprising that many constitutions assign labels such as *official, national*, or *state* language without spelling out their legal significance, such as how a government may act constitutionally or unconstitutionally regarding an official language provision. For example, Article 5 of the Haiti constitution declares that "Creole and French are the official languages of the Republic." Despite the expectations that labels such as *official language* create, this kind of constitutional proclamation of status does not tell us anything about rights and obligations. Unlike statutes, constitutions rarely specify the means to accomplish their functions, allowing legislative freedom to expound choice of means. In fact, some constitutional framing seems to intentionally preclude enforceable legal rights unless specifically provided later: the Hawaiian state constitution, for example, provides that "English and Hawaiian shall be the official languages of Hawaii, except that Hawaiian shall be required for public acts and transactions only as provided by law." It is ironic that an official language may hardly be used in any official communication. This situation is clearly intended where the number and choice of official languages far exceed what is bureaucratically manageable (such as the 37 indigenous languages

---

[2] Wesley Newcomb Hohfeld, "Fundamental Legal Conceptions as Applied in Judicial Reasoning," *The Yale Law Journal* 26, no. 8 (1917): 710–70.

[3] John Ely, *Democracy and Distrust* (Cambridge, MA: Harvard University Press, 1980), 1.

that have been awarded official status in Bolivia, including extinct languages). It is also common in post-colonial jurisdictions where the use of endogenous languages in official capacity remains aspirational. In Haiti, although both Creole and French enjoy official status, most government communications take place in French. In Paraguay, where Guaraní fared much better than most indigenous languages in Latin America in surviving colonialism and eventually gaining official status in 1992, Spanish still dominates public administration and schooling.[4]

Some constitutions provide more specificity by granting that certain languages "may" or "shall" be used for official purposes. By contrast, "must" is rarely used, unless the obligation is vaguely stated. Consider Article 3(2) of the Cyprus constitution:

> Legislative, executive and administrative acts and documents shall be drawn up in both official languages and shall, where under the express provisions of this Constitution promulgation is required, be promulgated by publication in the official Gazette of the Republic in both official languages.

The choice of modal verb is significant here, as it is in any other legal documents: "may" indicates permission to act; whereas in legislative texts, "shall" is generally understood to convey an imperative to act, it can also be construed as merely permissive or directory.[5] Even where it is understood to convey an imperative, the statement may be taken merely as a policy direction, with no specified consequence for non-compliance. Depending on how its language is constructed, constitutional recognition of a language may induce varying degrees of expectation in its citizens for the government to provide services in the language, but it rarely creates enforceable obligations on the government or individual rights for citizens. Where the constitution does not mandate specific government action, it is up to governments to translate such status into rights and obligations through implementing legislation.

Some constitutional provisions about language express aspirational moral commitments. The South African constitution, for example, provides that all official languages "must enjoy parity of esteem and must be treated equitably" (Article 6(4)), and that the state "must take practical and positive measures to elevate the status and advance the use of" indigenous languages (Article 6(2)). Despite the apparent strength of the modal verb "must," it remains a mystery how "parity of esteem" may be ensured and whether "equitably" can be interpreted as "fairly but less than equally." The obligation to elevate the status and advance the use of indigenous languages does not specify how much state

---

[4] Ito, "With Spanish, Guaraní Lives: A Sociolinguistic Analysis of Bilingual Education in Paraguay."

[5] Henry Campbell Black, *Black's Law Dictionary* (St. Paul, MN: West Publishing, 1990); Joseph Kimble, "Plain English: A Charter for Clear Writing," *Thomas M. Cooley Law Review* 9, no. 1 (1992): 1–58.

action is required. Similarly, Article 3 of the Cameroon Constitution provides that the state "shall guarantee the promotion of bilingualism throughout the country." Such aspirations are at times so nebulously articulated that there is almost a kind of built-in tolerance for minimal follow-up action.

LEGISLATIVE EFFORT

Legislation may be used to realize constitutional aspirations. Language legislation can be used to create obligations and rights and to establish a specialized public office that handles relevant matters. It can also be used to convey a policy direction without creating specific rights and obligations.[6] Implementing legislation puts official status conferred constitutionally into effect; where such constitutional provision is absent, official status may also be declared by statutes. In democratic societies, statutes are created by a political process involving elected legislators that represent different interest groups.[7] This means that there may be political obstacles to enacting legislation that protects minority interests.

Official status of Welsh is declared by statute. Neither Britain nor Wales has a written constitution.[8] A bilingual legislature—the National Assembly for Wales—was established by the Government of Wales Act of 1998 (amended in 2006). Although rights to use the Welsh language in legal proceedings in Wales were conferred in the Welsh Language Act of 1967, it is the Welsh Language Act of 1993 that gives the Welsh and English language equal official status in public life in Wales and obliges public institutions to provide bilingual services. The 1993 Act also established the Welsh Language Board, which had the mission of overseeing the implementation of the Act and promoting the use of the Welsh language. The Board was later replaced by the office of Language Commissioner, created through the Welsh Language (Wales) Measure of 2011.

By contrast, in Ireland, the official status of English and Irish is conferred constitutionally—but it took 81 years before the intended rights that flow from the constitutional recognition (in 1922 as Constitution of the Irish Free State; subsequently in the Constitution of Ireland of 1937) were underpinned in legislation. The Official Languages Act of 2003 sets out rules governing use of the Irish language by public bodies and creates the Office of An Coimisinéir Teanga (Office of the Language Commissioner[9]).

---

[6] When President George W. H. Bush signed the Native American Languages Act (NALA), he stated that he understands the Act to be a statement of general policy and does not "confer a private right of action on any individual or group"; cited in *Office of Hawaiian Affairs v. Department of Education*, 951 F. Supp. 1484 (D. Haw. 1996).

[7] Eskridge, Frickey, and Garrett, *Legislation and Statutory Interpretation*.

[8] The British Constitution is not codified in a single document, but is said to derive from a number of sources, including statutes, conventions, judicial decisions, and treaties. There has been discussion of a new constitutional settlement for Wales.

[9] Established in 2004; www.coimisineir.ie.

In addition to implementing legislation, amendments to other existing legislation may be needed to ensure compatibility with official multilingualism. For example, official status granted to multiple languages may affect the language requirement for citizenship, voting, and election. Although legislation on official languages predominately creates obligations on public actors, an official multilingual policy can also reach private sectors and external affairs. For example, private businesses may be required to adjust their products and services in order to comply with language-related regulation, such as that of publicly displayed commercial signs and of product labels (especially ingredients on food packaging[10] and health products). The language options for treaty making may also be updated along with state language policy.[11]

Statutes on official language can have such wide-reaching effects that they are essentially "super-statutes": statutes that "penetrate public normative and institutional culture in a deep way"[12] and have a broad and lasting effect on the legal system and public culture. Support for this claim can be found in *Canada v. Viola*[13] and *Lavigne v. Canada*,[14] where the Canadian Supreme Court holds that the Official Languages Act is not an ordinary statute, but a quasi-constitutional legislation that reflects "certain basic goals of our society" and takes precedence over other federal legislation.

JUDICIAL PUSH

Judges can play a significant role in advancing the legal development of official multilingualism, by challenging sluggish executive action in making institutional changes, or developing principles from vaguely worded law. In fact, Frith considers it a virtue that language status not have a fixed legal meaning, so that—in common law spirit—the term can be defined by courts through jurisprudence.[15] That said, official language law is often drafted to avoid granting enforceable rights and the possibility of legal challenges.

Canada provides a radical example of judicial activism. Although linguistic diversity has been a concern since the founding days of Canadian federation, the status equality of English and French in Canada was a much later judicial innovation.[16] Section 133 of the 1867 Constitution provides that all Acts of the Parliament of Canada and of the Legislature of Quebec have to

[10] Rendering a phenomenon of what is sometimes called "cereal box bilingualism."

[11] For example, Canada would seek to have treaties that it makes with other states authenticated in both official languages (Official Languages Act, 1985, Article 10(1)).

[12] William N. Eskridge and John Ferejohn, "Super-Statutes," *Duke Law Journal* 50, no. 5 (2001): 1215.

[13] *Canada v. Viola* [1991] 1 FC 373 (CA).

[14] *Lavigne v. Canada* [2002] 2 SCR 773.

[15] Cited in Lecomte, "Official Languages or National Languages?"

[16] Beaupré, *Interpreting Bilingual Legislation*.

be published in both English and French and that both languages "may" be used in the Parliament, legislature, and court proceedings. It was, however, the Supreme Court that established that the two language texts of federal law are equally authentic, in its decision of *R. v. Dubois*.[17] The principle was later placed on a statutory footing in the Official Languages Act of 1969, which stipulates the official and equal status of English and French in Canada and obliges federal institutions of Canada to offer services in both languages. The same Act also creates the Office of the Commissioner of Official Languages (OCOL). The Act has been further strengthened through amendments in 1988 and 2005, which made the rights enforceable. The official status of English and French is constitutionalized in the Canadian Charter of Rights and Freedoms, contained in Constitution Act of 1982, which confers the right to use either language to communicate with the federal government of Canada and some provincial governments. The significance of official multilingualism has continued to widen in Canada, not least thanks to the liberal approach the Canadian Supreme Court has taken in interpreting language rights. For example, in a 1999 decision, it held that language rights are not only a matter of formal equality, but also a means of supporting official language communities and their culture (*R v. Beaulac*[18]).

Legal development surrounding official languages in South Africa followed a different order of events. It started with constitutional recognition, the concretization of which was later propelled by judicial interpretation. The South African Constitution (Section 6, Act No. 108 of 1996) provides for equitable use of the 11 official languages. The Pan South African Language Board (PanSALB), envisioned in the constitution (Article 6(5)), was established through statute (the PanSALB Act) in 1995 to create the conditions for the development and the equitable use of all official languages. However, critics have long complained about the lack of effective implementation. In *Lourens v. President of South Africa and others*,[19] the High Court in Pretoria held that the government had failed to comply with its constitutional obligations to regulate and monitor the use of official languages (Section 6(4)). Local governments seem to have done even less in ensuring equitable use of all official languages.[20] In response to such criticisms, the Use of Official Languages Act was passed in 2012 to promote more equitable use of the official languages, to delineate the scope of language rights, and to offer guidance on language management in governmental institutions. The South Language Practitioners' Council Bill

---

[17] *R. v. Dubois* [1935] S.C.R. 378.

[18] *R v. Beaulac* [1999] 1 S.C.R. 768.

[19] *Lourens v. President of South Africa and others* [2010] ZAGPPHC 19; 2013 (1) SA 499 (GNP).

[20] Hennie Strydom, "Obstacles in the Way of a Multilingual South African State," in *Law, Language and the Multilingual State*, ed. Claudine Brohy et al. (Bloemfontein: SUN MeDIA, 2012), 31–44.

was also passed in 2014 to regulate the training and accreditation of language practitioners.

CONFORMING TO INTERNATIONAL LAW

One infrequently discussed consideration in the formation and interpretation of state language law is conformity to international law. In principle, international law does not restrict states from designating one or more languages as official language(s) and treating them differently than non-official languages, so long as the policy respects freedom of expression, procedural fairness, and non-discrimination. Other than the rights to understand and be understood in the courtroom, which are essential to a fair trial, international law only offers broad principles when it comes to language rights, and does not oblige state governments to use any particular language in any specific public domain.

The meaning of non-discrimination is, however, somewhat murky. In *Guesdon v. France*,[21] a French citizen whose first language is Breton was charged with damaging public property by defacing road signs in French. He and his 12 witnesses sought to testify in Breton and to have their testimony heard through the assistance of an interpreter, but their request was refused by trial and appellate courts in France. He claims that French courts violated his rights under Articles 14, 19, 26, and 27[22] of the International Covenant on Civil and Political Rights (ICCPR), but the United Nations Human Rights Committee rejected the claim and held that the provision for the use of one official court language is permissible. The Committee held that the claimant suffered no discrimination because anyone unable to speak or understand French is provided with the services of an interpreter. On the other hand, in one controversial, and certainly atypical, case regarding the use of non-official language in public domains (*J.G.A. Diergaardt et al. v. Namibia*[23]), the Human Rights Committee held that the Namibian government violated Article 26 of the ICCPR by intentionally restricting the use of Afrikaans and urged its officials to respond to citizens in languages other than the official one in a non-discriminatory manner. Article 3 of the Namibian Constitution declares English to be the only official language, but permits the enactment of legislation to allow the use of other languages. However, the Namibian government had attempted to block the passing of legislation that will allow the use of Afrikaans in administration, justice,

---

[21] *Guesdon v. France*, Communication No. 219/1986, U.N. Doc. CCPR/C/39/D/219/1986 (1990). See also the following similar cases: *Cadoret and Le Bihan v. France*, Communication No. 323/1988,U.N. Doc. CCPR/C/41/D/323/1988 (1991); *Bideault v. France*, Application No 11261/84, October 8, 1986, D. R. 48; *Isop v. Austria*, Application No. 808/60, March 8, 1962.

[22] Including his rights to a fair hearing, his right to have witnesses heard on his behalf, his right to have the assistance of an interpreter, his right to freedom of expression, his right to equal treatment, and the enjoyment of minority rights, such as the use of a minority language.

[23] *J.G.A. Diergaardt et al. v. Namibia* (Communication No. 760/1997), CCPR/C/69/D/760/1997.

education, and public life. The Committee also noted that public authorities have been instructed to ignore written or spoken information communicated to them in Afrikaans. In dissent, Committee member Abdelfattah Amor argues that all languages other than the official language are on equal footing, so there is no issue of discrimination; he also states that the right to use one's first language cannot take precedence over the official language law of a country. On the whole, it is fair to say that international law rarely challenges state authority on their conferral of official status to language(s) and their deployment of official language(s) in public domains.

Mechanisms for Implementation and Their Limitations

Languages that enjoy the same official status may have different starting points in their official life and rarely receive genuinely equal treatment in public institutions. The practice of institutional multilingualism may be considered a spectrum with its two ends marked by (i) parallel multilingualism, where all official communication takes place in all official languages and all official languages are treated equally, and (ii) functional multilingualism, where official languages are used for different purposes and are positioned in a hierarchy. Many multilingual jurisdictions have assigned equal status to multiple languages, but practice a hybrid model, where the languages may be upheld for some purposes (such as legal interpretation) but not others (such as official communication). Other jurisdictions have an open policy of functional multilingualism, clearly acknowledging that some languages have more currency in public institutions than others. Among jurisdictions that offer equal status to two or more languages, hardly any practice or manage to fully achieve parallel multilingualism.

While functional multilingualism may emerge from social structures (as in a class society) and historical practices (such as through retention of colonial diglossia), parallel multilingualism is always planned and strenuously maintained. In this section, we will focus on jurisdictions that have parallel multilingual practices, and examine what these jurisdictions have done to establish linguistic equality in their public institutions. The examples discussed in this chapter are not meant to be representative of all jurisdictions that proclaim parallel multilingualism. If anything, they are atypical in that they are relatively "advanced"[24] in their institutionalization of multilingualism. We will focus especially on the institutional structures that have been created to

[24] When I refer to "advanced" bilingual or multilingual jurisdictions in this book, I am pointing specifically to the relative amount of time and effort that have been devoted to developing legal multilingualism, instead of the relative level of socioeconomic development of a polity.

facilitate and monitor the implementation of official language law. By virtue of mutual learning, there are broad similarities in the institutions that different jurisdictions have created. This includes the setting up of a government watchdog to ensure that public bodies comply with official language law. In fact, a global network of language commissioners (www. languagecommissioners. org) has been formed for experience sharing. It is unlikely to be accidental that all members of this network come from jurisdictions that are working toward linguistic equality.

The analysis that follows shows that the supreme status of state language law may not only be compromised by the lack of implementing legislation, where it is implemented, but its strength is also undermined by entanglement in bureaucracy and politics, limited political goodwill to live up to constitutional aspirations, and a lack of involvement from respective language communities.

DEDICATED OFFICE

It has become a common practice for advanced bilingual and multilingual jurisdictions that assert linguistic equality to rely on a dedicated public office to facilitate and monitor the institutionalization of official multilingualism.[25] This office is primarily an administrative unit, which is sometimes also assigned some degree of adjudicatory and enforcement power, contributing to what is sometimes known as the administrative state.[26] The office is filled by an individual—often called a language commissioner, or a more structured organizational body, such as a language board or a language commission.[27] Its main job is to regulate the fulfillment of duties by public bodies as stipulated in language legislation. This regulatory structure emphasizes the duty of governments, rather than rights of individual citizens, and provides an administrative solution to problems that otherwise may lead to legal mobilization. These offices fit the classic model of Weberian bureaucracy: a hierarchical office created with an explicit purpose, roles with designated duties defined independently of the

[25] This is the central, and presumably independent, but not the only government office that has responsibilities regarding official languages. For example, in Canada, outside of the OCOL, Canadian Heritage is also responsible for promoting the official languages. The Canadian Parliament also has internal teams dedicated to official bilingualism in the Senate (the Standing Senate Committee on Official Languages) and in the House of Commons (House of Commons Standing Committee on Official Languages); both teams conduct research studies on official language policies and publish reports regularly.

[26] Referring to the concentration of powers in executive agencies. See Cynthia R. Farina, "Statutory Interpretation and the Balance of Power in the Administrative State," *Colombia Law Review* 89, no. 3 (April 1989): 452–528.

[27] The former model has a promotional advantage in that the Commissioner may be easily identifiable and relatable to the public; but the downside is that the effectiveness of the Commissioner is heavily dependent on the individual personality of the appointee. See discussion in Chapter 2 of Mac Giolla Chríost, *The Welsh Language Commissioner in Context*.

individuals who assume them, and rules delineating the scope of authority of the office. To understand the institutionalization of official multilingualism, we will take a look at who occupies these positions and what sort of power their offices have.

The first Language Commissioner in Canada was appointed in 1970, following the Official Languages Act of 1969. The Commissioner is appointed by and reports directly to the Parliament. Being accountable to the Parliament, the OCOL is, in theory, shielded from interference of sectorialized ministers. Although the Language Commissioner is a non-partisan role that is often filled by candidates from academia or journalism, some Language Commissioners had been active in electoral politics or have affiliation with the political party that holds majority in Parliament.[28] The Language Commissioner leads the OCOL, which has a mandate to ensure that the objectives of the Official Languages Act are met. Its three main objectives include ensuring equality of English and French in public bodies subject to the Act, supporting the preservation and development of official language minority communities, and promoting the equality of English and French in Canadian society.[29] In order to meet these objectives, the OCOL plays the role of ombudsman, in addition to being in charge of auditing, liaison, monitoring, promotion and education, court intervention and reporting. The court intervention role allows the OCOL to be proactive in its work: in addition to intervening in language rights cases, the Commissioner may also decide to file proceedings himself or herself to enforce language rights guaranteed under the Act (as amended in 1988). Some key cases that the Commissioner was involved in are instrumental in clarifying the scope of language rights and restoring the balance of power between right-holders and the government.[30]

Unlike his or her counterpart in Canada, the Irish Language Commissioner in Ireland is appointed by the President, the publicly elected head of state, with recommendations of both houses of Parliament. The Commissioner reports to Minister for Community, Rural and Gaeltacht Affairs, who is appointed by the Prime Minister (Taoiseach), head of the government. Despite the statutory guarantee of his or her independence (Article 20 of Official Languages Act 2003), such appointment and reporting arrangement gives the Commissioner less autonomy and democratic legitimacy than his or her counterpart in

---

[28] Chantal Hébert, "Madeleine Meilleur's Appointment Fails the Non-Partisan Smell Test," *The Star*, May 24, 2017, https://www.thestar.com/news/canada/2017/05/24/madeleine-meilleurs-appointment-fails-the-non-partisan-smell-test-hbert.html.

[29] "Mandate and Roles," accessed March 13, 2017, http://www.officiallanguages.gc.ca/en/aboutus/mandate.

[30] Graham Fraser, "Protecting Language Rights: Overview of the Commissioner's Interventions in the Courts 2006–2016" (Office of the Commissioner Official Languages, 2016).

Canada, for the Parliament is likely to represent more plural interests and make decisions more transparently.

In terms of roles and responsibilities, a major difference between the Irish and the Canadian model is that the Commissioner in the former does not play a role in promotion, education, and court intervention. The Official Languages Act of 2003 places the Minister for Community, Rural and Gaeltacht Affairs in the position to propose modifications to the Act and to make regulations for promoting the use of the Irish language for official purposes in the state. The Irish Language Commissioner's Office has three statutory functions:[31]

(1) to provide an ombudsman service;
(2) to act as compliance agency in relation to state services through Irish; and
(3) to provide advice on language rights and obligations.

In Wales, the first Language Commissioner was appointed by the First Minister, leader of the largest party in the National Assembly for Wales, in 2012. With authorities granted by the Welsh Language (Wales) Measure of 2011, the Commissioner promotes the use of the Welsh language, imposes standards on organizations, and conduct inquiries.[32] His or her office has to publish an annual report on the activities of the Commissioner and a five-year report on the position of the Welsh language for scrutiny by the Welsh Ministers, who are also appointed by the First Minister. Again, the appointment and reporting arrangement are not the most conducive to the independent functioning of the agency. Similar to the Canadian model, the 2011 Measure (Section 8-10) also empowers the Welsh Language Commissioner to intervene in court cases.

Usually a bilingual Language Commissioner is appointed in bilingual jurisdictions, so that he or she can—at least symbolically—represent the interests of the speakers of the two official languages. In the case of South Africa, where there are 11 official languages, the PanSALB Act stipulates that the board should be composed of 14 members who have language-related skills (such as interpretation, lexicography, and language planning) and who should be broadly representative of the diversity of the South African community (without mandating that each official language is represented). Candidates for the board are shortlisted by the Portfolio Committee on Arts and Culture and then selected by the Minister of Arts and Culture.[33] Unlike the Language

---

[31] Seán Ó Cuirreáin, "Translation of Speaking Notes at the Houses of the Oireachtas Joint Committee on Public Service Oversight and Petitions," December 4, 2013, https://www.coimisineir.ie/userfiles/files/SpeakingnotesAnCoimisineirTeanga04122013.pdf.

[32] See official website at http://www.comisiynyddygymraeg.org/english/Pages/Home.aspx.

[33] Minutes of meeting of the Portfolio Committee on Arts and Culture, "Procedure for the Appointment of Board Members to the Pan South African Language Board (PanSALB)," March 6, 2013. Available on https://pmg.org.za/committee-meeting/15518/. The minutes also revealed uncertainty as to who PanSALB should be answerable to—the Committee or the Minister.

Commissioners earlier discussed, PanSALB is chiefly responsible for promotion and research, and its compliance function is heavily qualified as an optional activity—it *may*, "on its own initiative," investigate language rights violations and, "in addition to any powers and functions conferred on or assigned to it by law," monitor observance of constitutionally provided language rights by public bodies (PANSALB Act of 1995; as amended in 1999; emphasis added). At the beginning of 2016, the Minister of Arts and Culture fired all the board members of PanSALB, citing a need to start on "a clean slate"[34] and complaining that the board showed poor performance and leadership.[35] The ease with which PanSALB was dissolved by a minister shows how politically dependent it is in organizational structure.

COMPLIANCE AND COMPLAINTS

Let us examine more closely what mechanisms these offices have in place to ensure compliance with state language law. Agencies responsible for official languages generally have the power to audit public bodies and to assess their compliance with existing statutory or constitutional obligations. For example, under the Official Languages Act, the Irish Language Commissioner has the power to obtain information from public bodies and to compel a person to attend before him in order to enable him to fulfill his duties. The Commissioner can also bring and prosecute proceedings for an offense committed by someone who fails or refuses to attend before the Commissioner and furnish information. Such power facilitates his or her ability to investigate complaints.

In 2014 alone, the Irish Language Commissioner's Office handled 709 complaints, most of which were resolved through an informal complaints resolution mechanism or through advising the complainants. Cases not resolved through these means are formally investigated. Since 2007, the Office has carried out more than a hundred investigations. By diverting grievances away from dispute resolution in formal courts, official language agencies prevent multilingual law from overburdening the judicial system. The adoption of administrative solutions to what may be constitutional or statutory violations has its pros and cons: on the one hand, it may weaken the force of the relevant law; on the other, these solutions are much more efficient and much less costly for the complainants than judicial recourse, especially considering that even if awarded, the size of damage in relevant cases tends to be small.

---

[34] Mpho Raborife, "Mthethwa Dissolves Pan South African Language Board," *News24*, January 13, 2016, http://www.news24.com/SouthAfrica/News/mthethwa-dissolves-pan-south-african-language-board-20160113.

[35] Prior to its dissolution, the board suffered from an ongoing administrative crisis and political saga, in relation to its bloated structure, soaring expenses on wages (amounting to 72% of their available funding), and alleged illegal employment (*Mail & Guardian*, April 2, 2015).

Although they are not usually legal professionals, in their capacity as ombudsman these commissioners practically play the role of an adjudicator working in the shadow of the law. Their reports are not binding decisions, but their opinions may lead to sanctions. The adjudicative nature of their investigations is evident in, for instance, the Irish investigative reports that have been published (available on the Commissioner's website). In these reports the Irish Commissioner acts as both the fact-finder and the trier of law. She or he decides whether a breach has occurred and offers rationale for the decision. His or her findings may be appealed on a point of law in the High Court; such an appeal has only been made once so far, by the Office the Revenue Commissioners, and the Court rejected it (*Na Coimisinéirí Ioncaim v. An Coimisinéir Teanga*[36]).

Apart from the authority of their decision, what distinguishes the Commissioner's opinion from adjudication is that these agencies do not generally have the power to punish violators or award damages to complainants whose language rights have been denied. Using the Irish example again, upon the Commissioner's reporting of a failure of compliance by a public body, it is the Minister for Community, Rural and Gaeltacht Affairs who has the power to order the public body to provide compensation to persons whose language rights have been denied. When a public body fails to implement recommendations following an investigation, the Commissioner may submit a report to the Houses of the Oireachtas.

The Canadian language commissioner has a similar scope of power. It investigates compliance, for example by having "language police" pose as travelers to monitor the level of bilingual services offered by airport security staff, retailers, and Air Canada.[37] In its ombudsman capacity, the OCOL receives and investigates complaints against federal institutions, but does not have the power to punish violators. Complaints are considered resolved when reports are produced and when federal institutions make certain commitments about their language provisions. After filing a complaint with the OCOL, a complainant may also choose to seek a court remedy from the Federal Court under the Official Languages Act. Although the Language Commissioner cannot impose sanctions, she or he does have the power to intervene in court cases should complainants decide to take legal action.

Since the primary goal of language commissioners is to ensure compliance instead of dispute resolution or enforcing accountability, their reports focus on improving the future behavior of the public bodies concerned, rather than on holding them accountable for the suffering of the complainants. Not only does the lack of enforcement power hinder their ability to ensure

---

[36] *Na Coimisinéirí Ioncaim v. An Coimisinéir Teanga* [2015] IEHC 110.

[37] A. H., "Canada's Airports: Beware the Language Police," *The Economist*, August 16, 2012, http://www.economist.com/blogs/gulliver/2012/08/canadas-airports.

compliance, the minimal consequences for breaching language rights may project the impression that language legislation can be taken less seriously than other legislation, contravening the apparent supreme status of such law, as earlier discussed. Under a managerial logic, non-compliance with language legislation is treated as a performance gap (discrepancy between a managerial aspiration and achievement[38]) rather than breaking the law, blurring the line between an administrative goal and a legal obligation. Similarly, language legislation in the United Kingdom limits opportunities for legal mobilization and instead emphasizes duties for public authorities,[39] thus encouraging administrative solutions for non-compliance. Recent developments in Wales may strengthen such administrative solutions. In addition to investigative powers, the Welsh Language Commissioner is newly empowered to impose civil penalties upon public bodies who fail to comply with the recently introduced language standards. Another innovation in Wales is the setting up of a specialized tribunal to handle appeals. The Welsh Language Tribunal will offer an opportunity for organizations to appeal against the Language Commissioner's decisions in relation to Welsh Language Standards. At the time of writing, the operational rules of the Tribunal are still being debated.

In Canada, the limited enforcement power of the Language Commissioner has been partly redeemed by an important federal program that complements the work of the OCOL—through the Language Rights Support Program (LRSP; 2008–2017) or the Court Challenges Program (CCP; 1978–2006 and 2017–present), which supports the use of judicial recourse to affirm, clarify, or effectively implement language rights. Between 1978 and 2012, the CCP and the LRSP funded over 300 language rights remedies.[40] The program, however, only funds litigations that are precedent-setting and are of national significance.

Language commissioners can also exhibit regulatory activism without resorting to legal remedies. In handling the cases of *Swinton* and *Admiral*, which involve companies refusing to offer services in Welsh to their customers, Mac Giolla Chríost alludes to pressure that the Welsh Language Commissioner has exerted on the companies even though there is no legal obligation for them to do so.[41]

---

[38] Lauren B. Edelman, Sally Riggs Fuller, and Iona Mara-Drita, "Diversity Rhetoric and the Managerialization of Law," *American Journal of Sociology* 106, no. 6 (2001): 1589–1641, https://doi.org/10.1086/321303.

[39] de Witte, "Language Rights: The Interaction between Domestic and European Development."

[40] Marie-Ève Hudon, "The Role of the Courts in the Recognition of Language Rights" (Legal and Legislative Affairs Division, Parliamentary Information and Research Service, Canada, 2013), http://www.lop.parl.gc.ca/Content/LOP/ResearchPublications/2011-68-e.htm.

[41] Mac Giolla Chríost, *The Welsh Language Commissioner in Context*.

SETTING GOALS AND MEETING STANDARDS

Another reason for the weak implementation of official multilingualism is the popularity of schemes-based approach over rights-based approach. Under a schemes-based approach, those who are being regulated get to decide what regulations should be imposed on them, and individual users do not have the power to launch claims directly against public service providers. In polities including Basque, Ireland, and Wales, the plans that public bodies make about their language use are known as "language schemes," referring to goals that they are asked to set for themselves regarding their language services provision. These schemes typically last for a few years. Instead of benchmarking them against a set of objectively defined standards imposed by the law, language commissioners appraise their ability to deliver their promises made in language schemes.

Despite legislative assurance that the Basque administration must be able to attend to people in the official language of their choice, instituted language schemes failed to guarantee the delivery of such standard of service. Williams summarizes a long list of reasons that explain the failure: bureaucratization, lack of targeted planning, conflict of interest between departmental interests and wider government policy, the absence of backing of language-planning officials by senior management, reluctance for civil servants to use some languages, and a top-heavy approach to language planning.[42]

In Ireland, despite the emergence of compliance professionals[43] in the form of Irish Language Officer or Irish Language Units in public bodies, the effectiveness of language schemes has also increasingly been questioned. First, the power to initiate schemes rests within the government office, rather than with the Commissioner. Commitment that public bodies make in the language schemes may be minimal—such as for reception staff to be able to say basic greetings in Irish and say the name of the department in Irish. Some departments are committed to provide pre-recorded telephone announcements bilingually but are silent about Irish-language service provision in interactive conversations. Many schemes include commitments to *improve* their existing service provision, rather than to meet an objectively set standard of service provision. Moreover, fewer and fewer language schemes have been submitted. Of the schemes that are in place, few of them have been satisfactorily implemented. In his 2014 annual report, the Irish Language Commissioner states that he is "firmly of the

---

[42] Colin Haslehurst Williams, "Perfidious Hope: The Legislative Turn in Official Minority Language Regimes," *Regional & Federal Studies* 23, no. 1 (March 1, 2013): 101–22, https://doi.org/10.1080/13597566.2012.754353.

[43] Lauren B. Edelman, "Legality and the Endogeneity of Law," in *Legality and Community: On the Intellectual Legacy of Philip Selznick*, ed. Robert A. Kagan, Martin Krygier, and Kenneth Winston (Lanham, MD: Rowman & Littlefield, 2002), 187–202; Lauren B. Edelman, *Working Law: Courts, Corporations, and Symbolic Civil Rights* (Chicago: University of Chicago Press, 2016).

view that the system of language schemes must be fundamentally altered."[44] He recommends that public bodies be required to provide a range of services as a matter of enforceable right, rather than as a voluntary pledge.

This is exactly where Wales is heading. Following the Welsh Language (Wales) Measure of 2011, language schemes are gradually being replaced by more robust statutory standards. Language standards will be imposed upon public bodies in the realm of services, policymaking, operation, promotion, and record keeping. The new Measure also gives the Welsh Language Commissioner new powers and duties to impose and enforce standards on organizations, including the power to impose a civil penalty of up to £5,000 in the case of non-compliance (Section 83). This essentially expands his or her adjudicatory and ombudsman role and strengthens his or her regulatory capacity. However, the move toward standards does not create individually enforceable rights. The power to seek legal redress remains with the Commissioner.

INTERIM ANALYSIS

The degree of independence and power granted to these agencies critically limits what they may achieve. Although the language commissioners in Canada, Ireland, and Wales are all presumed to be independent, the independence they enjoy is qualified by their appointment, reporting, and funding structure (more on the last point later in this chapter). When monitoring government compliance with law, they report to individuals or a group of individuals in the government, who are under the pressure of electoral politics. Regardless of whether political neutrality is maintained in their appointment process, the commissioners themselves are not elected and are essentially salaried bureaucrats who are not directly accountable to the language communities their work is supposed to benefit. There is little room for the voice of language communities to be heard in the office's promotion and safeguarding of language rights, other than through complaints that individual members of these communities may lodge. Although absolute independence may be undesirable because these commissioners are, after all, public policy actors holding publicly funded positions, there is room to improve the transparency and legitimacy of their work by introducing more public consultations and participatory governance.[45] An inherent dilemma in these offices is that they have been given roles with seemingly conflicting interests. As promoter of official languages, they are responsible for critiquing shortfalls in government policies; at the same time, part of their job is to make sure that these policy goals are

[44] An Coimisinéir Teanga, "Annual Report 2014," March 15, 2015, 5.

[45] Mac Giolla Chríost, *The Welsh Language Commissioner in Context*.

met.[46] If they perform their regulatory function too well, public offices may feel overburdened. A plan, which was ultimately scrapped, to merge the office of the Irish Language Commissioner with that of the Ombudsman is interpreted by some as a way of silencing a Language Commissioner who has been "too successful" in highlighting the deficiency of the Irish system.[47] On the other hand, if they do not push hard in their promotional role, their legitimacy in the eyes of the public is threatened. Although many of the language commissioners are well-regarded, their credibility as promoters of language rights derives more from their language skills, personal charisma, and devotion to the cause than the structure that creates their position.

A helpful framework of analysis here is Edelman's legal endogeneity theory,[48] which challenges the notion that law is a coercive and top-down force imposed upon those being regulated and offers an explanation of how organizations may actually shape the meaning of law. According to the exogenous view of law, law is formulated and defined before it is applied to those who are subject to it. By contrast, Edelman suggests that law is endogenous: that the meaning of law is "determined largely *within* the social arena that it seeks to regulate."[49] Vagueness in legislative language, an emphasis on procedure rather than substantive outcome and on duties rather than rights, and weak enforcement mechanisms are a recipe for organizational mediation of law. Using equal employment opportunity and affirmative action law in the United States as an example, Edelman shows that such law motivates organizations to derive formal compliance structures (in the form of offices, positions, rules, and procedures) but leaves enough leeway for them to construct the law in ways that cause minimal disturbance to the status quo. Courts come to accept these formal structures as evidence of good faith, which in the end make it more difficult for victims to establish the discrimination they suffered. Not only do these structures become standard elements of organizational governance, industry norms are eventually incorporated into legal definitions of fairness. Although Edelman's example concerns the compliance of the private sector with the law, her discussion about organizations can equally apply to public bodies, which are also subject to legal regulation. The theory also explains the managerialization of law and legalization of organizations, and their intertwined effects. The managerialization of civil rights law, Edelman argues, explains the ineffectiveness of such laws.

In the preceding analysis, we can see that managerial logic also seeps through the work of official language agencies. As part of a bureaucratic

---

[46] See Mac Giolla Chríost for a detailed account of conflict in roles in the case of the Welsh Language Commissioner.

[47] Williams, "Perfidious Hope," 115.

[48] Edelman, "Legality and the Endogeneity of Law"; Edelman, *Working Law*.

[49] Edelman, "Legality and the Endogeneity of Law," 192 (emphasis original).

structure, public bodies that are legally obliged to adopt official languages in their public communication come to define what it means to have fulfilled their obligations, significantly weakening the potential for multilingual law to increase linguistic access to public services for official language communities. Both language schemes and language standards are attempts to fill in gaps that the law leaves open. In particular, the system of language schemes resembles Edelman's endogenous definition of compliance[50]—those who are being regulated can negotiate the terms of compliance. Unlike the anti-discrimination law that Edelman considered, the threat of legal sanctions for non-compliance is negligible in the case of language legislation. The lack of imposed standards and the limited threat of sanctions encourage tokenistic compliance measures, or non-fulfillment of pledges. One interesting observation that Edelman has made about compliance measures that organizations come up with is that they have the potential to influence the way legal institutions understand the respective law. In this case, language schemes may come to define what it means to fulfill language rights and to set legal norms. Viewed in this light, the replacement of language schemes with language standards in Wales is an intervention to renegotiate the meaning of the official language law.

In contrast to the jurisdictions previously discussed, most former non-settler colonies do not have elaborate compliance structures, and their emphasis is usually placed more on developing and promoting the use of endogenous languages, so that they can be on par for official use with a colonial language. In these polities, speakers of an exogenous language are mostly local elites, rather than descendants of the former colonial power. For example, no dedicated office oversees the implementation of the official language law in Hong Kong and Malaysia. In Malaysia, the 1957 constitution declares Malay as the national language, but only provides guarantee for the use of English—for all official purposes for a period of 10 years after Merdeka Day (Article 152(2)) and thereafter until Parliament otherwise provides. The National Language Acts of 1963 and 1967 reverse the guarantee and provide that the national language should be used for all official purposes and the use of English may also be permitted. The government body Dewan Bahasa dan Pustaka (the Institute of Language and Literature) promotes and develops the Malay language, but there is no specialized compliance body that monitors the language rights conferred constitutionally or statutorily. In Hong Kong, the Official Languages Ordinance declares that both English and Chinese are official languages for the purposes of communication between the government and the public. Again, no dedicated office monitors government compliance with the ordinance. Many former non-settler colonies do not see bilingualism or multilingualism as a direction of development or a defining characteristic of the polity (as is typical in

---

[50] Edelman, "Legality and the Endogeneity of Law."

post-colonial jurisdictions), but rather as a transitional strategy. The existence of a dedicated agency, despite all the limiting factors to its effectiveness, signals the long-term vision of a multilingual state.

Resource Constraints

One obvious explanation for why public institutions fall short of full multilingualism is resource constraints. Depending on the linguistic demographics of the population, official multilingualism can indeed be a very costly enterprise. Even where there is political goodwill, many post-colonial states simply do not have the capacity to offer multilingual services, and cannot afford to develop such capacity. Since a functioning legal system is likely already in place and operates in a colonial language, retaining both the system and the language may be considered a cost-saving measure, despite aspirations expressed constitutionally.

Even where resources are available, politicians debate about whether official multilingualism is a wise use of money. In societies where one language dominates others, the demand for multilingual services may be low and some may question, as a matter of principle, whether it is worth investing in developing the institutional capacity to serve minority-language speakers. Government budgeting is generally subjected to electoral politics. Where resources have been spent to set up a government watchdog, as discussed in the preceding section, it is no secret that its leash may be tightened through funding cuts. Meri Huws, the first Welsh Language Commissioner, has raised doubts about the independence of her office given its funding structure, pointing out that it is essentially a government-funded body charged with the task of regulating the government.[51]

INVESTMENT ON HUMAN CAPITAL

What do public bodies need to spend on in order to develop a multilingual capacity? The largest investment is in human capital. Public bodies may employ compliance professionals—a language officer or a team of professionals in a language unit—to help them meet the demands of a multilingual language regime. These language professionals often include translators, interpreters, and lexicographers. However, in many situations, employing language professionals

[51] She was quoted as asking, "When we are a body that regulates the Government but are also simultaneously directly funded by the Government, is that constitutionally sound?" in the National Assembly for Wales Research Service blog; see https://assemblyinbrief.wordpress.com/2014/11/10/a-look-at-the-welsh-language-commissioners-work/.

alone is not sufficient. Other public servants may also be required to have requisite language competence.

In Ireland, a statutory provision that requires all staff of state agencies to be fluent in Irish was enacted in 1928, but its introduction was postponed 54 times until it was shelved in 1966.[52] The Supreme Court found in *Ó Beoláin v. Fahy*[53] that Irish citizens have the right to conduct all business with public bodies through Irish. However, as discussed earlier in the chapter, the government is still struggling to develop the capacity to ensure this right. Language schemes devised by public bodies are only practiced where resources permit. Some progress seems to be made in law enforcement with the passage of Garda Síochána Act of 2005, which requires that all Irish policemen stationed in Gaeltacht areas should be fluent in Irish. However, as of 2012, only one out of nine officers in a Garda station in a Gaeltacht area of County Donegal spoke Irish.[54]

Trials that require Irish- and Welsh-speaking judges are rare in Ireland and Wales, respectively, and thus the capacity for judges to handle cases in these languages has not been tested extensively. There are more judges who can speak Welsh in lower courts than in appellate courts. According to the HM Courts and Tribunals Service, there are one High Court Judge, seven Circuit Judges, one Deputy Circuit Judge, six District Judges, two District Judge Magistrates, seven Recorders, and 16 Deputy District Judges who are able to conduct court proceedings in the Welsh language. In Ireland, the Courts of Justice Act of 1924 states that a judge assigned to a district where the Irish language is used must be able to speak the language. When the previous Language Commissioner tried to investigate the Irish competence of a district judge appointed to Donegal, he was denied access to such information.[55]

The need for judges with the capacity to function in different official languages is conditional upon language rights conferred in a jurisdiction. Since relatively more language rights are granted in Canada, there is a greater demand for bilingual judges. Whether bilingual or multilingual language competence should be a requirement for judicial appointment[56] is contentious, and this debate is ongoing in Canada. Since Canada guarantees the right of an accused to be heard in the official language of his or her choice (Section 530 of the

---

[52] Ó Cuirreáin, "Translation of Speaking Notes at the Houses of the Oireachtas Joint Committee on Public Service Oversight and Petitions."

[53] *Ó Beoláin v. Fahy* [2001] 2 IR 279.

[54] Gavan Reilly, "Investigation Finds Only 1 of 9 Officers in Gaeltacht Garda Station Spoke Irish," *TheJournal.Ie*, April 24, 2012, http://www.thejournal.ie/only-1-of-9-officers-in-gaeltacht-garda-station-spoke-irish-report-427481-Apr2012/.

[55] John Fallon, "State Stops Probe into Judge's Irish Language Skills—Independent.Ie," *The Irish Independent*, April 9, 2008, sec. News, http://www.independent.ie/irish-news/state-stops-probe-into-judges-irish-language-skills-26436302.html.

[56] In vast majority of jurisdictions in the world, judges are appointed rather than elected (the US is a rare exception, where state court judges may be elected). Language requirement can be imposed in either scenario.

Criminal Code), a sufficient number of bilingual judges have to serve in each province and in the appeal courts. The Canadian Supreme Court is an exception to Sections 16 and 17 of the Official Languages Act, which outline the duty for federal courts to ensure that judges understand the proceedings without an interpreter. Although the Act does not require Supreme Court Justices to be bilingual, three out of nine of them must come from Quebec. Whether Supreme Court judges need to be bilingual has been a galvanizing question. Since May 2008, bills have been tabled six times in the House of Commons aiming to require Supreme Court justices to understand both official languages upon appointment. None has been successfully passed, though the last version of the bill was only defeated at the second reading.[57] Notwithstanding arguments that bilingual judges would improve the Court's status and fulfillment of its role as a national institution,[58] opponents are concerned that the additional language requirement will significantly reduce the pool of qualified candidates.[59] A 2016 government revision of the selection process has specified that appointees need to be functionally bilingual.

To improve the language competence of existing judges, the Office of the Commissioner for Federal Judicial Affairs offers language training to Superior Court judges, and the Minister of Justice of Canada provides a language-training program to federal and provincial court judges. The hope is that there will be sufficient francophone judges who can try complicated civil and criminal cases, particularly outside Quebec and New Brunswick. Apart from language training, it has also been suggested that judges be trained on substantive knowledge of language rights.[60] The Access to Justice in Both Official Languages Support Fund[61] offers legal and linguistic tools, workshops, and training to bilingual lawyers and other justice system officials, and provides legal education and information to the public.

Language requirements for judicial staff may be territorial-based. In Finland, judges need to be fluent in the majority language in any unilingual

[57] For a summary of the debate, see Marie-Ève Hudon, "Bilingualism in the Federal Courts" (Legal and Social Affairs Division Parliamentary, Information and Research Service, 2016).

[58] Sébastien Grammond and Mark Power, "Should Supreme Court Judges Be Required to Be Bilingual?" *Special Series on the Federal Dimensions of Reforming the Supreme Court of Canada*, 2011, 49.

[59] The Canadian Bar Association, "Institutional Bilingualism at Supreme Court of Canada," 2010; Matthew Shoemaker, "Bilingualism and Bijuralism at the Supreme Court of Canada," *Canadian Parliamentary Review* 35, no. 2 (2012): 30–35.

[60] "Access to Justice in Both Official Languages: Improving the Bilingual Capacity of the Superior Court Judiciary" (Study by the Commissioner of Official Languages of Canada in partnership with the Commissioner of Official Languages for New Brunswick and the French Language Services Commissioner of Ontario, 2013).

[61] Department of Justice Government of Canada, "Access to Justice in Both Official Languages Support Fund," accessed March 13, 2017, http://www.justice.gc.ca/eng/fund-fina/jsp-sjp/ol-lo/index.html.

or bilingual district, and they must also have the ability to "speak and write" the minority language if they are appointed in a bilingual district. However, in a unilingual district a judge must also show an ability to *speak* the other official language.[62] This ensures that citizens have a right to use any of the official languages in the courtroom anywhere in the country.[63] Other court staff also receive language training. In the Helsinki Court of Appeal, for example, Swedish language courses are held continuously. The Ministry of Justice also offers Swedish courses to front-line staff handling customer service.[64] Five of the 15 local prosecution offices are bilingual, and one is Swedish-speaking (in Åland); prosecutors in bilingual offices are required to have excellent oral and written skills in Swedish, in addition to Finnish. Even in Finnish-speaking offices, a Swedish-speaking prosecutor from another jurisdiction could be brought in by the Prosecutor General to handle criminal cases with Swedish-speaking parties.[65] Access to police services in both Finnish and Swedish is also safeguarded in Finland.[66] Section 16a (1032/2007) of the Decree on Police Administration (158/1996) imposes language proficiency requirements on police units according to the linguistic status of the unit's jurisdiction. The Police College of Finland has included a test of the second national language in the diploma of police studies they offer. However, recent government reports still found policemen's language proficiency in Swedish to be deficient, and in one situation, a Swedish-speaking individual had to drive to a police station to clear up his case after he had been approached by a traffic policeman who did not have sufficient knowledge of Swedish to understand him.[67] Bilingual proficiency requirements also have been extended to border control officers.

In Switzerland, since most lawyers practice only in one canton, they only need to know the language(s) used in their canton, but good knowledge of French and German is considered necessary "for legal research and professional advancement."[68] Multilingual skills are more in demand in bilingual and trilingual cantons, as well as for handling federal law. A federal court is obliged to use the same official language as when a case was first tried in the canton in which it originated.[69]

---

[62] Kenneth Douglas McRae, Mika Helander, and Sari Luoma, *Conflict and Compromise in Multilingual Societies: Finland* (Waterloo, ON: Wilfrid Laurier University Press, 1997), 272.

[63] Ministry for Foreign Affairs, "The Fourth Periodic Report of Finland on the Application of the European Charter for Regional or Minority Languages" (Unit for Human Rights Courts and Conventions (OIK-40), 2010).

[64] Ministry for Foreign Affairs.

[65] Ministry for Foreign Affairs.

[66] Ministry for Foreign Affairs.

[67] Ministry for Foreign Affairs.

[68] McRae, *Conflict and Compromise in Multilingual Societies*, 144.

[69] Known as the "starting language principle." See Richter, "The Model Character of Swiss Language Law."

Depending on the level of commitment, authorities may need to provide professional development opportunities for not only judges and interpreters, but also other courtroom staff such as clerks, court reporters, and registry officers, and law enforcement officers such as policemen, bailiffs, and probation officers. For example, as we shall see in the next chapter, stenographers need to be retrained in the Philippines to work in a new official language. Instead of providing training to staff directly, governments may also incentivize staff to acquire relevant language skills. Canada, for example, offers a "bilingualism bonus"[70] (C$800 a year) to federal employees who occupy a bilingual position, attaching a price tag to bilingual skills.

Apart from training existing staff, states that have a long-term vision in official multilingualism also need to make sure that future legal practitioners develop the necessary language competence. Since language competence is situation-specific, having some general ability to speak a language does not automatically enable the speaker to function in it professionally. Language training thus needs to be integrated with the legal education curriculum. This requires coordination with higher education institutions and possibly increased public funding.

THE BUDGET LEASH

This section provides a rough comparison of the monetary investment some advanced bilingual and multilingual jurisdictions have made in facilitating and maintaining official multilingualism. This includes money spent on monitoring and facilitating compliance, standardizing and developing the lexicon of new official languages, promotion of official languages, subsidizing education and training on official languages, and so on. The reader is cautioned against interpreting the figures as a direct indication of commitment to the cause, considering huge variation in local circumstances such as linguistic demographics, population size and their geographical distribution, and so forth. Importantly, there are also likely to be cross-jurisdictional differences in the kind of cost the estimates cover in the data available.

Canada invests more money, as a share of GDP per capita, than any other jurisdiction, in institutionalizing and promoting bilingualism. The Fraser Institute estimates that Canada spends C$2.4 billion (approx. US$1.88 billion) annually on federal and provincial bilingualism.[71] This amounts to

---

[70] National Joint Council, "Bilingualism Bonus Directive," accessed March 13, 2017, http://www.njc-cnm.gc.ca/directive/d1/en.

[71] François Vaillancourt and Oliver Coche, "Official Language Policies at the Federal Level in Canada: Costs and Benefits in 2006" (Fraser Institute, Studies in Language Policy, May 2009); François Vaillancourt et al., "Official Language Policies of the Canadian Provinces: Costs and Benefits in 2006" (Fraser Institute, Studies in Language Policy, January 2012).

approximately C$85 (approx. US$68) per capita,[72] or under 0.2% of GDP per capita. The federal estimate, amounting to C$1.8 of the C$2.4 billion, has taken into account direct spending and transfer payments for programs designed to foster the vitality of English- and French- minority communities, cost of translation and interpretation services, bilingualism bonus to federal employees, language training for public servants, spending for the OCOL, and "unobserved costs" (such as loss of productivity during language training). The Access to Justice in Both Official Languages Support Fund,[73] for example, has a five-year budget of approximately C$40 million (approx. US$31 million) to ensure that the Canadian judiciary has the institutional capacity to offer bilingual service. The Contraventions Act Fund (with a five-year budget of C$49.4 million, or approx. US$38.8 million, between 2008 and 2013) of Canada provides financial support for provinces and territories that have agreed to guarantee language rights provided under Part XVII of the Criminal Code and Part IV of the Official Languages Act.[74] At the provincial level, the most substantial spending is on minority primary and secondary education, followed by general government services.[75]

In Ireland, the Department of Community, Rural and Gaeltacht Affairs[76] spent €10.8 million (approx. US$11.4 million) in 2009 on promoting and supporting the use of the Irish language, of which €796,000 (approx. US$842,900) was the budget for the Office of An Coimisinéir Teanga.[77] Using 2009 population statistics, the investment amounts to €2.38 (approx. US$2.68) per capita, or 0.005% of GDP per capita. Citing that the Office had a staff level of 4.4 civil servants in 2013, the former Commissioner Ó Cuirreáin complained that it was never given adequate resources to perform its statutory obligations.[78] Budgetary constraint is acknowledged in a 2014 report that reviewed the Official Languages Act of 2003, one of its objectives having been to seek to amend provisions so that "expenditure arising from the legislation is cost-effective"[79]

---

[72] For 2006–2007, using the population statistics from the same year.

[73] Government of Canada, "Access to Justice in Both Official Languages Support Fund."

[74] Department of Justice Government of Canada, "Contraventions Act Fund for Implementation of Language Obligations Evaluation," accessed March 13, 2017, http://www.justice.gc.ca/eng/rp-pr/cp-pm/eval/rep-rap/12/loe-ole/p2.html.

[75] Vaillancourt et al., "Official Language Policies of the Canadian Provinces: Costs and Benefits in 2006."

[76] This Department was abolished in 2011 and its function to promote and support the Irish language is now the responsibility of the Department of Arts, Heritage and Gaeltacht Affairs.

[77] Colin Haslehurst Williams, "In Defence of Language Rights: Language Commissioners in Canada, Ireland and Wales," in *Law, Language and the Multilingual State*, ed. Claudine Brohy et al. (Bloemfontein: SUN MeDIA, 2013), 45–69.

[78] Ó Cuirreáin, "Translation of Speaking Notes at the Houses of the Oireachtas Joint Committee on Public Service Oversight and Petitions."

[79] Department of Arts, Heritage and the Gaeltacht, "Review of Official Languages Act 2003," 2014, 4.

(note that the rhetoric is managerial rather than legal). Each government department also has regular expenditure on translating and printing Irish language publications, documents, and so on. For example, in 2013 the Minister for Education and Skills spent €107,521 (approx. US$113,830) on translation.[80] An amendment bill of the Official Languages Act, tabled in 2014, proposed changes that include cost-cutting measures which may weaken the force of the existing legislation, such as reducing government obligation to publish public policy proposals in Irish and extending the duration of language schemes from three to seven years.

Wales has a population of just over 3 million. No overall estimate was found for Welsh investment in its bilingual policy. The Welsh Language Board, with 30 staff members, had a grant of £5.8 million in the fiscal year ending March 31, 1998.[81] A budget of £4.1 million was allocated for the Welsh Language Commissioner the first two years of his office (2012–2014), which suffered a 10% cut to £3.7 million for 2014–2015 and then a 8.1% cut to 3.4 million in 2015–2016. The budget dropped another 10% to £3 million in 2016–2017, amounting to a spending of £1 (approx. USD $1.22) per capita, or 0.006% of GDP per capita. A full-time equivalent of 47 officers are currently hired by the Commissioner.[82] The Commissioner complains that the budget cut imposed on her office has been more severe than reductions made in other government organizations, warning of a high risk of maladministration.[83] Apart from the Welsh Language Commissioner, the government spends regularly on translation services, S4C (a Welsh language television channel), bilingual public signs, and so on.

In 2013–2014, the Nation Language Service and the PanSALB in South Africa, a country of 54 million people, had an expenditure of R38.9 million (approx. US$3.1 million) and R95.7 million (approx. US$7.7 million), respectively, amounting to R134.6 million (approx. US$10.8 million) in total,[84] US$0.2 per capita, or 0.003% of GDP per capita. Between 2011 and 2014, PanSALB had a budget deficit of R30 million. Its soaring expenses and questionable audit reports led to a decision to fire 44 of its senior managers in 2015, saving R24 million in salaries. The organization had also spent R21 million in

[80] "Parliamentary Debates," Dáil Éireann Debate, Vol. 833, No. 2, Written Answers Nos. 68–74, March 5, 2014, http://oireachtasdebates.oireachtas.ie/debates%20authoring/DebatesWebPack.nsf/takes/dail2014030500076#N8.

[81] Colin Haslehurst Williams, "The Role of Para-Governmental Institutions in Language Planning," in *Languages, Constitutionalism and Minorities*, ed. André Braën, Pierre Foucher, and Yves Le Bouthillier (Markham, ON: LexisNexis Butterworths, 2006), 137–59.

[82] Welsh Language Commissioner, "Estimate for the Financial Year 2015–16," 2014.

[83] Meri Huws, "Welsh Language Commissioner's Budget 2016–17," Letter from Welsh Language Commissioner to the First Minister, January 27, 2016.

[84] Department of Arts and Culture, "Annual Report 2013–2014," 2014.

legal fees within five years "because staff members were suing each other."[85] The Telephone Interpreting Service for South Africa, which allows for access to an interpreter over the distance, cost R31 million (approx. US$2.5 million).

The Ministry of Home Affairs of India has a 2015–2016 budget of 56.42 crores of rupees (approx. US$8.9 million) under the heading of Official Language.[86] That amounts to per capita spending of approximately US¢0.007, or 0.0004% of GDP per capita.

Investment made in the multilingual policy in the European Union may be said to be proportional to the size of the supra-national union, which has been multilingual from the outset and currently covers over 500 million people in 28 countries.[87] If all institutions of the Union are taken into account, the European Union spends about 1% of its total budget on translation and interpreting[88] (amounts to approximately €1.1 billion/US$1.17 billion in 2008, or €2.5/US$2.67 per citizen, or 0.008% of GDP per capita[89]). In the European Parliament, the directly elected legislative body of the European Union, over a third of the total expenditure contributes to maintaining its multilingualism regime,[90] including salaries and office space, meeting rooms equipped with interpretation booths and facilities, computer systems, and administration, and so on, bearing in mind that the Union has allocated a relatively small budget for its own administrative activities.[91] The Union has also funded research initiatives, projects, and other programs related to multilingualism; recent opportunities include Creative Europe, Horizon 2020, and others. The previously mentioned Erasmus+ program has a seven-year budget of €14.7 billion (approx. US$15.7 billion), although it is unclear how much of it goes to multilingualism, which is among its priorities. As the Union expanded and austerity became the center of European politics, the Union has attempted to keep budgetary resources for multilingualism under control and to stay administratively efficient. For example, instead of translating parliamentary debates into all official languages,

---

[85] Siyabonga Mkhwanazi, "Language Board Blew R100m," *IOL*, March 4, 2015, sec. News, http://www.iol.co.za/news/politics/language-board-blew-r100m-1827057.

[86] Ministry of Home Affairs, "Notes on Demands for Grants 2015–2016," Demand No. 53, n.d., http://www.indiabudget.nic.in/ub2015-16/eb/sbe53.pdf.

[87] European Parliament, "Multilingualism in the European Parliament," accessed March 13, 2017, http://www.europarl.europa.eu/aboutparliament/en/20150201PVL00013.

[88] "Orban: Multilingualism 'Cost of Democracy' in EU," *EURACTIV.Com*, November 13, 2008, http://www.euractiv.com/section/languages-culture/interview/orban-multilingualism-cost-of-democracy-in-eu/; "A New Framework Strategy for Multilingualism," Communication from the Commission to the Council, the European Parliament, the European Economic and Social Committee and the Committee of the Regions, November 22, 2005.

[89] This cost has been compared to the price "for a cup of coffee." See European Commission, 2004.

[90] European Parliament, "Never Lost in Translation," Press Service, October 1, 2008.

[91] Peter A. Kraus, *A Union of Diversity: Language, Identity and Polity-Building in Europe* (Cambridge: Cambridge University Press, 2008).

proceedings will be recorded, with translation provided only upon request.[92] Many EU institutions practice selective multilingualism in internal communication.[93] Ash wrote that the heart of the democracy problem in Europe is not Brussels but Babel.[94] The Tower of Babel is a commonly used metaphor to express the fear that costs involved in maintaining official bilingualism or multilingualism may become uncontrollable. However, those who worry that the European Union might collapse under its own weight because of its language regime may be surprised that its per capita investment on multilingualism has not significantly increased, despite recent expansion of the Union.

Regardless of whether formal equality is given to their official languages, many post-colonial jurisdictions save costs by practicing functional rather than parallel multilingualism in selected domains. It is common, for example in Hong Kong, India, Pakistan, and Sri Lanka, to handle cases in lower courts in endogenous languages (where most discussions are about facts), and to use a colonial language in higher courts (where issues of law may be debated). There may also be functional separation within the same trial: proceedings and records may be in a colonial language such as English, and oral evidence may be given in an endogenous language (which may be a national language); this is the case in Botswana, Kenya, Tanzania, and in Francophone Africa.[95] Such a practice tends to improve administrative efficiency and costs by removing the need for interpretation in fact-finding.

Critics have called investment in official multilingualism unnecessary or wasteful,[96] arguing that language is a peripheral issue that should give way to more important matters such as economy and development, given the scarcity of resources. Multilingual language regimes thus often become a target of cost-cutting measures. However, we cannot only ask how much it costs to do something, and ignore how much it costs not to do something. One must not forget that even if a jurisdiction is monolingual, governments still need to

---

[92] Marc Hall, "EU Parliament Makes Cuts to Translation Budget," *EURACTIV.Com*, November 22, 2012, http://www.euractiv.com/section/languages-culture/news/eu-parliament-makes-cuts-to-translation-budget/.

[93] Kerstin Odendahl and Jan Scheffler, "The EU Principle of Integral Multilingualism: On the Road Towards Expansion or Restriction?" in *Language Rights Revisited: The Challenge of Global Migration and Communication*, ed. Dagmar Richter et al. (Oisterwijk; Berlin: Wolf Legal Publishers; Berliner Wissenschafts-Verlag, 2012), 97–111.

[94] Timothy Garton Ash, "Never Mind the Treaty Squabbles. Europe's Real Problem Is Babel," *The Guardian*, October 18, 2007, sec. Opinion, https://www.theguardian.com/commentisfree/2007/oct/18/comment.politics.

[95] Richard Powell, "Bilingual Courtrooms: In the Interests of Justice?" in *Dimensions of Forensic Linguistics*, ed. J. Gibbons and M. Teresa Turell (Amsterdam: John Benjamins, 2008), 131–59.

[96] For example, Wren comments that in the Canadian context, that "(t)he move toward bilingualism has been flawed and costly—critics would argue profligate." Christopher S. Wren, "Canada's Bilingual Adventure: Pardon My French," *The New York Times*, October 14, 1986, sec. World, https://www.nytimes.com/1986/10/14/world/canada-s-bilingual-adventure-pardon-my-french.html.

spend money on accommodating its multilingual citizens in essential services. It is also meaningless to consider costs without assessing benefits—economic or otherwise. Some polities have reported seeing economic value in practicing official multilingualism. For example, Finland's bilingualism is said to benefit both its domestic labor market and its trading with other Nordic countries.[97] In Hong Kong, official bilingualism in Chinese and English has been seen as a strength in its development as a knowledge-based economy, especially in the context of a rising China and the continued dominance of English in the international business environment. In fact, we have also seen in the preceding chapters that there is an emergent trend among African states to strategically adopt official multilingualism for gaining access to the global economy. Finally, there may be less tangible but significant benefits that official multilingualism could bring, such as political stability and enhanced government legitimacy.

Reality Check: Status Quo, Undisrupted

This chapter shows that apart from sluggishness in legal implementation, the institutionalization of official multilingualism also reveals the classic gap, as frequently pointed out by legal realists, between law on paper and law in action. In this case, though, the gap seems to be expected or even intended. Although cost is understandably a concern for any policy, the implementing institutions for official multilingualism seem to have limited power by design, due to their bureaucratic and funding structures. As government watchdogs, the independence of these agencies is critical to their function, but it is hardly ever attained. This is evident in the appointment and reporting process of language commissioners, the means available to them to achieve their assigned functions, and the funding structure of these agencies. They have limited power to sanction public bodies that fail to provide multilingual services. Their work may also be crippled by budget cuts.

This picture is consistent with the theoretical perspective presented in the preceding chapter. Since the symbolic capital of official language law may be harnessed without corresponding legal implementation, not all jurisdictions are interested in realizing the significance of official status in public institutions. Even where implementing measures are in place, the institutions created often serve to translate collective goals into matters of individual rights. It is only based on the latter that complaints may be lodged. Minority language communities may find it disappointing that their official language rights are only enforceable as individual rather than collective rights, given their interest

[97] "Strategy for the National Languages of Finland: Government Resolution" (Prime Minister's Office Publications, July 2012).

in cultural defense.[98] More peculiar is the fact that even some of the more advanced multilingual jurisdictions often do not grant agency to individuals to legally enforce their rights. Individuals have to depend on dedicated government offices to act on their behalf. Seen in this light, official language law in multilingual jurisdictions is thus less a language rights regime arising from a politics of difference, than an institutional strategy to de-politicize language matters and to ensure the political stability of the polity. The bureaucratic structure of the government watchdogs also limits their courses of action in implementing language law and allows little room for the participation of the speech communities whose life their work affects. Even though constitutionally provided official language law is supposed to bypass electoral politics, the institutional structures that implement the law are not insulated from the tyranny of the majority. On the other hand, the political voices of speech communities are silenced in the institutional structures that are derived from official language law, which have limited dialogic quality.

The findings are a reminder of the kind of critiques that Critical Legal theorists have made about rights. Rights discourse may be resource intensive, and it may not tackle—and may even potentially disguise—fundamental inequalities that rights claimers are actually facing. It diverts attention to individual rather than group experiences, converting social problems into individual entitlements.[99] The position of official language rights is even more precarious than that of other civil rights because of their entrenchment in bureaucratic structures.

FROM MULTILINGUAL LAW TO MULTILINGUAL BUREAUCRACY

Law seems to have the power to transform political demands to an administrative issue, containing grievances that may otherwise be channeled in higher-stake, riskier, or less structured domains. It puts a heavy procedural limitation on a national imagination of pluralism.

State language law loses its presumed strength when translated into institutional practice. Jurisdictions that aim for full equal treatment of official languages in public institutions find that the cost required may be prohibitive. Despite all the investment that has been made, official multilingualism seems to be taken less seriously than other constitutional or quasi-constitutional obligations. In some jurisdictions, state language law quickly turns into a bureaucratic structure and a managerial goal rather than a legal obligation.

---

[98] Ruth Rubio-Marín, "Language Rights: Exploring the Competing Rationales," in *Language Rights and Political Theory*, ed. Will Kymlicka and Alan Patten (2003; reprint, Oxford: Oxford University Press, 2007), 52–79.

[99] Wendy Brown, *States of Injury: Power and Freedom in Late Modernity* (Princeton, NJ: Princeton University Press, 1995).

It is true that the linguistic capital required for full multilingualism cannot be developed overnight, but that does not eliminate the question of whether existing practices will ever lead to where they aspire to be. The relative success of the Canadian model of Language Commissioner has attracted followers, but it cannot be easily replicated without adaptation to local realities. The current capacity of many language commissioners tends to be too limited for them to do their job. The first Irish Language Commissioner, Seán Ó Cuirreáin, who assumed service in 2004, resigned from his position 10 years later after expressing disappointment in the government's failure to comply with legislation on the use of Irish in public bodies and the limited power and resources that his office received to facilitate changes: "I had, in essence, come to the firm belief that in the two years which remained in my term of office, there would be little else that I could personally achieve in relation to language rights for Irish speakers and Gaeltacht communities." Upon his resignation, thousands of protestors marched in Dublin, calling for more recognition of the Irish language and complaining that people are not able to access state services in Irish, even in Gaeltacht areas. His successor, Ó Domhnaill, also criticized the weak commitment of language schemes and warned that too much flexibility allowed in policy implementation may hurt language rights.[100] A further setback that official bilingualism in Ireland suffered is the recent appointment of Joe McHugh as the Minister for Community, Rural and Gaeltacht Affairs, who is not a fluent speaker of Irish. Although McHugh improved his Irish language skills during his term of office, the appointment of a non-Irish speaker to promote the Irish language was taken as "a slap in the face" for Gaeltacht communities and drew criticisms from language groups.[101] Excessive leniency in implementation frustrates citizens' expectations and impedes the government's potential in becoming a role model for the wider community by showing equal respect for official language communities.

Access to public services in an official language is sometimes treated as a privilege, a policy direction, or an aspiration, respected at times of prosperity, rather than a right. When a polity faces budgetary constraints, implementation of language law becomes an easy target for cost-cutting. The question, ultimately, is not absolute cost but priority. Motivation for lawmaking may not align with priorities in legal implementation. The symbolic function that state language law serves in the national narrative may be deemed sufficient to achieve pragmatic goals, removing urgency in implementation. It is not an

---

[100] Rónán Ó Domhnaill, "Translation of Speaking Notes at the Houses of the Oireachtas Sub-Committee on the 20 Year Strategy for the Irish Language and Related Matters," May 27, 2014.

[101] "Irish Protest as 'Rusty' Minister Joe McHugh Books Course," *BBC News*, July 16, 2014, sec. Europe, http://www.bbc.com/news/world-europe-28327755; Éanna Ó Caollaí, "Kenny Criticised for Comments about Appointment of Minister for Gaeltacht," *The Irish Times*, July 27, 2015, http://www.irishtimes.com/news/politics/kenny-criticised-for-comments-about-appointment-of-minister-for-gaeltacht-1.2297843.

accident that where official multilingualism is promised but not fulfilled, the official languages that public institutions fail to cater for are less dominant languages. In the post-colonial world, especially in Africa, these are usually endogenous languages.

The bureaucratic structure created by official language law allows limited influence from those who interests are supposed to be represented by it, both in terms of the content of the legislation that concerns them and the ways such legislation is implemented. There is little accountability in existing language regimes. In other words, even where official language law offers formal equality to subordinated groups, their voice is still subordinated in the implementation of such law. Moreover, they cannot seek and assert rights in this structure without affirming its legitimacy and the legitimacy of the people behind it.

PUBLIC SECTOR EMPLOYMENT AND DISTRIBUTIVE JUSTICE

The administrative structure for implementing official multilingualism is not designed to include representation from speech communities that the law affects. Official multilingualism, by itself, does not directly enhance the autonomy and self-governance of minority communities whose language gained official status.

However, official multilingualism, if its implementation is taken seriously, may lead to increased demand for bilingual public servants. In Canada, for example, approximately 40% of positions in the federal public service are designated bilingual.[102] Enhanced public-sector employment opportunities can enhance upward social mobility, especially given that the government is one of the largest employers in modern societies.[103] Although this may not be planned for when a state decides to adopt official multilingualism, official multilingualism has the potential to promote distributive justice by diverting economic opportunities to people from marginalized communities who possess such bilingual skills.

This distributional effect, however, applies more to states with sub-state national groups than to post-colonial polities, which account for most bilingual and multilingual states in the world. In the latter case, official multilingualism usually means that colonial languages continue to be an important second language to acquire and remain languages of power. In fact, in many post-colonial polities, bilingual skills and public-sector employment remain a privilege of the elites. This means that official multilingualism can actually perpetuate social inequalities by blocking monolingual locals from public employment opportunities.

---

102 http://www.ocol-clo.gc.ca/en/resources/frequently-asked-questions#Q22

103 Patten and Kymlicka, "Introduction: Language Rights and Political Theory: Context, Issues, and Approaches."

CREATING INEQUALITY WITH EQUALITY: A PARADOX

Even if the boat of parallel multilingualism does not sink under the weight of bureaucracy, it will not reach the shore of linguistic equality. One of the paradoxes of linguistic equality is that equality across languages may worsen inequality among speakers of the same language.

Even though official bilingualism or multilingualism is expected to benefit monolingual members of official language communities, it gives rise to a bilingual or multilingual advantage, or sometimes called bilingual or multilingual privilege.[104] Those who are brought up to be bilingual or multilingual have better access to public service employment (from front-line staff all the way up to political leaders), which in many places is an opportunity for upward social mobility. Thus the socioeconomic impact of multilingual law needs to be assessed not just across ethnolinguistic communities, but also across socioeconomic classes who have differential access to multilingual education and resources (including learning materials, private tutors, immersion experiences, etc.). The gravity of this problem depends on local circumstances, such as education policy (for example, whether bilingual or multilingual education is provided in state-sponsored education and how effective that education is) and the geographical distribution of language speakers (for example, where isolated monolingual communities have fewer opportunities of coming into contact with other languages). As mentioned earlier, in many post-colonial states, bilingualism or multilingualism is still a privilege of the elites.

Even though official multilingualism is supposed to be an obligation on the state instead of the citizens, individuals may be motivated to learn another official language to increase their competitive edge in the job market. This has the potential of promoting the vitality of a minority official language by increasing its pragmatic value, while at the same time exerting pressure on minority communities to acquire a majority language, which may in turn speed up assimilation.

Where minority communities have a much higher bilingual rate than majority community, as in the case of French Canadians, the monolingual majority may complain that official bilingualism gives minority communities an unfair advantage. However, it must be recognized that not all individual multilingualism is a privilege. In fact, in some societies it is minorities who bear the "burden" of bilingualism; that their linguistic capital becomes useful under official multilingualism cannot be considered unjust. One cannot tell minorities that it is their responsibility to learn the majority language in order to integrate

[104] The problem of bilingual privilege has been raised in Canada when it comes to judicial appointment; see Barbara Kay, "Of Course Justin Trudeau Wants Bilingual Judges: He's the Product of Bilingual Privilege," *National Post*, July 28, 2015, sec. Comment, http://news.nationalpost.com/full-comment/barbara-kay-of-course-justin-trudeau-wants-bilingual-judges-hes-the-product-of-bilingual-privilege.

into the society, and then turn around and say that they are privileged to be in a bilingual environment.

Multilingualism becomes a privilege when it is a dominant pathway to resources, but its door is shut for people with less socioeconomic power. Contrary to common sense that defines privilege as the opposite of meritocracy, in states such as the United States, meritocracy has become the new aristocracy, in that class privilege is transferred across generations through investment in educational and training opportunities.[105] Michael Young, who coined the term *meritocracy* in his 1958 satire *The Rise of the Meritocracy*, explains that meritocracy becomes dangerous when it is used to block social mobility:

> It is good sense to appoint individual people to jobs on their merit. It is the opposite when those who are judged to have merit of a particular kind harden into a new social class without room in it for others.[106]

Meritocracy is in fact more deceptive than aristocracy in that it seems to be more morally defensible. Through the lens of meritocracy, the privileged and the underclass appear to deserve what they get. Language skills are certainly capable of contributing to meritocracy,[107] and official language policy can influence the equalization of opportunities, in positive or negative ways, by skewing demands and supply in the linguistic market.

---

[105] Daniel Markovits, *Snowball Inequality: Meritocracy and the Crisis of Capitalism* (Harvard University Press, forthcoming).

[106] Michael Young, "Down with Meritocracy," *The Guardian*, June 29, 2001, sec. Politics, https://www.theguardian.com/politics/2001/jun/29/comment.

[107] Although, when compared with formal education qualifications, the means of developing languages skills may be said to be less monopolized.

Chapter 5

Creating Multilingual Legal Texts

DOMINATION AND DEPENDENCE

> Translation is uniquely revealing of the asymmetries that have structured international affairs for centuries. In many "developing" countries . . . it has been compulsory, imposed first by the introduction of colonial languages among regional vernaculars and later, after decolonisation, by the need to traffic in the hegemonic lingua francas to preserve political autonomy and promote economic growth. Here translation is a cultural practice that is deeply implicated in relations of domination and dependence, equally capable of maintaining or disrupting them.
>
> —Lawrence Venuti[1]

Precision is a paramount goal of legislative drafting because of the desire for legal certainty. On the other hand, there has to be sufficient open-texture in the language of the law to allow for its flexible application to changing circumstances in the future. The balance is not easy to strike. Achieving this balance in a language that is non-native to a legal system, or maintaining the balance to the same extent in parallel language texts, is even more challenging.

Translation is perhaps the first task that people think of in the preparation of multilingual legal texts. The risk is that a failure to achieve translation equivalence compromises legal certainty. Equivalence aside, there are also deeper political tensions in the process of legal translation: power struggles among speakers of the source and target language may be reflected in translation strategies adopted.

And translation is not the only task required. The legislature needs to revise drafting procedures to ensure that different language versions of the law are consistent with one another, and that they respect linguistic equality where it is emphasized by the law. Where the new official language has not developed

[1] Lawrence Venuti, *The Scandals of Translation: Towards an Ethics of Difference* (London: Routledge, 1998), 158.

a legal vocabulary and a formal register, further linguistic engineering may be necessary. Sometimes ideological engineering is also called for. The case study at the end of this chapter details the deployment of a combination of linguistic and ideological engineering in an attempt to create a new "language" for official purpose.

Legislative texts are not the only kind of legal texts that a multilingual polity produces. Šarčević identifies three types of legal texts based on their functions: those whose communicative function is primarily prescriptive (i.e., legislative texts such as laws, regulations, codes, treaties and conventions); those that are primarily descriptive but also prescriptive (such as judicial decisions and litigation documents); and those that are purely descriptive (such as law textbooks, commentaries, and journal articles).[2] Many advanced bilingual and multilingual jurisdictions ensure that primary prescriptive legal texts are available in all official languages, but are much more relaxed when it comes to language use in descriptive or semi-prescriptive texts. We will therefore not devote attention to descriptive legal texts in this chapter.[3]

Challenges in Legal Translation

We will start by considering translation work that is needed in producing multilingual legislation. The expectation for textual equivalence is especially high where the source and the target texts have equal legal status, as compared with legal translation in monolingual jurisdictions, where the target text is provided for reference and carries no legal force. Translation is also particularly demanding where an official language shares a different cultural root with the legal system in place and where translation across legal systems is required.

ACHIEVING TEXTUAL EQUIVALENCE

No two words—taken from the same or different languages—are fully equivalent in all dimensions of meaning, especially if we take into account not just denotation but also connotation, collocation, social and affective meaning, as well as frequency of usage (an infrequently used word is often linguistically marked, raising the question of not only what is said, but also how something is said[4]). Take the word *law* as an example. In any European language you can

---

[2] Susan Šarčević, "Challenges to the Legal Translator," in *The Oxford Handbook of Language and Law*, ed. Peter M. Tiersma and Lawrence M. Solan (Oxford: Oxford University Press, 2012), 187–99.

[3] Although one should note that in many cases, the communicative function of a legal text and a translation may be different; for example, the translation of a prescriptive text may have descriptive function only (such as the English version of Chinese law).

[4] Basil Hatim, "The Translation of Style: Linguistic Markedness and Textual Evaluativeness," *Journal of Applied Linguistics* 1, no. 3 (2004): 229–46.

usually find two words, derived from Latin *lex* and *jus*, that roughly correspond to the English word *law*. The French equivalents, *loi* and *droit*, are derived from Roman law. Although *loi* is often translated as *law*, its scope of meaning is narrower than the English equivalent, referring to a rule or a command that has legal authority,[5] such as legislation, statute, or an act. *Droit*, which may denote subjective "right," extends to cover the more abstract concepts of law, legal order, and legality. The English word *law*, by contrast, refers to legal order as a whole, including both specific acts and abstract conceptions of law. The meaning of a word also changes according to its immediate linguistic context. For example, the French term *droit commun* (not to be confused with English *common law*) refers to ordinary law that is generally applicable to every case unless exceptions are specified. In contrast, the meaning of *droit* in *droit d'achat* (right of pre-emption) is much narrower, referring to a legal title or claim. In German the two equivalent terms are *Gesetz*, which refers to positive or written law, and *Recht*, which is often translated as *right, natural law*, or *justice*. Thus laws (*Gesetze*) can be unlawful (*rechtswidrig*), although this sounds awkward in English.[6] To take the comparison further, the Chinese word for law, *fa*, has a much more punitive connotation[7] than any of the equivalents discussed in the preceding. Suffice it to say that perfect translation is an unreachable goal, if it makes sense to set such a goal at all.

Although translatability is a problem that faces any type of translation, the problem is most acute in the production of authentic legislative texts in bilingual and multilingual jurisdictions, where uniform application of law is a top priority. The primary challenge is in translating legal terminology that has no conceptual equivalence in the target language. Although the reverse is not always true, where there is no concept, there is no word. Legal terminology is system-bound, for it evolves alongside legal concepts and principles within a legal tradition. For example, the common law concepts of *consideration* and *equity* have no equivalents in the civil law tradition; similarly, *compétence* in civil law, which describes the heart of the relationship between citizens and the state, does not translate into common law.[8] This is the kind of challenge faced by the bijural jurisdiction of Canada which has to develop a terminology of common law in French and one of civil law in English. David and Brierley go

---

[5] Barbara Cassin et al., *Dictionary of Untranslatables: A Philosophical Lexicon* (Princeton, NJ: Princeton University Press, 2014).

[6] Marc Jacob, *Precedents and Case-Based Reasoning in the European Court of Justice: Unfinished Business* (New York: Cambridge University Press, 2014).

[7] Liang Zhiping, "Explicating Law: A Comparative Perspective of Chinese and Western Legal Culture," *Journal of Chinese Law* 3 (1989): 55.

[8] Bénédicte Sage-Fuller, Ferdinand Prinz sur Lippe, and Seán Ó Conaill, "Law and Language(s) at the Heart of the European Project: Educating Different Kinds of Lawyers," in *Current Legal Issues*, Vol. 15: *Law and Language*, ed. Michael Freeman and Fiona Smith (Oxford: Oxford University Press, 2013), 493–512.

as far as saying that English legal terms cannot be translated effectively into Latin languages such as French, and that "if a translation must be made, whatever the price, the meaning is most often completely distorted."[9] The challenge seems almost insurmountable when it comes to concepts derived from case law, such as "Wednesbury unreasonableness," a term that comes to denote a standard of unreasonableness in assessing an application for judicial review following the English case *Associated Provincial Picture Houses Ltd v. Wednesbury Corporation*.[10] The impossibility of effectively translating such terms means that the burden of comprehension has to be shifted to the interpreter to discover the meaning of the terms in the universe of case references.

Translation between languages within the same legal tradition, say across continental Europe, is relatively straightforward,[11] but translating between legal systems requires the implantation of concepts into terms that often cannot stand alone during interpretation. The problem of translatability is epitomized in colonial and post-colonial jurisdictions where the legal system is imported from a foreign culture, bringing in legal concepts that not only know no equivalence in native language(s),[12] but also may clash with local understandings of the world[13]—in fact, the claim that locals lacked the Western concept of property law was a colonial excuse for seizing native land.[14] Transplantation thus involves not only individual concepts, but a web of interrelated concepts, a whole conceptual system, and an entire legal lexicon.[15] To bridge the cross-cultural semantic gap, paraphrasing, borrowing, or coinage of new terms may be used to represent foreign concepts, and each approach has its ramifications. Legislative bodies can publicize translation equivalents in an official glossary or gazette to block unintended interpretation of translated words. However, ensuring that the translated text is transparent and readable is a challenge.

Let us take the former British colony of Hong Kong as an example. The difference in orthography generally prevents direct borrowing from legal English into Chinese (although use of mixed code may be permitted occasionally in

---

[9] René David and John E. C. Brierley, *Major Legal Systems in the World Today: An Introduction to the Comparative Study of Law*, 3rd ed. (London: Stevens & Sons, 1985), 334–35.

[10] *Associated Provincial Picture Houses Ltd. v. Wednesbury Corporation* [1948] 1 KB 223.

[11] Mattila, *Comparative Legal Linguistics*.

[12] In European colonization, the lack of conceptual equivalence for "property" in the local culture was used as a basis for holding that natives could not be entitled to property rights.

[13] Sometimes a compromise is made by the parallel retention of some customary law, notably when it comes to family and religious matters.

[14] Stuart Banner, "Why Terra Nullius? Anthropology and Property Law in Early Australia," *Law and History Review* 23, no. 01 (2005): 95–131.

[15] The likely starting point for the development of a legal lexicon is customary legal concepts, especially concepts that have more congruence between the local and the foreign systems of law, according to a diachronic study that analyzes the translation of legal English into Maori. Stephens and Boyce, "The Struggle for Civic Space between a Minority Legal Language and a Dominant Legal Language: The Case of Māori and English."

informal documents or in the spoken medium, and transliteration is not uncommon in informal domains of language use). The Latin phrase *habeas corpus ad subjiciendum* (literally, "you should have the body"), a writ requiring a person under arrest to be brought into court, is translated into Chinese as a monstrous compound word 解交被拘押者並說明其拘押日期及原因令狀 (literally, a writ for releasing and handing over the arrestee which states the arrest period and reasons) by the Department of Justice.[16] The translated phrase, which is Anglicized and perhaps unavoidably clumsy, relies on paraphrasing and the adoption of an unusual term 解交 (gaai2 gaau1), which is not a verb compound found in modern Chinese. In ancient Chinese, it refers to the ritual of officials bowing to each other at the change of office. It appears that the meaning of the verb compound has been reinvented here. I can only infer, through back translation, that the meaning of "releasing" and "handing over" comes separately from the characters 解 (gaai2; to separate or untie) and 交 (gaau1; to hand over, deliver, or submit).

Paraphrasing is useful for explaining the meaning of the original phrase, but it adds to the lengthiness and complexity of the translation and may compromise readability. It also has the potential of introducing uncertainties into the target language text, where indeterminacies arise from the paraphrasing. On the other hand, transliteration or coinage of new terms may fill a lexical gap, but frustrates comprehensibility. Before a transliterated term or a newly coined term gains sufficient currency, the translated text has to be understood by reference to the source text, making one official language less autonomous than another.

The system specificity of legal language not only makes translation of certain lexical items challenging. Etymological complexities, which may be exemplified in the case of common law English as a source language, also limit the possibility of stylistic equivalence in legal translation. Due to its trajectory of development, common law English is actually composed of many source languages: namely Latin, Norman French, and Anglo-Saxon. Many doublets or triplets in legal English are formed by juxtaposing Latin, French, and Anglo-Saxon words, as in *fair and equitable*, *full and complete*, and *rest, residue, and reminder*. This stylistic feature, adopted to ensure understanding during transitions of legal language and thus bearing historical significance, is impossible to reproduce in a language that does not share the same historical development. If literally translated, the translation will simply read inexplicably repetitive. One may only hope to render a target language text that is functionally equivalent. Apart from etymology, other stylistic features of legal English, such as distinctiveness in register, archaic expressions, and redundancy, do not

---

[16] The English-Chinese Glossary of Legal Terms: http://www.legislation.gov.hk/eng/glossary/homeglos.htm.

make translation impossible, but may influence how the translation is perceived. For example, common law rendered in Chinese conveys less formality and does not seem to project the same air of authority, despite its official status.[17]

Translation may seem easier between languages with closer heritage links, but there the translator is more prone to encounter false friends—words that look deceptively similar but differ in meaning. The risk of encountering false friends is especially high when translating across legal systems. For example, despite the shared Latin origin, *jurisprudence* in French is confined to meaning judicial decisions, but in English it refers to the discipline of legal theory.[18] Other examples include *contract* and *contrat*,[19] and *equity* and *équité*.[20] In translating across legal systems, the legal translator must therefore also take on the role of a comparative lawyer.

LOCATING THE OBJECT OF FIDELITY

It is not difficult to spot a parallel between debates in translation theories and theories of statutory interpretation, captured roughly by the dichotomy between "the letter" and "the spirit." While a judge may choose to adhere to the literal meaning of a statute ("the letter"), or to what they believe is the purpose of the law or the intent of the lawmakers ("the spirit"), the translator may also choose between a more literal ("the letter") or a freer approach ("the spirit") to translation. The dichotomy is a coarse one, for among translation theorists alone one may find diverse opinions regarding the kind of equivalence one should aim for (such as terminological, textual, formal, functional, dynamic, communicative, etc.), and a legal interpreter with professional integrity can neither completely ignore what the text of the law says nor what purpose a piece of law is meant to serve.

The traditional approach to legal translation is founded on the principle of fidelity to the source text. Literal translation has been the golden rule, especially in the translation of legislation,[21] as the letter of the law is seen as sacred. As Poon has put it, although translation styles might be more liberal today,

---

[17] Kwai Hang Ng, *The Common Law in Two Voices: Language, Law, and the Postcolonial Dilemma in Hong Kong* (Stanford, CA: Stanford University Press, 2009).

[18] Sage-Fuller, Prinz sur Lippe, and Ó Conaill, "Law and Language(s) at the Heart of the European Project: Educating Different Kinds of Lawyers."

[19] The French term does not carry with it the concept of consideration; the English term does not include certain agreements (such as bailments, trusts, and conveyances) that fall within the definition of the French term. See Rodolfo Sacco, "Language and Law," in *Ordinary Language and Legal Language*, ed. Barbara Pozzo (Milan: Giuffrè, 2005), 1–22.

[20] The English term refers to the principles developed in the Court of Chancery; the French term refers to the principles of fairness and reasonableness. See Šarčević, "Challenges to the Legal Translator."

[21] Didier (1990), cited in Susan Šarčević, "Legal Translation and Translation Theory: A Receiver-Oriented Approach," *Genéve 2000: Actes*, 2000, http://www.tradulex.com/Actes2000/sarcevic.pdf.

the first consideration in legal translation is still "fidelity to the original text."[22] Even today, the UN Instructions for Translators states that fidelity to the original text "must be the first consideration" in official translation,[23] and the literal method of translation still dominates the drafting of EU legislation.[24]

This approach is, however, not unchallenged. In her seminal work on legal translation, Šarčević argues that fidelity should be given to legal intention rather than the source text, for the reason that presumption of equal intent is a better way of preserving the unity of the single legal instrument than that of equal effect and equal meaning.[25] She calls her proposal a "receiver-oriented approach" to legal translation, holding that legal considerations must prevail in selecting translation strategies. Her approach was challenged by Poon, who questions the ability of a translator to foresee how a text will be interpreted by the court and how the same legal effect might be achieved by the target text, especially given the indeterminacy of word meaning. Poon argues that translators "must endeavour to give a faithful translation closest to the meaning of the source text" by producing "a semantically and syntactically literal translation," and leave interpretation issues with the court.[26] Wolff also criticizes Šarčević's approach for its assumptions that legal translators need to have legal knowledge, which to him poses a "practical impossibility," and that legal intent is fixed and discoverable, which is not a "sustainable" argument.[27]

As will be shown later on in this chapter, some multilingual jurisdictions have indeed moved toward relying on professionals trained in both translation and law in legislative drafting. There is truth to Wolff's claim that legal intent may be elusive, but so are legal effect and textual meaning. Countering Poon's idea, I argue that in a multilingual jurisdiction, the translator cannot afford to ignore how his or her output will be read. Where it is in place, linguistic equality changes the game of legal interpretation, making it impossible for multilingual jurisdictions to claim that one text of the law better reflects the intended legal meaning. This has led courts to move away from textualism. In resolving linguistic indeterminacy in bilingual and multilingual jurisdictions, a contextual and purposive approach to interpretation is not only licensed but often necessitated (see Chapter 6 for further elaboration on this). This changing approach to legal interpretation fuels a conceptualization of the law that is distant from the text that formulates it. The question is no longer whether a translation is an accurate representation of the source text, but also whether language

22 Wai Yee Emily Poon, "The Cultural Transfer in Legal Translation," *International Journal for the Semiotics of Law* 18, no. 3–4 (December 1, 2005): 315, https://doi.org/10.1007/s11196-005-9004-7.

23 Šarčević, *New Approach to Legal Translation*, 16.

24 Baaij, "Fifty Years of Multilingual Interpretation in the European Union."

25 Šarčević, *New Approach to Legal Translation*.

26 Poon, "The Cultural Transfer in Legal Translation," 322.

27 Leon Wolff, "Legal Translation," in *The Oxford Handbook of Translation Studies*, ed. Kirsten Malmkjær and Kevin Windle (Oxford: Oxford University Press, 2011), 238.

per se can accurately represent legislative intention. Such distancing between legal meaning and linguistic meaning encourages rethinking of the role of the legal translator and what legal translation should be faithful to. Traditional perspectives in translation see translation as either a derivative text or an independent text.[28] Neither of these conceptualizations seems to appropriately describe the status of an authenticated translation of statutes, which, as the next chapter will further explain, is part of a mega text. To the extent that understanding how a reader approaches their work can influence how translators do their job, it is useful for legal translators to become aware of how multilingual legal texts are increasingly read by courts as a whole, with versions juxtaposed with each other. Therefore, their work forms part of a unitary legal instrument, rather than a new representation of an existing instrument. A purposive approach to statutory interpretation does not logically warrant any particular translation strategy in the preparatory process of the law, but it diminishes the value of textual fidelity which Poon advocates for, and it aligns with Šarčević's approach that gives primacy to legal rather than textual meaning.

IDEOLOGICAL AND POWER STRUGGLES

In a monolingual jurisdiction, where translation or interpretation is provided for someone who does not speak an official language, it is normally the interpreted or translated words, rendered in an official language, that become part of the official record. The original utterances or texts are evanescent and legally unimportant. This is also the case when foreigners or minority language speakers communicate in a non-official language in the courtroom of bilingual and multilingual jurisdictions. In all these cases, an official language is more powerful than a non-official language; in other words, the perceived value of the languages is consistent with their legal status. When it comes to translating multilingual legislation, official legal status does not provide a full picture of power relationships between the source and target language. More often than not, the source language—an existent official language—is a politically more powerful language than the target language—a later introduced official language.[29] It is not a mere coincidence that legal vocabulary and concepts are often borrowed from more powerful languages into less powerful ones.

Multilingual jurisdictions that emphasize linguistic equality attempt to conceal such power disparity, through prescribing ways of talking about

[28] Cees Koster, "The Translator in between Texts: On the Textual Presence of the Translator as an Issue in the Methodology of Comparative Translation Description," in *Translation Studies: Perspectives on an Emerging Discipline*, ed. Alessandra Riccardi (Cambridge: Cambridge University Press, 2002), 24–37.

[29] This is where my view of legal translation diverges from that of Šarčević, who equates authority with legal status.

translation. Bilingual and multilingual jurisdictions often discourage legal practitioners from calling a translation "a translation" and translation errors "translation errors." Instead, one must refer to them as "text" or "version" and "difference" or "discrepancy of meaning."[30] In effect, such jurisdictions paint out the translation process and the translators from the image of law they create. This intentional effort of concealment lies at the core of the treatment of translation equivalence as a legal fiction[31]—purposeful make-believe devices that, through conscious pretense, allow judges to use settled law creatively to deal with unforeseen situations. Under the equal authenticity principle, language versions of legislative texts are a priori equivalent, regardless of how the translation turns out. The legal fiction of equivalence preserves the perception that there is only one law, notwithstanding potential linguistic indeterminacies introduced by multilingualism. From this perspective, "authentication" is a step that completes the fiction. It not only assigns legal force to a text, but also attempts to remove inferior connotations stemming from identifying a text as a translation. Such connotations might otherwise subvert the principle of equal authenticity[32] by projecting the impression that some language versions may be more powerful than others. An authenticated translation is no longer treated as "translation" (and becomes "an authenticated text"). Such effort aims to induce an ideological change, an attempt to balance the power relations between languages that have acquired equal legal status but may not be perceived to have equal social status.

Ideological choices are also made in the process of translation. The classic dichotomy in translation is between a source-oriented and a target-oriented approach. A source-oriented approach emphasizes fidelity to the source text, and may entail the use of techniques such as borrowing, transliteration, neologisms, or literal translation. Translation that is done through this approach may thus retain traces of foreignness that the target language reader finds hard to comprehend. A target-oriented approach, on the other hand, focuses on the comprehensibility of the translated text, and is associated with free[33] or idiomatic[34] translation. A radical example of this approach involves substitution of a foreign concept with a native equivalent (e.g., from *baguette* to *naan*), a process that may be understood as domestication. Translation done this way tends

---

30 E.g., "A Paper Discussing Cases Where the Two Language Texts of an Enactment are Alleged to be Different," Law Drafting Division, Department of Justice, Hong Kong, May 1998.

31 Janny H. C. Leung, "Translation Equivalence as a Legal Fiction," in *The Ashgate Handbook of Legal Translation*, ed. Le Cheng, King Kui Sin, and Anne Wagner (London: Routledge, 2014), 57–69.

32 This refers to the principle that official language texts have equal authority, as applied in Hong Kong, Canada, the EU, etc. This is discussed further in the next chapter.

33 "Free" translation is not completely unconstrained. The "free" translator pays attention to what the source text says, but less to *how* it is said.

34 Idiomatic translation focuses on the target language and its readers, seeking to achieve alignment with relevant language habits. It conceals the apparent foreignness of the source text.

to be more readable, but such readability may be deceptive because cultural differences are masked.

I have argued elsewhere that by assuming that language versions that have the same legal status will perform the same legal function, legal translation theories have failed to take into account sociopolitical realities[35] and to acknowledge the potential influence that power relations have on processes of translation. Approaches to legal translation reflect an underlying power structure and social struggle among the languages involved.[36] A powerful source language tends to attract a literal, or source-language-oriented approach to its translation, as is typical in colonial settings. There are, for example, complaints that common law written in Chinese in Hong Kong is too Anglicized. In fact, the judiciary makes clear that common law Chinese is not written for the layperson, but for people who have some familiarity with common law.[37] A translation produced with a source-oriented approach has limited interpretive autonomy, for its interpretation relies on its indexical relationship with the source text.[38] A jurisdiction that emphasizes equality among its official languages might give greater respect to the inherent characteristics of the target language.[39] In some bilingual and multilingual jurisdictions, it has been argued that citizens should have the right not just to receive the law in all official languages, but to receive law that is rendered in an idiomatic way. For example, in Switzerland, where the Swiss Civil Code was translated from German to French and Italian, the francophone population has demanded for the Code to be written in natural French.[40] In tracing changing approaches in legal translation from English to Maori, Stephens and Boyce report a shift in recent times from a source-oriented translation strategy involving heavy borrowing (such as the transliteration of the English word *court* as *kooti* in Maori) to neologisms that draw on resources of the Maori language.

Malta presents a curious case for discussion. Although in cases of discrepancy, the Maltese version of the law in Malta prevails over the English version, bills are drafted in English and then translated into Maltese using a literal translation approach.[41] This peculiarity results from post-colonial efforts

---

[35] Janny H. C. Leung, "Ideology and Political Meaning in Legal Translation," in *Meaning and Power in the Language of Law*, ed. Janny H. C. Leung and Alan Durant (Cambridge: Cambridge University Press, 2018), 236–55.

[36] The relationship between translation and power asymmetry has been noted by Venuti in the quote at the beginning of the chapter. Venuti, *The Scandals of Translation*.

[37] "Discussion Paper on the Laws in Chinese," Attorney General's Chambers Hong Kong, 1986.

[38] Kwai Hang Ng, "Legal Translation and the Problem of Heteroglossia," in *Comparative Law: Engaging Translation*, ed. Simone Glanert (Milton Park, Abingdon, UK; New York: Routledge, 2014), 49–66.

[39] Supranational jurisdictions such as the EU might be an exception, given the overriding concern for uniformity.

[40] Šarčević, "Legal Translation and Translation Theory: A Receiver-Oriented Approach."

[41] Where legal concepts have no Maltese equivalent, the English terms are not translated but are borrowed into the Maltese text.

to reverse the subjugated status of Maltese in legal interpretation and to promote its use in public domains. Despite the superior legal status assigned to Maltese, the way their bilingual law is drafted reveals that English still practically enjoys prestige in the country. Moreover, subsidiary legislation may be published in English only.[42] The case of Ireland is somewhat similar, but with the initial drafting being English-led rather than entirely in English, and the Irish version—which trumps the English text in case of conflict in bilingual statutes[43]—produced mostly subsequently.

In sum, the task of legal translation involves the making of not only linguistic but also ideological choices. In fact, the way a legal text is translated can become a very politically sensitive matter. Despite official bilingualism in Canada, for example, the French translation of many of the documents of the Constitution Act of 1982 has never been formally adopted, at least in part due to the challenge in producing a version that will receive unanimous support from the federal government and all provinces.[44]

Reinventing Legal Drafting: Translation and Beyond

Translation is undoubtedly the major facilitator of cross-linguistic communication in bilingual and multilingual jurisdictions. Traditionally, drafting and translation are seen as distinct and sequential stages of textual production. By definition, a translation does not come into existence before the source text. Thus it is difficult to imagine a translation having an impact on the drafting of the original, or a translation coming into existence with the original at the same time. As a means of ensuring linguistic equality, these seemingly anachronistic events are happening in some advanced bilingual and multilingual jurisdictions in the world, thanks to innovation in legislative drafting.

In Hong Kong, legislation is typically drafted in English before being translated into Chinese. One major challenge in translating English statutes is that they are written in long and complicated sentences, whereas modern Chinese sentences tend to have a much simpler sentence structure. In view of such divergence, the English text of a statute is now drafted in plain English wherever possible. This has made the task of translation easier and is an

---

[42] Vanni Bruno, "Ensuring the Quality of Drafting of Legislation in a Multilingual Context," September 20, 2013, http://ec.europa.eu/dgs/legal_service/seminars_en.htm.

[43] According to Article 25.4 of the Irish Constitution. See also Dáithí Mac Cárthaigh, "Interpretation and Construction of Bilingual Laws: A Canadian Lamp to Light the Way?" *Judicial Studies Institute Journal* 2 (2007): 211–28.

[44] Hugo Choquette, "Translating the Constitution Act, 1867: A Critique," *Queen's Law Journal* 36, no. 2 (June 1, 2011): 503–50.

example of how the prospect of translation has changed the way the source language text is written.[45]

Translation of EU legislation is particularly tricky given its overlay with national law. In view of the need to translate legislative texts into all its 24 official languages, concepts that are anticipated to pose translation difficulties are avoided in the drafting language (which is mostly English, sometimes French). Terms that are neutral—in the sense that their use is not specific to any one national legal system—are preferred (for example, *subsidiarity* is preferred to the UK-specific term *devolution*). The drafting language is deculturalized (which is sometimes also known as deterritorialized) to maintain distance with national legal cultures and to make it more translatable.[46] In order to do so, lexical and grammatical simplification and creation of new terms[47] (such as *right of withdrawal* to refer to consumer's right to withdraw from contracts for goods and services) may be necessary. Through this translation practice, a pan-European legal language (derogatorily referred to as Eurospeak by those who find EU terminology and acronyms confusing or incomprehensible) has been developed, which is derived from the existing languages of its member states but alienated from their native speakers at the same time. Umberto Eco famously said, "The language of Europe is translation." Perhaps there is an additional layer of truth to this statement now, as compared to when it was originally conceived. There are complaints that legal French in the European Union does not read like French at all,[48] and this may partly have to do with the fact that many non-native speakers are involved in drafting. The challenge that this drafting practice poses to the idea that the native speaker is an unquestioned linguistic authority may, however, be seen as a positive ideological development[49]. Legal translation in the European Union is no longer entirely a matter of cross-cultural transfer, as translation is commonly perceived, but the creation of a new legal culture. The deculturalization practice in EU drafting allows for translation to feed back into the drafting process, even before it takes place, based on the cumulative wisdom of an institutionalized multilingual regime. In fact, comments made by translators may lead to the altering of the original, as stipulated in

---

[45] Tony Yen, "Bi-Lingual Drafting in Hong Kong," *The Loophole (Journal of the Commonwealth Association of Legislative Counsel)* (August 2010): 65–69.

[46] Biel, "Translation of Multilingual EU Legislation as a Sub-Genre of Legal Translation"; T. J. M. van Els, "The European Union, Its Institutions and Its Languages: Some Language Political Observations," *Current Issues in Language Planning* 2, no. 4 (December 1, 2001): 311–60, https://doi.org/10.1080/14664200108668030.

[47] But as the corpus builds up, the creativity of the translator is restricted.

[48] The phenomenon is found not only in legislative language but in the language of the case law of the ECJ as well. See McAuliffe (2011) for the development of "Court French."

[49] For a summary of contested assumptions that people make about "native speakers," see Rampton, "Displacing the 'Native Speaker': Expertise, Affiliation and Inheritance."

the Joint Practical Guide[50]. In the European Parliament and Council, both the original draft (which is usually authored by non-native speakers of the drafting language) and the translation go through legal-linguistic revision by interdisciplinary specialists, known as lawyer-linguists, before they become finalized.[51]

The qualification of legal translators is another noteworthy feature of legal translation in the European Union. Translators in the European Court of Justice (ECJ) are lawyer-linguists who are qualified lawyers with competence in at least three EU official languages, including French. Unlike other EU institutions, the ECJ has a single internal working language—French. Lawyer-linguists translate documents submitted by the parties in the language of procedure (which can be in any official language) into French, and translate judgments written by judges and their *référendaires*[52] (in French) and advocates generals and their *référendaires* (usually in English or French) into all official languages. The most prominent feature about legal translation in the European Union is its scale, arising from the multiplicity of official languages in the union. The number of official languages in the Union (24 at the time of writing) means that direct translation in all language combinations is no longer viable. Pivot languages (French, English, German, Italian, Spanish, and Polish in the ECJ and English, French, German, Italian, Spanish, and Polish in the European Parliament) have been used to cope with the expansion of the Union and its official languages.[53] Where direct translation is not possible, texts written in an official language may have to be translated into one of the pivot languages, which then becomes the new source language for translation into another official language. In view of the complex and costly translation regime, some have talked about reviving Latin or adopting a form of legal Esperanto in the Union, and others have suggested that English be made superior to other official languages. However, there is no sign yet that member states are willing to give up the status of their language. The politics of recognition has not receded.

Canada revolutionized the method of multilingual legislative drafting with its introduction of co-drafting in the late 1970s. To ensure the harmony of their legal texts, the Canadian federal government and the province of New Brunswick have abandoned the idea of original/translation or source/target language altogether in their legislative drafting process. In the spirit of both

---

[50] Luxembourg: Office for Official Publications of the EC, "Joint Practical Guide of the European Parliament, the Council and the Commission for Persons Involved in the Drafting of European Union Legislation (2nd Ed.)," 2013.

[51] European Commission Directorate-General for Translation, *Lawmaking in the EU Multilingual Environment*, Studies on Translation and Multilingualism (Luxembourg: Publications Office of the European Union, 2010).

[52] These personal legal assistants to the judges are qualified lawyers with a reasonable command of French. See McAuliffe, "Language and Law in the European Union."

[53] Pozzo, "Multilingualism, Legal Terminology and the Problems of Harmonising European Private Law"; McAuliffe, "Language and Law in the European Union."

bilingualism and bijuralism, a Francophone, usually trained in civil law, and an Anglophone, usually trained in common law, work in partnership in drafting federal legislation.[54] They are guided by bilingual instructing officers who are legal advisors from the sponsoring department. They attend all meetings so they both fully understand the background of the bill that they need to draft. They work together in each assignment, going back and forth to discuss each section of the draft, with the help of jurilinguists[55] (members of the Jurilinguistic Services Unit in the Legislative Services Branch) who are specialists in the language of the law. The jurilinguists ensure the linguistic quality of the texts (with a focus on style, terminology, and phraseology) and their equivalence in meaning.[56] The output is then reviewed by legislative revisers and paralegals. Both the English and the French texts are treated as an original expression of the law and are printed side by side. Since the translator and the draftsperson are one, it may be said that this method of bilingual textual production has bypassed translation, at least in the traditional sense of the term. It is believed that co-drafting produces legislative texts that are idiomatic and of consistently good quality in both language versions.

The Canadian model has inspired legislative drafting in other bilingual and multilingual jurisdictions, such as Belgium, Switzerland, and Wales. In Belgium, the French and Dutch versions of the law are co-drafted by a native speaker of each language. A German translation is produced afterward for reference only. This drafting method shows respect to the internal structure of each drafting language and has replaced an earlier approach where the Dutch version followed the French text word for word. Every bilingual draft has to be vetted before approval. The drafting procedures are detailed in a manual published by the Council of State.[57] In Switzerland, co-drafting may be more accurately described as co-revising. Federal legislative drafting usually starts with German and is translated into other official languages, in a way that prioritizes the naturalness of the target language text. Co-revising takes place at an intermediary stage as a quality-assurance procedure, when linguists and jurists who are speakers of different official languages discuss and suggest revisions to the drafts both in form and content, and may even spot textual issues not restricted to questions of linguistic equivalence.[58] In Wales,

---

[54] Lionel A. Levert, "The Cohabitation of Bilingualism and Bijuralism in Federal Legislation in Canada: Myth or Reality?" *Harmonization and Dissonance: Language and Law in Canada and Europe*, May 7, 1999, http://www.justice.gc.ca/eng/rp-pr/csj-sjc/harmonization/hfl-hlf/b1-f1/bf1e.html.

[55] They are the Canadian equivalents of the European lawyer-linguists.

[56] Privy Council Office Government of Canada, "Guide to Making Federal Acts and Regulations: Part 2: Making Acts: 2.3 Preparation and Cabinet Approval of Bills," accessed February 26, 2017, http://www.pco.gc.ca/index.asp?doc=legislation/chap2.3-eng.htm&lang=eng&page=information&sub=publications.

[57] http://www.raadvst-consetat.be/?page=technique_legislative&lang=en.

[58] Lötscher, "Multilingual Law Drafting in Switzerland."

for over two centuries legislation had been typically drafted in English and then translated into Welsh. However, having drawn from the Canadian experience, co-drafting has been adopted since 1999 so that Welsh and English versions of legislation are now drafted alongside each other. Some have argued that co-drafting can be more cost-effective and time-efficient than translation. There also have been calls for co-drafting in Ireland, where the Irish legislative text enjoys a higher status than the English text.[59]

Constructing and Developing a Legal Language

Introducing a new legal language sometimes involves not just translation, but also a great deal of linguistic engineering, most importantly the standardization and expansion of the lexicon. Such engineering is often viewed as necessary to "cure" the "deficits" of native languages that make them "unfit" as legal languages. In post-colonial polities, it is often argued that an endogenous language has not developed a vocabulary for legal arguments or formal register required by the solemnity of the courtroom, casting doubt as to whether it is fit for serving as a legal language of an imported legal system.[60] The argument is particularly strong where endogenous languages do not have a written or standardized form. Such arguments are used to justify the perpetuation of colonial languages, or hypothetically until an endogenous language has acquired the same level of "sophistication."

Many jurisdictions have invited lexicographers to coin new words in a new official language to prepare it for its legal role. New words are rarely entirely new. They tend to derive one way or another from existing native or foreign words. Take Malaysia as an example. Similar to many other former British colonies, the Malaysian judiciary is also charged with the task of translating English common law into the local language. The adoption of a Latin script in Malay has provided the condition for an approach that involves not only translation, but also a great deal of linguistic innovation. This approach may be described as the Malayanization of Latin and English, resulting in terms such as *artikel* ("article"), *isemen* ("easement"), and *devis dan bekues* ("devise and bequest"). Sometimes loan words from English are adopted (e.g., *alibi*). Orthographic and/or phonological modification may be involved (e.g., *caj* for "charge"; *ejen* for "agent"). Ordinary words may acquire new legal meanings by extension (e.g., *amanah* for "trust"). Translation may be done word for word (loan translation, such as *aset cair* for "liquid asset") or through conceptual

[59] Harry McGee, "Experts Say Constitutional Changes Should Look at Subtlety of Irish Translation," *The Irish Times*, February 21, 2015, sec. News, http://www.irishtimes.com/news/politics/experts-say-constitutional-changes-should-look-at-subtlety-of-irish-translation-1.2111749.

[60] Leung, "Negotiating Language Status in Multilingual Jurisdictions."

transfer (e.g., *cek tak layan*, literally "unserviced check," for "dishonored check")[61]. Despite the localization efforts, today many Malaysian lawyers still prefer using English to Malay and consider Malay lacking in the precision, sophistication, and elegance that English is presumed to have.[62]

For the sake of cost-saving or easing intergroup tensions, some governments have engineered a new official language that attempts to bridge dialectal differences in local tongues. Romansh, which became a national language in Switzerland in 1938 and a semi-official language in 1996, is one such example. It has five regional varieties (sometimes known as idioms): Putèr, Sutsilvan, Surmiran, Sursilvan, and Vallader. What the government adopted is a pan-regional standardized variety of Romansh (called Romansh Grischun, RG) created by linguist Heinrich Schmid in 1982. The move was meant not only to save costs of translating from other official languages to these regional varieties, but also to save Romansh by unifying the speakers, phasing out the regional differences, and giving the language a critical mass to survive. RG is used as the target language in the translation of official documents and is the language of textbooks in public education in the canton of Graubünden/Grisons where Romansh speakers are concentrated. The plan, however, backfired and divided more than it united. Romansh speakers expressed strong opposition, calling RG "a bastard language" that nobody speaks. In Norway, a similar effort to merge Bokmål and Nynorsk into a pan-Norwegian variety Samnorsk during the first half of the twentieth century also failed amid resistance and was abandoned. The creation of a new language or variety by authorities is not only a linguistic challenge, but also a battle against the ideology of linguistic purism and identity politics. This struggle is similar to the more general debate on language standardization, which may be characterized as competition between rationalism—the ideology that a neutral medium of communication facilitates mutual understanding and participation, and romanticism—the ideology that language is not just communicative but also expressive of one's identity.[63]

From Linguistic to Ideological Engineering

In order to prepare a new official language for its legal role, both linguistic and ideological engineering are necessary. Let us take a closer look at an Asian

[61] See Richard Powell, "Vernacularising the Law: Malaysia's Bilingual Policy as a Model for Postcolonial Common Law Systems." (Melbourne Graduate School of Education, 2014), http://minerva-access.unimelb.edu.au/handle/11343/51109. Powell offers a detailed discussion of the work that has been done to vernacularize common law English in Malaysia.

[62] Leung, "Negotiating Language Status in Multilingual Jurisdictions."

[63] Dirk Geeraerts, "Cultural Models of Linguistic Standardization," in *Cognitive Models in Language and Thought: Ideology, Metaphors and Meanings*, ed. Rene Dirven, Roslyn Frank, and Martin Putz, reprint ed. (Berlin: Mouton de Gruyter, 2012), 25–68.

example—the Philippines, which has made one of the most long-lasting efforts in creating and promoting a new legal language in the country.

The Philippines was under Spanish rule between 1565 and 1898 and subsequently under US rule between 1898 and 1946. At the end of three centuries of colonial presence in the Philippines, Spanish was spoken by only a small number of powerful elites. US colonialization, despite being much shorter, brought a golden age for the English language in the Philippines that lasted beyond the colonial period, until the 1970s, through post-war neo-colonial relations.[64]

Under the influence of a monolingual nationalist ideology, Manuel Quezon, the first president (1935–1944) of the commonwealth of the Philippines (a transitional administration in operation between 1935 and 1946), yearned to reduce the dominance of colonial languages and adopt a single unifying homegrown language in its nation-building project. Thanks to free education that the US colonial government provided, by the 1930s English had largely replaced Spanish as the dominant language in official functions in the Philippines, had established itself as a lingua franca in the country, and had become a language of Philippine literature (in what is sometimes known as Philippine English). Even though English had become the most commonly spoken language in the country at the time, the transitional administration believed that a national language with local roots was necessary. Elected delegates to the 1934 Constitutional Convention, who were charged with the task of writing a constitution for an independent Philippines, had to decide what this national language would be. Since Spanish was still the language of law (although in courts English had already replaced it), and use of English was widespread,[65] the delegates affirmed English and Spanish as official languages in the 1935 Constitution. They also made a provision for an indigenous national language. A unifying endogenous language did not exist, and choosing one native language over others would have ignited sectionalism. The delegates thus decided that this national language would be a "new" language based on existing native languages. The provision was later amended such that the new language would be based on *one* of the existing native languages.[66]

The Institute of National Language, composed of seven members who each represented a native linguistic group, was created in 1936 to find the most suitable native language that would form the basis of the new national language. The Institute found that Tagalog, being the first language of about a

---

[64] Vicente L. Rafael, "Taglish, or the Phantom Power of the Lingua Franca," in *Philippine English: Linguistic and Literary*, ed. M. Lourdes S. Bautista and Kingsley Bolton (Hong Kong: Hong Kong University Press, 2008); Thompson, *Filipino English and Taglish*.

[65] Thompson, *Filipino English and Taglish*.

[66] Article 14, Section 3, of the Philippine Constitution of 1935 mandated that "Congress shall take steps toward the development and adoption of a common national language based on one of the existing native languages."

quarter of the population of the Philippines at the time, was the best fit, and they went on to engineer this national language with an approach that has been described as puristic. They indigenized the orthography by replacing the 32-letter Spanish-based Abecedario with the 20-letter Abakada, which follows the pre-colonial alpha-syllabic writing system Baybayin. Neologisms were created to replace loan words from foreign languages. A frequently cited example is the coining of the word *salumpuwit* to replace the widely used term *silya* (derived from Spanish *silla* for "chair").[67] The outcome of their work was published as dictionary and grammar books for the teaching of Tagalog as a subject in the classroom. *Balarila ng Wikang Pambansa* (Grammar of the National Language) was published by Lope K. Santos in 1940. The purist approach was met with resistance and was seen as not conducive to intellectualizing the national language such that it can function effectively as a medium of instruction.[68]

A National Language Week has been held since the Philippines became fully independent in 1946 through the Treaty of Manila.[69] In 1959, the national language was rebranded as Pilipino to remove ethnic association. Through government efforts in promoting the national language and its adoption by the media, the national language gradually gained popularity in usage, but its adoption in the public domains was mostly cosmetic. For example, all government buildings and offices were renamed in it, and all government letterheads were translated into it.[70] However, English, also an official language, remained the sole language of administration, law, and education. English was perceived as a language of upward social mobility. The indigenized version of it, Filipino English, had become associated with Filipino identity until a wave of nationalistic student activism and social unrest in the early 1970s brought the golden age of English to an end.[71]

The 1972 Constitution Convention reaffirmed English and Pilipino as official languages but mandated "the development and formal adoption of a common national language to be known as Filipino" (Article 15, Section 3(2)). This also implied that Pilipino (with a P) ceased to be the national language. The transition of Pilipino to Filipino (with an F) signals a change in approach and conception, a way of consoling non-Tagalog (especially Cebuano) speakers who had been questioning the decision to use Tagalog as the basis of the national language and complaining that it was too difficult to learn. The situation was peculiar in that, when Filipino received its constitutional status in 1973, it was still gestating.[72] Although Filipino is primarily based on Pilipino, from

---

[67] Darrell T. Tryon, ed., *Comparative Austronesian Dictionary: An Introduction to Austronesian Studies* (Berlin; Boston: De Gruyter Mouton, 1994), 336, https://doi.org/10.1515/9783110884012.

[68] Thompson, *Filipino English and Taglish*.

[69] From 1997 onward, the entire month of August has been declared National Language Month.

[70] Eldrige Marvin B. Aceron, *Ateneo Law Journal* 38, no. 1 (1993): 76–94.

[71] Thompson, *Filipino English and Taglish*.

[72] Aceron.

this point onward, a more pragmatic and liberalized approach to the national language was taken. Spanish and English influences were openly embraced. Elements from other native dialects and languages (such as Cebuano, Ilocano, and Waray-Waray) were to be incorporated. The Tagalog-based alphabet Abakada was modified in the 1976 Filipino Orthography Reform, which reintroduced 11 Spanish letters[73] that are used in other Philippine languages but not in Tagalog. Popular words and phrases, especially in specialized domains such as law, sciences, and administration, were selected from other Philippine and foreign languages for inclusion into the corpus of the language.

It was only after 40 years of developmental effort that the national language was finally adopted as a medium of instruction, along with English, in a bilingual educational policy that began in 1974. Filipinos educated through this system ended up preferring to speak neither pure English nor pure Filipino but Taglish, a hybrid of Tagalog and American English with some Spanish overlay.[74] Although in formal situations, pure English or pure Filipino may be used, on the street and in the media it is Taglish that is spoken. The tension between promoting the national language and maintaining an English standard has not been and will not likely be resolved. Due to the country's reliance on remittance from overseas Filipino Workers (OFW) with high English proficiency, it would not be practical for Filipino to completely replace English in school.

The present Constitution, of 1987, provides that English and Filipino are official languages,[75] and affirms Filipino as the national language. Article 14 acknowledges that Filipino is still under development:

> The national language of the Philippines is Filipino. As it evolves, it shall be further developed and enriched on the basis of existing Philippine and other languages.

The Constitution also created the Commission on the Filipino Language (CFL; Komisyon ng Wikang Filipino),[76] which was set up in 1991. Its mission is to make Filipino an effective instrument of national development and to develop and preserve other Philippine languages. It has 11 commissioners who represent major Philippine languages, including Tagalog, Cebuano, Ilocano, Hiligaynon, and the major languages of Muslim Mindanao. The Commission reformed the Filipino alphabet again to its current 28-letter form.

---

[73] C, CH, F, J, LL, Ñ, Q, RR, V, X, and Z.

[74] Thompson, *Filipino English and Taglish*.

[75] Article 14, Section 7: "For purposes of communication and instruction, the official languages of the Philippines are Filipino and, until otherwise provided by law, English." The way this section is worded suggests that English will eventually be removed as an official language.

[76] In Article 14 of the 1987 Constitution: "The Congress shall establish a national language commission composed of representatives of various regions and disciplines which shall undertake, coordinate, and promote researches for the development, propagation, and preservation of Filipino and other languages."

Despite the linguistic work that has gone into developing and branding Filipino, the language is still widely perceived to be Tagalog in disguise. Some minority language speakers consider the imposition of a dominant language a domestic form of imperialism, questioning the legitimacy of choosing one native language over another and fearing that this will lead to or reinforce the political dominance of one language group over others. Although resistance persists, Filipino has been steadily gaining ground[77] and has become a national lingua franca, especially through education, commerce, media, and popular culture. The 2000 census reports that 65 million out of 76 million Filipinos are able to speak the national language as a first or second language.[78] The increased number of speakers across the country has facilitated its development away from Tagalog[79] and has helped to promote acceptance across the country. When speakers of two different Philippine native languages meet, Filipino has become the language they switch to. The fall in English competence has become a concern because of the OFW contribution to the Philippine economy, and recent successions of government have emphasized the importance of restoring English proficiency.

However, Filipino has still not displaced English as the language of court proceedings. Although witnesses may testify in Filipino or Taglish in the courtroom, English is still the default language of courtroom interaction and written documents. Development of Filipino for legal use has lagged behind social and other official domains. It was not until 2007 that the Senate passed a resolution to recommend the expansive use of Filipino ("and other prevailing dialects in pertinent provinces of the country") by the judiciary. The Philippine legal system is a hybrid of foreign influences including Anglo-American common law, Malay customary laws, Spanish civil law, and Islamic law for Philippine Muslims. Although the Filipino language has been engineered for almost 80 years, there is still public and professional opinion that argues that it is not ready as a legal language. English still occupies superior status in legal interpretation.[80] Laws are largely drafted in English. In case of textual discrepancies, the English version of legislation prevails. Case law is written in English. Proficiency in English is still essential for a legal career. The bar examination is conducted in English.

---

77 Fortunato Gupit and Daniel T. Martinez, *A Guide to Philippine Legal Materials* (Manila: Rex Book Store, 1993).

78 Isabel Pefianco Martin, "Expanding the Role of Philippine Languages in the Legal System: The Dim Prospects," *Perspectives in the Arts and Humanities Asia* 2, no. 1 (March 29, 2012), https://doi.org/10.13185/121.

79 Ernesto Constantino et al., "Proposals to the Con-Com: Provisions for the National Language (1986)," in *The Language Provision of the 1987 Constitution of the Republic of the Philippines*, ed. Andrew Gonzalez and Wildrido V. Villacorta (Manila: Linguistic Society of the Philippines, 2001), 71–81.

80 Gupit and Martinez, *A Guide to Philippine Legal Materials*; Palmer, *Mixed Jurisdictions Worldwide: The Third Legal Family (Second Edition)*.

Most linguistic engineering involved in preparing Filipino for legal use has focused on the development of terminology. Retired judge Cezar Peralejo published an English-Filipino legal dictionary in 1995, for example. Another one was published by Norma Sia-Chionglo in 2011. Filipino legalese contains a lot of loan words from English (such as *arraignment* and *litigant*), Spanish (such as *abogado* for "attorney" and *akusado* for "accused") and indigenous languages (such as *nasaskdal* for "defendant" and *sabi-sabi* for "hearsay").[81]

Judge Peralejo has also translated the Civil Code, Penal and Family Codes, and the Revised Rules on Civil Procedure from English into Filipino, and he had other retired judges edit the translation to ensure accuracy. Overall, relatively few pieces of legislation have been translated into Filipino so far.[82] In 2006, the Supreme Court set up a committee[83] to translate important judgments into Filipino.

Since legal education is offered in English, all legal professionals are proficient in English but not necessarily Filipino. Training seminars have been organized for judges, lawyers, and court employees on the use of Filipino in court proceedings.[84] Nevertheless, many are still not used to communicating legal concepts in Filipino.

Generally speaking, the language of the trial is still English. Witnesses who choose to testify in Filipino or another local language will have their testimony translated into English. However, recently there have been repeated attempts to increase the use of Filipino in criminal court proceedings. This was piloted for six months in 2008 in Bulacan in seven regional trial courts in Malolos city and one in Guiguinto. Filipino was used in the hearing and resolution of motions and in the conduct of pre-trial conferences, trials, and rendition of judgments.[85] Translation between Filipino and English was eliminated because all participants understood Filipino. The trial process was thus expedited. A linguistic problem that has been raised concerning the use of Filipino in the court relates to the written record of trial proceedings. Court stenographers are trained to do shorthand in English, but few know how to do it in Filipino. They have steno machines designed for note taking in English.[86] During the

---

[81] Richard Powell, "English in Southeast Asian Law," in *English in Southeast Asia: Features, Policy and Language in Use*, ed. Ee Ling Low and Azirah Hashim (Amsterdam: John Benjamins, 2012), 241–66.

[82] Martin, "Expanding the Role of Philippine Languages in the Legal System."

[83] Committee on Linguistic Concerns to Translate Landmark Supreme Court Decisions into Filipino and Other Major Philippine Dialects. Martin, "Expanding the Role of Philippine Languages in the Legal System."

[84] Dino Balabo, "Filipino in Court Proceedings Gains Headway," *The Philippine Star*, November 22, 2009, http://www.philstar.com/nation/525158/filipino-court-proceedings-gains-headway.

[85] Office of the Court Administrator, "Pilot-Testing the Use of Filipino in Trial Court Proceedings," 2009, http://oca.judiciary.gov.ph/?page_id=175.

[86] Vivencio O. Ballano, "The 'Rule of Law,' Oral Textuality, and Justice in Criminal Court Proceedings," *Loyola Schools Review* 1, no. 1 (2001): 105–30.

pilot, stenographers were trained to use Ikilat, the Filipino stenography, and all records were documented in Filipino.[87] The stenographers found their job more challenging because courtroom interactions were faster without interpretation.[88] Despite initial positive results,[89] the pilot scheme has been halted, but courts were allowed to continue with it if they wished.[90] Only one court[91] continued for five years until 2013.[92]

Resistance from educated elites, especially legal professionals, has contributed to the limited application of Filipino in the legal system. There is strong reluctance among elites to give up English, which has clear instrumental value in their status maintenance and access to the globalizing economy. Columnist Amadora argues that English allows the Filipino people to be internationally competitive and give them an edge over its Asian neighbors. She is concerned that giving up English would make them "insular-thinking" and "narrow-minded."[93] More specifically, for legal professionals, the continued use of English can help them maintain their status quo and serve the interests of the ruling class. Although few deny that the use of Filipino in courts can enhance access to justice,[94] elites continue to argue that Filipino is not good enough or fully developed as a legal language. A 2003–2004 survey showed that 76% of the regional trial court and lower-level court judges did not agree to the use of local languages in court proceedings.[95] At least some of the inertia seems to be based on the association between language and social class, given that English is predominantly used by elites and Filipino is linked with illiterate people at the lower end of the social hierarchy. Publisher Teodoro Locsin, Sr., writes in a newspaper article that, unlike English, which is "the language of knowledge for Filipinos," Tagalog is "the language of ignorance" and

---

[87] Martin, "Expanding the Role of Philippine Languages in the Legal System."

[88] Powell, "English in Southeast Asian Law."

[89] Margaux Ortis, "SC: Use of Filipino Language in Courts 'Positive,'" *Philippine Daily Inquirer*, July 1, 2008.

[90] Supreme Court Administrative Circular No. 16-2010: "In view of the difficulties encountered in the use of Filipino in court proceedings manifested by the Presiding Judges and the court stenographers . . . as expressed in their letters dated January 12, 2010 and January 7, 2010, to the Chancellor of PHILJA, the use of the national language therein shall be optional and on a per case basis." Martin, "Expanding the Role of Philippine Languages in the Legal System."

[91] Regional Trial Court 80 in Malolos City, a Special Court for Drug Cases in Bulacan, led by Judge Buhat.

[92] Marilu Rañosa-Madrunio, "Power and Control in Philippine Courtroom Discourse," *International Journal of Legal English* 2, no. 1 (2014): 4–30.

[93] Zeneida Amadora, *Manila Bulletin*, September 17, 1988.

[94] A Public Opinion Survey on the Courts (POSC) conducted in 2003 reported that 46% of respondents said they could not understand proceedings in English. Martin, "Expanding the Role of Philippine Languages in the Legal System."

[95] Mahar Mangahas, "Social Climate: Survey on Access to Court Justice," *Inquirer.Net*, July 5, 2008.

Filipino is "stupid and idiotic."[96] Feelings toward a linguistic community are often projected onto perceptions of the language that the community speaks; thus political discourse may masquerade as linguistic discourse. For example, Filipino is said to be insufficiently intellectualized for judicial purposes.[97]

There is no doubt that the building of a linguistic infrastructure for legal operations takes time. However, given that historically the language of many legal systems has changed over time, this task should not be unthinkable. In other words, a strong form of linguistic determinism—that a language is inherently unfit for a task—is untenable in this context. For one thing, English was at one point a vernacular that was criticized as being too imprecise as a legal language when compared to French.[98] The struggle is as much ideological as linguistic. The dilemma that the Philippine judiciary is facing is very similar to that faced by many other post-colonial jurisdictions. On the one hand, promoting the vernaculars is an essential part of decolonization, and using them facilitates access to justice. On the other hand, the colonial language is still an important connection to the legal tradition and to the outside world.

Clearly more work is to be done, most notably the translation of all laws (including judgments) into Filipino,[99] an official publication of a bilingual lexicon, and introduction of Filipino into legal education. Implementation may begin in more strategic areas. For example, Martin suggests that use of Filipino in the *barangay* justice system, a state-powered local administration in charge of dispute resolution, will probably be welcomed because of its relative informality.[100] Although the Philippines is officially bilingual, in the legal context the country is still attempting to put the policy into practice. The bilingual policy is meant to be transitional, but it is anticipated to remain in place in the foreseeable future. Legal conservatism and language ideologies have both contributed to resisting radical changes to the status quo.

---

[96] Locsin (1993), cited in Teresita Gimenez Maceda, "The Filipino National Language: Discourse on Power," in *Papers from the Seventh Annual Meeting of the Southeast Asian Linguistics Society*, ed. Karen L. Adams, Thomas John Hudak, and F. K. Lehman (Tempe: Arizona State University, Program for Southeast Asian Studies, 2003), 99.

[97] An intellectualized language is defined as a language that can be used as a medium of a complete education in any field of knowledge from kindergarten to the university and beyond. To intellectualize a language requires extensive translation, corpus, and acquisition planning. Bonifacio P. Sibayan, "The Intellectualization of Filipino," *International Journal of the Sociology of Language* 88, no. 1 (1991): 69–82, https://doi.org/10.1515/ijsl.1991.88.69.

[98] Tiersma, *Legal Language*.

[99] Lawmaker Magtanggol T. Gunigundo proposed in 2010 House Bill 217 to the House of Representatives to mandate the creation of the Sentro ng Batas sa Wika, which would be responsible for translating laws, rules and regulations, and jurisprudence and for conducting researches in law in Filipino. There does not seem to be traceable follow-up to this proposal. Abigail A. Modino, "Creation of Sentro Ng Batas Sa Wika Sought" (Press release, House of Representatives, Republic of the Philippines., August 12, 2010), http://www.congress.gov.ph/press/details.php?pressid=4346.

[100] Martin, "Expanding the Role of Philippine Languages in the Legal System."

The Impossibility of Textual Equality

I will end this chapter with a quick recap of the insights developed. Our discussion on legal translation makes clear that that no existing translation approach can perfectly balance the needs of a multilingual jurisdiction: to have legislative texts that are equally authentic without compromising readability and accuracy. The translation of bilingual and multilingual legislation often has the hallmarks of a hybrid text—texts that are created in the target language but contain textual features borrowed from the source language that may seem out of place in the target language culture, as a result of choice instead of poor translation. This is the case for EU texts and for translation produced following a source-oriented approach, and it is often also the case in post-colonial jurisdictions where the local vernacular is deemed ill-equipped to fill the shoes of a colonial language in a colonial legal system. Jurisdictions that have a stronger symmetry between the official languages may adopt a more target-oriented approach to legal translation. Where one official language is dominating, the less powerful language tends to be more textually dependent on the more powerful language. The choice is not easy: a hybrid text may be less comprehensible to the target reader, but a more idiomatic translation can potentially compromise accuracy. At either extreme, the goal of improving access to justice may be defeated. Innovations in drafting techniques, such as co-drafting and merging of legal and linguistic expertise, have provided a possible solution to this dilemma. This solution, however, works well only when no new language attains official status after the law is prepared. In most multilingual post-colonial polities, endogenous languages are added as official languages in a legal system that is already entrenched in a colonial language.

Another inherent dilemma is that sometimes so much linguistic engineering is applied to make an endogenous language fit for its official purpose that the resultant language loses authenticity and its connection to the people who speak it and identify with it. In other words, the text that is being held as equal to others is written in a modified form of the language. In some cases, such modification is moderate, approximating the distance between ordinary and specialized use of any language. In cases where a language is spread over a larger geographical region and variation is significant, a standardized variety that is created and adopted may not be recognizable to people who are presumed to speak the language.

The fundamental obstacle to textual equality is that legal designation of equality between two texts does not make people perceive the languages equally or read the texts the same way. Social forces outside the law affect the perception of an official language. Official status may increase people's motivation to learn a language, boost its vitality, and increase its competitive value in the linguistic market to some extent. However, formal equality is not sufficient to subvert established social hierarchy, especially where a dominant language continues to have higher instrumental value outside the law and where language use is socially stratified. The Philippine example shows clear efforts not only in creating a new official language but also in branding and rebranding it, in the hope of increasing public acceptance and inducing ideological change. Identity interests about a national language have to compete with utility interests of a colonial language that now functions as a global lingua franca. Such clash of interests is typical in the post-colonial world. A further irony is that resistance to adopt an endogenous language frequently comes from local elites, especially through conservatism in the legal profession, and the tension between equality and privilege is often expressed in terms of linguistic shortcomings of this language. As Fanon[101] observes, the colonized are rarely freed by decolonization. Rather, during decolonization, power is transferred to the national elites, who tend to align in value with the departed colonial forces.

[101] Frantz Fanon, *The Wretched of the Earth* (New York: Grove Press, 1965).

Chapter 6

Interpreting Multilingual Legislation

THE LIMITS OF LANGUAGE AND THE CERTAINTY OF UNCERTAINTY

> Many of the possible interpretations of legal rules are lost, or at least are not consciously present, in the mind of the interpreter who looks to the rules in only one language. Rather than seizing upon a second language in order to enrich legal understanding and to gain more sophistication in legal interpretation, the jurist [or interpreter] who looks to only one text accepts incomplete normative descriptions and relies on jejune interpretive methods.
>
> —Roderick A. MacDonald[1]

Multiple Expressions, One Law?

> Had the lower court read the Chinese text of the Basic Law, it would have ruled in the church's favour, he (Martin Lee SC) said.[2]
>
> —*South China Morning Post* (Hong Kong, October 4, 2011)

> Tam Yuk-ha could have been guilty under the law in English but innocent according to the Chinese translation, Mr Justice Wally Yeung Chun-kuen said.[3]
>
> —*South China Morning Post* (Hong Kong, October 31, 1996).

Not only do legislatures in a bilingual or multilingual state need to write their laws in two or more languages, their judiciary also needs to decide how the bilingual or multilingual texts of the law should be read. Quotes like the preceding

---

[1] MacDonald, "Legal Bilingualism," 156.

[2] Referring to the case *The Catholic Diocese of Hong Kong Also Known as the Bishop of the Roman Catholic Church in Hong Kong Incorporation v. Secretary for Justice*, FACV No. 1 of 2011.

[3] Referring to the case *HKSAR v. Tam Yuk Ha* [1997] 2 HKC 531.

illustrate how legal indeterminacy in bilingual or multilingual jurisdictions could shake public confidence in the legal system, and challenge the belief that there is a single right answer to every legal question, as famously articulated by Ronald Dworkin.

Interpretation of written law is not only a feature of the civil law tradition. Codification of the law is increasingly frequent in common law jurisdictions as well, notwithstanding their reputation as being case-centered and judge-centered. Although written laws apply smoothly in most cases,[4] statutory language sometimes fails to produce clear results.

As Quine has famously asserted, linguistic meaning is indeterminate, and the same text can be read in different ways.[5] Linguistic indeterminacy is a main source of legal indeterminacy. Since certainty is generally seen as the most important property of law,[6] courts have developed various canons of construction to help judges interpret legal texts with consistency. Nevertheless, interpretive gaps still permit argument on both sides of an issue.[7] Legal indeterminacy has attracted much attention from legal theorists, as it casts doubt on the extent to which the law controls judicial decisions, and thus threatens the legitimacy of law. The indeterminacy thesis, a radical argument for legal realism, suggests that the judge often must choose between two or more legally acceptable solutions to a case. In other words, legal questions lack single right answers.[8]

Linguistic indeterminacy may trigger the use of certain rules of statutory interpretation, whose use can influence the outcome of a case. In English courts, statutes are first interpreted using the plain meaning of language (the Literal Rule). Where the statutory language is found to be obscure or ambiguous, courts may depart from the ordinary meaning of the text if its application leads to an absurd outcome (the Golden Rule), if the secondary (i.e., less ordinary) meaning better rectifies the "mischief and defect" that a statute targets (the Mischief Rule), or if the secondary meaning is favorable to the accused in a criminal case (the Rule of Lenity). To help resolve ambiguity, courts may consider the contextual circumstances and external evidence such as preparatory documents leading up to the legislation, and consult dictionaries or

---

[4] Lawrence Solan, *The Language of Statutes: Laws and Their Interpretation* (Chicago: University of Chicago Press, 2010); Solan, "Multilingualism and Morality in Statutory Interpretation."

[5] Robert Kirk, "Indeterminacy of Translation," in *The Cambridge Companion to Quine*, ed. Roger F. Gibson (Cambridge: Cambridge University Press, 2004), 151–80.

[6] Sir Matthew Hale, "Reflections by the Lord Chief Justice Hale on Mr. Hobbs His Dialogue of the Law," in *A History of English Law (7th Edn) Volume 1*, ed. Sir William Holdsworth (London: Methuen, Sweet & Maxwell, 1956), 505.

[7] Solan, *The Language of Statutes*.

[8] Kenneth J. Kress, "Legal Indeterminacy," in *Philosophy of Law and Legal Theory: An Anthology*, ed. Dennis Patterson, 1st ed. (Malden, MA: Wiley-Blackwell, 2003), 253–91.

sometimes corpora.[9] These discretionary considerations may be exercised only if indeterminacy is identified.[10]

Writing and reading the law in two or more languages potentially amplifies linguistic indeterminacy. It would be a nightmare for a bilingual or multilingual jurisdiction if the application of two or more language versions of the law to the same case leads to two or more different legal outcomes. Such legal indeterminacy could give rise to chaos. Just imagine opposing parties in a trial each holding on to one language version of the law, and arguing that theirs is a better representation of legislative intent. Indeed, these nightmares have periodically haunted bilingual and multilingual jurisdictions, given—as discussed in the preceding chapter—that translation is rarely perfect. Established rules of legal interpretation, having been derived with the assumption that there is only one official text of the law, are not always helpful in resolving interpretation problems in a multilingual jurisdiction. Most obviously, the Literal Rule would not get us anywhere when we have two or more literal readings that differ from each other (assuming that there can be agreement about the literal reading of a text). The Golden Rule is not useful if none of the divergent interpretations arising from the language versions is absurd. A shift in interpretation dynamics has been deemed necessary in bilingual and multilingual jurisdictions, in a bid to extract one law from two or more textual representations.

The nature of the challenge that legal multilingualism poses to interpretation hinges on the legal status assigned to the different language versions of the law. We will therefore briefly consider alternatives in status management before focusing on specific challenges in attempts to uphold status equality in multilingual legal interpretation.

To Be Equal or Not to Be Equal

How does a jurisdiction weigh the meaning contained in one language version of the law against another? The question may be answered differently depending on whether a jurisdiction assigns an equal status to its official languages.

Languages that have received the same formal status may nevertheless have unequal authority when it comes to practical matters such as legal interpretation. This solution may be politically challenging but legally painless.[11]

---

[9] A corpus is a body of written texts, or recorded and transcribed speech, collected from actual language use in authentic contexts. A corpus provides the basis for systematic textual analysis by corpus linguists, usually with the assistance of computer software. For an extraordinary debate about the applicability of corpus linguistics in legal interpretation, see *State v. Rasabout*, 2015 UT 72.

[10] Janny H. C. Leung, "The Object of Fidelity in Translating Multilingual Legislation," *Semiotica* 2014, no. 201 (2014): 223–38, https://doi.org/10.1515/sem-2014-0026.

[11] This is not to say that linguistic indeterminacy does not exist in statutory interpretation in these jurisdictions. A single text may contain linguistic indeterminacies.

Whenever the texts of the law disagree, the language version that has superior authority is deemed to have a higher reference value and prevails. In these jurisdictions, statutory interpretation is akin to that in monolingual jurisdictions.[12] In Malta, Maltese shall prevail in case of conflict between the Maltese and the English texts of the law. In Ireland, the constitution and statutes are passed and signed bilingually, but the Irish text prevails over the English-language text.[13] In Belgium, although German is one of three official languages, only legislative texts published in French and Dutch are considered authentic; the German version of the law is published only for informative purposes. In Malaysia, English prevails in legislations enacted before 1967, and the now national language Malay prevails in legislations enacted afterward.[14] In Brunei, both the English and the Malay version of the law are authentic; in case of discrepancy between the English and Malay legislative texts, English prevails over Malay in any bill, written law, or instrument, and Malay prevails over English in the Constitution, the Succession and Regency Proclamation, or the Nationality Legislation.[15] In the Pacific, where there is conflict across different language versions of legislative texts, the English text prevails over the local language equivalent in Samoa, Kiribati, and Fiji; in the Marshall Islands, Marshallese and English texts of the constitution are equally authentic, but Marshallese prevails over English in case of conflict. In Rwanda, where law is published in French, English, and Kinyarwanda, in case of conflict the version in which the law was adopted—which technically could be any of the three official languages but practically is mostly Kinyarwanda—shall prevail.[16] In Louisiana, a US state with a French tradition where bilingualism was officially practiced between 1845 and 1868,[17] the French version of some older laws still has a lingering effect in statutory interpretation and in practice prevails over the English text, even though the latter is the only authoritative language today.[18]

Although such unequal form of legal bilingualism or multilingualism is practiced in many jurisdictions, giving one language more legal force than another potentially provokes conflicts among linguistic communities. In the

---

[12] That said, the preference for a dominant text may not be an absolute principle in unbalanced bilingual or multilingual jurisdictions. In Ireland, it has been suggested that preference for the Irish text is a canon of interpretation used at the discretion of the court, and is usually applied only after attempts at reconciliation fail. Mac Cárthaigh, "Interpretation and Construction of Bilingual Laws: A Canadian Lamp to Light the Way?"

[13] Mac Cárthaigh, "Interpretation and Construction of Bilingual Laws."

[14] Powell, "Bilingual Courtrooms: In the Interests of Justice?"

[15] http://www.unesco.org/most/lnbrune.htm.

[16] Nzanze, "Challenges of Drafting Laws in One Language and Translating Them: Rwanda's Experience."

[17] Roger K. Ward, "The French Language in Louisiana Law and Legal Education: A Requiem," *Louisiana Law Review* 57, no. 4 (1997): 1283–1324.

[18] George A. Bermann, "Bilingualism and Translation in the U.S. Legal System: A Study of the Louisiana Experience," *The American Journal of Comparative Law* 54 (2006): 89–102.

case of post-colonial jurisdictions, different kinds of tension may be created depending on whether a higher status is assigned to an endogenous language (e.g., in the form of conflicts among endogenous communities, or dissatisfaction from professional classes who are usually better acquainted with the former colonial language) or to a former colonial language (e.g., in the form of neocolonial control). The practice essentially relegates one or more official legislative texts to merely reference texts. This solution is therefore not a politically viable move in all jurisdictions.

The alternative, which is to ascribe equal importance to each official language, is politically painless but legally challenging. It practically restructures the process of statutory interpretation. The rest of the chapter will be devoted to jurisdictions that have tried to maintain equality among the language versions of their legal texts.

Equal Authenticity

Equality among different language versions of a legal text is maintained by what is known as the equal authenticity principle, which has its origin in international law. As discussed in Chapter 1, certain languages in different regions of the world, such as Latin, French, and Arabic, had for a long time served as diplomatic languages for international communications. With the rise of the nation-state ideology and the concurrent elevation of a national language facilitated by the print medium,[19] in modern times it has become extremely common for treaties to be drawn up in two or more languages that represent each of the contracting parties.[20] Most treaties specify the status of the different language versions in one of the final clauses. For instance, some treaties may grant some language versions the status of "authentic" or "official" texts, and some may designate one text to be authoritative in case of divergence. If there is no such provision, the International Law Commission (ILC) of the United Nations considers each version of the treaty as authentic and authoritative for purposes of interpretation. That both texts of a bilateral treaty are equally binding, unless otherwise negotiated by the parties concerned, is based on the principle of equality of states, thought to originate from the Treaty of Westphalia 1648. The principle assumes legal equality across sovereign states despite their varied political strength.

---

[19] A single language variety propagated as a national language through print capitalism is an important precursor of modernity.

[20] I rely heavily on Tabory (1980) in this section, as it is one of the few monographs dedicated to this topic. In fact, it was a major piece of reference that the Hong Kong judiciary used in drafting its method for bilingual statutory interpretation.

Equal authenticity has long been a presumption in the interpretation of treaties. In *Foster v. Neilson*,[21] the Supreme Court of the United States ruled that the Treaty of Amity signed between the United States and Spain in 1819 had to be executed by the legislature before it became law. The court came to the opposite conclusion and ruled that the same treaty executed itself, in *United States v. Percheman*,[22] when the Spanish version of the text came to its attention and influenced its reading of the English version.[23]

The 1969 Vienna Convention on the Law of Treaties (VCLT), as the product of an initiative taken by the ILC between 1962 and 1966, codifies existing customary international law governing multilingual treaties (i.e., treaties authenticated in two or more languages). Treaty interpretation, a highly controversial and difficult subject, is formulated in Section 3 (Articles 31–33) of the VCLT. Articles 31 and 32 lay down general rules and supplementary means of treaty interpretation, whereas Article 33 specifically addresses multilingual treaties:

Art. 31: General rule of interpretation

1. *A treaty shall be interpreted in good faith in accordance with the ordinary meaning to be given to the terms of the treaty in their context and in the light of its object and purpose.*
2. *The context for the purpose of the interpretation of a treaty shall comprise, in addition to the text, including its preamble and annexes:*
   - *(a) any agreement relating to the treaty which was made between all the parties in connexion with the conclusion of the treaty;*
   - *(b) any instrument which was made by one or more parties in connexion with the conclusion of the treaty and accepted by the other parties as an instrument related to the treaty.*
3. *There shall be taken into account, together with the context:*
   - *(a) any subsequent agreement between the parties regarding the interpretation of the treaty or the application of its provisions;*
   - *(b) any subsequent practice in the application of the treaty which establishes the agreement of the parties regarding its interpretation;*
   - *(c) any relevant rules of international law applicable in the relations between the parties.*
4. *A special meaning shall be given to a term if it is established that the parties so intended.*

[21] *Foster & Elam v. Neilson*, 27 U.S. (2 Pet.) 253 (1829).

[22] *United States v. Percheman*, 32 US (7 Pet.) 51 (1833).

[23] The court comments, "The treaty was drawn up in the Spanish as well as in the English language. Both are originals, and were unquestionably intended by the parties to be identical."

Art. 32: Supplementary means of interpretation

Recourse may be had to supplementary means of interpretation, including the preparatory work of the treaty and the circumstances of its conclusion, in order to confirm the meaning resulting from the application of article 31, or to determine the meaning when the interpretation according to article 31:

(a) leaves the meaning ambiguous or obscure; or

(b) leads to a result which is manifestly absurd or unreasonable.

Art. 33: Interpretation of treaties authenticated in two or more languages

1. *When a treaty has been authenticated in two or more languages, the text is equally authoritative in each language, unless the treaty provides or the parties agree that, in case of divergence, a particular text shall prevail.*
2. *A version of the treaty in a language other than one of those in which the text was authenticated shall be considered an authentic text only if the treaty so provides or the parties so agree.*
3. *The terms of the treaty are presumed to have the same meaning in each authentic text.*
4. *Except where a particular text prevails in accordance with paragraph 1, when a comparison of the authentic texts discloses a difference of meaning which the application of articles 31 and 32 does not remove, the meaning which best reconciles the texts, having regard to the object and purpose of the treaty, shall be adopted.*

The VCLT provides broad and general principles rather than detailed rules, and refrains from ranking elements of interpretation or specifying the means through which "the meaning which best reconciles the texts, having regard to the object and purpose of the treaty" may be arrived at. It is also noticeably silent on contested issues such as whether comparison between different authentic versions should be obligatory, what value un-codified interpretative rules have, and how to evaluate co-drafted versus translated versions of multilingual documents. This is because the VCLT is a product of negotiation, containing only uncontroversial provisions that all conference delegations were ready to accept.[24]

The equal authenticity principle contained in the VCLT and its variants have been adopted in treaty interpretation and by many supranational bodies such as the European Union and the World Trade Organization (WTO). It also has been absorbed by bilingual and multilingual jurisdictions such as Belgium,[25]

[24] Tabory, *Multilingualism in International Law and Institutions*.

[25] French and Dutch versions of the law are equally authentic in Belgium; German version of the law is for information only.

Canada,[26] Finland,[27] Hong Kong,[28] Kosovo,[29] Wales,[30] and Switzerland,[31] which emphasize equality among their official languages. It is from these jurisdictions that the kind of media quotes in the epigraph of this chapter may be found.

Textual Equivalence as Legal Fiction

If authentic language versions of a legal text are truly equal in meaning and status, then any single language version should carry the intended legal meaning,[32] and multilingual legal interpretation should not differ significantly from monolingual legal interpretation. However, that authentic language texts carry the same meaning, which the equal authenticity principle is premised on, is but a legal fiction.[33] This legal fiction, spelled out in Article 33(3) of the VCLT, is *sine qua non*, or essential, for the adoption of the equal authenticity principle in bilingual and multilingual jurisdictions. To the extent that translation is relied upon in bilingual and multilingual legislative drafting, the assumption is that a translated text shall be identical to the original text. Even if co-drafting is practiced and translation is kept at a minimal, bilingual or multilingual jurisdictions sometimes fail to produce the same meaning in two or more language versions of their law. Textual discrepancies may arise not only from mistranslation, but also from interlingual indeterminacies that are not obvious until context draws attention to them.

---

[26] It applies to federal legislation and legislation in some provinces. See Section 133 of the Constitution Act, 1867; Section 16(1) of the Canadian Charter of Rights and Freedoms; and Section 2 of Official Languages Act 1988.

[27] Section 17 of the Constitution grants Finnish and Swedish equal status.

[28] See 3(2) of the Official Languages Ordinance. The equal authenticity principle applies to statutory interpretation in Hong Kong, but not to interpretation of the Basic Law, which is known as the mini-constitution of Hong Kong.

[29] Article 5(1) of the Constitution grants Albanian and Serbian official status. The Law No. 02/L-37 on the Use of Languages (2006) further expressly provides that the languages enjoy equal status and rights.

[30] Government of Wales Act 2006, s. 156, provides that the English and Welsh texts of the law should have equal standing.

[31] Legislative enactments, including the constitution, are equally authentic and binding in German, French, and Italian in Switzerland.

[32] Tabory, *Multilingualism in International Law and Institutions*.

[33] Lawyers and legal scholars have heard the term "legal fiction" for more than a century. Over time it has come to include concepts such as "implied conditions," "attractive nuisance," and "corporate personality." An implied condition is assumed to be part of a contract, even if no party to the contract has ever considered it. Children are taken as invitees rather than trespassers on a property containing an attractive nuisance. The action of an agent is an action of the corporation. Legal fictions may appear paradoxical because they are not literally true, yet they are not meant to deceive. In fact, they function to ensure the stability of the justice system, by enabling an old law to encompass a new situation without having to bend the existing rule. Sanford Schane, *Language and the Law* (London; New York: Continuum, 2006).

Many bilingual and multilingual jurisdictions require the interpreters of their law to temporarily suspend their disbelief and pretend that original and translated texts carry exactly the same meaning. As mentioned before, these jurisdictions have invented alternative labels for translation and translation errors, as though they are throwing translators and the translation process down a "memory hole." In the European Union, the term *translation* is pegged to the legal status of a legislative text, rather than to its origin. Only non-authentic language versions of the law are published as *translations*.

The legal fiction of equivalence can sometimes motivate judges to find equivalence where there is none. Take the Hong Kong case *The Queen v. Tam Yuk Ha*[34] as an example, where the point of dispute was whether the placing of metal trays and other items in front of a fresh provisions shop would be considered as an "alteration or addition"[35] that would result in a material deviation from its approved building plan. The equivalent phrase used in the Chinese text is *zeng jian gong cheng* (增建工程, literally, "additional construction"). In the first appeal of the case, Justice Yeung utilized his intuition as a Chinese speaker and stated that

> '增建工程' *(zeng jian gong cheng) plainly means "building additional construction or building works." No one who understands the Chinese language would, by any stretch of the imagination, come to the conclusion that the placing of metal trays and other items in front of the shop would be a* '增建工程' *(zeng jian gong cheng).*

But that was exactly what was decided subsequently in *HKSAR v. Tam Yuk Ha*,[36] where the Court of Appeal argued that the same Chinese expression is not inconsistent with the English one, effectively ignoring the ordinary meaning of the Chinese phrase.

When discrepancies are alleged, judges determine whether the two or more versions are equal by comparing the relevant authentic texts. An underlying assumption in this determination is that there *is* a truth of the matter, one way or the other, and that this truth can be discovered. Contrary to this assumption, Quine asserts that "the whole idea of meaning and sameness of meaning is a little more than a convenient way of talking, without solid empirical foundation."[37] Unlike classic legal fictions such as "attractive nuisance" or "implied conditions," the falsity of the fiction of textual equivalence highlighted by the work of Quine, and many others since, rarely seems to enter judicial consciousness, at least as reported in proceedings that insist on the connectedness of

---

[34] *The Queen v. Tam Yuk Ha* [1996] MA No. 933.

[35] In By-law 35 of the Food Business (Urban Council) By-laws, Cap. 132.

[36] *HKSAR v. Tam Yuk Ha* [1997] 2 HKC 531. All three judges carry a Chinese surname (Chan, Liu, and Wong) and are likely to be Chinese speakers.

[37] Kirk, "Indeterminacy of Translation," 152.

facts, legal reasoning, and outcome as being essential in upholding the law. Some judges may genuinely believe they are locating an objective truth when comparing the sameness of texts. Others may feel they have arrived at a correct solution when a particular way of reconciling a particular discrepancy has been found (sometimes through cherry-picking possible word meanings). Either way, the underlying presumption generates not only external but also internal deception,[38] and creates a false impression of legitimacy. The contrasting possibility, that there is no ready-made truth of fixed meaning but only active judgment, nevertheless repeatedly resurfaces in the frequency with which judges disagree among themselves over the versions of truth on such matters.

There is a deeper danger inherent in the fiction of translation equivalence, as a result. This lies in only partial awareness of how the principle conceals the subjectivity involved in the exercise of judgment.[39] Therefore, even in cases where courts deem language versions of the law to be equivalent, their interpretation is not necessarily safe from the undercurrents of interlingual discrepancies.

Legislative History and Implicit Preference

Bilingual and multilingual jurisdictions that have openly adopted the equal authenticity principle differ in how closely they adhere to it. Here I shall continue with the Hong Kong example, where equal authority has been granted to its two official languages, but the judiciary shows implicit preference to one language version of the legal text over another during statutory interpretation.

Although the interpretation of bilingual legislation in Hong Kong is modeled on the same principle laid down in VCLT 33, as expressed in Interpretation and General Clauses Ordinance 10(B),[40] Hong Kong courts had habitually relied on the English text of the law during most of the colonial period, and have been somewhat half-hearted in upholding the equal authenticity principle after it became bilingual just before the handover in 1997. Earlier laws (including 532 principal ordinances and around 1,000 pieces of subsidiary

---

[38] Lon Luvois Fuller, *Legal Fictions* (Stanford, CA: Stanford University Press, 1967).

[39] Leung, "The Object of Fidelity in Translating Multilingual Legislation."

[40] 10(B):

(1) The English language text and the Chinese language text of an Ordinance shall be equally authentic, and the Ordinance shall be construed accordingly.

(2) The provisions of an Ordinance are presumed to have the same meaning in each authentic text.

(3) Where a comparison of the authentic texts of an Ordinance discloses a difference of meaning which the rules of statutory interpretation ordinarily applicable do not resolve, the meaning which best reconciles the text, having regard to the object and purposes of the Ordinance, shall be adopted.

legislation[41]) in Hong Kong were enacted first in English and later translated into Chinese. After 1989,[42] laws have been enacted simultaneously in English and Chinese.[43]

Despite the equal authenticity principle, Hong Kong courts give more weight to the English text given its original status in cases involving earlier laws, as in *HKSAR v. Lau San Ching and Others*,[44] where the meaning of the Chinese and English texts of Section 4(28) of the Hong Kong Summary Ordinance was found to differ:[45]

> . . . if the Ordinance was initially enacted in English, the English text was the original official text from which the Chinese text was subsequently prepared and declared authentic. In ascertaining the ordinance's legal meaning, the English text should be taken as more accurately reflecting the legislature's intent at the time it was originally enacted. In this case, the meaning borne by the original official English text, which was already in existence as early as 1932, should take precedence over the Chinese authentic text.

The argument was made immediately after the court held that the difference between the Chinese and the English text was not reconcilable, without invoking a consideration of the object and purposes of the specific ordinance involved. Similarly, in *Chan Fung Lan v. Lai Wai Chuen*,[46] where the differences between the Chinese and the English texts were found to be irreconcilable,[47] the court also bolstered the idea that the authenticated Chinese text had a humble start as a translation:

> One must bear in mind that the authenticated Chinese text started life simply as a translation of the original legislation and if there are errors

---

[41] Emily Poon Wai-yee, "The Pitfalls of Linguistic Equivalence: The Challenge for Legal Translation," *Target: International Journal of Translation Studies* 14, no. 1 (January 1, 2002): 75–106, https://doi.org/10.1075/target.14.1.04poo.

[42] This is after the Official Language (Amendment) Ordinance came into operation in April 1989. The first Chinese version of an Ordinance was authenticated in 1992, via promulgation in the Gazette by an order made by the Governor in Council, and the authentication of the Chinese version of all existing legislation was completed by the change of sovereignty in 1997.

[43] The Hong Kong Basic Law, which stipulates the basic policies of the PRC toward the Hong Kong Special Administrative Region, is a notable exception to the bilingual legal policy of Hong Kong. As a national law of the PRC, the Chinese version is the authentic language.

[44] *HKSAR v. Law San Ching and Others*, HCMA 98/2002.

[45] The Chinese text leaves out the word "may" in the sentence "Any person who without lawful authority or excuse . . . does any act whereby injury or obstruction whether directly or consequentially, *may* accrue to a public place or to the shore of the sea, or to navigation, mooring or anchorage, transit or traffic . . . shall be liable to a fine of $500 or to imprisonment of 3 months" (italics added).

[46] *Chan Fung Lan v. Lai Wai Chuen*, HCMP 4210/1996.

[47] The Chinese text contains the word "charge," which does not appear in the English text, in s 18 of the Estate Duty Ordinance.

> in the translation, which are bound to arise in such a mammoth undertaking, such errors should not be given effect simply because under Section 10(B) of the Interpretation Ordinance the two texts are said to be equally authentic.

The same idea was relied upon in a later Lands Tribunal case, *The Commissioner of Rating and Valuation v. Chan Ho-Chin Colin*,[48] to undermine the Chinese version of the law.

If the presumption is for the original text to prevail, any discrepancy with another authentic text is dealt with as a translation error. Such an approach is not practically different from jurisdictions practicing a limited form of bilingualism, where in case of divergence, one text prevails. But equal authenticity raises false expectations about language equality that are in tension with the kind of implicit preference displayed.

In fact, in the *Young Loan Arbitration*[49] case, the Arbitral Tribunal confirmed that the earlier international practice of referring to the original text as an aid to interpretation is incompatible with the equal authenticity principle in VCLT 33. Sullivan and Driedger have also argued that "[i]t is inconsistent with the equal authenticity rule to resolve discrepancies between two language versions by giving automatic preference to one."[50] In the European Union, reference to the translation history of legislation violates the legislative culture.[51]

Instead of relying purely on fiction and suppressed memory, Canada has taken a rare and proactive step to prevent legislative history from undermining the equal authenticity principle, through repealing existing laws and re-enacting bilingual laws to "erase" the effect of legislative history and to overcome an inferior complex associated with translation.

A Teleological Approach to Legal Interpretation

Even for jurisdictions that are determined to uphold the equal authenticity principle, the presumption that all authentic texts carry equal meaning sometimes fails, and thus interpretation approaches need to be developed for handling these cases.

---

[48] *The Commissioner of Rating & Valuation v. Chan Ho-Chin Colin*, LDMR 48/2000.

[49] *Young Loan Arbitration* [1980] 59 ILR 494. The case concerned discrepancies between the English, French, and German versions of the London Debt Agreement. The court gave no weight to the fact that the clause had been drafted in English and held that the object and purpose of the disputed clause was fully achieved by the German text.

[50] Ruth Sullivan and Elmer A. Driedger, *Driedger on the Construction of Statutes*, 3rd ed. (Markham, ON: Butterworths, 1994), 218.

[51] Solan, "Multilingualism and Morality in Statutory Interpretation."

While a monolingual text may often be read in more than one way and therefore may be ambiguous, discrepancies may also arise when two clearly written, equally authentic language versions of the same statute are incongruent with each other. The identification of linguistic indeterminacy prompts the use of certain rules of statutory interpretation. To help resolve ambiguity, courts may consider the contextual circumstances and external evidence, such as preparatory documents leading up to the legislation, dictionaries, and sometimes even corpus data that provide some evidence about common usage of language.[52] These discretionary considerations may be exercised only if indeterminacy is identified, as stated by Lord Reid in *Black-Clawson v. Papierwerke*:[53]

> In the comparatively few cases where the words of a statutory provision are only capable of having one meaning, that is an end of the matter and no further enquiry is permissible.

Although rules of interpretation are ordinarily predicated on the certainty of the language of the law, judges are "generally astute to find the necessary 'ambiguity' which enabled them to interpret the document in proper context" in trying to avoid injustice (Lord Hoffmann in *Kirin-Amgen v. Hoechst*[54]). The potential for finding such ambiguity seems to be expanded by legal bilingualism or multilingualism, under which not only intralingual (i.e., within-language) but also interlingual (i.e., between-language) indeterminacy[55] may emerge from different versions of the law.

Bilingual and multilingual jurisdictions have come up with various approaches to tackle discrepancies between equally authentic language versions of the law. In Finland, if textual discrepancies occur in cases that involve citizen rights, courts are bound to adhere to the version more favorable to the individual.[56] The shared meaning rule, which requires the court to determine the common meaning of two language versions as far as possible, is generally applicable in Canada (affirmed in *R v. Dubois*;[57] reaffirmed in *Quebec (Revenue) v. Caisse populaire Desjardins de Montmagny*[58]). According to Bastarache,[59] where both versions are clear, the court will look for a shared meaning between

---

[52] The question of whether corpus linguistics should be used in legal interpretation was debated in *Utah v. Rasabout*, 356 P.3d 1258 (Utah 2015).

[53] *Black-Clawson International Ltd v. Papierwerke Waldhof-Aschaffenburg AG* [1975] AC 591 [1975] 2 WLR 513 [1975] 1 All ER 810 [1975] UKHL 2.

[54] *Kirin-Amgen v. Hoechst* [2004] UKHL 46.

[55] Referring to textual discrepancies/inconsistencies. Both intralingual and interlingual indeterminacies are subtypes of linguistic indeterminacy.

[56] McRae, Helander, and Luoma, *Conflict and Compromise in Multilingual Societies*.

[57] *R v. Dubois* [1935] S.C.R. 378.

[58] *Quebec (Revenue) v. Caisse populaire Desjardins de Montmagny*, 2009 SCC 49 [2009] 3 SCR 286.

[59] Bastarache, "Bilingual Interpretation Rules as a Component of Language Rights in Canada."

them.[60] Moreover, where one is clear and the other one is ambiguous, the clear version is preferred (as in *Canada (A.G.) v. Brown*[61]). Where one meaning is broad and the other is narrow, the narrow meaning is generally preferred (as in *Côté v. Canadian Employment and Immigration Minister*[62]). However, none of these rules is determinative, as any outcome arrived at needs to be checked against linguistic context (i.e., the rest of the provision) and legislative intent. This is in line with the guiding principle provided in VCLT, which provides that the law must be interpreted in light of its object and purpose (Article 31).

Although in jurisdictions with three or more official languages it is theoretically possible to increase legal certainty by simply resorting to the majority meaning (i.e., majority rule) where legislative texts are found to diverge, this interpretive solution is not available to bilingual jurisdictions, and is not usually explicitly adopted. In fact, there is some EU jurisprudence against majoritization, even where one language version diverges from the rest because of clear mistakes.[63] In Switzerland, where all three official texts of the law are found to differ, or where one version differs substantially from the other two, no particular version may be preferred. Other elements of interpretation, such as the purpose and context of the provision, have to be considered.[64]

One of the most common problem cases involves texts that contain supposedly equivalent terms of different semantic scope. For example, the case of *Doré v. Verdun*[65] concerned the discrepancy in meaning between the term *disposition* in the French version of Article 2930 of Civil Code of Québec, and the equivalent term *stipulation* in the English version. The English term has a narrower, exclusively contractual connotation. The Canadian Supreme Court refused to be bound by the meaning shared by both language versions of the law, instead adopted an interpretation based on the French term and Parliamentary history, and argued that the interpretation is consistent with legislature's intention.

In bilingual and multilingual jurisdictions, the converging trend is to use purpose as the overriding consideration in resolving interlingual indeterminacy.[66] The approach places equal intent above equal effect and equal meaning and is in accord with legislative supremacy. Of course, the teleological

---

[60] If no shared meaning can be found, the conflict is considered "absolute," as in *R v. Klippert* [1967] S.C.R. 822.

[61] *Canada (A.G.) v. Brown* [2005] FC 1683.

[62] *Côté v. Canadian Employment and Immigration Minister* [1986] A.C.F. no 447, 69 N.R. 126 (Fed. C. A.).

[63] See discussion in Michal Bobek, "The Multilingualism of the European Union Law in the National Courts: Beyond the Textbooks," in *Linguistic Diversity and European Democracy*, ed. Anne Lise Kjær and Silvia Adamo (Surrey, England; Burlington, VT: Ashgate, 2011), 123–42.

[64] Lötscher, "Multilingual Law Drafting in Switzerland."

[65] *Doré v. Verdun (City)* [1997] 2 S.C.R. 862.

[66] Leung, "Statutory Interpretation in Multilingual Jurisdictions."

approach has been widely adopted not only by bilingual but also monolingual jurisdictions, and is not in itself a novelty. But the approach has taken on a new dimension of meaning, functionality, and significance in a bilingual and multilingual legal environment. It is attractive to bilingual and multilingual jurisdictions because it allows for the preservation of unity of the law, despite its potentially divergent linguistic representations. However, some have expressed concern that interpreters may be encouraged to look for discrepancies among language versions in order to depart from the texts of the law altogether.[67] Moreover, given the departure of legal meaning from the texts that represent it, another inevitable drawback of the teleological approach is that citizens may not be able to fully understand the law based on a single authentic text.

Routine Comparison and Textual Interdependency

In bilingual and multilingual jurisdictions, statutory interpretation typically starts with one language version of a statute. Another language version is brought up if an intralingual indeterminacy is discovered, if a discrepancy is alleged, or if the court simply wishes to confirm its interpretation of one text using another authentic text. Otherwise a unilingual judge in a bilingual or multilingual jurisdiction may decide a case based on one version of the law, as in the case of monolingual jurisdictions.

That this could be a problem was raised in *R. v. Mac*,[68] where the Ontario Court of Appeal had to determine the meaning of the English word *adapted* in the phrase "adapted and intended to be used to commit forgery" in the Criminal Code, which is ambiguous between the meanings of "suitable for" or "modified or altered." The court decided that both meanings are plausible and therefore the meaning favorable to the defendant should be adopted. However, when the case reached the Supreme Court of Canada, the court found that the ambiguity could have been quickly resolved if the French version of the law was referred to (for French uses different terms *modifié* and *adapté* where the English term *adapted* was used).

Since then, the Supreme Court of Canada has modified its Rules to require parties to present the Court with every provision to be interpreted in both languages, where they have been published.[69] In at least a few other bilingual and

---

[67] Bobek, "The Multilingualism of the European Union Law in the National Courts: Beyond the Textbooks."

[68] *R. v. Mac* [2002] 1 S.C.R. 856.

[69] Bastarache, "Bilingual Interpretation Rules as a Component of Language Rights in Canada." Admittedly, this requirement will only achieve its purpose if the trial judge is bilingual; in many cases they are not. Therefore, one extra-legal factor to statutory interpretation in bilingual and multilingual jurisdictions is the language competence of the judge(s).

multilingual jurisdictions, routine comparisons between language versions are also encouraged, even in the absence of an apparent discrepancy. The WTO occasionally compares its authentic legal texts without being prompted by parties raising arguments based on a comparison of the texts.[70] The French and Spanish texts have been used to confirm its interpretation of the English text. In *US—Oil Country Tubular Goods Sunset Reviews*,[71] the Appellate Body confirmed via the French and Spanish versions of an anti-dumping agreement that the "definition" and "determination" of injury cannot be equated. The Appellate Body also remarked, *obiter dictum* in the same case,[72] that "routine comparison of authentic texts would be a good practice." In the European Union, comparison of language versions has been called for in over 30 judgments through the years and is now considered "settled case law."[73]

The existence of more than one language version of the law can be immensely helpful in resolving intralingual ambiguities. According to Beaupré, many cases would not have reached the courts "had the parties compared the two versions of the law in the first place."[74] In translation studies, Berman has also argued that "clarification is inherent in translation, to the extent that every translation comprises some degree of explication."[75] Comparison may lead to an even higher level of clarity in jurisdictions with three or more official languages. In one Swiss case,[76] for example, the ambiguity in a German term *in der Regel* ("as a rule")—whether it refers to *monatlich* ("monthly") or *monatlich und zum voraus* ("monthly and in advance")—was clarified by comparison with the French (*en règle générale*) and Italian (*di regola*) version of the law, both of which cover both terms (*mensuellement et d'avance* and *in anticipo mese per mese*, respectively).

Sometimes the court does not simply adopt one meaning of an ambiguous term and discard another. Courts may arrive at a blended meaning between two texts of the law, which cannot be established by relying on either text alone. In the Canadian case of *Aeric Inc. v. Canada Post Corp.*,[77] it was not clear whether *the principle business/l'activité principale* refers to only profit-making activities, as suggested by the English text, or a wider sense captured by the French

---

[70] For six of such cases, see Bradly J. Condon, "Lost in Translation: Plurilingual Interpretation of WTO Law," *Journal of International Dispute Settlement* 1, no. 1 (February 1, 2010): 191–216, https://doi.org/10.1093/jnlids/idp007.

[71] *United States – Sunset Reviews of Anti-Dumping Measures on Oil Country Tubular Goods from Argentina*, WT/DS268/AB/R, WTO Appellate Body Report, December 17, 2004.

[72] WTO decisions are not formally precedential, but they have clear reference value.

[73] Baaij, "Fifty Years of Multilingual Interpretation in the European Union."

[74] Beaupré, *Interpreting Bilingual Legislation*, 2–3.

[75] Antoine Berman, "La Traduction Comme Épreuve de l'étranger [Translation and the Trials of the Foreign, Translated by Lawrence Venuti] (1985)," in *The Translation Studies Reader*, ed. Lawrence Venuti (Routledge, 2000), 289.

[76] Detailed in Lötscher, "Multilingual Law Drafting in Switzerland."

[77] *Aeric Inc. v. Canada Post Corp.* [1985] 16 D.L.R. (4th). 686.

text. The Court harmonized the meaning of the possible interpretations and concluded that the phrase may refer to non-profit-making activities that were related to a business carried out by the person.

It is inadequate to consider the interpretation of multilingual legal texts only from the perspective of the legal decision-maker. An official multilingual policy creates the expectation that the corresponding language communities could have better linguistic access to the law, and potentially participate in a trial conducted in their own language (more on language rights in Chapter 7). Since each language version of the law is supposed to be authentic, one would expect that citizens could rely on a version they understand to regulate their conduct. However, the preceding discussion makes clear that bilingual and multilingual jurisdictions often see the need to compare and combine the meaning of all authentic texts in interpreting a statute, and sometimes refer to legislative documents that the public do not have easy access to. If this becomes a regular practice, it will take not just legal knowledge, but also mastery of not one but all official languages, to comprehend the law. Expert consultation will become necessary, and legal effects seem less foreseeable to the layperson. The need to read all versions together has been described as "an inherent vice of legal bilingualism."[78] The paradox of multilingual interpretation is that making the law linguistically available to more language communities may only improve accessibility to the law to a limited extent. Despite these limitations, there does not seem to be any alternative model of multilingual interpretation that can avoid this paradox.

The European Union as a Radical Example

Integrating Europe provides a radical example of the multiplicity of legislative languages. Multilingualism in the European Union has been described as being fundamentally distinctive, since the notion prominently symbolizes European historical, political, and cultural diversity, a legal imperative, a political necessity, a democratic accountability and representation tool, and a guarantee of public access to Community documents.[79] It is a necessary corollary to the principle of direct effect and the doctrine of supremacy of Community law. This explains the Union's strong commitment to avoid linguistic discrimination and to ensure uniformity in interpretation across nations. Language equality is enshrined in Council Regulation No. 1,[80] which guarantees that the languages

[78] Eric T. M. Cheung, "Bilingualism: Where Are We Heading?," in *Reform of the Civil Process in Hong Kong*, ed. J. R. Burton and R. M. Wilkinson (Singapore: Butterworths Asia, 2000), 251.

[79] Phoebus Athanassiou, "The Application of Multilingualism in the European Context," *Legal Working Paper Series No. 2*, European Central Bank, February 2006.

[80] OJ L 17, 6.10.1958, p. 385, as amended.

of all member states are both official and working languages of the institutions of the Union (Article 1). Articles 21, 290, and 314 of the Treaty establishing the European Community and Regulation No 1/58 (as amended by successive Acts of Accession) provide a legal basis for multilingualism in the European Union. According to Article 314, Community law provisions must be interpreted and applied in light of the versions established in the other Community languages.

Ensuring that all the 24 authentic texts of EU legislation carry the same meaning is seen as practically impossible. A search in legal databases returns numerous results of cases involving discrepancies between language versions of legislative texts. Baaij has found that between 1960 and 2010, 246 European Court of Justice (ECJ) judgments have included comparison of language versions, among which 170 of them were found to contain discrepancies between language versions.[81]

Baaij further found that in 95[82] out of those 170 judgments (approx. 56%), the ECJ was able to resolve the case[83] through comparing different authentic versions of the legislative texts.[84] In two-thirds of these cases, the court preferred a meaning carried by the majority of language versions ("majority argument"). In one-third of the cases, it preferred a clearer version than others ("clarity argument").[85] The comparative method was established clearly in *CILFIT*,[86] a leading authority on the scope of the obligation imposed by the third paragraph of Article 177 of the EEC Treaty, which aims to ensure that Community law is interpreted and applied in a uniform manner in all the member states. In the judgment, the Court of Justice stated that since Community legislation is drafted in more than one authentic language, "an interpretation of a provision of Community law thus involves a comparison of the different language versions." Despite the clear direction that the ECJ has given to domestic courts in *CILFIT*, the ECJ usually compares language versions only on the initiative of the parties.[87] Bobek suggests that this may be a good thing, not least because

---

[81] Baaij, "Fifty Years of Multilingual Interpretation in the European Union."

[82] Note that Baaij refers to the comparative method as "the literal approach." I argue that the comparative method is qualitatively different from the literal rule of statutory interpretation as traditionally constructed, in that courts have to deal with competing literal meanings, and additional guiding principles (such as the majority or clarity argument) are necessary to resolve the textual conflict.

[83] I.e., by using the comparative method as a primary argument in the judgment. Note that in other cases, the comparative method may still be used for making supplementary arguments.

[84] Some sample cases are *Erich Stauder v. City of Ulm*, Case 26/69 [1969] ECR 419; *Birden v. Stadtgemeinde Bremen*, Case C-1/97 [1998] ECR I-7747; *Codan*, Case C-236/97 [1998] ECR I-8679; *Sumitomo Chemical*, Joined Cases T-22/02 and T-23/02 [2005] ECR II-04065.

[85] Baaij, "Fifty Years of Multilingual Interpretation in the European Union."

[86] *Srl CILFIT and Lanificio di Gavardo SpA v. Ministry of Health* (Case 283/81) ECLI:EU:C:1982:335 [1982] ECR 3415, October 6, 1982.

[87] Joxerramon Bengoetxea, "Multilingual and Multicultural Legal Reasoning: The European Court of Justice," in *Linguistic Diversity and European Democracy*, ed. Anne Lise Kjær and Silvia Adamo (Surrey, England; Burlington, VT: Ashgate, 2011), 97–122. For a review of the limited extent

the comparative method is used to solve rather than create problems.[88] When national courts experience doubt in their interpretation of EU legislation, they also consult other language versions—but they usually select only one or two of them, which tend to be well-known languages such as English and French.[89]

Driven by the need for a uniform interpretation of EU regulations, the purpose and general scheme of the law is an overriding consideration, even if it means that sometimes the ordinary meaning of one or more texts has to be disregarded. For the same reason, the common denominator is not always the best solution in resolving discrepancies, and the clear meaning in one language version does not always override the ambiguous meaning contained in another version. In practice, the ECJ goes with the majority argument most of the time, and is more likely to rely on the teleological approach when it has to justify departure from the majority-language versions or when there is no clear majority.[90] In *Fonden Marselisborg Lystbådehavn v. Skatteministeriet*,[91] French, English, Italian, Spanish, Portuguese, German, and Finnish versions of Article 13B(b) of the Sixth Council Directive use a term for "vehicles" that covers general means of transport,[92] while the Swedish, Dutch, Greek, and Danish equivalents have a more limited meaning, covering only land-based transport. Although the Danish word *kjøretøjer* clearly refers to land-based transport on wheels, the court held that "vehicles" used in that provision must be interpreted as covering all means of transport, by reference to the purpose and general scheme of the rules of which it forms a part—that as a general rule, value added tax (VAT) should be charged on all taxable transactions unless derogations are expressly provided for, and as exceptions to the rule, the scope of derogations should be interpreted strictly.

Erla María Sveinbjörnsdóttir v. The Government of Iceland[93] is a comparable case, which concerns whether claims put forward by certain relatives of an insolvent person will be recognized as privileged claims. In point 24 of Annex

---

to which national courts engage in such routine comparisons in interpreting EU law, see Bobek, "The Multilingualism of the European Union Law in the National Courts: Beyond the Textbooks."

[88] Bobek, "The Multilingualism of the European Union Law in the National Courts: Beyond the Textbooks."

[89] Mattias Derlén, "In Defence of (Limited) Multilingualism: Problems and Possibilities of the Multilingual Interpretation of European Union Law in National Courts," in *Linguistic Diversity and European Democracy*, ed. Anne Lise Kjær and Silvia Adamo (Surrey, England; Burlington, VT: Ashgate, 2011), 143–66.

[90] Baaij, "Fifty Years of Multilingual Interpretation in the European Union."

[91] *Fonden Marselisborg Lystbådehavn v. Skatteministeriet* (Case C-428/02) [2005] ECR I-1527.

[92] In 13B(b)(2), "the letting of premises and sites for parking vehicles" is listed as an exception to the tax exemption laid down for the leasing and letting of immovable property.

[93] *Erla María Sveinbjörnsdóttir v. The Government of Iceland* Case E-9/97, December 10, 1998. This is not an ECJ but an EFTA case. The EEA covers 27 EU states and three of the EFTA states. The EFTA Court has jurisdiction with regard to EFTA states that are parties to the EEA Agreement (at present Iceland, Liechtenstein, and Norway) and is closely modeled upon the ECJ.

XVIII to the European Economic Area (EEA) Agreement, an expression meaning "direct relative" as used in the English, Norwegian, Danish, Greek, German, Swedish, Portuguese, Dutch, and Italian versions must be understood as covering siblings, but the corresponding term in Icelandic is *ættmenni í beinan legg*, which means "a line of ascendants and descendants" that does not cover siblings. Despite the clarity of what this term does not cover in Icelandic, the court held that "an error in the translation into Icelandic cannot change the meaning of the Directive." An Icelandic citizen cannot reasonably be expected to have read many language versions of the law, or to know that there might be an error or ambiguity in the text of the law they are relying on. However, as shown in this and the preceding case discussed, both the ECJ and the European Free Trade Association (EFTA) Court gave priority to uniformity of application of law over legitimate expectations from individuals.

EU courts sometimes even insist that one version of a text should never be considered in isolation, in order to ensure uniform application of EU law in all the member states. This was stated in *Erich Stauder v. City of Ulm*.[94] In this case, it was found that, unlike the French and Italian texts of an EC decision (Official Journal 1969 L 52/9), the German and Dutch texts imply that the sale of butter at a reduced price under certain warfare schemes is conditional on revealing to retailers the name of the beneficiary. Although the original decision was based on the French version, the court did not automatically give preference to it. Instead the court argued that

> [w]hen a single decision is addressed to all the Member States the necessity for uniform application and accordingly for uniform interpretation makes it impossible to consider one version of the text in isolation but requires that it be interpreted on the basis of both the real intention of its author and the aim he seeks to achieve, and in the light in particular of the versions in all four languages.

Taking a liberal interpretation of the four texts, the court held that the provision in question must be interpreted as not requiring—although it does not prohibit—the identification of beneficiaries by name. For the same reason, an EU lawyer who does not examine different authentic versions of the law may be accused of negligence.[95]

Although comparison across texts is often made, EU courts are extremely careful not to give the impression that one language is favored over another, even if the final outcome of interpretation coincides with the meaning

---

[94] *Erich Stauder v. City of Ulm* (Case 26/69) [1969] ECR 419. In this particular case, the court held that the most liberal interpretation should prevail, provided that it is sufficient to achieve the objectives pursued by the decision in question. The point was also made in *Sociale Verzekeringsbank v. Van der Vecht* (Case 19/67) [1967] ECR 345.

[95] Gambaro, "Interpretation of Multilingual Legislative Texts."

contained in one or more language versions. For instance, in *Helmut Müller GmbH v. Bundesanstalt für Immobilienaufgaben*,[96] the court drew no legal consequences from the discrepancies found in the terminology of "public works contract" across language texts, but based its interpretation on the purpose and general scheme of the law. It states that one should not be fixated with the text of the law, especially with a single text that represents it:

> The existence of these textual problems is a strong incentive for not attempting to find the "correct" interpretation of provisions through a strictly literal analysis of the provisions in question, especially if that analysis is confined to a single language version. In fact, the only possible guides in seeking the meaning to be attributed to the provisions are systematic interpretation and teleological interpretation, combined with a good sense of interpretation. (para 25)[97]

In *European Commission v. French Republic*,[98] where different language versions of the VAT Directive were found not to correspond, the court explicitly discusses how discrepancy between language versions increases indeterminacy. A term was rendered as *œuvre* ("an individual act") in French, while its English, Danish, Italian, Finnish, and Swedish counterparts refer to "an activity" in the general sense, and the German and Polish versions use even more general terms that refer to "a sector" or "a field." The court found that

> [a]n extrinsic ambiguity results from those variations between the language versions which strengthens the intrinsic ambiguity of the terms used in the French version of point 15 of Annex III to the VAT Directive. (para 53)

Although bilingualism and multilingualism might amplify indeterminacy, and the need to refer to multiple texts of the law might compromise accessibility to justice, some believe that it may have some jurisprudential advantages, especially where the number of language versions is three or more. For instance, Solan has argued that the proliferation of languages actually *assists* the ECJ in its interpretation of statutes by making it easier to discover the intended meaning of the law. He quotes Augustine: "The great remedy for ignorance of proper signs is knowledge of languages."[99] Baaij's data suggest that this

---

[96] *Helmut Müller GmbH v. Bundesanstalt für Immobilienaufgaben* [2010] Case C-451/08.

[97] A similar idea is conveyed in *Maatschap M.J.M. Linthorst, K.G.P. Pouwels en J. Scheren c.s. v. Inspecteur der Belastingdienst/Ondernemingen Roermond* [1997] Case C-167/95, where the court states in para. 14: "When interpreting a provision of Community legislation the Court seeks to develop a uniform interpretation of the text which accords with the real intention of the Community legislature and which is not necessarily influenced by the peculiarities of any one linguistic version of the various equally authentic texts."

[98] *European Commission v. French Republic* [2010] Case C-492/08. The case concerns whether France has failed to fulfill its obligations as an EU member state by reducing the rate of VAT for service providers of the government legal aid scheme.

[99] Solan, "The Interpretation of Multilingual Statutes by the European Court of Justice."

claim is true about one-third of the time. In 109 of the 170 ECJ judgments (approx. 64%) where discrepancies were discovered, the discrepancies were treated as an interpretive problem. In the remaining 61 judgments (approx. 36%), discrepancies were used as an interpretive tool that was used to support argument for an interpretation.[100] Lötscher argues similarly that in the case of Switzerland, the availability of three authentic versions of the law adds additional guide to interpretation and helps reveal problems in interpretation that may otherwise remain unnoticed if the legal instrument were written in one language only.[101] Of course, such benefit may only be reaped by an interpreter who has multilingual competence.

Rethinking Legal Interpretation

Bilingual and multilingual jurisdictions must make a difficult choice about language equality when they design their language law. Establishing a linguistic hierarchy might eliminate some potential complexities in statutory interpretation, but it comes with political and social costs. If language equality is upheld, on the other hand, then a legal fiction about translation equivalence, a shift toward teleological interpretation, and a widening distance between law and the texts that represent it seem to be inevitable consequences in legal interpretation. Where bilingual or multilingual texts of the law are equally authentic, it may be considered negligent to rely only on one version of the law, but the obligation to read all language versions is also a burden for the average citizen and may compromise transparency and predictability of the law. However, it is important to make clear that the problems of bilingual or multilingual interpretation are not created by the equal authenticity principle. Textual discrepancies may also be found between a legal text and its un-authenticated translations. By not granting translations legal force (such that they are for information purposes only), the state is simply transferring the consequences of textual discrepancies to the readers of such translation.

Monolingual jurisdictions tend to favor plain meaning,[102] and alternative interpretation methods are only explored when the plain meaning of the legislation is not clear or if it leads to an absurd result. In bilingual and multilingual jurisdictions, plain meaning is also a starting point of interpretation, but the very notion of the existence of a single textual meaning is abandoned, and routine comparison may take place even without alleged discrepancies. This is a profound change in legal interpretation: the presumption of where authority

---

[100] Baaij, "Fifty Years of Multilingual Interpretation in the European Union."
[101] Lötscher, "Multilingual Law Drafting in Switzerland."
[102] It is a basic rule of statutory construction in English courts.

resides is shifted away from the text, which becomes only one source of evidence for legislative intent. Jurisdictions adopting the equal authenticity rule often need to consider the combined meaning of all the authentic texts, and by so doing, effectively ignore the meaning of some of the individual texts. From this perspective, the literal meaning of one or more authentic texts might not have any regulatory value, despite its legal status. Legal meaning needs to be constructed from a mega text made up of all the authentic texts, in a process of harmonization during which part of the text dissolves and disappears. In a way, the fact that each text is authentic essentially means that no text is authentic. It is equivalent to saying to someone that the law will be written in your language, but you should not rely on it. This could be frustrating, and potentially devastating, to citizens governed by it, especially when it comes to criminal matters. While ignorance of the law is no defense, the fictional assumption that citizens can understand their rights and obligations may become even flimsier when citizens have no way of ascertaining what the law says by reading it in an official language that they can understand. A legal paradox seems inevitable in a multilingual legal order: the cost of linguistic inclusivity is that each constituent group of a multilingual jurisdiction has to surrender predictability of legal outcome derivable from a single-language version of the law.

Few would dispute that interpretive weight should be given to the purpose and object of the law. In fact, it may be a good thing that bilingual and multilingual interpretation forces attention to purpose. Judges are not obliged to focus on purpose when there is only one text of the law, which may or may not capture the intent of the legislature. However, judicial discretion widens as incongruent language versions of the law open up more candidates for correct interpretation by adding inter-lingual uncertainties on top of intra-lingual uncertainties, which are usually not discovered until the relevant sections are compared when applied in cases. There may also be interpretive freedom when it comes to which purpose of a statute should be prioritized, as the court navigates the sea of legislative history and debates. Therefore, even someone competent in all official languages could not reliably predict which purpose of a statute the court will give more weight to in the interpretation process. It is no longer true in this context that meaning may be found within the four corners of a legal document. Lord Oliver in *Black-Clawson* has said that "(i)ngenuity can sometimes suggest ambiguity or obscurity where none exists," and this may help to avoid injustice. In bilingual and multilingual jurisdictions, the amount of ingenuity for the task will be reduced, for two language versions of a text are almost bound to contain differences, even in the absence of blatant translation errors. Seen from this perspective, certainty of the law may diminish in a bilingual or multilingual jurisdiction, opening up the danger of ex post facto (after the facts) law[103] to a certain degree. In resolving interlingual discrepancies, judges need to mitigate between fair notice and fair adjudication.

On the other hand, the multiplicity of languages can also be seen as a resource to restrict the scope of judicial interpretation, as additional language versions provide unique cues to legal meaning that are not available in a monolingual jurisdiction[104] and that may resolve uncertainties arising from vagueness and ambiguity.[105] Opposing forces therefore compete to increase and decrease legal certainty, and the way these forces balance out may depend on individual cases and jurisdictions. In the context of international law, Butler reports that the multiplicity of authentic texts of international treaties has not led to a dramatic increase in international disputes that turn on textual disparity.[106]

From the perspective of individual cases, interlingual indeterminacies threaten to enlarge legal uncertainty and judicial discretion, but it may be argued that the resolution of indeterminacy in individual cases produces greater determinacy in the wider system going forward. The law implicitly or explicitly changes when intralingual indeterminacies are resolved, but the problem of indeterminacy may be eased by the iterative practice of judicial interpretation over time. This is how case law generally works in common law jurisdictions. However, this systems perspective does not eliminate concerns about the problem of indeterminacy in individual cases and the limited linguistic access to the law by lay people. In order to access the relatively determinate meaning of a legislative text as established by case law, lay people will need the competence to navigate interpretive history. Depending on the availability and competence of legal representation, private parties to a case may have very unequal starting points in their grasp of the law. In essence, the kinds of interpretive problems that multilingualism brings about are not necessarily distinctive, but they exacerbate problems that always exist.

Furthermore, the multiplicity of legal languages forces us to rethink the relationship between language and the law, and to re-assess the capacities and limitations of human language. As mentioned earlier, courts in multilingual jurisdictions do not confine themselves to "any or even all of the texts,"[107] but may search for the true legislative intent of the given provision. In other words,

---

[103] Law applied retroactively to a past action that changes its legal consequences; this is generally prohibited and frowned upon.

[104] Solan argues that multiplicity of languages gives courts more room to achieve fidelity to the intention of the legislation, but he also cautioned that if the languages are too different, the amount of discretion available to a court might become too broad. Solan, "The Interpretation of Multilingual Statutes by the European Court of Justice."

[105] Deborah Cao, "Inter-Lingual Uncertainty in Bilingual and Multilingual Law," *Journal of Pragmatics* 39, no. 1 (January 2007): 69–83, https://doi.org/10.1016/j.pragma.2006.08.005.

[106] W. E. Butler, "Comparative Approaches to International Law," *Recueil Des Cours* 190, no. 9 (1985): 58–61.

[107] Klimas and Vaiciukaite, "Interpretation of European Union Multilingual Law," 9.

multilingual interpretation forces the interpreter to see that legal knowledge transcends language, or that language does not fully capture the law. This insight, made visible by the bilingual and multilingual context, applies to any jurisdiction. As one of the pioneering scholars of legal bilingualism MacDonald has observed,

> Between the illusion of homogeneous, neutral, determinate legal language and the illusion of contingent, arbitrary, indeterminate legal language lies the insight of legal bilingualism. Legal bilingualism (or more radically, legal multilingualism) takes as given that the complete normative content of the law cannot be expressed by a particular set of words in one or any number of languages; but it also takes as given that language is a privileged communicative symbolism for apprehending law's normativity. All law, given this insight, is multilingual.[108]

Legal multilingualism makes it more defensible to depart from the text of the law. A central issue in legal theory is whether judges "make" law rather than "find" law that has been laid down by the legislature.[109] US Supreme Court Justice Antonin Scalia criticizes judge-made law and argues that legal interpretation should be based on the original, textual meaning of statutes (a position known as textualism, which may be considered a kind of originalism, in the sense of original meaning rather than original intent). Textualists believe that "judges must seek and abide by the public meaning of the enacted text, understood in context."[110] Neither textualism nor the Plain Meaning Rule (or Literal rule) in statutory construction sits well with the idea that language may not fully capture legal meaning. On the other hand, the foundations of multilingual statutory interpretation seem to be compatible with both classical intentionalism, which treats meaning as what the speaker intends to convey, and the purposive theory, which upholds the importance of legislative purpose.

Although much of this chapter highlights what may happen when discrepancies occur, Solan reminds us that hard cases should not be overstated, and that, notwithstanding the indeterminacy of language, most of the time law works fairly well.[111] Indeed, interlingual discrepancies are found only in a minority of cases, in all the jurisdictions referred to in this chapter. However, these are also jurisdictions that have a mature legal system, with ample resources for legislative drafting. When thinking about the phenomenon of legal multilingualism at a global scale, separation of powers, rule of law, reliable

---

[108] Macdonald, "Legal Bilingualism," 126.

[109] Hutton, *Language, Meaning and the Law*; Solan, *The Language of Statutes*.

[110] John F. Manning, "Textualism and Legislative Intent," *Virginia Law Review* 91 (2005): 420.

[111] See Solan, *The Language of Statutes*, focusing on monolingual statutes in the United States; Solan, "Multilingualism and Morality in Statutory Interpretation," focusing on bilingual and multilingual legislation in Canada and the European Union.

legal translation, and democracy (a basis for legislative supremacy) cannot be treated as a given, and the implications of widening judicial discretion cannot be underestimated. The risk that textual discrepancies are exploited by judicial mischief needs to be assessed in the local context.

Considering the political circumstances that drive the establishment of a multilingual regime, judges arguably have a special moral duty to be faithful to legislative goals in constructing bilingual and multilingual laws, as Solan argues:

> The goal in creating such regimes is in large part to balance the ceding of political power to a higher order governmental structure, while at the same time showing respect for the autonomy of the individual groups whose power has been ceded. . . . When the question is a matter of respect for national sovereignty as it is in the EU, or of respect for a large minority in exchange for their remaining in the larger legal order, as it is in Canada, the stakes go up.[112]

On the whole, official multilingualism appears to challenge legal certainty. However, legal certainty, which helps people understand the law they are governed by, is not an absolute good. The interpretive space that is opened by official multilingualism may potentially be exploited to promote minority interests and to provide room for pluralistic conceptions of justice. However, such potential is at the mercy of judicial consciousness.

112 Solan, "Multilingualism and Morality in Statutory Interpretation," 19.

Chapter 7

Conferring Official Language Rights in Legal Communication

ACCESS TO JUSTICE AND CONFLICT OF LAWS

> . . . the most brutal of truths: that, in the ordinary course of things, power produces rights, not rights power; that law is itself a product of the political, not a prime mover in constructing social worlds; that law, alone, is not what separates order from chaos or an equitable society from a state of savagery.
>
> —John Comaroff and Jean Comaroff[1]

We have seen that implementing legislation of official multilingualism can lead to the creation of duties on the part of the government, mostly in terms of multilingual service provision by public bodies. This chapter turns to the question of the extent to which official multilingualism has also created enforceable rights in legal processes.

Linguistic barriers may be encountered in any type of legal communication, even where everyone supposedly speaks the same language, for legalese is characteristically difficult to understand.[2] The most severe types of barriers are typically removed by mandating linguistic accommodation where non-communication or gross miscommunication is likely. This is part of due process and fair trial rights that are derived from a natural justice rationale. To understand the nature of official language rights, two questions are asked in this chapter. The first is a practical one—whether and how official language law enhances language rights for the communities concerned. A comparative approach will be taken to answer this question. The second question is a philosophical one. Should language rights that are derived from official status be distinguished from language rights that are derived from fair trial rights? Are the former more like privileges than rights? Since natural justice rationale only

---

[1] John L. Comaroff and Jean Comaroff, "Criminal Justice, Cultural Justice: The Limits of Liberalism and the Pragmatics of Difference in the New South Africa," *American Ethnologist* 31, no. 2 (2004): 192.

[2] Tiersma, *Legal Language*.

seeks to ensure effective communication and fair trial, and is indifferent to the choice of particular languages, the enlargement of language rights through official status must be justified through additional principles. Courts in multilingual jurisdictions have been trying to come up with persuasive principles that justify the derivation of language rights from official status. Such rights have been granted based on a constitutional promise about linguistic equality, the cultural survival of official language communities, or respect for the cultural identity of these communities. These rights may conflict with other legal norms and lead to conflict of rights.

The Notion of Language Rights

Language-specific rights in national laws and international treaties as a component of minority protection actually predate the contemporary notion of human rights by more than a century.[3] Language-related rights penetrate all three generations of human rights[4] and encompass a broad array of issues, from freedom of expression to personality and educational rights. The first two generations of human rights—focused on individual freedom and equality—prohibit discrimination based on language,[5] whereas the third generation of human rights instruments[6] attempt, in a non-legally binding way, to promote linguistic diversity and the collective rights of minority groups[7]. Since the freedom to use any language in a private domain is guaranteed in international law as a component of the freedom of expression,[8] contention about language rights mostly concerns the public domain.

---

[3] André Braën, "Language Rights," in *Language Rights in Canada*, ed. Michel Bastarache (Montréal, Que: Les Editions Yvon Blais, 1987), 3–67; Stephen Tierney, "Reflections on the Evolution of Language Rights," in *Languages, Constitutionalism and Minorities*, ed. André Braën, Pierre Foucher, and Yves Le Bouthillier (Markham, ON: LexisNexis Butterworths, 2006), 3–27.

[4] The first generation of rights is civil-political, the second socioeconomic, and the third is known to be collective-developmental. See Fernand de Varennes, "The Existing Rights of Minorities in International Law," in *Language, a Right and a Resource: Approaching Linguistic Human Rights*, ed. Miklós Kontra et al. (Budapest; New York: Central European University Press, 1999), 117–46.

[5] Such as the Universal Declaration of Human Rights of the United Nations (1948) and the European Convention on Human Rights (1950).

[6] Such as the UN Declaration on the Rights of Persons belonging to National or Ethnic, Religious and Linguistic Minorities (1992), the European Charter for Regional or Minority Languages (1992), the Oslo Recommendations regarding the Linguistic Rights of National Minorities (1998), and the UN Declaration on the Rights of Indigenous Peoples (2007).

[7] For an excellent overview, see Robert Dunbar, "Minority Language Rights in International Law", *International and Comparative Law Quarterly* 50, No. 1, (January 2001): 90–120.

[8] In *Ballantyne, Davidson, McIntyre v. Canada* (Communications Nos. 359/1989 and 385/1989), a case that deals with the banning of English-language advertising in Quebec, the UN Human Rights Committee held that "a State may choose one or more official languages, but it may not exclude, outside the spheres of public life, the freedom to express oneself in a language of one's choice." See also Article 19, 26, and 27 of the International Covenant on Civil and Political Rights.

The development of *language rights*, or its variant *linguistic human rights* (LHR), as a stand-alone concept is relatively recent, and has not fully achieved internal coherence. These concepts typically refer to newer formulations of language-related rights (e.g., see the Universal Declaration of Linguistic Rights of 1996,[9] or related advocacy[10]) that seek positive measures from governments in the protection of languages and accommodation of minority language use in the public domain. Language rights advocacy mainly focuses on the right to instruction and public services in one's language, especially for minority-language speakers, with the hope of ensuring language survival across generations. The right to learn an official language has also been discussed. Although states generally have the autonomy to decide their own official language policy, de Varennes argues that there is an increased expectation—though not a legal obligation—for states to offer public services in minority languages on a sliding-scale basis (i.e., the larger the minority community, the higher the expectation).[11]

Some language rights are protected by means of fundamental human rights such as freedom of expression, right to education, right to a fair trial, and non-discrimination. Consider, first, three cases that concern freedom of expression and non-discrimination. In *Sidiropoulos and others v. Greece*,[12] applicants who claim to be of Macedonian ethnic origin applied to form a non-profit association called "Home of Macedonian Civilisation" in Florina, northern Greece. The Florina Court of First Instance refused to register the association, citing that the association's promotion of "the idea that there is a Macedonian minority in Greece" is "contrary to the country's national interest." The Salonika Court of Appeal affirmed the rejection, using extensive historical research to argue that the Macedonian language was one of the oldest Greek dialects and the Macedonian civilization is but part of Greek civilization, and calling the proposed association's aims "dubious" propaganda. The decision was upheld in the Court of Cassation. In a similar case, *Yazar and others v. Turkey*,[13] the Turkish Constitutional Court ordered to dissolve a Kurdish association, the People's Labour Party, pointing out that propaganda based on racial difference threatens Turkey's national and territorial integrity. When these two cases reached the European Court of Human Rights, the state in question was held to offend the freedom of association.[14] In the third case,[15] the banning of publications of

[9] Available on http://www.unesco.org/cpp/uk/declarations/linguistic.pdf. The document has been signed by the International PEN Club, and some institutions and nongovernmental organizations, but has not been ratified by the United Nations or UNESCO.

[10] Skutnabb-Kangas, *Linguistic Genocide in Education—or Worldwide Diversity and Human Rights?*

[11] Fernand de Varennes, "Language as a Right in International Law: Limits and Potentials," in *Language Rights Revisited: The Challenge of Global Migration and Communication*, ed. Dagmar Richter et al. (Oisterwijk; Berlin: Wolf Legal Publishers; Berliner Wissenschafts-Verlag, 2012), 41–61.

[12] *Sidiropoulos and others v. Greece*, Application No. 26695/95, July 10, 1998.

[13] *Yazar and others v. Turkey*, Application No. 22723/93, April 9, 2002.

[14] Article 11 of the Convention for the Protection of Human Rights and Fundamental Freedoms.

[15] *Ekin Association v. France*, Application No. 39288/98, July 17, 2001.

foreign origin in France was deemed to violate freedom of expression and potentially also non-discrimination (a question that the court found unnecessary to determine). Language rights may also be derived from the right to education. The European Court of Human Rights ruled in a Belgian case[16] that the right to education, a basic human right, does not entail the right to be educated in the language of one's parents. On the other hand, in *Cyprus v. Turkey*,[17] the provision of primary schooling in Greek by the Northern Cyprus government without follow-up at the secondary school level was held to be a breach of the right to education.

Language rights may also flow from other legal rights that are not universal human rights. In Europe, some language rights are derived from other freedoms and rights proffered in European laws, and a supranational standard of language rights has emerged.[18] In *Anton Las v. PSA Antwerp NV.*,[19] the Court of Justice of the European Union held that although member states have the freedom to adopt an official language policy, a decree that requires employment contracts to be drafted in Dutch (where the place of business is in the Dutch-language region) violates the freedom of movement for workers within the European Union. In other words, parties should be free to draft their cross-border employment contract in a language other than an official language of the member states concerned. Language rights may also lead to decisions that have implications that are far from purely linguistic. In Canada, the closure of a francophone hospital in Ontario was successfully challenged based on protection of rights of the francophone minority (*Lalonde v. Ontario*[20]).

Language rights that are derived from basic legal rights (such as fair trial) are applied universally. Such universally applicable language rights, whether granted by nations or international human rights instruments, tend to be limited in scope. For example, Section 32 of the South African Constitution provides that every person shall have the right to instruction in the language of his or her choice where this is reasonably practicable, leaving no doubt that this right is far from being an absolute right and that its realization is subject to resource constraints.

Language rights that flow from minority rights are not applied universally. There are a few international human rights instruments[21] that focus on the rights of certain linguistic minority groups—usually by distinguishing old and new migrants. These language rights tend to focus on the communicative needs

---

[16] *Cases Relating to Certain Aspects of the Laws on the Use of Languages in Education in Belgium*, Applications No. 1474/62; 1677/62; 1691/62; 1769/63; 1994/63; 2126/64, July 23, 1968.

[17] *Cyprus v. Turkey*, Application No. 25781/94, May 10, 2001.

[18] de Witte, "Language Rights: The Interaction between Domestic and European Development."

[19] *Anton Las v. PSA Antwerp NV.*, Case C-202/11 [2013], ECLI:EU:C:2013:239.

[20] *Lalonde v. Ontario*, 2001 CanLII 21164 (ON CA).

[21] Such as UN Declaration on the Rights of Persons Belonging to National or Ethnic, Religious and Linguistic Minorities and Framework Convention for the Protection of National Minorities.

of minorities and cultural expressions in the private domain, and do not entertain their identity claims in dealing with public authorities.[22]

By contrast, language rights that are derived from the official status of a language are legal rights conferred by a government, or deduced by judges when they interpret the meaning of such status. They usually apply to particular languages, and may be claimed by individuals based on a personality or territoriality principle.[23] For example, the right to receive education in one's first language has been derived from the official status of a language or granted as a minority right in some states. The Sami Language Act 2003, for example, guarantees this right for Sami in Finland.

Following from the discussion in Chapter 4, since official status does not have a fixed meaning, there is no language right inherently tied to it. But official status provides the ground for asserting and negotiating language rights. Although official language rights affect numerous aspects of public and private life, the most direct sites that they impact are public institutions and legal processes. Having examined how official language law affects public institutions in Chapter 4, the next section will focus on its relevance to legal processes and will consider what kinds of language rights have been derived from official status.

Official Language Rights in Multilingual Courtrooms

Language rights affect many aspects of trial proceedings, from the medium of a trial to the translation of documents. Of course, some basic language rights are also recognized in monolingual jurisdictions, but here we will specifically focus on language rights derived from official status in a multilingual environment.

THE RIGHT TO AN INTERPRETER

Quality of courtroom interpretation is a problem facing any jurisdiction when local or foreign speakers of non-official languages come into contact with the legal system. Given that the relevant literature is sizable[24] and that this problem

[22] Mowbray, *Linguistic Justice*. See also Paz for a comprehensive review of case law in the international language rights regime, which reveal a huge gap between promise and practice. Moria Paz, "The Failed Promise of Language Rights: A Critique of the International Language Rights Regime," *Harvard International Law Journal* 54, No. 1 (2013): 157–218.

[23] Under the personality principle, citizens can claim the official language right anywhere within the jurisdiction of a polity; under a territorial principle, the right may be claimed within a geographical region of the polity, and different territories of a polity may have different official language policies. Official bilingualism in Canada follows a personality principle, and official language rights in Switzerland follow a territorial principle. See discussion in Patten and Kymlicka, "Introduction: Language Rights and Political Theory: Context, Issues, and Approaches."

[24] See, for example, Berk-Seligson, *The Bilingual Courtroom*; Sandra Beatriz Hale, *The Discourse of Court Interpreting: Discourse Practices of the Law, the Witness, and the Interpreter* (Amsterdam: John Benjamins, 2004).

is not specific to bilingual and multilingual jurisdictions, it will not receive detailed treatment here. Rather, this section will discuss the more basic issue of access to courtroom interpretation, and interpretation problems that are more peculiar to bilingual and multilingual courtrooms.

Defendants in criminal cases have the basic human right to receive the assistance of an interpreter in court if they do not understand or cannot speak the language of the court. This is provided in the International Covenant on Civil and Political Rights (ICCPR). However, at the time of writing, 26 UN states[25] have not yet ratified or acceded to the ICCPR. Approximately one-fifth of the world's population (or 21%, according to 2015 data on www.cia.gov) live in these states. Even signatory states sometimes fail to appoint an interpreter, set a questionably low language proficiency standard in deciding whether a person needs a court interpreter, or offer an interpreter who does not speak the same language variety.[26] The point is that it cannot be taken for granted that this right is fully respected. It should also be noted that the right to an interpreter only applies to criminal defendants. As pointed out by Eades, "there is no such right addressing witnesses (i.e., those who are not defendants), parties in a civil court, or indeed L2 speakers in any other legal contexts, such as lawyer interview, mediation session, or police interview."[27]

In a monolingual jurisdiction, access to interpreter is provided only to ensure fair trial, and is thus typically contingent upon one's ability to understand or speak the language of the court. In other words, no interpreter is provided to someone who is able to communicate in the language of the court. For example, if you are a native German speaker appearing in German court, you cannot suddenly request to speak in Swahili and ask for an interpreter. In France, a Breton[28] native speaker was charged with defacing road signs in French by painting over them and making them bilingual in French and Breton. The French court did not allow him to testify in Breton and have his testimony interpreted in French. Even though he claims that he expresses himself best in Breton, he was deemed to be capable of speaking and understanding French. The UN Human Rights Committee held that the right to have

---

[25] States that have signed but not ratified include China, Comoros, Cuba, Nauru, Palau, Sao Tome and Principe, and Saint Lucia. States that have neither signed nor ratified include Antigua and Barbuda, Bhutan, Brunei, Fiji, Kiribati, Malaysia, Marshall Islands, Federated States of Micronesia, Myanmar, Oman, Qatar, Saint Kitts and Nevis, Saudi Arabia, Singapore, Solomon Islands, South Sudan, Tonga, Tuvalu, and United Arab Emirates.

[26] See Lynn W. Davis et al., "The Changing Face of Justice: A Survey of Recent Cases Involving Courtroom Interpretation," *Harvard Latino Law Review* 7 (2004): 1, for some of such cases that took place in the United States.

[27] Diana Eades, "Participation of Second Language and Second Dialect Speakers in the Legal System," *Annual Review of Applied Linguistics* 23 (March 2003): 114, https://doi.org/10.1017/S0267190503000229.

[28] Breton is a minority language native to Brittany in France.

the assistance of an interpreter could only be claimed if he did not understand or speak the language of the court (*Guesdon v. France*[29]). In a UK case,[30] an Irish speaker in Northern Ireland was not permitted to lodge a court application for an occasional liquor license drafted in Irish. The applicant argued that the Administration of Justice (Language) Act (Ireland) of 1737, which requires that court proceedings take place in English in Northern Ireland, is incompatible with the European Charter for Regional and Minority Languages and the European Convention on Human Rights and Fundamental Freedoms. However, the court held that his rights were not violated because he fully understood English. In cases like this, the request for linguistic accommodation was made not to tear down a communication barrier, but to bring an identity struggle into the courtroom, by challenging the existing language practice of a legal regime.

In some jurisdictions that practice official multilingualism, by contrast, one may choose to use another official language and request an interpreter even if one is fluent in the official language that the trial takes place in. This applies not only to criminal defendants but also to litigants, witnesses, and other courtroom participants. For example, since becoming an official language in New Zealand, Maori may be used in legal proceedings by any member of the court, party, witness, counsel, or any person with leave of the presiding officer, whether or not they can understand or communicate in English (Māori Language Act 1987, s4). An interpreter will then be assigned to them. This is an example of language rights that are assigned to particular languages and are derived from official status.

A challenge to determining the right to an interpreter is the elusive definition of "language": for example, whether an official "language" comprises one or more varieties,[31] and whether dialectal speakers of an official "language" are entitled to an interpreter. This is a difficult issue that tends to be decided on an ad hoc, case-by-case basis. Varieties of a language may be mutually intelligible, unintelligible, or somewhere along the scale. In Hong Kong, other Chinese dialects are routinely interpreted to and from Cantonese, even when all participants can understand both the original and the interpreted utterances. On the other hand, interpretation is usually not provided between varieties of English, which is also an official language of Hong Kong. An ethnographic study done across the border in mainland China reports that defendants whose

---

[29] *Guesdon v. France*, Communication No. 219/1986, U.N. Doc. CCPR/C/39/D/219/1986 (1990).

[30] *In re the Administration of Justice (Language) Act (Ireland)* 1737 [2009] NIQB 66.

[31] This has been publicly debated in Hong Kong, where Chinese and English are official languages, with no conclusive outcome. Justice Hartmann in *Cheng Kai Nam, Gary v. HKSAR* (2001) commented, *obiter*, that he assumes Chinese to refer to "Cantonese, as opposed to other languages/or dialects that fall under the description of 'Chinese'" for Cantonese is spoken by the great majority of the local population. On the other hand, in 2014 the website of the Education Bureau stirred up a storm by claiming that Cantonese is just a "dialect" and "not an official language."

first language is Nigerian Pidgin English received assistance from English-Chinese interpreters who have limited sensitivities to non-standard varieties of English and have difficulty understanding the defendants.[32] Speakers of non-standard varieties are likely to face the same challenge in many parts of the world.

THE RIGHT TO SPEAK IN AN OFFICIAL LANGUAGE OF ONE'S CHOICE

Inseparable is the right to speak in an official language. Can someone who is proficient in the language of the trial nevertheless request to speak in another official language? Even though a person may be able to communicate in a designated official language, this may not be the language the speaker identifies and feels most comfortable with, considering that multilinguals tend to use their language skills in different contexts. One is likely to for example, feel more emotional resonance with the first language that one learns to speak.[33] Insisting on using one's first language in an official context may of course also be a way of making an identity and cultural claim in language politics, through asserting the legitimacy of a minority language in an official setting. The right to speak in an official language of one's choice is provided in some relatively advanced multilingual jurisdictions, such as Canada,[34] Finland,[35] Ireland,[36] and Hong Kong.[37]. This right can potentially enable defendants and litigants to better express themselves and feel less stressed in the formal courtroom environment, and thus arguably improve access to justice. But of course this improvement is available only to speakers of official languages.

This right is not recognized in all bilingual and multilingual jurisdictions, especially where some languages have been granted official language status for symbolic purposes only, or where resources are limited. Despite the official status of the Hawaiian language (alongside with English) in State of Hawaii, Tagupa, a plaintiff of Native Hawaiian ancestry, was not allowed to respond in Hawaiian in his oral disposition. He claimed that this violated the Hawaii Constitution and the 1990 Native American Languages Act and appealed to the United States District Court (D. Hawaii).[38] The court rejected

---

[32] Biyu Du, "The Bilingual Trial: Access to Interpreting, Communication, and Participation in Chinese Criminal Courts" (The University of Hong Kong, 2016).

[33] Nelson Mandela has this famous quote, "If you talk to a man in a language he understands, that goes to his head. If you talk to him in his language, that goes to his heart."

[34] Section 133 of the Constitution Act 1867: ". . . either of those Languages may be used by any Person or in any Pleading or Process in or issuing from any Court of Canada established under this Act."

[35] Finnish and Swedish may be used in any court cases (Language Act 2003); Sami may also be used in some municipalities (Sami Language Act 2003).

[36] Article 8 of Official Languages Act 2003.

[37] Cap. 5 of Official Languages Ordinance.

[38] *Tagupa v. Odo*, 843 F.Supp. 630 (D. Haw. 1994).

his claim, reasoning that neither the Hawaii Constitution nor the Native American Languages Act grants the right of giving oral deposition testimony in the Hawaiian language. It further argued that because the plaintiff is fluent in English, using a Hawaiian interpreter "would needlessly complicate and delay the deposition process," which is contrary to the Federal Rules of Civil Procedure. Here the court limited language rights to fair trial considerations and did not wish to extend language rights based on official status, unless such rights are explicitly provided for in the law. By contrast, official recognition of Welsh has brought about the right to speak in an official language in Wales. Under the Welsh Courts Act of 1942, it was a matter of judicial discretion whether a Welsh-speaking person could testify in Welsh in court, and the applicant's English proficiency was part of the consideration. Since the repeal of said Act and the enactment of the Welsh Language Act in 1993, the English and the Welsh language are to be treated equally in the public sector, and the Welsh language may be spoken by any party in any legal proceedings in Wales (S22), regardless of their proficiency in English. This means that linguistic equality, rather than fair trial, is the guiding principle here.

There are associated procedural issues that come with this right. For example, where the accused enjoys the right to use an official language of his or her choice, the question arises as to whether the accused is properly informed of it. This was one of the issues raised in a review of Part XVII of the Criminal Code (Language of Accused) published by The House of Commons of Canada.[39] Under this law, the judge bears the responsibility of ensuring that an accused is informed of his or her right, either personally or by counsel. Where the obligation to advise is breached, a common remedy is to order a new trial.

THE RIGHT TO BE UNDERSTOOD IN AN OFFICIAL LANGUAGE OF ONE'S CHOICE

How often does the right to speak in an official language (by a litigant/defendant) translate into the right to be understood (directly, not via an interpreter) in that language? The right to argue a case in one's own language is of strategic value in adversarial trials, where rhetorical resources may be crucial in legal argumentation but may be lost in translation. Can a defendant demand that a particular official language be used as the medium of trial proceedings, or that a judge who can understand a particular official language presides over his or her trial? Should the approval of such an application be conditioned upon the defendant's language proficiency? How might this proficiency be measured, and by whom?

---

[39] "Statutory Review of Part XVII of the Criminal Code" (The Standing Committee on Justice and Human Rights, House of Commons, 41st Parliament, Second Session, April 2014).

The official status of a language leads to the expectation that one is free to choose it as the medium of a trial. But only a few bilingual and multilingual jurisdictions have derived the right to be understood from its official language law.

One of these is Canada, which grants the right to be heard by a judge who understands the official language of one's choice in all criminal cases (Section 530 of the Criminal Code allows for a case to be tried by a judge or judge and jury who speak the official language of the accused's choice), in civil cases before federal courts (other than the Supreme Court of Canada), and in some provincial courts. Earlier court decisions were conservative about conferring this right. In a trilogy of cases involving the interpretation of section 133 of the Constitutional Act 1867,[40] the Supreme Court of Canada held that the right to "use" an official language in courts is a speaker right and does not apply to recipients of communication. The court was concerned about conflict of rights—granting the right to be understood may deprive other people's freedom to use the language of their choice. A more generous interpretation was applied in the landmark case of *R. v. Beaulac*,[41] when the Supreme Court of Canada was called on to analyze section 530 of the Criminal Code. The court granted the accused a new trial before a judge and jury who speak both official languages, and established that this right is not derived from the right to a fair trial, but rather from the country's guarantee of equality between the two official languages. It is absolute and substantive. The defendant's native language and ability to speak the other official language are irrelevant, because the accused should be able to freely and subjectively assert either official language as part of his/her cultural identity. The court argued that

> [l]anguage rights are not negative rights, or passive rights; they can only be enjoyed if the means are provided. This is consistent with the notion favoured in the area of international law that the freedom to choose is meaningless in the absence of a duty of the State to take positive steps to implement language guarantees. (para 20)

But the right may be denied to an applicant who cannot competently speak the official language of his or her choice, for otherwise the purpose of the relevant provisions would be defeated. This was the case in *Ontario (Attorney General) v. Fleet Rent-a-Car Ltd.*[42] and *Children's Aid Society of Toronto v. W.F.*,[43] where

---

[40] *MacDonald v. City of Montreal*, 1 S.C.R. 460 (1986); *Société des Acadiens v. Association of Parents*, 1 S.C.R. 549 (1986); *Bilodeau v. A. G. Manitoba*, 1 S.C.R. 449 (1986).

[41] *R. v. Beaulac*, 1 S.C.R. 768 (1999).

[42] *Ontario (Attorney General) v. Fleet Rent-A-Car Ltd.* [2002] O.J. No. 4693, 2002 CarswellOnt 428629, C.P.C. (5th) 315.

[43] *Children's Aid Society of Toronto v. W.F.* [2014] O.J. No. 4338, 2014 ONCJ 480 (CanLII).

applicants who had limited French requested that their trial be held in French in an apparent attempt to stall proceedings.

Criminal cases are prosecuted by the state, which typically bears the legal burden of linguistic accommodation. Civil cases, on the other hand, are disputes between private parties, and balancing their language rights is a more complicated issue. In Canada, provincial policies differ, and bilingual jury is only available in certain areas for civil cases. In Ontario, French litigants enjoy the right to a bilingual court, as guaranteed by the Courts of Justice Act.[44] In bilingual proceedings, the judge, prosecutor, registrar/clerk, and the court reporter/monitor are all bilingual. This right is not qualified by judicial discretion, even in a case where a party was seemingly attempting to delay the proceedings by manipulating the bilingual obligation of the courts (*Belende v. Patel*[45]).

Where the language preference of different trial participants appears to be in conflict, the trial judge can order a bilingual trial when the circumstances warrant it. In *Sarrazin*[46] and more recently in *Munkonda*,[47] one or more of the defendants petitioned for the trial to be conducted in English only, and the rest asked for a French-only trial. In both cases it was decided that the proper thing to do would be to conduct a bilingual trial, which does not vitiate the defendants' right to be tried in the official language of their choice. An alternative approach was adopted in the case of *Armeni*,[48] where one defendant was French speaking and the other one was English speaking. The Quebec Superior Court ordered separate trials for the defendants to reduce the amount of simultaneous translation needed in a bilingual trial. In justifying the decision, Brunton, J., expressed concern that one of the official languages will inevitably become dominant in a bilingual trial.

A similar, somewhat less extensive, right has also developed in Ireland. With the purpose of reinstating the use of the Irish language in public bodies, the Official Languages Act of 2003 provides in Section 8 that a person has the right to use and be heard in the official language of his or her choice, in any civil or criminal proceedings.[49] For criminal trials, in the leading case *Ó Beoláin v. Fahy*,[50] the defendant was deemed to have the right to defend his case in Irish and to have the relevant statutes and rules of court served to him in Irish. It is established that as far as practicable, a judge who speaks Irish would be assigned if so requested, in Courts of Districts that include Irish-speaking

---

[44] Section 126(1): "A party to a proceeding who speaks French has the right to require that it be conducted as a bilingual proceeding."

[45] *Belende v. Patel*, 2008 ONCA 148.

[46] *R. v. Sarrazin* [2005] 196 O.A.C. 224 (CA).

[47] *R. v. Munkonda*, 2015 ONCA 309.

[48] *Armeni v. R.* [2007] Q.J. No. 3821 (Quebec Superior Court, District of Terrebonne).

[49] Note, however, that the 1948 Irish Constitution does allow the legislature to make provisions for the exclusive use of one official language for particular official purposes (Article 8).

[50] *Ó Beoláin v. Fahy* [2001] 2 IR 279.

areas.[51] However, when it comes to requests for an Irish-speaking or bilingual jury, applications have been rejected on multiple occasions (*MacCárthaigh v. Éire*;[52] *Ó Maicín v. Éire*[53]), based on the ground that this linguistic criterion will exclude a significant portion of the population who are eligible to serve as jurors. As for civil cases, where the state is party to the case, the official language chosen by the other party shall be used. In case there are two or more persons to the party and they do not agree on the use of an official language, the state shall use an official language that is reasonable in regard to the circumstances (Section 8 of the Official Languages Act of 2003). Between private parties, the right to have a case heard in an official language of one's choice is confined to a right to conduct the litigant's own side of the case in that language (reinforced in *Ó Monacháin v. An Taoiseach*[54]).

In Wales, the scope of the right reflects the limited sovereignty of the country. Civil trials and hearings before magistrates may take place in Welsh or bilingually, but trials in Crown Courts are in English.[55] A Welsh-speaking judge is assigned wherever practicable in cases where the Welsh language may be used,[56] but jurors may not be selected on the basis of Welsh language ability.[57] However, the geographical restriction of the 1993 Welsh Language Act means that when cases go on higher appellate courts, as in the case of *Williams v. Cowell*[58] when an employment dispute escalated from a local tribunal to the Employment Appeal Tribunal in London, they will have to take place in English.

Finland offers constitutional protection of the right to use Finnish or Swedish before courts of law and to receive official documents in that language (Section 17 of the Constitution of Finland). When a court is located in a bilingual municipality, the official language spoken by the defendant will be used as the language of the trial. In the event that different parties to the trial request

---

[51] S71 of the Courts of Justice Act 1924: "So far as may be practicable having regard to all relevant circumstances the Justice of the District Court assigned to a District which includes an area where the Irish language is in general use shall possess such a knowledge of the Irish language as would enable him to dispense with the assistance of an interpreter when evidence is given in that language."

[52] *MacCárthaigh v Éire* [1999] 1 IR 186.

[53] *Ó Maicín v. Éire* [2010] IEHC 179.

[54] *Ó Monacháin v. An Taoiseach* [1986] ILRM 660.

[55] Justice Thomas et al., "Bilingual Lawmaking and Justice: A Report on the Lessons for Wales from the Canadian Experience of Bilingualism" (Office of the Counsel General, April 4, 2006).

[56] III.23.7 of The Consolidated Criminal Practice Direction: "The listing officer, in consultation with the resident judge, should ensure that a case in which the Welsh language may be used is listed (a) wherever practicable before a Welsh speaking judge, and (b) in a court in Wales with simultaneous translation facilities."

[57] III.23.5 of The Consolidated Criminal Practice Direction: "The law does not permit the selection of jurors in a manner which enables the court to discover whether a juror does or does not speak Welsh or to secure a jury whose members are bilingual to try a case in which the Welsh language may be used."

[58] *Williams v. Cowell* [2000] 1 WLR 187.

to use different official languages, the court decides on the language of the proceedings with regard to the rights and interests of the parties. If the language cannot be decided on this basis, local demographics will be considered—the language of the majority in the court district will be used (Section 12-17 of Language Act 2003). The Sami Language Act 2003 also provides for the use of the Sami language in Finnish courts that covers the jurisdictions of Enontekiö, Inari, Sodankylä, and Utsjoki.

In EU courts, the language of a case may be Irish[59] (Gaelic) or any of its official languages.[60] The language of a case is chosen by the applicant in the case of direct actions, except where the defendant is a member state, in which case the official language of the member state will be used, or where the parties agree otherwise.

The right to be heard in an official language is not recognized in the bilingual jurisdiction of Hong Kong, where the language of the trial is a matter of discretion for the judge (Section 5 of Official Languages Ordinance). The judge can decide to try a case in English, in Chinese, or in a combination (for example, Cantonese for oral evidence and English for submissions). In *Cheng Kai Nam*,[61] the defendant, who is conversant in English, requested that his case be presided by a judge who can understand his first language, Cantonese, instead of a monolingual English judge. The defense lawyer posited that a constitutional right to use Cantonese in the courts of Hong Kong should include two elements: "first, the right to speak Cantonese and, second, the right to be understood by the courts in Cantonese without the intervention of an interpreter" (para. 14). Justice Hartmann rejected the application, holding that "that right to employ or utilize the language does not imply a reciprocal obligation on the part of the court to speak and read that language" (para. 19). The decision has been widely criticized. Experienced court interpreter Ester Leung questions the assumption that people who are dependent on interpreting services have equal access to justice.[62] Others have argued that not allowing a Cantonese speaker to

---

[59] Irish is highlighted because it has a limited official status during a transitional period. This derogation is expected to end in 2022. At the time of writing, EU institutions are not able to provide full translation and interpretation services into and out of Irish, but Irish may be used as the language of a case at the ECJ.

[60] Article 36 of Consolidated version of the Rules of Procedure of the Court of Justice, as of September 25, 2012.

[61] *Re Cheng Kai Nam* [2002] 2 HKLRD 39. This was a judicial review case that took place at the Court of First Instance. It represents the current position of the judiciary; see Legislative Council Secretariat (2011/2012).

[62] Ester S. M. Leung, "Interpreting for the Minority, Interpreting for the Power," in *Dimensions of Forensic Linguistics*, ed. John Gibbons and M. Teresa Turell (Amsterdam: John Benjamins, 2008), 197–211.

use his or her first language throughout the proceedings perpetuates suppression and injustice from the city's colonial past.[63]

In South Africa, the Justice Department has not yet formulated a policy on the use of official languages other than English and Afrikaans. Section 35(3)(k) of the South African Constitution does not confer on an accused person a right to have a trial conducted in the language of his or her choice, but only a right to be tried in a language that he or she understands, "or, if that is not practicable, to have the proceedings interpreted in that language." This means that fair trial instead of linguistic equality is the overriding consideration. Thus in *Mthethwa v. De Bruin NO and Another*,[64] a defendant who understood English was not successful in demanding that his trial took place in his native language isiZulu. On the other hand, due to the lack of interpreters between IsiXhosa and English/Afrikaans, two trials did take place in IsiXhosa, which happened to be spoken by every trial participant in those cases (*Matomela*[65] and *Macebo Damoyi*[66]). In a review of the latter case, Judge N. J. Yekiso held that the proceeding was in accordance with justice, but provided utilitarian reasons[67] to urge that English be used as the only language of record in court proceedings.

The implications of granting a right to be understood without interpreter mediation are particularly complicated in jury trials. We will consider the issue of jury trials more thoroughly later in this chapter.

THE RIGHT TO ACCESS PUBLIC LEGAL INFORMATION IN AN OFFICIAL LANGUAGE OF ONE'S CHOICE

Public legal information refers to legal texts published officially, including acts, statutes, legislative proposals, judgments, and reference documents. Generally, states are committed to publishing the law in their official languages, but they vary greatly in their efficiency of getting this done and their commitment in making the full range of legal materials available in all official languages. Other than supranational and international bodies such as the European Union, few bilingual or multilingual jurisdictions have translated all their case law in all their official languages. Some have chosen to translate or summarize important judgments only; others see the task as too formidable to attempt. This issue is

---

[63] Phil C. W. Chan, "Official Languages and Bilingualism in the Courtroom: Hong Kong, Canada, the Republic of Ireland, and International Law," *The International Journal of Human Rights* 11, no. 1–2 (March 1, 2007): 199–225, https://doi.org/10.1080/13642980601176332.

[64] *Mthethwa v. De Bruin NO & Another*, 1998(3) BCLR 336(N).

[65] *S v. Matomela*, 1998(3) BCLR 339 (Ck).

[66] *S v. Macebo Damoyi* (24441, A210/02, 44/02) [2003] ZAWCHC 65.

[67] The judge argued that the use of English as the only language of record will be both economical and in the best interest of justice. "After all, English is already a language used in international commerce and international transactions are exclusively concluded in the English language."

particularly problematic in common law jurisdictions where precedent is very much part of the law.

Under the pressure of equality of states and the principle of direct effect (i.e., that EU laws are directly applicable to citizens within the Union), the European Union is diligent in ensuring that its law is accessible in all its official languages. The Union publishes its constitutive treaties and secondary legislation (regulations, directives, decisions, etc.) in all its 24 official languages.[68] Although the internal working language of the ECJ is French, and thus the case documents and case law in the ECJ are drafted in French, the report for a hearing is translated into the language of the trial. Judgments, orders of the court, and the advocate's general opinions are subsequently translated into all the official languages of the Union.[69] Unlike EU law, which is authentic in all its official languages, judgments are authentic only in the language of the trial, even though they are first drafted in French and are available in all official languages.

Although Canada is often considered a leading bilingual jurisdiction, ironically Canada's Constitution Act of 1982 still does not have an authenticated French translation (as discussed in Chapter 5). Generally speaking, Canadian federal legislation has to be published in both official languages, but the rule that applies to provincial legislation varies. In *Re Manitoba Language Rights*,[70] the Supreme Court of Canada found that, in light of section 23 of the Manitoba Act of 1870, Manitoba laws that had been published only in English for 125 years had no legal force or effect, for they did not fulfill the constitutional requirement of being bilingual. The court, however, allowed the laws to be temporarily valid until translation could be re-enacted in order to avoid a legal vacuum. On the other hand, Alberta has no constitutional obligation to publish its provincial laws in French (*R. v. Caron*[71]). Judgments of federal courts are published bilingually. Bastarache points out that Canadian law has not made clear whether the two versions of a court's judgment are equally authentic, but argues that they should be, for "judgments define and develop the law."[72]

Section 30 of Language Act 2003 in Finland provides that acts, statutes, decrees, and legal rules are published in Finnish and Swedish. However, legislative proposals and reports are published in Finnish with a Swedish summary, or with a full Swedish translation where the report is deemed to be of considerable importance to the Swedish population in the country (Section 31). On the

---

[68] McAuliffe, "Language and Law in the European Union."

[69] McAuliffe.

[70] *Re Manitoba Language Rights* [1985] 1 S.C.R. 721.

[71] *R. v. Caron*, 2014 ABCA 71.

[72] Bastarache, "Bilingual Interpretation Rules as a Component of Language Rights in Canada," 173.

other hand, if a legislative proposal or report is of significance primarily to the Swedish-speaking population or to the Åland Province, it may be published in Swedish with a Finnish summary and a Finnish text of the legislative proposal.

In Ireland not all legislation has been translated into Irish. The Irish case *Ó Beoláin v. Fahy*[73] established, based on a linguistic equality argument, that there is a constitutional duty (pursuant to Article 25.4.4) for Ireland to make statutes available in all its official languages. Given that state funds have been used to provide the English version of court rules, equal treatment must also be afforded to Irish speakers (O'Hanlon J. in *Delap v. An tAire Dlí agus Cirt agus an tArd-Aighne*[74]). Following this judgment, the Official Languages Act (Ireland) of 2003 stipulates that "as soon as may be after the enactment of any Act of the Oireachtas, the text thereof shall be printed and published in each of the official languages simultaneously" (Section 7). Statutes are now being translated as they are enacted, and a backlog of 20 years (circa 1980–early 2000s), during which virtually no official Irish translation had been provided, is being cleared. The 2010 case of *Ó Murchú v. An Taoiseach & chuid eile*[75] reaffirmed that the Irish translation of statutes and statutory instruments should be made available as soon as practicable, but the Supreme Court was cautious in extending the right to translation by basing its reasoning narrowly on the argument that the absence of translation of legal procedures might impede the applicant's (a solicitor's) conducting of legal affairs. It refused to deal directly with the significance of the primary official status of Irish as provided in Article 8 of the Constitution, or to grant right of access to "all legal materials in Ireland"[76] in Irish.[77]

All legislation in Hong Kong is available in both English and Chinese. Judgment is published in the language of the trial, but those that are of jurisprudential value have been translated and have been made available on the judiciary website since 2008. Since 1995, 426 pieces of Chinese judgments have been translated into English, and leading judgments in English are also translated into Chinese. As of October 31, 2011, 17,192 Chinese judgments and 50,872 English judgments had been uploaded onto the Judiciary website (Legislative Council Secretariat, 2011–2012). The judiciary is also making available bilingually Reasons for Sentence handed down by the High Court and the District Court, Practice Directions, and one set of Specimen Directions in Jury Trial. In addition, the judiciary is producing a Bilingual Common Law

---

73 *Ó Beoláin v. Fahy* [2001] 2 IR 279.

74 *Delap v. An tAire Dlí agus Cirt agus an tArd-Aighne* [1990] IRSR (1980–1998) 46.

75 *Ó Murchú v. An Taoiseach & chuid eile* [2010] IESC 26.

76 Which "would logically extend to the text of judgments delivered by the courts, administrative circulars and other materials."

77 Mark De Blacam, "Official Language and Constitutional Interpretation," *The Irish Jurist* 52 (2014): 90–114.

Series. The first casebook on criminal law was published in 2003, land and employment cases in 2005 and 2006, respectively.

When a jurisdiction becomes bilingual or multilingual, priority is usually given to making legislation available in all official languages, and effort sometimes runs out of steam once this task is completed. Since case law has prescriptive function in common law jurisdictions, its translation is important but often ignored. From a practical perspective, some may argue that laypersons do not read case law anyway, and legal professionals usually have the linguistic ability to read case law in its original language. However, unrepresented litigants also need access to sources of law (see later discussion in this chapter).

THE RIGHT TO ACCESS CASE MATERIALS IN AN OFFICIAL LANGUAGE OF ONE'S CHOICE

Does a defendant or litigant have the right to receive case documents in an official language of one's choice? If such a right exists, who should bear the cost of translation—the defendant/litigant, the other party, or the judiciary?

For criminal cases in Canada, the right to receive translated case documents was initially developed based on both the right to a fair trial (i.e., such that the accused can understand the charges against them) and the right to elect the official language of the trial. In *Boudreau v. New Brunswick (N.B.C.A.)*,[78] the court ordered that a breathalyzer certificate written in English, which was adduced in evidence at trial, be translated into French for the French-speaking defendant to ensure a fair trial. In *Simard*,[79] it was held that the right to have the charge orally translated into the official language of a defendant's choice was absolute, but an accused did not have an absolute right to have a written translation of the information. An amendment that came into force on October 1, 2008, section 530.01(1) of Criminal Code, clarified the matter by providing that a prosecutor shall, on application by the accused, offer a translation[80] of information or indictments against them in the official language of the accused. Similar rights are also afforded to defendants in summary offense cases at the provincial level (*Canada (Commissioner of Official Languages) v. Canada (Department of Justice)*[81]). There is no duty for the prosecutor to provide a translation of all the evidence that was disclosed (*Stadnick*[82] and *Stockford*[83]).

---

[78] *Boudreau v. New Brunswick* [1990] N.B.J. No. 846, 59 C.C.C. (3d) 436 (N.B.C.A.).

[79] *R. v. Simard* (Ont. Ct. (Gen. Div.)) [1994] O.J. No. 1769.

[80] In the case of a discrepancy between the original and the translation, the original version shall prevail. See s530.01(2).

[81] *Canada (Commissioner of Official Languages) v. Canada (Department of Justice)* [2001] F.C.J. No. 431.

[82] *R. v. Stadnick* [2001] Q.J. No. 5226 (Que. S.C.).

[83] *Stockford v. R.* [2009] Q.J. No. 8369.

Civil cases are quite a different matter. Generally speaking, one cannot insist that the other party has to file documents and communicate in a particular official language, or provide a translation (*Casselman Electrique Ltée v. Gaudreau*[84]), if they do not wish to do so. In certain areas in Ontario identified by 126(2) of the Courts of Justice Act, a party may file pleadings and other documents written in French; elsewhere, a party may file pleadings and other documents in French with the consent of the other party. In *LeBlanc v. York Catholic District School Board*,[85] the Ontario Superior Court of Justice held that litigants could not refuse to receive documents served to them by the other party only because the documents are written in an official language that they do not prefer.

In Finland, notices, summonses, and letters that are sent by courts of law or other authorities to someone being notified of a pending case or a case that is to be taken up for consideration, regardless of the language of proceedings, have to be sent "in the language of the recipient if this is known or can reasonably be ascertained, or in both Finnish and Swedish" (Section 19(3) of Language Act 2003). This may also be in the Sami language (Sami Language Act of 2003) for a Sami recipient. Section 20 further specifies that the state shall provide an official translation, free of charge, of summons, judgment, decision, record, or other documents, to the extent that the matter relates to his or her rights, interests, or obligations. But for civil cases between private parties, the parties are generally responsible for their own translation needs, "unless with regard to the nature of the matter the court decides otherwise."

In Ireland, defendants cannot compel the other party to provide translation of legal notices in Irish, even where the plaintiff is the state or a public body. In *Attorney General v. Coyne and Wallace*,[86] the defendants were served notices of intention to prosecute written in Irish for traffic offenses that took place in Gaeltacht. Although the defendants did not understand Irish, the Supreme Court held that it was sufficient that the Garda (national police of Ireland) who served the notices explained their effect. Moreover, based on Article 8 of the Constitution, Kingsmill Moore, J., argued that either English or Irish might be used "unless provision had been made by law that one language only was to be used for any one or more official purposes." This was reaffirmed in *An Stát (Mac Fhearraigh) v. Neilan*[87] and *Ó Conaire v. MacGruairc*.[88] However, the court also noted that the duty to translate may arise if required by rules of natural justice or fair procedures.

---

[84] *Casselman Electrique Ltée v. Gaudreau* [1997] O.J. No. 2005.
[85] *LeBlanc v. York Catholic District School Board* [2002] O.J. No. 4640.
[86] *Attorney General v. Coyne and Wallace* [1967] 101 ILTR 17.
[87] *An Stát (Mac Fhearraigh) v. Neilan* [1984] IRSR (1980–1998) 38.
[88] *Ó Conaire v. MacGruairc* [2010] 3 IR 30.

In Hong Kong, for both civil and criminal proceedings, documents must be submitted in the language of the trial (Official Languages (Translation) Rules, Cap 5B). Courts also have discretion to order the provision of translation from one official language to another. According to High Court Civil Procedure (Use of Language) Rules (Cap 5C), a party to a proceeding who has been served in an official language with which he or she is not familiar may request the other party to provide him or her with a translation in the other official language. The translation cost incurred shall be costs in the cause of the proceedings. This means that, subject to the discretion of the trial judge, the loser is liable to covering such costs, and so translation requests can increase the stake of a civil trial.

Cases that arise in EU courts are rather different in nature. The most common kind of direct action is launched against member states for failing to fulfill their treaty obligations. The language of application, which can be any of the 24 EU official languages, is the language of the case. The general principle is that all documents submitted must be in the language of the case, but summaries may suffice for lengthy documents (*European Commission v. Grand Duchy of Luxemburg*[89]).

THE RIGHT TO USE A NON-STANDARD VARIETY OF AN OFFICIAL LANGUAGE

Many people speak a language variety that is somewhat different from the standard variety officially recognized, prescribed, or developed by a government. Well-known examples include creole languages[90] have often emerged as a result of language contact, and such languages may have linguistic features that are distinctive from a standard variety from which they are supposed to originate. Non-standard varieties, however, do not have to be created by special historical circumstances. More often than not, they acquire a marginal status when another variety is designated as standard.

The use of a non-standard but mutually intelligible variety of an official language is usually tolerated but not explicitly provided for. Official language policies almost invariably imagine a language as something spoken by a homogenous population and are usually silent about dialects. This language ideology, which renders some people, activities, or elements invisible or ignored, is what Irvine and Gal call "erasure."[91]

---

[89] *European Commission v. Grand Duchy of Luxembourg*, C-526/08 [2010] ECR I-6151.

[90] There is nothing exceptional about creole languages other than the social and historical context in which they originated. Michel DeGraff, "Linguists' Most Dangerous Myth: The Fallacy of Creole Exceptionalism," *Language in Society* 34, no. 4 (2005): 533–591.

[91] Judith T. Irvine and Susan Gal, "Language Ideology and Linguistic Differentiation," in *Regimes of Language: Ideologies, Polities, and Identities.*, ed. P. V. Kroskrity (Santa Fe: School of American Research Press, 2000), 35–84.

Traditionally, respect for the judge and his or her courtroom is partly maintained by the formal register of language use. The use of non-standard varieties in the courtroom is sometimes said to threaten courtroom formality.

Non-Standard Form

There is usually no objection to the use of a mutually comprehensible variety of an official language. In fact, the use of such varieties often goes unacknowledged. Interpretation services may be provided where the variety used is perceived to be significantly different from the standard variety expected in the courtroom. However, linguistic accommodation cannot be taken for granted, which is problematic given the political nature of the distinction between language and dialect. In Chinese courtrooms, Chinese defendants who are speakers of rural dialects are sometimes asked to use the standard dialect Putonghua despite their limited proficiency in it.[92]

Speakers may adopt different varieties of an official language as a communicative strategy. Style switching has been reported in monolingual jurisdictions as an indicator of audience awareness. Fuller documents how Southern black attorneys switched the style of their language from Standard English to African American Vernacular English (AAVE) in order to convey solidarity, alignment, and humility in front of African American jurors.[93] In the bilingual jurisdiction of Malaysia, Powell and Hashim have observed switching—by trial participants including judges—between more international and more local varieties of English in the courtroom, depending on the addressee.[94] In one such example, the counsel switches between Malaysian English and Standard English depending on whom he is addressing, and the judge responds to him in Malaysian English:

> Counsel [to clerk]: This one lah [giving bundle of documents to clerk].
>
> Counsel [to judge]: I humbly request for a short break, Yang Arif (Your Honour).
>
> Judge [to counsel]: Short one is it, ah?
>
> —(High Court, Terengganu 2005.11)

Standard English is regarded as the polite form. When the interlocutor feels less concerned about formality (e.g., from counsel to clerk or from judge to counsel), they switch to Malaysian English. The use of sentence-final particles (such as *lah* and *ah*) in Malaysian English is derived from language contact

---

[92] Du, "The Bilingual Trial: Access to Interpreting, Communication, and Participation in Chinese Criminal Courts."

[93] Janet Fuller, "Hearing between the Lines: Style Switching in a Courtroom Setting," *Pragmatics* 3, no. 1 (December 21, 2009): 29–43.

[94] Richard Powell and Azirah Hashim, "Language Disadvantage in Malaysian Litigation and Arbitration," *World Englishes* 30, no. 1 (2011): 92–105.

between English, Malay, and varieties of Chinese (such as Cantonese and Hokkien). In combination with lexical tones (not marked in the original transcript), stress, and duration, such switching may serve a wide range of semantic and pragmatic functions (e.g., expression of solidarity, sarcasm, and emphasis). Although the scarcity of spoken records leaves uncertain the extent to which such switching between English varieties was observable during colonial days, one may speculate that official bilingualism in English and Malay has made such switching more tolerable in post-colonial Malaysian courtrooms. The pattern of mixing is particularly interesting given the superior status that Malay enjoys over English in the legal system. This official preference does not accord with existing language ideologies that people hold: use of Standard English still projects a higher level of formality than a domesticated variety of the language.

For many others, the use of a non-standard variety may not be a choice or a conscious decision, raising questions of communicative disadvantage, which is not mitigated by court interpreters. Speakers of Aboriginal English, for example, have distinctive ways of seeking and sharing information and giving information at a level of specificity that is different from non-Aboriginal speakers. Importantly, few of them have bicultural competence (i.e., the ability to switch between Aboriginal and non-Aboriginal ways of interacting). Apparent fluency may be misleading, as sociocultural differences are sufficient to cause miscommunication (e.g., gratuitous concurrence being taken as a confession).[95] Eades thus suggests that cross-cultural interpreters be provided.[96] Her suggestion draws attention to blind spots in court interpretation and to internal variations among speakers who are supposedly proficient in the same "language." Varieties of a language may share identical grammatical forms but have substantial pragmatic differences. Interpreting is not just a matter of translating words and sentences and may be necessary even when a court participant appears to speak the official language of the courtroom.

Mixed Use of Official Languages

Code-mixing (the insertion of words or phrases of a language variety into speech conducted in a primary-language variety), code-switching (the shift from one language variety to another between clauses), and lexical borrowing (the adaptation of a foreign word into a language, sometimes with morphological or phonological adjustment) are commonplace in everyday communication. In places such as Hong Kong and Malaysia, such mixed use of languages

---

[95] Diana Eades, "A Case of Communicative Clash: Aboriginal English and the Legal System," in *Language in the Law*, ed. John Gibbons (London; New York: Longman, 1994), 234–64.

[96] Even then, Eades argues, there will still be insurmountable clashes between Aboriginal communities and the legal process. For example, in Aboriginal societies, only certain people have rights to certain knowledge, but a law enforcer might expect an Aboriginal suspect or witness to supply information.

is a marker of a society's cultural heritage and its history of language contact. While code-mixing may be habitual, the pattern it creates is not random.[97] In many post-colonial jurisdictions, insertions are linguistically marked and mirror power struggles between the ex-colonizer's language and the local language.

Where people habitually mix languages in their daily life, should such manner of speech be allowed in the courtroom, if the languages involved are officially recognized? If mixing is allowed, what implications might it have for the judicial system? For example, would language mixing confuse the court interpreter, complicate record keeping, or compromise courtroom formality?[98]

Returning to the Malaysian example, apart from switching between varieties of English, code-switching and code-mixing between English and Bahasa Malay are also commonplace in the Malaysian courtroom.[99] Powell and Hashim[100] have observed the following interaction:

> C: *Minta* deterrent sentence. *Mangsa seorang yang kurang 16 tahun.*
> (We are asking for) (The victim is under 16)
> J: She had the *surat akuan* in 1992.
> (statutory declaration)
> W: *Saya* off*kan* handphone *sebab takut ayah atau* nurse *hubungi saya.*
> (I switched off) (being afraid father or his) (would contact me)

During this short interaction, the counsel and witness used Malay as a base language in their turn and the judge used English. Both ordinary (*handphone* and *nurse*) and legal (*deterrent sentence* and *surat akuan*) terms had been inserted into the base languages.[101] It can be seen from the frequency of lexical insertion and judicial participation that code-mixing is endemic in the Malaysian courtroom, showcasing how deeply rooted cultural habits may penetrate judicial formality in common law and how fluid and multilayered the relationship between language and identity may be.

In Kenya, high court proceedings take place in English, but both English and Swahili may be used in magistrates' courts. David and Powell[102] give the

---

[97] Carol Myers-Scotton, *Duelling Languages: Grammatical Structure in Codeswitching* (Oxford: Oxford University Press, 1993).

[98] Elena De Jongh and Ana Roca, "Interpreting Spanish Codes in Southern Florida: The Preparation of Court Interpreters," in *Sociolinguistics of the Spanish-Speaking World: Iberia, Latin America, United States*, ed. Carol A. Klee and Luis A. Ramos-Garcia (Tempe, AZ: Bilingual Press, 1991), 349–58.

[99] Maya Khemlani David et al., eds., *Code Switching in Malaysia* (Frankfurt am Main: Peter Lang, 2009).

[100] Powell and Hashim, "Language Disadvantage in Malaysian Litigation and Arbitration."

[101] The dominant language, which provides the grammatical structure for the sentence as a whole, is also sometimes called "matrix language" in code-switching studies. Carol Myers-Scotton, "The Matrix Language Frame Model: Developments and Responses," in *Codeswitching Worldwide II*, ed. Rodolfo Jacobson (Berlin; New York: Mouton de Gruyter, 2001), 23–58.

[102] David and Powell (2003), cited in Powell, "Bilingual Courtrooms: In the Interests of Justice?"

following example, where both the defendant and the judge speak in a mix of English and Swahili in a Kenyan magistrates court:

> D: Your honour *naomba unipunuzie* bond *kwa sababu*
> (Your honour I beg you to reduce the bond because)
> family *yangu imeshindwa kufikisha* two hundred thousand.
> (my family cannot come up with two hundred thousand)
> J: *Siwezi kupunguza* bond *kwa sababu umekuwa* accused
> (I cannot reduce the bond because you were accused
> *umeiba gari na ninaona shilingi elfu mbili ni* fair.
> (of stealing cars and I believe 2,000 shillings is fair)

In the Philippines, Ballano has observed witnesses using Taglish[103] in the courtroom, sometimes because they struggle to speak entirely in English or Tagalog.[104] Such code-mixing seems to be tolerated, which reduces the burden for court participants, but only English is used for records.[105] This means that what is supposed to be a transcription of courtroom interaction actually involves translation.

Civil procedures in Hong Kong stipulate that mixing of codes in the spoken form in court is acceptable (s.5 of the Official Languages Ordinance (Cap. 5)) but not in the written form. In *Chan Kong v. Chan Li Chai Medical Factory (Hong Kong) Ltd.*,[106] the Court of Appeal held that pleadings written partly in Chinese and partly in English (at times with both languages used in a single sentence) was unacceptable, based on r.4(1) of the High Court Civil Procedure (Use of Language) Rules (Cap. 5C) which states that such documents must be served in *either* of the official languages. Witnesses and litigants in person have been observed to insert English lexical items, especially legal terms, in their Cantonese utterances. This is done presumably to borrow authority from the English language, which is perceived to be the more powerful official language.[107] It is not laypersons alone who use code-mixing or lexical borrowing in the courtroom. Legal professionals in Hong Kong habitually mix codes in Cantonese trials, but never in English trials, giving rise to a differential level of judicial formality between trials that take place in the two official languages. Such mixing is especially prominent during in-group communication between legal professionals participating in a trial (i.e., as opposed to legal-lay

[103] Taglish is a mix of not only Tagalog and American English but also has bits of Spanish. It is used by educated Filipinos not only on the street but also in tabloids, radio, and television. Thompson, *Filipino English and Taglish.*

[104] Ballano, "The 'Rule of Law,' Oral Textuality, and Justice in Criminal Court Proceedings."

[105] Martin, "Expanding the Role of Philippine Languages in the Legal System."

[106] *Chan Kong v. Chan Li Chai Medical Factory (Hong Kong) Ltd.*, Civil Appeal No. 161 of 2006.

[107] Janny H. C. Leung, "Lay Litigation Behaviour in Postcolonial Hong Kong Courtrooms," *Language and Law / Linguagem e Direito* 2, no. 1 (2015): 32–52.

interaction), as in the following exchange between a judge (J) and counsel (C) in a Cantonese trial:[108]

C:	咁under without prejudice (. . .) 佢地就講緊 (.) without prejudice is to the maker itself ↑ 咁個maker 既admission (.) in essence 個個maker waive 左個個 (.) without prejudice right 就可以=	*Then under without prejudice (. . .). They are talking about (.) without prejudice is for the maker itself ↑ The maker's admission (.) in essence if the maker waives the without prejudice right that should be ok=*
J:	=當然唔得啦 (.) 你咁樣會影響到個court的官感架嗎↑	*=Of course not(.) This way you will affect the court's impression↑*
C:	But (.) 就算如果係咁的情況我地有個open offer 出左黎呢 (.) even by way↑ of summons (.)去到法庭呢個係open offer 黎架喎(.) It's NOT even without prejudice.	*But (.) even if that is the case we have an open offer proposed (.) even by way ↑of summons (.) In court this is still an open offer (.) It's NOT even without prejudice.*
J:	It's sanction offer. Sanction offer is a sanction offer.	*It's a sanction offer. Sanction offer is a sanction offer.*
C:	It's superseded by an:: obligation to the court (.) by way of summons.	*It's superseded by an:: obligation to the court (.) by way of summons.*
J:	點解一個summons 就可以可以可以解除左呢個order (.) 22 rule 25 呢件事呢？你可唔可以enlighten 我呢？	*How can a summon lift the order (.) 22 rule 25? Can you enlighten me?*
C:	我唔係話(.) 我唔係話解除 (.) 因為sanction offer 係一個我地:被告人(.)之前比的sanction offer.	*I'm not talking (.) I'm not talking about lifting (.) because the sanction offer is a sanction offer that our: defendant (.) previously gave.*
J:	Yea	*Yea*

Both lexical borrowing and inter-sentential code-switching took place in this short excerpt, where most of the English insertions involved legal terminology. This is probably because legal professionals in Hong Kong are trained in English.

Unlike Hong Kong, Finnish law explicitly provides for written documents to be drafted in mixed codes, subject to judicial discretion. Section 19(2) of the Language Act of 2003 states:

108 Reported in Matthew W. L. Yeung and Janny H. C. Leung (forthcoming) "I have no idea what they were talking about: Miscommunication between unrepresented litigants and legal professionals."

> In accordance with the discretion of an authority, documents related to the preparation and consideration of a matter may be drafted in part in Finnish and in part in Swedish. Nonetheless, a decision and a judgment shall be issued in one language only.

Although official status may affect its acceptability, language mixing is not exclusive to bilingual and multilingual jurisdictions. It is also observable in monolingual jurisdictions, especially in informal courts. In an ethnographic study of small claims courts in New York, Angermeyer found that Spanish defendants inserted English words in their statements to preserve cohesion.[109]

The Language Criterion in Jury Selection

Although the use of non-standard varieties of language may challenge the solemnity and formality of the courtroom, it does not directly challenge substantive principles of law or constitutive rules for the functioning of the legal system. However, if a jurisdiction recognizes a right to be heard in an official language without interpreter mediation, its implication has the potential of rupturing fundamental assumptions in existing legal practice. While adding a linguistic criterion to judicial appointment may limit the pool of potential candidates and thus may be seen by some as undesirable, a linguistic criterion in jury selection raises deeper questions, for it may come into conflict with the basic rationale of jury trials.

The right to trial by a jury of peers was enshrined in the Magna Carta of 1215, which states:

> No freemen shall be taken or imprisoned or disseised or exiled or in any way destroyed, nor will we go upon him nor send upon him, except by the lawful judgment of his peers or by the law of the land.

The use of the word *peer* is here ambiguous: it may be used to refer to equals, or people of a high rank (primarily in Britain). Both senses have been used, during different time periods, in the notion of trial by peers. In its early incarnation, the right to be tried by one's equals was reserved for the nobility. This privilege was later extended to commoners, such that nobilities were tried by nobilities, and commoners by commoners. Trial by peers, in the sense of peerage, was abolished in the United Kingdom in 1948.

In the contemporary understanding of trial by peers, *peer* refers to equals. Trial by a jury of peers—as distinguished from a trial by the government[110]—is

---

[109] Philipp Sebastian Angermeyer, "Lexical Cohesion as a Motivation for Codeswitching: Evidence from Spanish-English Bilingual Speech in Court Testimonies," in *Selected Proceedings of the First Workshop on Spanish Sociolinguistics*, ed. Lotfi Sayahi (Somerville, MA: Cascadilla Proceedings Project, 2003), 112–22.

[110] Lysander Spooner, *Essay on the Trial by Jury* (Boston: John P. Jewett, 1852).

a measure to safeguard against power abuse. It is used to ensure that the decision-maker is impartial and to instill public confidence in the criminal justice system. Jury trials are conducted mostly in criminal cases, but also sometimes in civil cases. As fact finders, jurors decide, based on evidence presented to them in court, whether facts of the case have been proven to be true.

In common law jurisdictions, a jury is typically made up of a randomly selected sample that represents a cross-section of the population. There are usually practical restrictions imposed on the selection of jurors, including citizenship, age, and proficiency in the language of the trial. It is also common to exclude former convicts, legal professionals, law enforcers, holders of public offices, medical practitioners, and people whose mental or physical disabilities prevent them from performing the duties of jury service. There are jurisdictional variations in the selection, criteria, and vetting (for example, whether lawyers are allowed to raise preemptive challenges) of jurors.

The jury system has been a subject of controversy. There has been talk of abolishing it both in the United Kingdom and the United States. Some argue that criminal and civil disputes today, with all the legal and evidential rules invoked in trials, have become too complex for laypersons to understand. Jurors are also often found to be biased and unpredictable in their decision-making.[111] The controversy becomes more complex when a bilingual or multilingual jurisdiction needs to determine whether official language law ought to have an impact on jury selection criteria. As the subsequent discussion will show, there is a clear divide in how these jurisdictions have responded to the question. Juror selection based on a linguistic criterion is a sensitive matter, as it could easily spill over into questions of race and ethnicity.[112]

In some multilingual jurisdictions, official language policy has been allowed to affect jury selection. The Canadian Criminal Code gives the defendant an absolute right to be tried by a judge or judge and jury who speak the official language of the accused (s530 Criminal Code), giving rise to the possibility of an English-speaking jury, a French-speaking jury, or a bilingual jury. In South Tyrol, jurors are expected to be bilingual in German and Italian. In Hong Kong, before the legal system became bilingual, all persons with insufficient command of English were excluded from serving as jurors, effectively limiting participation by a majority of the public. Now jurors may serve on trials as long as they can understand the language of the proceedings, which may be Chinese or English. The bilingual policy thus facilitated wider participation in

---

[111] Valerie P. Hans and Neil Vidmar, "Jurors and Juries," in *The Blackwell Companion to Law and Society*, ed. Austin Sarat (Malden, MA: Blackwell, 2004), 195–211.

[112] The issue of whether the exclusion of Hispanic jurors, seemingly based on language competence, constituted racial discrimination was considered in the *Hernandez* case in the United States (discussed in the next subsection); the Supreme Court held that it did not, as a race-neutral explanation of the exclusion could be offered.

the criminal justice system in this case. All these examples show that official language law has the potential of renegotiating the meaning of *peer*.

On the other hand, in the bilingual jurisdictions of Wales and Ireland, speakers of the majority official language (i.e., English) can speak and be heard in their language in court, but those who speak a minority official language (i.e., Welsh in Wales and Irish in Ireland) do not enjoy the same treatment, despite equal or higher status given to the latter. Both countries have seen vigorous debates on this matter recently. The Welsh Parliament debated and decided against including a bilingual jury in the Welsh Language Act of 1993. Twelve years later, a consultation paper on the bilingual jury was published in 2005, but the bill was voted down in 2010.[113] In Ireland, the implication of the official status of Irish for jury composition is not clearly spelled out in legislation. The question was brought before the Irish Supreme Court in two cases. In both instances, the court turned down the request for an Irish-speaking or bilingual jury. In both jurisdictions, the main concern was whether the selection of jury members based on a linguistic criterion undermines representativeness, where an official language is spoken by a small minority.

UNIFORMITY OF INFORMATION, EQUAL PARTICIPATION, AND UNMEDIATED ACCESS TO EVIDENCE

Linguistic competence of jurors is also an issue for monolingual jurisdictions. Where a testimony is given in a language other than the language of the trial, jurors who have bilingual competence may understand the original utterances before they are interpreted, creating a situation where jurors have differential access to information. This was deemed a problem in *Hernandez v. New York*,[114] where the United States Supreme Court upheld a decision by a New York State court to exclude Hispanics from serving on the jury. Since a substantial amount of evidence would be submitted in Spanish, Spanish-speaking jurors might listen to the original testimony instead of relying on the English interpretation. But it is the English interpretation that would become the official record of what was said. The court accepts that uniform deference to the official translation is an acceptable race-neutral explanation of juror exclusion. That the decision has disparate impact on a linguistic minority was not a concern as long as it did not have a discriminatory purpose.

In an entirely opposite spirit, some jurisdictions have allowed people who do not speak the language of the trial to serve as jurors through interpretation, thus prioritizing equal participation over linguistic uniformity. This is practiced in the Supreme Court in New Mexico, which decided in 2000 that

---

[113] The Ministry of Justice (2010) concluded that the jury system and the Welsh language formed a dichotomy and the government must choose between the two.

[114] *Hernandez v. New York*, 500 U.S. 352 (1991).

non-English-speaking persons were entitled to serve as jurors and to receive interpreter services throughout the proceedings.[115] Similarly, following an amendment to the Jury Act,[116] in jury trials in the Northwest Territories and Nunavut in Canada, any person who is able to speak and understand one of the 11 official languages is qualified to serve on the jury in a trial that may be conducted in English or French.

Yet other jurisdictions prioritize the right of official language speakers to be understood without mediation, seeking to avoid the use of court interpreter wherever possible. When the relevant section in the Criminal Code of Canada was debated (as Bill C-42 then) in the House of Commons,[117] a strong consensus supports a right to be tried by a judge or judge and jury who speak the official language of the accused. The main concern was not principle but implementation—whether it is feasible to recruit enough jurors with the required language competence in different parts of the country. The Canadian parliament considers the right to be heard in an official language a matter of minimum standards of official language rights. This approach improves linguistic access to justice for official language communities and eliminates problems arising from court interpretation. While numerous studies have reported misinterpretation as a source of injustice and unmediated access to evidence is therefore ideal, the current international standard for fair trial rights fully accepts interpreter-mediated access to legal proceedings. If unmediated access to evidence is where the bar is set, then many defendants (such as immigrants and other aliens) can never be said to have a fair trial. Generally, the presence of an interpreter is considered sufficient mitigation for language barrier. The expectation that one can use and be heard in an official language in a trial only arises with official status given to that language.

AVAILABILITY AND IDENTIFICATION OF JURORS

Apart from an English- or French-speaking jury, a bilingual jury may also be summoned in certain areas in Canada (for example, where two defendants in the same case request to be tried in different official languages). Based on population statistics, Canada has a large enough French-speaking population who may serve as jurors, even in English-dominant territories, although identifying them is sometimes a problem. Constituting a bilingual jury is also "relatively easy,"[118] given that speakers of a minority official language tend to be bilingual

---

[115] Benmaman (2002), cited in Eades, "Participation of Second Language and Second Dialect Speakers in the Legal System."

[116] R.S.N.W.T. 1988, c. J-2.

[117] "House of Commons Debates, 30th Parliament, 3rd Session: Volume 6," June 23, 1978, http://parl.canadiana.ca.

[118] "House of Commons Debates, 30th Parliament, 3rd Session: Volume 6," 6703.

in any province. Moving the venue of the trial to another territorial division within the same province provides a further resort, although it may incur additional costs and delays.

Even where minority language jurors are available, there may be the concern that some language groups feel more burdened with jury duty than others. This seems inevitable. The extension of rights for official language communities also comes with responsibilities.

In practice, trials that require French-speaking jurors are rare in many Canadian territories. A mistrial was declared in Yellowknife, in the Northwest Territories of Canada, in 2013 after the court had difficulty finding more than two French-speaking jurors in a pool of 1,200 randomly selected residents.[119] To rectify the situation, the Northwest Territories are now trying to amend their Jury Act and create a francophone jury list.[120]

This brings us to the question of not just whether linguistically competent jurors are available, but where to find them. A prospective juror list is often adopted from electoral rolls and may not contain information about language skills. As one could imagine, the challenge typically lies in identifying speakers of a minority official language.

Each province in Canada has its own way of compiling a juror list. Some provinces create their French jurors list by obtaining access to directories of francophone associations. French-speaking and bilingual citizens may also be systematically identified by asking people in the citizens database of assessment authorities or health-care system about their language competence, as recommended by a study of juror recruitment in British Columbia.[121] Ontario has already sorted its juror list into English, French, and bilingual speakers, following the Jurors Act of 1990.

If a bilingual jury were to be adopted in Wales and Ireland, there would be less of a problem of identifying bilingual speakers, for almost all Welsh and Irish speakers also speak English. However, Welsh and Irish speakers are not identified in the jurors list. In fact, in England and Wales, the current Criminal Practice Directions forbids such identification:

> 3K.6 The law does not permit the selection of jurors in a manner which enables the court to discover whether a juror does or does not speak Welsh,

---

[119] Jake Edmiston, "Judge Declares Mistrial after Court Fails to Find More than Two French-Speaking Jurors for Sexual Touching Trial," *National Post*, August 14, 2013, sec. News, http://news.nationalpost.com/news/canada/judge-declares-mistrial-after-court-fails-to-find-more-than-two-french-speaking-jurors-for-sexual-touching-trial.

[120] "N.W.T. Proposes Creating List of French-Speaking Jurors," *CBC News*, February 3, 2015, http://www.cbc.ca/news/canada/north/n-w-t-proposes-creating-list-of-french-speaking-jurors-1.2942577.

[121] Association des juristes d'expression françaisede la Colombie-Britannique (AJEFCB), "Recruiting French-Speaking and Bilingual Jurors in British Columbia," 2008.

> or to secure a jury whose members are bilingual, to try a case in which the Welsh language may be used.

Apart from legal restrictions, another challenge to identifying jurors based on linguistic abilities is reliability. Such identification chiefly depends on self-report. The language competence of jurors is rarely assessed. Their self-assessment may not be accurate—people often understate or overestimate their language ability. Language competence is also situation-specific—people who are fluent in a language for a particular purpose (e.g., child-rearing) may struggle with it in another context (e.g., professional presentation). Competence may also decline without regular use, and thus information obtained may become out of date. Finally, there may be lack of good faith in self-report. Prospective jurors may or may not want to serve for personal reasons. In Nova Scotia, it has been reported[122] that some francophones stated that they did not speak French in order to avoid jury duty.

The question of reliability was raised in Wales in a statement made by the then Lord Chancellor Lord Hailsham in the House of Lords, based on a report produced by Lord Justice Edmund Davies. Hailsham recounted a trial that had taken place the year before, where every member of the jury expressed a preference to take the oath in Welsh. English translation was provided for Welsh evidence presented in the trial. It later surfaced that although all jurors claimed that they understood Welsh, eight out of 12 of them considered that such translation had been necessary. He remarked,

> One juror who had even passed the School Certificate with oral proficiency in Welsh said that his understanding of the evidence given in Welsh was improved by its translation into English, as those participating had spoken Welsh of such a high standard.[123]

Although, in the broad Gaeltacht area, approximately two-thirds of the community is recorded as speaking Irish on a daily basis, the court in *Ó Maicín v. Éire*[124] raised doubts as to whether all of those recorded as being capable of speaking Irish "may be able to do so to a sufficient level as would enable them to conduct the difficult task of following evidence and argument in Irish without assistance." The court argued that there is no evidence available to show whether these people have such a level of competence in Irish that they could fully understand legal proceedings without any material difficulty.

---

122 http://www.parl.gc.ca/HousePublications/Publication.aspx?DocId=6460298&Language=E&Mode=1.

123 Hailsham of Saint Marylebone, "Use of Welsh in Courts in Wales," Hansard, House of Lords, Vol 343, cc532-40, June 12, 1973.

124 *Ó Maicín v. Éire* [2010] IEHC 179.

Due to the notoriously complex and atypical nature of courtroom discourse, it is difficult to guarantee that any layperson, even if fluent in the language of the trial, would fully understand legal proceedings. The risk of misunderstanding evidence is amplified when jurors have to work in their second or weaker language, without opportunities for seeking clarification. Presumably this risk is graver than the risk of mistranslation by professional interpreters. Note that a bilingual trial does not actually remove the need for translation and interpretation. The risk of mistranslation, however, is compensated to a certain extent by the hope that any significant errors might be caught by bilingual speakers, especially the judge, present in the case.

REPRESENTATIVENESS AND LEGITIMACY

Where the population of a minority official language is sufficiently large, the practical concern of finding the right jurors does not seem to be insurmountable. The most fundamental challenge to a right to receive a bilingual jury, or a jury consisting of speakers of a minority official language, is the argument that it might compromise the representative character of the jury.

The issue of representativeness comes up in how a jury list is formed. One way of identifying French-speaking jurors in Canada, currently being practiced in some provinces, is by accessing membership lists of francophone school boards.[125] The drawback of this method is that Francophone speakers identified this way are therefore all parents with young children, who may not be representative of the wider population in the province.

What poses a more contentious theoretical paradox is whether the formation of a minority official language jury frustrates the representativeness and thus legitimacy of the jury. This is the strongest reason for not forming an Irish or Welsh jury in Ireland and Wales. In the Irish case of *MacCárthaigh v. Éire*,[126] the court rejected the defendant's request for a jury who can understand Irish without the assistance of an interpreter based on the limited availability of Irish-speaking jurors in Dublin. Later, in *Ó Maicín v. Éire*,[127] where the alleged offense had occurred in a Gaeltacht area, the native Irish-speaking defendant requested that his case be tried before a bilingual jury. Difficult legal questions arose as the court dealt with two apparently conflicting constitutional rights: the right of citizens to conduct their business with the state in Irish (Article 8) and the constitutional right to a trial by jury (Article 38.5). Article 38.5 does not in fact define the right to a trial by jury, but based on *de*

---

[125] Association des juristes d'expression françaisede la Colombie-Britannique (AJEFCB), "Recruiting French-Speaking and Bilingual Jurors in British Columbia."

[126] *MacCárthaigh v Éire* [1999] 1 IR 186.

[127] *Ó Maicín v. Éire* [2010] IEHC 179.

Búrca v. Attorney General,[128] the Supreme Court held that a constitutionally compliant jury is one that is drawn from "a pool broadly representative of the community so that its verdict will be stamped with the fairness and acceptability of a genuinely diffused community decision." The court thus rejected the applicant's request, and argued that the right to a trial by jury is not only a right of the defendant, but it entails an obligation for the state to ensure that he is tried by a jury that represents a fair cross-section of the community. In the judgment the court also expressed concern that having a narrow pool of jurors leads to further exclusion because of a possible connection between the jurors and parties or witnesses to the case. The decision has been criticized[129] for failing to reconcile its stance with the primary position given to Irish as the first official language of the state in Article 8 of the Constitution.[130]

The court decision is partly influenced by a similar argument made by Lord Hailsham presented in the Welsh context.[131] Hailsham argues that since jury service is not just a duty but also a privilege of citizenship, debarring a third-quarter of the population from serving on the jury in a particular case based on their inability to understand Welsh "would involve a radical departure from that random formation of the jury panel which Blackstone described as a 'palladium' of our liberties." Therefore, he concludes that a Welsh-speaking jury should not be empanelled, even if practically achievable. He is satisfied that a simultaneous translation apparatus can resolve communication challenges.

Interestingly, there was questionable jury representativeness to speak of when Lord Hailsham made his statement or when Blackstone made his commentary. When the Hailsham report was made in 1973, only property owners were eligible for jury service.[132] Property ownership was also an important reason Blackstone believed that jurors could be expected to discharge their duties properly. Evans suspects that Blackstone would be "appalled" by the inclusion of all adults on the jury list.[133] In fact, Blackstone believed that an alien litigant or defendant should be tried by a jury *de medietate linguae* (a tradition from 18th C England), a special jury of mixed language abilities consisting of six Englishmen and six foreigners. He said this would make the trial "more impartial."[134]

---

128 *de Búrca v. Attorney General* [1976] IR 38.

129 R. Gwynedd Parry, "'An Important Obligation of Citizenship': Language, Citizenship and Jury Service," *Legal Studies* 27, no. 2 (June 1, 2007): 188–215, https://doi.org/10.1111/j.1748-121X.2007.00048.x; De Blacam, "Official Language and Constitutional Interpretation."

130 Article 8 also stipulates that departure from the official languages provision may be created by legislation; however, the Juries Act (Ireland) of 1976 does not provide for such a departure. See Parry, "'An Important Obligation of Citizenship.'"

131 Hailsham of Saint Marylebone, "Use of Welsh in Courts in Wales."

132 The property qualification was abolished by the Jury Act of 1974.

133 Roderick Evans, "Bilingual Juries?" (The Centre for Welsh Legal Affairs' Seventh Annual Lecture, November 25, 2006).

134 Evans, "Bilingual Juries?"

Parry also criticized the logic of these decisions.[135] The idea of representativeness, based on random selection, in jury selection is a means of ensuring that the panel is independent and impartial. It is only a means to an end. Lay magistrates appointed in England and Wales are not necessarily representative of the local community, but their legitimacy is not invalidated as a result. Unless the minority-language population is extremely small, there is no reason to believe that jurors randomly selected from a minority-population group are any less fair-minded than those drawn from the entire population, or are less likely to promote public confidence of the jury system.

Another point that Parry made is based on a historical perspective. He observes that the jury, as a marker of citizenship, has been composed differently as the concept of citizenship evolved. In England, from the Middle Ages to the early 1970s,[136] jury had been a matter of trial by superiors rather than peers. Jurors then were predominantly middle-aged male property owners. With gradual social and political emancipation, eligibility for jury service widened to include the great majority of adults, which, coinciding with the widening of suffrage, essentially redefined citizenship. In an age that celebrates multiculturalism, Parry urges rethinking of bilingual jury as a group instead of individual right, and of citizenship not as a universal attribute but as differentiated and inclusive of group identities (thus "multilingual citizenship"). However, Parry offers little insight as to why certain group identities should be prioritized over others in an official language regime, and how to resolve the problems of conflicting group identities (such as identities based on gender, race, language, and political orientation).

Furthermore, other than the few jurisdictions mentioned in the preceding that offer interpretation service for jurors, there is almost always a linguistic criterion for jury eligibility (such as a requirement to understand English in the UK[137]). It is inevitably the proficiency of a language spoken by a politically dominant group (whether majority or minority) that is required. In discussing whether British citizens of limited English could serve as jurors, Douglas Carswell, Member of Parliament, was quoted as having said, "The jury system is founded on the idea that we are all tried by our peers. If your peers cannot speak English, or read or write it properly, how can you have confidence you will get justice?"[138] Of course, for minority defendants, random selection only makes it likely that they will be judged by jurors from dominant groups.

---

[135] Parry, "'An Important Obligation of Citizenship.'"

[136] See Criminal Justice Act of 1972 and Juries Act of 1974.

[137] Criminal Practice Directions VI Trial 39C.2: The court may exercise its power to excuse any person from jury service for lack of capacity to act effectively as a juror because of an in sufficient understanding of English.

[138] Steve Doughty, "Can't Read or Write English? You Could Still Serve on a Jury under New Rules Designed to Help Immigrants," *Mail Online*, April 25, 2011, http://www.dailymail.co.uk/news/article-1380538/Cant-read-write-English-You-serve-jury-new-rules.html.

Random selection for small samples is not sensitive to plurality and does not guarantee representativeness. And representativeness does not guarantee impartiality, especially given in-group and out-group bias in human decision-making. In Canada, Aboriginal Justice Inquiry of Manitoba (AJI) reported in 1991 that indigenous peoples who spoke only indigenous languages have been routinely excluded from jury service. This, along with other reasons, has led to persistent underrepresentation of indigenous jurors.[139] Perhaps perceptions of legitimacy, which representativeness is ultimately about, ought not be taken only from the perspective of the majority. It is possible to argue that jurors randomly drawn from a particular language community may actually bring us closer to the true meaning of trial by peers.

Having said that, in reality the meaning of *peer* is not negotiated based on judgment of fairness in bilingual and multilingual jurisdictions. After all, the right to a jury in a minority language, if granted, flows from official status instead of from access to justice. Even jurisdictions that recognize the right to a minority official language jury do not give the same treatment to all minority languages, perhaps for fear of opening a floodgate, especially in linguistically diverse territories. Despite having granted official status to indigenous languages in some territories, Canada has consistently refused to form an indigenous jury for indigenous populations (see *Lamirande*[140] and *Teerhuis-Moar*[141]), and speaking only an indigenous language has been a reason why indigenous persons have been excluded from jury service.[142]

Although often justified in legal terms, divergence in practice across jurisdictions and conflicting lines of reasoning suggest that there is no clear overriding legal rationale for supporting one practice over another. Including a linguistic criterion changes the pool from which random samples are drawn, and it is debatable whether this challenges representativeness and legitimacy. On the other hand, allowing defendants or litigants speaking an official minority language to be heard directly without mediation improves their access to justice, assuming that the jurors chosen really have the competence to understand them. Multiplicity of official language status adds a new dimension of complexity to the already thorny area of jury studies, and has the potential of clashing with established legal principles.

---

[139] Richard Jochelson et al., "Revisiting Representativeness in the Manitoban Criminal Jury," *Manitoba Law Journal* 37, no. 2 (2015): 365–98.

[140] *R. v. Lamirande*, 2002 MBCA 41.

[141] *R. v. Teerhuis-Moar*, 2007 MBQB 165.

[142] Jochelson et al., "Revisiting Representativeness in the Manitoban Criminal Jury."

Unrepresented Litigants

Before the Conquest, an Englishmen could be his own advocate, for the law was in English. When French became the language of pleading, Englishmen had no choice but to "have recourse to the shrine of the lawyer."[143] Early colonists in the English colonies of North America were eager to create law books that an ordinary person could read and understand without the help of a lawyer. Massachusetts had at one point forbade lawyers from serving in its legislature and required all parties to a case to represent themselves.[144] These historical facts remind us not only that litigating through a legal representative has not always been a norm, but also that legal language(s) significantly affects the configuration of a trial and access to justice.

A surge in self-representation has been reported all over the world,[145] especially in the civil justice system, not least because of the extortionate cost of legal representation and the limited reach of legal aid. Many unrepresented litigants, including those who have limited proficiency in the official language of a legal system, have no option but to represent themselves, in courtrooms where interpreters may or may not be available. In Canada, for example, the vast majority of unrepresented litigants could not afford a lawyer.[146] A report of the Supreme Court Self-Help Information Centre in British Columbia reveal that over half of its users speak a language other than English at home (the majority of them speaking Asian languages; 5.6% use French at home); 8.3% of the surveyed users of the Centre found English-only services a problem.[147]

Unrepresented litigants in Canada interviewed by Macfarlane found navigating the justice system on their own very difficult, even though most of them are native speakers of the language of a trial.[148] In fact, they encounter language difficulties even before their case goes to trial. For example, many have difficulty comprehending the terminology used in court forms. Even monolingual legal systems have realized the need to provide multilingual support services; 19% of the unrepresented litigants who used the Citizens Advice Bureau (CAB), located within the Royal Courts of Justice in the United

---

143 John Warr, cited in Tiersma, *Legal Language*, 35.

144 Tiersma, *Legal Language*.

145 There are reports on this from the United Kingdom, the United States, Australia, and New Zealand. See Leung (2015).

146 Trevor C. W. Farrow et al., "Addressing the Needs of Self-Represented Litigants in the Canadian Justice System," A White Paper Prepared for the Association of Canadian Court Administrators, 2012.

147 John Malcolmson and Gayla Reid, "British Columbia Court Self-Help Information Centre," Final Evaluation Report, August 2006.

148 Julie Macfarlane, "The National Self-Represented Litigants Project: Identifying and Meeting the Needs of Self-Represented Litigants," Convocation: Treasurer's Advisory Group on Access to Justice (TAG) Working Group Report, May 2013.

Kingdom, speak English as a second language[149]. The Supreme Court Self-Help Information Centre in British Columbia[150] is translating materials into other languages in the hope of offering a basic orientation for its multilingual population. The Law Commission of New Zealand has also recommended the provision of legal information in key community languages.[151]

There is added pressure on bilingual and multilingual jurisdictions to make all aspects of their legal services available in their official languages, especially reference materials that are useful for case preparation, including information about procedural rules, relevant legislation, and case judgments. In Newfoundland and Labrador, for example, legal information is being translated into French and into Inuktitut, Innueimun, and Mi'kmaw.

Official multilingualism may augment unrepresented litigation. In post-colonial jurisdictions, where legal systems had been operating in a former colonial language and precluding self-representation by the majority, introducing a vernacular as an additional legal language may enable litigation that was otherwise unthinkable. When a legal system presents itself as being more linguistically accessible, litigants may feel more confident to go to court without a lawyer. That said, they may not be aware that the vernacular as newly introduced into the legal system may be very different from the everyday language they are used to, given that many legal concepts remain foreign imports. Moreover, being unfamiliar with the process, they may have unrealistic expectations of the justice system and consume more court time and judicial resources than normal.

A vast amount of literature suggests that unrepresented litigants are at a disadvantaged position. Although increasing linguistic access enables participation in legal processes, overt linguistic barriers exist even when litigants are "native speakers" of the language of the trial. For example, they may adopt styles of speech that discount their credibility (e.g., hyper-formality and over-elaboration[152]) or have difficulty adjusting to the formality of the courtroom.[153] In the former British colony of Hong Kong, cases may now be tried in Cantonese or English. Although official reference texts provided by the Resource Centre for Unrepresented Litigants (http://rcul.judiciary.gov.hk) are available in Chinese, they are largely anglicized and incomprehensible

---

[149] Joyce Plotnikoff and Richard Woolfson, *A Study of the Services Provided under the Otton Project to Litigants in Person at the Citizens Advice Bureau at the Royal Courts of Justice* (Great Britain, Lord Chancellor's Department, Research Programme, 1998).

[150] Malcolmson and Reid, "British Columbia Court Self-Help Information Centre."

[151] "Delivering Justice for All: A Vision for New Zealand Courts and Tribunals," Law Commission Report 85 (Wellington, New Zealand, March 2004).

[152] William M. O'Barr, *Linguistic Evidence: Language, Power, and Strategy in the Courtroom* (New York: Academic Press, 1982).

[153] Ng, *The Common Law in Two Voices*.

to the layperson.[154] Little help may be found from the online glossary that the Department of Justice provides, which lists Chinese-English translation equivalents of legal terms, without offering any explanation of what the terms mean. My earlier study of unrepresented litigation in Hong Kong shows that litigants may misunderstand procedures (e.g., using objections as a means to express disagreement, or being confused by the difference between a statement and a testimony), waive their rights (e.g., to cross-examine) without fully understanding the implications, and fail to distinguish what is legally relevant, even though the trial takes place in their native language, Cantonese.[155] Some litigants destruct courtroom formality by bringing in Cantonese mannerisms (e.g., haggling, exaggeration, and name-calling) into an English common law courtroom, only to be reprimanded by the judge.

The situation is arguably worse when one tries to litigate in a second language. One highly educated unrepresented litigant who chose to litigate in English (a second language that she speaks with apparent fluency) had a tendency to use chains of intensifiers and adjectives to emphasize her points: "every single," "never ever," "malicious, humiliating, discriminatory, degrading, abusive," all of which prompted the judge to doubt her sensitivity to the English language and to remind her more than once how serious her allegations were:

> Judge: "manipulative," "abusive," . . . you know how strong these words are? You know your words?

If extending linguistic access to justice may be considered one objective of official multilingualism,[156] the discussion so far suggests that such extension alone is not sufficient to empower unrepresented litigants, especially in post-colonial contexts. Even though litigants may now litigate in their first language, they may not have the pragmatic competence to advocate for themselves successfully in a common law courtroom. In fact, chances are that they may lose a case that they could have won if they had legal representation.

A more substantive issue, which has been elucidated in Chapter 6, is peculiar to bilingual and multilingual law. For jurisdictions that have adopted the equal authenticity principle, unrepresented litigants cannot be expected to know how one language version of a piece of legislation should be interpreted in relation to another, especially where there are textual discrepancies.

---

[154] Matthew W. L. Yeung and Janny H. C. Leung, "An Empirical Study of Lay Comprehension of Chinese Legal Reference Texts in Hong Kong," *International Journal of Speech Language and the Law* 22, no. 1 (May 11, 2015): 79–110, https://doi.org/10.1558/ijsll.v22i1.17224.

[155] Leung, "Lay Litigation Behaviour in Postcolonial Hong Kong Courtrooms."

[156] The governor of Hong Kong, for example, said in 1985, "It is right that laws should be available in the language of the majority of the population." See Attorney General's Chambers (1986).

Paradox of Language Rights

Not all language rights issues that may arise in the course of interaction between citizens and official language law could be covered in this chapter. For example, language use in police cautions and pretrial investigation is omitted. The question of whether duty lawyers need to be fluent in an official language spoken by the defendant has arisen in some jurisdictions, as has the question of whether language rights derived from official status may be equally enjoyed by non-citizens who also speak that official language.[157]

This chapter shows that despite the expectations that it may create in the mind of citizens, official multilingualism does not in itself guarantee the expansion of language rights, given the divergent practices. The extent of rights is open to interpretation, and is an outcome of balancing against other competing considerations. Overall, it is more likely that citizens in multilingual jurisdictions have more language choices available to them in their dealings with the law than their counterparts in monolingual jurisdictions. Some leading multilingual jurisdictions not only have allowed their citizens to speak in an official language, but also have allowed them to be heard in the official language of their choice. These decisions are not straightforward in that judiciaries need to balance the language rights of different parties involved in legal processes, as in the case of civil trials, and also to resolve conflicts between official language rights and other established legal principles, as exemplified in the discussion of jury selection.

On the whole, official multilingualism may also pose challenges to a judicial system by increasing the volume of unrepresented litigation and by threatening courtroom formality. In some post-colonial jurisdictions, official multilingualism has allowed informal language practices (such as code-mixing) to be brought into the courtroom. This may be seen as damaging to the symbolic means (such as decorum) through which law establishes its authority.

Due to the widening of language options, people with multilingual abilities may be said to have an advantage over monolingual citizens in a multilingual jurisdiction. This reiterates the argument that equality across language communities may inadvertently create inequality within language communities. In some cases, bilingual litigants can make decisions about their choice of language strategically, for example, by deliberately involving interpreters in order to buy thinking time, or by asking for documents to be translated for them in

---

[157] This was the moot point in the European case of *Bickel and Franz* (C-274/96), November 24, 1998, where the Luxembourg court had to decide whether a German tourist in South Tyrol, Italy, is entitled to be tried in German, an entitlement granted to the German-speaking community of the Province of Bolzano. Although in this case the court held that Italy could not discriminate based on nationality, in national courts facing no similar treaty obligation it is unclear which way the decision will go.

order to delay trial or add to the stake of the trial, especially if the other party is less financially resourceful. It has also been noted that in Canada, some bilingual defendants choose to proceed in an official language that allows for an earlier trial in order to shorten their detention,[158] because shortage of bilingual judges means a longer wait time for a trial in a minority language. In southern Manitoba, some defense counsels have also chosen to conduct a trial in English in order to avoid a certain francophone judge who is known to be strict.[159] Although the issue of linguistic privilege is not unique to bilingual and multilingual jurisdictions, such strategic deployment of language choices is enabled by official multilingualism.

A fundamental question is the philosophical and moral basis of language rights derived from official status. Common justifications for the granting of language rights are derived from human dignity as an individual (which give rise to freedom, equality, and personality rights), as a community (with degrees of autonomy leading up to the right of peoples to self-determination), and the protection of linguistic diversity (as though it is a kind of biodiversity). These justifications can lead to conflicting policy directions. According to the Oslo Recommendations Regarding the Linguistic Rights of National Minorities (1998), where members of a minority are significant in number, they should have the right to access state services or to communicate with public entities in their language. This sliding-scale logic is based on principles of equality and proportionality: the bigger a language group, the more linguistic accommodation they should receive from the government.[160] On the other hand, if the purpose is to maximize linguistic diversity, stronger protection should be given to less dominant languages to ensure their survival. But official language rights do not clearly follow any of these approaches. Indeed, it has been argued that "language rights" that are tied to the concept of "nation" are not "rights," but are better characterized as "privileges"[161] or entitlements. As such, it is questionable whether they should be considered absolute rights. When deriving language rights from official status, courts have been articulating rationales that appear to be circular: because these languages enjoy special legal status, they should be treated generously. They simply have to show deference to political decision-making.

---

158 Mike Wallace, "Statutory Review of Part XVII of the Criminal Code: Report of the Standing Committee on Justice and Human Rights," House of Commons, Canada, April 2014.

159 "Standing Committee on Justice and Human Rights: Evidence," Number 014, 2nd Session, 41st Parliament, House of Commons, Canada, March 4, 2014.

160 de Varennes, "Language as a Right in International Law: Limits and Potentials."

161 Jens Normann Jørgensen, "Language and Languages in European Ideology, Political Documents and Real Life," in *Linguistic Diversity and European Democracy*, ed. Anne Lise Kjær and Silvia Adamo (Surrey, England; Burlington, VT: Ashgate, 2011), 208–20.

Chapter 8

Concluding Remarks on Linguistic Equality, Strategic Pluralism, and Linguistic Justice

> The more languages there are that receive public recognition the more it is likely that such recognition will become a meaningless formality and the real work will be done in the dominant language.
>
> —Alan Patten[1]

Despite the lack of universal agreement about what justice means, equality is generally seen as a requirement for justice. Since equality is a foundation of liberalism and a moral norm, the value of linguistic equality is easily taken for granted.

Linguistic equality has become a sort of legal spectacle in multilingual jurisdictions: the sheer number of official languages in some jurisdictions has been a source of amazement, and often these languages are paraded with pride. What exactly does upholding equality among these languages mean? Note that I am not discussing here an abstract, utopian notion of linguistic equality, but the kind of linguistic equality that arises specifically from official multilingualism, the kind that is being practiced and used in legal reasoning. Building upon the analyses conducted in earlier chapters, I offer a characterization of linguistic equality as it is claimed and practiced in bilingual and multilingual jurisdictions today. I call it *shallow equality*, and argue that it must not be confused with popular conceptions of equality that have a universal basis.

Both symbolic jurisprudence and shallow equality are properties of a policy of strategic pluralism. The symbolic nature of official language law and the shallow character of linguistic equality do not prevent official multilingualism from serving legitimate goals. Neither official monolingualism nor multilingualism is inherently just or unjust; official multilingualism is not morally superior to official monolingualism. Both are viable strategies for the survival of a polity. Although this book has been primarily concerned with

[1] Alan Patten, "Who Should Have Official Language Rights?" in *Languages, Constitutionalism and Minorities*, ed. André Braën, Pierre Foucher, and Yves Le Bouthillier (Markham, ON: LexisNexis Butterworths, 2006), 245.

the descriptive and analytical questions of how to make sense of official multilingualism, I will conclude with some insights that may illuminate normative questions about linguistic justice.

Inherent Dilemmas about Upholding Linguistic Equality

We will start this discussion by taking stock of some of the insights gained in the preceding four chapters about the consequences of upholding equality among official languages in public institutions and legal processes. Even where there is political goodwill to achieve linguistic equality, it appears that the goal cannot be fully realized without creating new kinds of inequalities and compromising other social goods. While it is not surprising that social goods compete and conflict with one another, evaluation of the social value of linguistic equality helps us weigh these goods. Where linguistic equality does not achieve as much good as it is anticipated to achieve, we will also analyze where the shortcomings come from. Apart from political inertia, which may be linked with instrumental motivations in law-making, some of the shortcomings arise from inescapable properties of language and their clashes with ideals of law, social forces outside of law, and from mismatches between what legal equality can offer and the needs it is expected to meet.

LINGUISTIC ACCESS TO JUSTICE

As shown in Chapter 6, multiple authenticity enlarges the distance between legal and textual meaning in legal interpretation. While a teleological approach can arguably better approximate legislative intent than a textualist approach, such that adoption of the former may be seen as a positive development in judicial interpretation, when it comes to lay access to the law, the impact of this approach is ambivalent. If legislative texts are equally authentic in two or more languages, legal meaning is located in all versions combined. In other words, even if a language enjoys equal official status, its monolingual speakers can only gain a partial understanding of the law. Multilingual laws are best interpreted by multilingual readers who have legal competence. In other words, multilingual law makes it easier for more people to know roughly what the law says, but simultaneously makes it harder for them to know it exactly what it means. One may say that the latter has always been impossible, even for native speakers of a monolingual jurisdiction, but multiplicity in language texts does add intertextual indeterminacy to legal interpretation. All these may not be transparent to the unrepresented litigant who feels ready to litigate without a lawyer because she or he can speak an official language.

Another area where multiplicity of language may affect lay participation in the legal system is jury selection. We have seen in Chapter 7 that adopting a linguistic criterion may compromise random selection. From the perspective of meaningful participation in trial, being directly heard by linguistically competent legal decision-makers certainly carries less risk of miscommunication than communicating through mediation (though communication without mediation is not required by the right to fair trial). However, depending on the size of a minority language community, restricting the pool of potential jurors to speakers of a minority language may raise questions about whether the jurors drawn may be affected by in-group bias in their decision-making. This is an example of a clash in ideology between linguistic equality and access to law, on one hand, and adjudicatory neutrality embedded in the notion of trial by peers, on the other.

AUTONOMY

Law only sets minimum standards of behavior. Although many language rights advocates seek legal protection of minority languages, the dependence on legal intervention for the vitality of minority languages is a worrying trend.[2] This warning is particularly acute considering the misalignment between the motivations of law-making and the needs of language communities.

Chapter 4 reviewed the kind of bureaucratic structure that institutional multilingualism operates in. Although this structure monitors compliance and handles complaints, it does not incorporate representative governance of language matters. In fact, this institutional structure has the practical effect of handling group-based demands as a matter of individual rights, offering no space for political negotiation. This is surprising considering that official multilingualism and linguistic equality arise as an inter-group relationship. Group-based actions are especially relevant to minority communities concerned with cultural survival. It is foolish to depend on bureaucrats, however much good faith some of them may have, to safeguard one's heritage. Even where linguistic equality is held as a fundamental principle, its implementing bodies may be subject to institutional constraints such as budget cuts. Autonomy requires agency, which existing institutions dispossess minority speakers of in favor of a bureaucrat acting as their spokesperson. There are limited signs that official multilingualism has directly enhanced the self-governing capacity or political representation of sub-state national minorities or endogenous communities in post-colonial polities.

Where minority nationalism thrives, as in the case of Catalonia and Quebec, official multilingualism may be used by the state to contain political resistance within an institutionalized space and to redirect grievances from

[2] Williams, "Perfidious Hope." See also Vanessa Pupavac, *Language Rights: From Free Speech to Linguistic Governance* (Basingstoke, Hampshire; New York, NY: Palgrave Macmillan, 2012).

outside to inside the system. An institutional structure set up under such a premise naturally offers limited scope to create radical change.

AUTHENTICITY

The official use of a language necessitates its standardization (i.e., the development of a relatively uniform variety of a language) and popularizes the standard language ideology,[3] threatening the perception of authenticity. Seen from this perspective, improving linguistic access to the law by adding new legal languages is akin to shooting a moving target, as the institutionalization and standardization of a language for official purposes invariably change the language. This is highly significant for many language communities because affirmation of authenticity is a chief motivation in the politics of recognition. Romansch and Filipino provide extreme examples of loss of authenticity, where a new language variety is artificially created for administrative convenience or political neutrality. The creation of a new language is accompanied by the creation of an imaginary speech community. Law is used to bridge reality with this imagination, not always successfully.

That institutionalization threatens authenticity is not unique to multilingual jurisdictions. Even in a monolingual English jurisdiction, everyday English is significantly different from legal English. The problem, however, is exacerbated in post-colonial contexts, where the amount of linguistic engineering needed to adapt an endogenous language to a colonial legal system is particularly burdensome. The resultant legal language may be barely recognizable to the native speakers of that language.

The tension between authenticity and utility seems to be an inherent property of language: increasing the utility of a speech variety requires elimination of linguistic differences through standardization, but such linguistic differences may precisely be markers of identity. On the other hand, refusal to agree on a standardized form can hasten the decline of languages spoken by a small population.[4] This tension arises because language serves both communicative and identity functions, and these are not always in accord.

SOCIAL AND ECONOMIC FORCES OUTSIDE OF LAW

In both the translation and interpretation of multilingual law, we have seen that despite official declarations of equality, popular perception that one official language is more authoritative or better than another still affects decision-making

---

[3] James Milroy and Lesley Milroy, *Authority in Language: Investigating Standard English*, 3rd ed. (London; New York: Routledge, 1999).

[4] N. Louanna Furbee and Lori A. Stanley, "A Collaborative Model for Preparing Indigenous Curators of a Heritage Language," *International Journal of the Sociology of Language* 154 (2002): 113–28.

in implicit ways. Legal equality asserted by states rarely subverts social hierarchy, and is not usually sufficient to counteract external forces, such as the dominance of English in the global linguistic market. These forces penetrate not only private domains but also public institutions and legal processes.

In post-colonial polities, despite all the effort that may be put into the corpus planning of an endogenous official language, its popularization is likely to be met with resistance when it continues to be seen as socially inferior. The ideology that a colonial language is better suited for law serves entrenched interests, notably those of the educated elites.

THE SLIPPERY SLOPE OF LINGUISTIC BOUNDARIES

"(T)the politicization of language, while helping one group to achieve its goals, is likely to create new problems for others."[5] Coulmas illustrates his point with the Greek language movement that was critical to the Greek secession from the multilingual Ottoman Empire. In the new state where Greek served as the national language, new minorities were created, and a new struggle against linguistic dominance began. Kraus also notes that nationalist groups in Eastern Europe that have successfully created new states are "sometimes less tolerant towards linguistic differences in their territory than the previous imperial administration had been."[6]

Not only may linguistic equality create new minorities and new inequalities, such as inequality within a language group that has differential access to bilingualism, even people who are taken to be speakers of an officially recognized language may not benefit from its elevated status. Consider Limburgish, a language spoken in regions near the Dutch–Belgian–German border that is said to have 550 dialects. It does not exist as a uniform language, but it was recognized collectively as a language in 1997 by the European Charter for Regional or Minority Languages, providing yet another example of the law carving out an imaginary speech community from a dialectological heteroglossia.[7] Similarly, the Evenki language, an indigenous language in Russia, is spoken by very scattered populations. The standardized form of the language is practically a foreign language for the people, and they refuse to speak it. In these cases, it is practically impossible for a government to communicate to its citizens in all of these varieties. Perhaps this is one reason why the European Charter for Regional or Minority Languages explicitly states that dialects of official languages should not be included as regional or minority languages—they just do not know how to deal with the challenge of dialectal differences.

---

[5] Coulmas, "What Are National Languages Good For?" 12.

[6] Kraus, "Neither United nor Diverse? The Language Issue and Political Legitimation in the European Union," 21.

[7] Bakhtin, "Discourse in the Novel."

This classic slippery-slope problem arises from the fact that language does not exist as a bound object, as notions of official status and linguistic equality assume it to be. Any attempt at drawing the boundary of a language makes one realize that language is far from homogenous and that marginal members exist. Further recognizing dialects may not resolve the problem, as variation also exists within dialects. Dialectal speakers are therefore often simply erased from the picture.

THE EQUALITY QUANDARY AND THE DIVERSITY PARADOX

Although it may signal equality, parallel usage of a language can lead to competition and redundancy. In a diglossic society, functionally distinct languages are arguably complementary. Fishman conjectures that if the roles of languages are not kept functionally separate, it is easier for a more powerful language to displace a less powerful language.[8] When a less powerful language is functionally redundant and is less preferred to another language due to persistent ideology, people may see its parallel existence as merely decorative. Ironically, in a less "equal" world, functional compartmentalization and geographical isolation may facilitate the survival of less powerful languages.

Linguistic equality is also caught in a kind of diversity paradox. The more linguistically diverse a society is, the more there is a need for a lingua franca,[9] and the higher the market value of multilingual proficiency becomes. This may reduce the incentives for people living in this society to remain monolingual, a situation that speeds up language shift and diminishes the significance of linguistic equality.

The Shallow Character of Linguistic Equality

The first and most important sense in which linguistic equality in contemporary multilingual legal orders may be said to have a *shallow* character is that this kind of equality fits neither a difference-blind nor a difference-aware conception of equality. The latter, deeper forms of equality form the basis of human rights instruments, traditional liberal philosophies, and the doctrine of state equality. A universalist conception of equality assumes that all human beings deserve equal treatment and respect. In more recent times, communitarian theories have tried to expand this notion to collective identities and posit that all cultures are also of equal worth. Shallow equality is not founded on this assumption, whether held at the individual level or extended to groups. Equality

---

[8] Joshua A. Fishman, "Societal Multilingualism: Stable and Transitional," in *Language in Sociocultural Change* (1968; repr., Stanford University Press, 1972), 135–61.

[9] De Swaan, "Endangered Languages, Sociolinguistics, and Linguistic Sentimentalism."

is shallow when it is selectively applied to certain individuals or groups, and the criteria for inclusion does not promote equality.

Selectivity alone is not the deal breaker. It is unreasonable to expect unbound inclusivity in national policy-making. No jurisdiction in the world today can afford to name all languages official, and to do so would completely devalue the currency of official recognition anyway. A difference-aware conception of equality permits selectivity, when selectivity promotes the equalization of individuals and groups living under disparate social conditions. For example, some international human rights instruments focus on minority or indigenous populations to protect their rights against oppressive states. The argument is that in order to treat people equally, we need to treat them differently because people are born into different socioeconomic conditions.

Official multilingualism is not a uniform phenomenon. As we have seen, it is a response to different types of challenges, such as nation-building, intergroup conflicts, migration, and globalization. Although the inclusion criteria of official multilingualism can only be deduced instead of discovered, I argue in this book that the most reliable predictor of inclusion is whether the inclusion promotes the political and economic capital of the polity. This neoliberal approach does not give all languages in a polity an equal opportunity of being included. It is not based on universal respect for languages, and it is never purely an intervention on endangered languages. Legal recognition of language status does not aim to bring disadvantaged languages to an equal starting point with others—thus bringing about a difference-aware kind of equality, but instead is a mechanism of establishing and maintaining distinctiveness, based on a politics of recognition. Some other criteria have a universal basis, including compensation for historical injustice and linguistic demographics, but these criteria seem to only apply when the interests of the groups concerned coincide with the political or economic interests of a dominant group.

At the international level, linguistic equality as a legal expression of the doctrine of state equality is manifested in international agreements but to a much more limited extent in IGOs. Linguistic equality tends to be upheld among only a few dominant world languages in IGOs and even then, English and French remain the principal languages of institutional operation. Even in the European Union, where all official languages are equal, some languages are more equal than others.

It is important to distinguish between shallow and deep equality because of the conflation that the term *equality* causes in discourses concerning official multilingualism. Official rhetoric about official multilingualism often takes advantage of this conflation, while simultaneously muting voices about deep equality. One may say that if we accept that equality as a fundamentally moral principle, perhaps half a loaf of bread is still better than no bread: equality among only some languages is still better than no equality between any languages. However, in most political contexts this conclusion is difficult to swallow, as many groups are getting no bread at all. Imagine where adjacent pieces of land conquered by two powerful imperialist groups are joined to become a single polity, and these groups decide that their two languages shall be equal, ignoring the hundreds of native languages spoken on the land. The kind of linguistic equality being upheld may be said to have social value in that it prevents violent conflicts between the imperialist powers, but the moral claim based on the assertion of equality is weak not only because the kind of equality maintained is very limited, but also because their criterion for inclusion is morally arbitrary. According to Weinstock, even historical connection and population size are morally arbitrary criteria because the former may reward colonialism and the latter may be a colonial consequence.[10]

The second sense in which linguistic equality may be called shallow comes from its formality. The banality[11] of linguistic equality is crystallized in my mind in a photograph published in the *New York Times* on April 11, 2016, in a follow-up story to the Brussels bombings that happened a month prior.[12] The photograph features a dozen Belgian federal policemen wearing vests—on half of the vests the French word *Police* is printed above the Flemish/Dutch word *Politie*, and on the other half *Politie* is printed above *Police*. When I searched for more images of the Brussels police force online, I found that they also have jackets on which the words are printed horizontally next to each other. Some of the jackets have *Politie* on the left and *Police* on the right, others with *Police* on the left and *Politie* on the right. According to Van Parijs, the two languages are allocated an equal amount of space and their order carefully alternated in bank notes, postage stamps, official documents, and national monuments in Belgium.[13] The effort that went into ensuring the "linguistic equality" of the bilingual logos is remarkable, and can only be justified by the symbolic function of language.

The formal pursuit of linguistic equality has implications about not only cost (see government spending, reported in Chapter 4), but also distribution of cost. It has the potential of displacing resources and energy that could have been put into empowering minorities and dominated populations in more substantive ways. This may include top-down provision of minority-language education in state-funded schools, or bottom-up effort in building civil society, protecting cultural heritage, and promoting minority language arts, and so on.

---

[10] Daniel M. Weinstock, "The Antinomy of Language Policy," in *Language Rights and Political Theory*, ed. Will Kymlicka and Alan Patten (repr., Oxford: Oxford University Press, 2007), 250–70.

[11] Following Billig, "banality" here refers to everyday, as opposed to dramatic or radical expressions. Billig, *Banal Nationalism*.

[12] I am grateful to Yale Law Professor Issa Kohler-Hausmann for drawing my attention to this photograph.

[13] Philippe Van Parijs, *Linguistic Justice for Europe and for the World* (Oxford; New York: Oxford University Press, 2011), 121.

Linguistic equity does not have to come from formal equality. In fact, insistence on formal equality may obscure the different conditions endured by languages and their speakers in the first place.

A deeper risk is that formal equality may give a fictional impression of democratic legitimacy to authoritarian governments, which may refuse to commit to any substantive redistribution of resources for marginalized communities, deny political participation by people that it claims to represent, or consistently allow the ruling class to exploit others. Official displays of tolerance may be accompanied by strong assimilationist practices, in polities that are prone to sham constitutionalism.[14] This is not an insignificant risk, considering that many officially multilingual states are found in Asia, Africa, and Eastern Europe, where electoral authoritarian regimes concentrate. To prevent the abuse of linguistic equality as a façade to authoritarianism, enhanced autonomy of minority groups and their political representation in the wider polity are necessary safeguards.

In an essay entitled "Boutique Multiculturalism," Fish distinguishes between *boutique multiculturalism* and *strong multiculturalism*. He characterizes the former as having a "superficial or cosmetic relationship to the objects of its affection."[15] By contrast, strong multiculturalism takes seriously the core values of cultures that it embraces. The two kinds of multiculturalism may be differentiated in the event of conflict between another culture and a core value of one's own. Official multilingualism has a boutique character. By embracing linguistic diversity in the law, a polity projects an air of inclusivity when pursuing a politics of difference. Where such inclusivity conflicts with economic and political interests, however, linguistic equality is almost always a lesser priority.

Linguistic equality expresses a presumption of equal worth among some languages that has limited political reality, and its potential to change this political reality is limited. In fact, the fiction of equality has the effect of hiding relationships of dominance and inequality.

The legal doctrine of equality of states, whether expressed linguistically or otherwise, has hardly made states more equal in international politics. By the same token, formal equality of languages does not make their speakers more equal politically or socially. It has been argued that even as a legal fiction, it may nevertheless create a sense of moral responsibility for more powerful states to treat weaker states on equal footing. This may work well under normal situations, but the fiction dissolves quickly as soon as conflict arises.[16] The same

---

[14] David S. Law and Mila Versteeg, "Sham Constitutions," *California Law Review* 101, no. 4 (August 2013): 863–952.

[15] Stanley Fish, "Boutique Multiculturalism, or Why Liberals Are Incapable of Thinking about Hate Speech," *Critical Inquiry* 23, no. 2 (1997): 378.

[16] Bart Landheer, *On the Sociology of International Law and International Society* (Dordrecht: Springer, 1966).

goes for linguistic equality. It may work formally to some extent, but social reality kicks in when more substantive interests are at stake.

Similarly, at the state level, as long as official multilingualism remains a nationist or nationalist agenda, asserted legal equality has limited relevance to conditions of social inequalities faced by language minorities or to reversing the subordinate position of endogenous languages. Multiplicity of official languages at the state level seems to signal a move away from linguistic nationalism, under the influence of equality of citizens. But linguistic nationalism has not died. Its grip on linguistic hegemony has been loosened by political reality, especially in states where powerful linguistic communities continue to use language to define their group identity. For example, bilingualism and biculturalism have come to define Canadian national identity, and this identity entails the recognition that both Anglophones and Francophones have a need to hold on to their linguistic expression and cultural identity. The revival of Gaelic and Welsh in Ireland and Wales is precisely a nationalistic expression, as is the promotion of endogenous languages in post-colonial polities. When exogenous languages have fused with native languages, the resultant hybrid (such as Singlish in Singapore) may also become a common heritage and thus a nationalist symbol. The nationalist tie to language policy has not been severed as official multilingualism flourishes. The fact that status given to official languages is frequently enshrined constitutionally attests to the observation that language still lies at the heart of national narratives. Linguistic equality in the European Union works in the same way, but toward a supranational narrative.

Given the prevalence of the phenomenon, as well as the length of time and the amount of effort that some jurisdictions have put into their multilingual institutions, it is astonishing that we have not seen a single example where the use of languages in a legal system is fully symmetrical, even where languages are given equal authority and are expected to be treated equally. Despite what their legal status might say, one official language is more accessible, dominant, and influential than another, corresponding with wider social structures and popular language ideologies. This is especially true where the number of official languages proliferates, as the epigraph of this chapter encapsulates.

By calling the existing conception of linguistic equality shallow, I expose the frequent mismatch between what it is and what it appears to be, but I do not wish to suggest that an even broader, or universalist conception of linguistic equality is necessarily socially desirable. It is rational for polities to limit the number of languages they recognize officially. At the other extreme, linguistic equality for all is not only politically and economic untenable, it is also a sociolinguistic impossibility, for language simply does not fall into discrete units that one can treat equally. The preceding analysis does not suggest that shallow equality is morally deficient, but cautions against the unchallenged assumption that linguistic equality as seen in multilingual jurisdictions today is an unqualified social good.

The Linguistic Justice Debate

That official multilingualism tends to be entrenched in symbolic law and that the kind of linguistic equality it endorses tends to be shallow in nature do not necessarily suggest that such law is unjust. Of course, whether such law is just depends on how one understands justice. Here I will briefly introduce the literature in political philosophy on *linguistic justice*,[17] and then discuss what insights the descriptive and analytical work of this book may offer to normative questions in the debate.

There are two major reasons why liberalism cannot handle linguistic diversity in the same way that it handles cultural and religious diversity. The first concerns compatibility of values. Since some cultures and religions may contain ideas that are incompatible with core liberal values and legal norms such as equality and individual freedom, there may be reasonable ground to not tolerate illiberal practices. Since there are no inherent values in language, there is no clear ground for exclusion. The selection of languages for official recognition is never based on their inherent properties, but rather on their capacity as a proxy for the political significance of their corresponding community of speakers, or their instrumental value as a politically neutral or marketable tool of communication. The second has to do with the impossibility of political neutrality about language. The standard liberal response to identity conflict is that polities can stay out of it by maintaining neutrality. This works for religion and culture, but not language. Linguistic neutrality is not an option in public communication, for polities cannot function in a linguistic vacuum. On the other hand, adopting one language, or some languages but not others, inevitably benefits some speakers but not others, violating the egalitarian foundation of liberalism. Given that adopting all languages is not practicable, how polities can manage linguistic diversity in an equitable way has thus become a puzzle for liberalism.

This puzzle may be illustrated through applying the Rawlsian notion of fairness to language policy. John Rawls famously argues that conditions of equality must be agreed upon by free and equal persons who do not have unfair advantages over others that are accumulated from the past.[18] Principles of justice should therefore be determined in the original position, a hypothetical scenario where nobody knows his or her position in society, thereby eliminating the influence of status quo. Applying the Rawlsian veil of ignorance to the question of linguistic justice, a just official language law should be imagined

---

[17] For a useful summary, see Helder De Schutter and David Robichaud, "Van Parijsian Linguistic Justice: Context, Analysis and Critiques," *Critical Review of International Social and Political Philosophy* 18, no. 2 (March 4, 2015): 87–112, https://doi.org/10.1080/13698230.2015.1023627.

[18] John Rawls, *Justice as Fairness: A Restatement*, ed. Erin Kelly (Cambridge, MA; London, England: The Belknap Press of Harvard University Press, 2001).

from the point of view of someone who does not know what first language she or he speaks in this hypothetical world. Solutions that meet the Rawlsian notion of fairness seem to be either impractical or unavailable. One of them is for everyone to learn all other languages, which is an impossibility. Two other possibilities, which are for no one to learn another language or for everyone to learn another language (with an even distribution of second languages being learned), will not satisfy the communicative needs of the globalized world. Perhaps the solution that ensures most linguistic equality is when a government operates in an artificial language (similar to Esperanto) that nobody speaks as a first language, and equal resources will be provided to everyone to acquire that language as a second language.[19] But this solution is highly inefficient. Alternatively, the burden may be completely shifted to the government instead. A government may operate in all languages, and risk collapsing under its own weight. Perhaps one day this solution may be made viable through technological advancement in artificial intelligence. Just like personal assistant programs in smartphones and home assistant machines that people now install in their residence, we may not be far from a future where government services can be provided through a combination of voice recognition and machine translation (whether people will be happy to communicate with an automaton is a separate question). Until then, our problem remains.

Compared with the communicative functions of language considered in the preceding thought experiment, equality in identity interests may be even harder to achieve, given that universal recognition depletes the meaning of recognition, and official recognition works as a resource only thanks to its scarcity. Weinstock argues, however, that states do not have to attach any symbolic significance to their linguistic choice. In his anti-symbolism proposal, the state should do nothing more than what is minimally required to effectively communicate with its citizens.[20] In other words, polities can offer linguistic accommodation to all without engaging in a politics of recognition.

In stark contrast to the anti-symbolism proposal, some political theorists urge polities to accommodate people's collective identity associated with language and question the individualist basis of liberalism. Holding that collective identity and cultural membership are important components of individual autonomy and dignity, communitarians such as Michael Sandal and Charles Taylor, and more recently multiculturalists such as Will Kymlicka, argue that state recognition and support for certain cultural or linguistic groups is compatible with liberalism and that the preservation of certain languages, cultures, and values is a legitimate collective goal.

---

[19] Jonathan Pool, "The Official Language Problem," *The American Political Science Review* 85, no. 2 (1991): 495–514, https://doi.org/10.2307/1963171.

[20] Weinstock, "The Antinomy of Language Policy."

Presenting a hybrid model that attempts to take care of both identity and non-identity interests, Van Parijs situates his analysis of linguistic justice in the global context and names at least three dimensions of linguistic justice: as fair cooperation, as equal opportunity, and as parity of esteem. He argues that the first two dimensions justify the promotion of English as global lingua franca, because the ascendency of English can break down linguistic borders, enhance cross-cultural understanding, and facilitate democratic deliberations in global governance.[21] The injustice that a global lingua franca creates is anticipated to shrink as English spreads, and is best compensated by the free provision of English resources to the non-Anglophone world. To uphold the parity of esteem, however, linguistic communities should be allowed to impose their language as the language of official communication and public education in some territory as long as the community itself is willing to bear the cost. The assumption is that respect for local linguistic practices will be reciprocated when populations move across these territories.[22]

Although it is not the purpose of the book to evaluate whether official multilingualism promotes justice, the analysis may inform the linguistic justice debate by pointing out nuances in the pursuit of identity and non-identity interests that underlie the competing senses of justice presented in the literature.

For those in support of linguistic convergence in the interests of efficiency, democracy, and equality of opportunity,[23] they may be surprised that official multilingualism does not have to be an obstacle to these goals. This is the case when recognition is primarily symbolic, which is observed in many polities. Moreover, even if policy implementation is taken seriously and that efficiency is compromised by an elaborate multilingual regime, multiplicity of official languages actually encourages the development of a lingua franca in the long run. Therefore, recognition of many languages could, somewhat counterintuitively, promote linguistic convergence. This is, of course, bad news for those who seek to reverse or slow down the loss of linguistic diversity.

For those who would like to see more recognition of collective identity, they may be pleased to know that a substantive number of polities are already doing this. However, they need to be aware that symbolic recognition is an unlikely tool for subverting power relations, even though it does present a norm-setting opportunity. Moreover, official recognition does not necessarily enhance the autonomy of a group or individuals in the group, or help preserve the authenticity or purity of their languages, considering the prospects

---

[21] Philippe Van Parijs, "Linguistic Justice," *Politics, Philosophy & Economics* 1, no. 1 (February 1, 2002): 59–74, https://doi.org/10.1177/1470594X02001001003; Van Parijs, *Linguistic Justice for Europe and for the World.*

[22] This regime has, of course, limited practicality for small and dispersed linguistic communities.

[23] De Schutter and Robichaud, "Van Parijsian Linguistic Justice: Context, Analysis and Critiques."

of linguistic standardization and bureaucratic management that are likely to accompany official recognition.

It may be helpful to clarify conceptually that identity and non-identity interests do not map neatly onto the symbolic and instrumental functions of language. Symbolic language law can be used to pursue non-identity interests such as pacification. On the other hand, identity interests in cultural survival and heritage preservation may be best protected by promoting the instrumental value of a language.

Since identity and non-identity interests that underlie both the symbolic and instrumental functions of language are competing, there is no language policy that everybody will find just. Obsession about linguistic justice may risk losing sight of the big picture. People's feelings of fairness are tied to socio-political context, especially for groups that have suffered historical injustice. A practical question, which can only be assessed contextually, is of course what a "just" linguistic policy may cost, both economically and politically. As Van Parijs observes, a linguistically just solution may not be a peaceful solution;[24] just imagine the chaos that may ensue if territories are redistributed along linguistic lines, in order to uphold the parity of esteem. Alternatively, one may also wish to consider whether everyone may be better off if investment on maintaining a multilingual regime is spent directly on measures that enhance democracy and equality of opportunity.

Pluralism as a Strategy

There is a deeply seated ideology that homogeneity is good and that heterogeneity leads to disorder. In various religions and mythologies, linguistic diversity is portrayed as a punishment from god or a plan of evil.[25] In law, certainty is a prized feature; courts of law work by eliminating alternatives in favor of one interpretation and acceptance of one system of judicial hierarchy. Divergent textual meanings that have equal authority, as illustrated in cases of multilingual statutory interpretation, are the worst nightmares in legal interpretation. In politics, the integrity of a polity is premised upon the idea of sovereignty, and atrocities are often tolerated in the name of national unity. In contrast, contemporary liberal celebrations of multiculturalism seem to suggest that the more diversity, the merrier. Linguistic homogeneity is oppressive, and linguistic pluralism is tolerant. Supporting the spread of English is imperialistic, and

---

[24] Van Parijs, *Linguistic Justice for Europe and for the World.*

[25] Apart from the famous biblical story of Babel, in Greek mythology Hermes invented many tongues to create discord among men, and in Hindu legend, Brahma, the god of creation, punished a tree for almost reaching heaven by cutting off its branches, which when cast down to earth made differences of belief and speech. See discussion in Liu, *Standardizing Diversity*.

preserving minority languages is noble. So the logic goes. Both ideologies are too simplistic to capture the complex interactions between linguistic diversity, historical and sociopolitical changes, and the contextual implications of language policies.

Both official monolingualism and official multilingualism are based on a politics of difference, and both may be sensible strategies for the legitimate goal of survival. An officially multilingual polity cannot claim absolute moral superiority over an officially monolingual counterpart; the number of officially recognized languages should not be taken as a moral barometer. Without looking into contextual factors such as implementation measures and sociopolitical conditions, official multilingualism cannot serve as a model for linguistic justice, a minimum standard, or a benchmark for best practice in the management of linguistic diversity.

Both *shallow equality* and *symbolic jurisprudence* are properties of a policy of *strategic pluralism* that underlies official multilingualism. These characterizations facilitate understanding of how official multilingual law works, and should not be taken as moral criticisms. In fact, social good may flow from official multilingualism, even if the consequence is indirect.

Researchers have speculated on the relationship between linguistic management and the health of a polity. Fishman, for example, notes that "[l]inguistically homogenous polities are economically more developed, educationally more advanced, politically more modernized, and ideologically-politically more tranquil and stable."[26] Such an observation, however, seems to focus on correlation rather than causation, ignoring the fact that many territories that were subjected to colonial exploitation in the past and unfair trade relations in the present happen to be in linguistically diverse regions. It also has been argued that giving supremacy to a politically neutral lingua franca, as is commonly done in post-colonial contexts, avoids polarizing the population, promotes a sense of equality among ethnic groups, and facilitates economic development by lowering transaction costs.[27] On the other hand, Patten and Kymlicka have observed that countries that offer more regional language rights and status recognition are "amongst the most peaceful, prosperous, free, and democratic societies around."[28] Tierney argues that given the grim prospect for self-determination, which remains an unresolved issue in international law, most sub-state national societies now focus their political aspirations on

---

[26] Fishman, "The Status and Prospects of Bilingualism in the United States," 150.

[27] Liu argues that the language regime of Indonesia plays a decisive role in its economic success post-independence. Indonesia is home to more than 700 languages and the only official language is a link language—Malay—which is a common trade language of the East Indies. According to Liu, such a language regime neutralizes power and mitigates the negative effects of ethnolinguistic heterogeneity. Liu, *Standardizing Diversity*.

[28] Patten and Kymlicka, "Introduction: Language Rights and Political Theory: Context, Issues, and Approaches," 5.

state recognition, seeking increased political representation in the public sphere and self-government.[29] The risky path of political independence is only pursued if their sense of autonomy and unique identity cannot be preserved within a state. In other words, official recognition, if seen as a form of power sharing and a sign of respect, can indeed be one step toward peaceful coexistence and reconciliation.

Looking at it from the perspective of speech communities whose language gains status recognition, it may be said that official recognition contributes to identity promotion and cultural security and may facilitate their political negotiation of rights. Status recognition may improve feelings and relationships in ways that are irrelevant to legal rights, including a sense of mutual interest[30] among groups whose languages are recognized. In the context of post-colonial polities, endogenous communities may enjoy a national pride and a sense of regaining ownership and autonomy that official recognition of their language offers. If a nation is a socially constructed, imagined community, as Anderson[31] suggests, perhaps symbolic recognition is the perfect solution to a problem that arises from this social imaginary.

But perhaps an unintended consequence of strategic pluralism carries also its most precious value: its potential to create and reinforce pluralist ideologies and influence social norms. According to Cover, law can only be interpreted within the nomos in which it is situated, and the dominating narrative that gives law its meaning changes over time. Therefore, official language law that has been interpreted narrowly today may acquire an broader significance later on, as social norms evolve.[32] Official multilingualism encourages a multiculturalist conception of national identity, which may be particularly crucial in transitional democracies that have to deal with inter-group conflicts. Such law creates a narrative that stretches reality toward an imagined alternative, providing a way of imagining a nation that is bound together by shared values, rather than by a shared language. The normalization of plurality may act as a small counterforce to the recent resurgence of nationalism, which is sometimes synonymous with xenophobia and intolerance, triggered by the pressures that global economic integration exerts on some local sectors.

A Tale of Caution and Opportunity

The account of official multilingualism offered in this book is neither utopian nor dystopian. What it has offered is a panorama of the phenomenon, a

---

29 Tierney, *Constitutional Law and National Pluralism.*

30 Tierney, *Constitutional Law and National Pluralism.*

31 Anderson, *Imagined Communities.*

32 Cover, "Foreword."

realistic assessment of its causes amidst competing narratives, and a comparative analysis of the complexity of its consequences. Some insights that converge from the analyses will be summarized here.

The shift from a monolingual to a multilingual state usually takes place under both sub-national and supranational pressure. Just like official monolingualism, official multilingualism is adopted by states when it is seen as useful to secure the survival of the state. Official multilingualism in international organizations is similarly a state-centered policy.

The presumption that official language status is necessarily a democratizing, liberating, and empowering force should not go unexamined. In the great majority of cases, the status is granted by symbolic law written in underspecified language. Even when implementation is taken seriously, the changes created may be extensive but not radical. Importantly, linguistic equality hardly ever changes underlying power relations. It is difficult to come up with any example where empowerment through linguistic equality has successfully challenged social hierarchy. By becoming less ethnocentric and more inclusive than traditional conceptions of linguistic nationalism, official multilingualism has responded and adapted to contemporary ethics and politics, but this transformation seems to be made largely to preserve existing power relations (i.e., preservation through transformation). That said, the norm-setting potential of official pluralism should not be underestimated.

Shallow equality may serve legitimate goals, but it must not be confused with the kind of difference-blind equality that has the backing of universalism, nor the kind of difference-aware equality that focuses on the equality of outcomes. Shallow equality in official multilingualism may very well be perceived by the citizens of the polity as just, if the basis of selection is widely accepted; but such acceptance cannot be taken for granted. The formal nature of linguistic equality may also conceal the disparate positions that speakers of these languages occupy in terms of economic and political power. From legal drafting to interpretation, existing power relations seep into decision-making despite formal equality. Potential forces in legal and political mobilization are contained or diverted by the bureaucratic structure of multilingual regimes. Even if there is goodwill behind linguistic equality, inter-group equality may inadvertently accentuate intra-group inequalities. There is a risk that over-investment in linguistic equality may also deprive resources from the promotion of more substantive equality for all.

Official language rights have the potential to extend access to justice for some communities, although arguably such access could also be provided through linguistic accommodation, rather than status recognition. Moreover, just like linguistic equality, official language rights are derived from a politics of difference. It is questionable whether they should be considered absolute rights. Since there is no strong reason why identity interests should automatically trump other public interests, legal norms, and individual rights, official language rights need to be weighed against other legal principles and social goods during legal interpretation and policy deliberation.

Strategic pluralism is a balancing act between identity and non-identity interests. Whether it is official monolingualism pursued by a state, or a demand for recognition advanced by a sub-state national group, history lessons have taught us that feverish pursuit of identity interests can be dangerous. Hutton has reminded us that Nazism started as a response to a perceived threat to one's mother tongue and to the horror of assimilation.[33] The best method of protecting one's language and culture is territorial separation, and the best way of increasing the influence of one's language and culture is through territorial expansion. The defense of language and culture can easily become a proxy for war. Moreover, linguistic and cultural survival concerns not only the current but also future generations. Ensuring intergenerational transmission of language and culture requires illiberal measures that deprive future generations of the freedom of choice. Balance must be maintained such that collective identities do not override our fundamental identity as human beings.

It should not be assumed that official multilingualism will have a net positive effect on linguistic diversity, or that official language communities will all thrive together. Both official monolingualism and official multilingualism are capable of promoting linguistic homogeneity. The more languages that are recognized, the more symbolic this recognition will be. The more seriously the multilingual regime is taken, the more there is a need for a lingua franca. As long as some officially recognized language is seen as instrumentally valuable and other officially recognized languages are seen as having only sentimental value, parallel multilingualism will not last, except in a purely symbolic form.

It follows that despite the supreme legal status that official language law often enjoys, linguistic minorities cannot depend on law for cultural preservation or linguistic survival. In particular, official multilingualism at the state level does little to protect minorities from transnational forces in the global linguistic market, which work through soft power. Most fundamentally, law helps disguise politics through its tendency toward universalization and neutrality,[34] and is ill-equipped to intervene with the particular conditions of linguistic minorities. As this study of official multilingualism shows, law readily lends itself as a discursive resource for both *recognition* and *misrecognition*, the granting of which is well within the bounds of sovereign power and liberal democratic governance.

---

[33] Hutton, *Linguistics and the Third Reich*.

[34] Pierre Bourdieu, "The Force of Law: Toward a Sociology of the Juridical Field," trans. Richard Terdiman, *The Hastings Law Journal* 38 (1987): 805–53.

BIBLIOGRAPHY

"A New Framework Strategy for Multilingualism." Communication from the Commission to the Council, the European Parliament, the European Economic and Social Committee and the Committee of the Regions, November 22, 2005.

"Access to Justice in Both Official Languages: Improving the Bilingual Capacity of the Superior Court Judiciary." Study by the Commissioner of Official Languages of Canada in partnership with the Commissioner of Official Languages for New Brunswick and the French Language Services Commissioner of Ontario, 2013.

Aceron, Eldrige Marvin B. *Ateneo Law Journal* 38, no. 1 (1993): 76–94.

Aeric Inc. v. Canada Post Corp. [1985], 16 D.L.R. (4th). 686.

Ager, Dennis. *Motivation in Language Planning and Language Policy*. Buffalo, NY: Multilingual Matters, 2001.

Ainsworth, Janet. "Law and the Grammar of Judgment." In *Meaning and Power in the Language of Law*, edited by Janny H. C. Leung and Alan Durant, 259–76. Cambridge: Cambridge University Press, 2018.

Alexander, Neville. "The Potential Role of Translation as Social Practice for the Intellectualization of African Languages." 2005. Keynote address delivered at the XVII World Congress of the International Federation of Translators held at Tampere, Finland, August 4–7, 2005.

Amadora, Zeneida. *Manila Bulletin*. September 17, 1988.

Amar, Akhil Reed. "The Central Meaning of a Republican Government: Popular Sovereignty, Majority Rule, and the Denominator Problem." *University of Colorado Law Review* 65 (1993): 749–86.

An Coimisinéir Teanga. "Annual Report 2014." March 15, 2015.

An Stát (Mac Fhearraigh) v. Neilan [1984], IRSR (1980–1998) 38.

Anchimbe, Eric A. "Functional Seclusion and the Future of Indigenous Languages in Africa: The Case of Cameroon." In *Selected Proceedings of the 35th Annual Conference on African Linguistics*, edited by John Mugane. Somerville, MA: Cascadilla Proceedings Project, 2006, 94–103.

Anderson, Benedict. *Imagined Communities: Reflections on the Origin and Spread of Nationalism*. Reprint, London; New York: Verso, 1992.

Angermeyer, Philipp Sebastian. "Lexical Cohesion as a Motivation for Codeswitching: Evidence from Spanish-English Bilingual Speech in Court Testimonies." In *Selected Proceedings of the First Workshop on Spanish Sociolinguistics*, edited by Lotfi Sayahi, 112–22. Somerville, MA: Cascadilla Proceedings Project, 2003.

Anghie, Antony. *Imperialism, Sovereignty and the Making of International Law*. 2004. Reprint, Cambridge: Cambridge University Press, 2007.

Anton Las v. PSA Antwerp NV., Case C-202/11 [2013], ECLI:EU:C:2013:239.

Armeni v. R. [2007], Q.J. No. 3821 (Quebec Superior Court, District of Terrebonne).

Ash, Timothy Garton. "Never Mind the Treaty Squabbles. Europe's Real Problem Is Babel." *The Guardian*, October 18, 2007, sec. Opinion. https://www.theguardian.com/commentisfree/2007/oct/18/comment.politics.

Associated Press. "Latvians Reject Russian as Official Language." *The Guardian*, February 19, 2012, sec. World news. https://www.theguardian.com/world/2012/feb/19/latvians-reject-russian-official-language.

Associated Provincial Picture Houses Ltd. v. Wednesbury Corporation [1948], 1 KB 223.

Association des juristes d'expression françaisede la Colombie-Britannique (AJEFCB). "Recruiting French-Speaking and Bilingual Jurors in British Columbia." 2008.

Athanassiou, Phoebus. "The Application of Multilingualism in the European Context." *Legal Working Paper Series No. 2*, European Central Bank, February 2006.

Attorney General v. Coyne and Wallace [1967], 101 ILTR 17.

Baaij, Cornelis J. W. "Fifty Years of Multilingual Interpretation in the European Union." In *The Oxford Handbook of Language and Law*, edited by Peter M. Tiersma and Lawrence M. Solan, 217–31. New York: Oxford University Press, 2012.

Baker, Colin, and Sylvia Prys Jones. *Encyclopedia of Bilingualism and Bilingual Education.* Buffalo, NY: Multilingual Matters, 1998.

Bakhtin, Mikhail M. "Discourse in the Novel." In *The Dialogic Imagination: Four Essays*, edited by Michael Holquist, translated by Caryl Emerson and Michael Holquist, 259–422. Austin; London: University of Texas Press, 1981.

Balabo, Dino. "Filipino in Court Proceedings Gains Headway." *The Philippine Star*, November 22, 2009. http://www.philstar.com/nation/525158/filipino-court-proceedings-gains-headway.

Ball, Deborah. "Swiss Effort to Save a Language Opens a Rift." *Wall Street Journal*, September 1, 2011, sec. World News. http://www.wsj.com/articles/SB1000142405311 1903352704576540252076676760.

Ballano, Vivencio O. "The 'Rule of Law,' Oral Textuality, and Justice in Criminal Court Proceedings." *Loyola Schools Review* 1, no. 1 (2001): 105–30.

Ballantyne, Davidson, McIntyre v. Canada, Communications Nos. 359/1989 and 385/1989, U.N. Doc. CCPR/C/47/D/359/1989 and 385/1989/Rev.1 (1993).

Banner, Stuart. "Why Terra Nullius? Anthropology and Property Law in Early Australia." *Law and History Review* 23, no. 01 (2005): 95–131.

Barushka, Katerina. "After Decades of Russian Dominance, Belarus Begins to Reclaim Its Language." *The Guardian*, January 28, 2015, sec. World news. https://www.theguardian.com/world/2015/jan/28/-sp-russian-belarus-reclaims-language-belarusian.

Bastarache, Michel. "Bilingual Interpretation Rules as a Component of Language Rights in Canada." In *The Oxford Handbook of Language and Law*, edited by Peter M. Tiersma and Lawrence M. Solan, 159–74. New York: Oxford University Press, 2012.

Bastarache, Michel, ed. *Language Rights in Canada*. Montréal: Les Editions Yvon Blais, 1987.

Bastarache, Michel, Naiomi Metallic, Regan Morris, and Chris Essert. *The Law of Bilingual Interpretation.* Markham, ON: LexisNexis Canada, 2008.

Beaupré, Rémi Michael. *Construing Bilingual Legislation in Canada*. Toronto: Butterworths, 1981.

Beaupré, Rémi Michael. *Interpreting Bilingual Legislation.* Toronto: Carswell, 1986.

Beauvois, Daniel. "Linguistic Acculturations and Reconstructions in the ULB Group (Ukraine, Lithuania, and Belarus)." In *Language, Nation, and State: Identity Politics in a Multilingual Age*, edited by Tony Judt and Denis Lacorne, 201–13. London: Palgrave Macmillan, 2004.

Belende v. Patel, 2008 ONCA 148.

Bell, Derrick A. "Brown v. Board of Education and the Interest-Convergence Dilemma." *Harvard Law Review* 93, no. 3 (1980): 518–33. https://doi.org/10.2307/1340546.

Bengoetxea, Joxerramon. "Multilingual and Multicultural Legal Reasoning: The European Court of Justice." In *Linguistic Diversity and European Democracy*, edited by Anne Lise Kjær and Silvia Adamo, 97–122. Surrey, England; Burlington, VT: Ashgate, 2011.

Berk-Seligson, Susan. *The Bilingual Courtroom: Court Interpreters in the Judicial Process*. 1st edition. Chicago: University of Chicago Press, 2002.

Berman, Antoine. "La Traduction Comme Épreuve de l'étranger [Translation and the Trials of the Foreign, Translated by Lawrence Venuti] (1985)." In *The Translation Studies Reader*, edited by Lawrence Venuti, 240–53. Routledge, 2000.

Berman, Harold J. *Law and Language: Effective Symbols of Community*. Edited by John Witte Jr. Revised edition. New York: Cambridge University Press, 2013.

Berman, Harold J. "The Origins of Western Legal Science." *Harvard Law Review* 90, no. 5 (1977): 894–943.

Bermann, George A. "Bilingualism and Translation in the U.S. Legal System: A Study of the Louisiana Experience." *The American Journal of Comparative Law* 54 (2006): 89–102.

Bickel and Franz (C-274/96), November 24, 1998.

Bideault v. France, Application No. 11261/84, October 8, 1986, D. R. 48.

Biel, Lucja. *Lost in the Eurofog: The Textual Fit of Translated Law*. Bern: Peter Lang, 2014.

Biel, Lucja. "Translation of Multilingual EU Legislation as a Sub-Genre of Legal Translation." In *Court Interpreting and Legal Translation in Enlarged Europe 2006*, edited by D. Kierzkowska, 144–63. Warszawa: Translegis, 2007.

Bigirimana, Jean-Baptist. "Translation as a Dynamic Model in the Development of the Burundi Constitution(s)." In *Translation Issues in Language and Law*, edited by F. Oslen, A. Lorz, and D. Stein, 193–212. London: Palgrave Macmillan, 2009.

Bilaniuk, Laada. "A Typology of Surzhyk: Mixed Ukrainian-Russian Language." *International Journal of Bilingualism* 8, no. 4 (December 1, 2004): 409–25. https://doi.org/10.1177/13670069040080040101.

Bilaniuk, Laada. *Contested Tongues: Language Politics and Cultural Correction in Ukraine*. Ithaca, NY: Cornell University Press, 2005.

Billig, Michael. *Banal Nationalism*. Los Angeles: Sage, 1995.

Bilodeau v. A. G. Manitoba, 1 S.C.R. 449 (1986).

Birden v. Stadtgemeinde Bremen, Case C-1/97 [1998], ECR I-7747.

Black-Clawson International Ltd v. Papierwerke Waldhof-Aschaffenburg AG [1975] AC 591, [1975] 2 WLR 513, [1975] 1 All ER 810, [1975] UKHL 2.

Black, Henry Campbell. *Black's Law Dictionary*. St. Paul, MN: West Publishing, 1990.

Blaut, J. M. *The Colonizer's Model of the World: Geographical Diffusionism and Eurocentric History*. London: Guilford Press, 1993.

Blommaert, Jan. "Situating Language Rights: English and Swahili in Tanzania Revisited." *Journal of Sociolinguistics* 9, no. 3 (2005): 390–417.

Bobek, Michal. "The Multilingualism of the European Union Law in the National Courts: Beyond the Textbooks." In *Linguistic Diversity and European Democracy*, edited by Anne Lise Kjær and Silvia Adamo, 123–42. Surrey, England; Burlington, VT: Ashgate, 2011.

Bohl, Dominik. "Language Rights in the World Polity: From Non-Discrimination to Multilingualism." In *Language Rights Revisited: The Challenge of Global Migration and Communication*, edited by Dagmar Richter, Ingo Richter, Reetta Toivanen, and Iryna Ulasiuk, 113–28. Oisterwijk; Berlin: Wolf Legal Publishers; Berliner Wissenschafts-Verlag, 2012.

Boudreau v. New Brunswick [1990], N.B.J. No. 846, 59 C.C.C. (3d) 436 (N.B.C.A.).

Bourdieu, Pierre. *Language and Symbolic Power*. Edited by John Thompson. Translated by Gino Raymond and Matthew Adamson. Cambridge: Polity Press, 1991.

Bourdieu, Pierre. "The Force of Law: Toward a Sociology of the Juridical Field." Translated by Richard Terdiman. *The Hastings Law Journal* 38 (1987): 805–53.

Braën, André. "Language Rights." In *Language Rights in Canada*, edited by Michel Bastarache, 3–67. Montréal, Que: Les Editions Yvon Blais, 1987.

Brown, Wendy. *States of Injury: Power and Freedom in Late Modernity*. Princeton, NJ: Princeton University Press, 1995.

Bruno, Vanni. "Ensuring the Quality of Drafting of Legislation in a Multilingual Context." Presented at the Commission Legal Revisers Group, Legal Service, European Commission, September 20, 2013. http://ec.europa.eu/dgs/legal_service/seminars_en.htm.

Bunnag, Sirikul. "English Skills Receive Boost." *Bangkok Post*, July 6, 2010, sec. News. http://www.bangkokpost.com/learning/news/185082/english-skills-receive-boost.

Butler, W. E. "Comparative Approaches to International Law." *Recueil Des Cours* 190, no. 9 (1985): 58–61.

Cadoret and Le Bihan v. France, Communication No. 323/1988, U.N. Doc. CCPR/C/41/D/323/1988 (1991).

Canada (A.G.) v. Brown [2005], FC 1683.

Canada (Commissioner of Official Languages) v. Canada (Department of Justice) [2001], F.C.J. No. 431.

Canada v. Viola [1991], 1 FC 373 (CA).

Cao, Deborah. "Inter-Lingual Uncertainty in Bilingual and Multilingual Law." *Journal of Pragmatics* 39, no. 1 (January 2007): 69–83. https://doi.org/10.1016/j.pragma.2006.08.005.

Cao, Deborah. *Translating Law*. Buffalo, NY: Multilingual Matters, 2016.

Caoimhin MAC Giolla Cathain v. The Northern Ireland Court Service [2010], NICA 24; 2010 WL 5126438.

Cases Relating to Certain Aspects of the Laws on the Use of Languages in Education in Belgium, Applications No. 1474/62; 1677/62; 1691/62; 1769/63; 1994/63; 2126/64, July 23, 1968.

Casselman Electrique Ltée v. Gaudreau [1997], O.J. No. 2005.

Cassin, Barbara, Emily Apter, Jacques Lezra, and Michael Wood. *Dictionary of Untranslatables: A Philosophical Lexicon*. Princeton, NJ: Princeton University Press, 2014.

Chan Fung Lan v. Lai Wai Chuen, HCMP 4210/1996.

Chan Kong v. Chan Li Chai Medical Factory (Hong Kong) Ltd., Civil Appeal No. 161 of 2006.

Chan, Phil C. W. "Official Languages and Bilingualism in the Courtroom: Hong Kong, Canada, the Republic of Ireland, and International Law." *The International Journal of Human Rights* 11, no. 1–2 (March 1, 2007): 199–225. https://doi.org/10.1080/13642980601176332.

Cheung, Eric T. M. "Bilingualism: Where Are We Heading?" In *Reform of the Civil Process in Hong Kong*, edited by J. R. Burton and R. M. Wilkinson, 241–252. Singapore: Butterworths Asia, 2000.

Children's Aid Society of Toronto v. W.F. [2014], O.J. No. 4338, 2014 ONCJ 480 (CanLII).

Choquette, Hugo. "Translating the Constitution Act, 1867: A Critique." *Queen's Law Journal* 36, no. 2 (June 1, 2011): 503–50.

Chua, Amy. *Day of Empire: How Hyperpowers Rise to Global Dominance—and Why They Fall*. Reprint edition. New York: Anchor, 2009.

Chumbow, Beban Sammy. "Towards a Legal Framework for Language Charters in Africa." In *Law, Language and the Multilingual State*, edited by Claudine Brohy, Theodorus du Plessis, Joseph-G. Turi, and José Woehrling, 1–26. Bloemfontein: SUN MeDIA, 2012.

Codan, Case C-236/97 [1998], ECR I-8679.

Cohn, Bernard S. *Colonialism and Its Forms of Knowledge: The British in India*. Princeton, NJ: Princeton University Press, 1996.

Comaroff, John L., and Jean Comaroff. "Criminal Justice, Cultural Justice: The Limits of Liberalism and the Pragmatics of Difference in the New South Africa." *American Ethnologist* 31, no. 2 (2004): 188–204.

"Combined Periodic Report of the Republic of Niger 2003–2014 on the Implementation of the African Charter on Human and Peoples' Rights." Republic of Niger, July 2014. http://www.achpr.org/files/sessions/16th-eo/state-reports/2-2003-2014/periodic_report_2003_2014_eng.pdf.

Condon, Bradly J. "Lost in Translation: Plurilingual Interpretation of WTO Law." *Journal of International Dispute Settlement* 1, no. 1 (February 1, 2010): 191–216. https://doi.org/10.1093/jnlids/idp007.

Constable, Marianne. *Our Word Is Our Bond: How Legal Speech Acts*. Stanford, CA: Stanford University Press, 2014.

Constantino, Ernesto, Consuelo J. Paz, Rosario Torres-Yu, and Jesus Fer. Ramos. "Proposals to the Con-Com: Provisions for the National Language (1986)." In *The Language Provision of the 1987 Constitution of the Republic of the Philippines*, edited by Andrew Gonzalez and Wildrido V. Villacorta, 71–81. Manila: Linguistic Society of the Philippines, 2001.

Cooray, L. J. Mark. *Changing the Language of the Law: The Sri Lanka Experience*. Québec: Presses de l'Université Laval, 1986.

Côté v. Canadian Employment and Immigration Minister [1986], A.C.F. no 447, 69 N.R. 126 (Fed. C. A.).

Coulmas, Florian. "What Are National Languages Good For?" In *With Forked Tongues: What Are National Languages Good For?*, edited by Florian Coulmas, 1–24. Ann Arbor, MI: Karoma, 1988.

Coulombe, Pierre A. *Language Rights in French Canada*. New York: P. Lang, 1995.

Coulthard, Malcolm, and Alison Johnson, eds. *The Routledge Handbook of Forensic Linguistics*. Reprint edition. London; New York: Routledge, 2013.

Coulthard, Malcolm, Alison Johnson, and David Wright. *An Introduction to Forensic Linguistics: Language in Evidence*. 2nd edition. Abingdon, UK; New York: Routledge, 2016.

Cover, Robert M. "Foreword: Nomos and Narrative." *Harvard Law Review* 97 (1983): 4–68.

Cover, Robert M. "Violence and the Word." *Yale Law Journal* 95 (1985): 1601–29.

Creery, Jennifer. "Taiwan to Make English an Official Language Next Year, Says Official." *Hong Kong Free Press*, August 31, 2018. https://www.hongkongfp.com/2018/08/31/taiwan-make-english-official-language-next-year-says-official/

Crystal, David. *English as a Global Language*. Cambridge: Cambridge University Press, 1997.

Crystal, David. *Language Death*. Cambridge: Cambridge University Press, 2000.

Cutts, Elmer H. "The Background of Macaulay's Minute." *The American Historical Review* 58, no. 4 (1953): 824–53. https://doi.org/10.2307/1842459.

Cyprus v. Turkey, Application No. 25781/94, May 10, 2001.

Dacey, Jessica. "Make English an Official Language, Study Urges." *SWI Swissinfo.Ch*, February 18, 2009. http://www.swissinfo.ch/eng/make-english-an-official-language--study-urges/7224750.

David, Maya Khemlani, James McLellan, Shameem Rafik-Galea, and Ain Nadzimah Abdullah, eds. *Code Switching in Malaysia*. Frankfurt am Main: Peter Lang, 2009.

David, René, and John E. C. Brierley. *Major Legal Systems in the World Today: An Introduction to the Comparative Study of Law*. 3rd edition. London: Stevens & Sons, 1985.

Davis, Lynn W., Michael N. McKell, Jaysen R. Oldroyd, and Brian C. Steed. "The Changing Face of Justice: A Survey of Recent Cases Involving Courtroom Interpretation." *Harvard Latino Law Review* 7 (2004): 1.

De Blacam, Mark. "Official Language and Constitutional Interpretation." *The Irish Jurist* 52 (2014): 90–114.

de Búrca v. Attorney General [1976], IR 38.

De Jongh, Elena, and Ana Roca. "Interpreting Spanish Codes in Southern Florida: The Preparation of Court Interpreters." In *Sociolinguistics of the Spanish-Speaking World: Iberia, Latin America, United States*, edited by Carol A. Klee and Luis A. Ramos-Garcia, 349–58. Tempe, AZ: Bilingual Press, 1991.

De Schutter, Helder, and David Robichaud. "Van Parijsian Linguistic Justice: Context, Analysis and Critiques." *Critical Review of International Social and Political Philosophy* 18, no. 2 (March 4, 2015): 87–112. https://doi.org/10.1080/13698230.2015.1023627.

De Swaan, Abram. "Endangered Languages, Sociolinguistics, and Linguistic Sentimentalism." *European Review* 12, no. 4 (October 2004): 567–80. https://doi.org/10.1017/S1062798704000481.

DeGraff, Michel. "Against Creole Exceptionallism." *Language* 79, no. 2 (June 2003): 391–410.

DeGraff, Michel. "Linguists' Most Dangerous Myth: The Fallacy of Creole Exceptionalism." *Language in Society* 34, no. 4 (2005): 533–91.

Delap v. An tAire Dlí agus Cirt agus an tArd-Aighne [1990], IRSR (1980–1998) 46.

"Delivering Justice for All: A Vision for New Zealand Courts and Tribunals." Law Commission Report 85. Wellington, New Zealand, March 2004.

Department for Business, Innovation and Skills. "International Education: Global Growth and Prosperity: An Accompanying Analytical Narrative." July 2013. www.gov.uk/bis.

Department of Arts and Culture. "Annual Report 2013–2014." 2014.

Department of Arts, Heritage and the Gaeltacht. "Review of Official Languages Act 2003." 2014.

Derlén, Mattias. "In Defence of (Limited) Multilingualism: Problems and Possibilities of the Multilingual Interpretation of European Union Law in National Courts." In *Linguistic Diversity and European Democracy*, edited by Anne Lise Kjær and Silvia Adamo, 143–66. Surrey, England; Burlington, VT: Ashgate, 2011.

Derlén, Mattias. *Multilingual Interpretation of European Union Law*. Alphen aan den Rijn: Kluwer Law International, 2009.

"Development of a Cultural Strategy for the Island." Education, Sport and Culture Committee, July 19, 2005.

Directorate-General for External Policies, Policy Department. "The Situation of National Minorities in Crimea Following Its Annexation by Russia." European Parliament, 2016.

"Discussion Paper on the Laws in Chinese." Attorney General's Chambers Hong Kong, 1986.

Doczekalska, Agnieszka. "Drafting and Interpretation of EU Law: Paradoxes of Legal Multilingualism." In *Formal Linguistics and Law*, edited by Günther Grewendorf and Monika Rathert, 339–70. Berlin; New York: Mouton deGruyter, 2009.

Doré v. Verdun (City) [1997], 2 S.C.R. 862.

Doughty, Steve. "Can't Read or Write English? You Could Still Serve on a Jury under New Rules Designed to Help Immigrants." *Mail Online*, April 25, 2011. http://www.dailymail.co.uk/news/article-1380538/Cant-read-write-English-You-serve-jury-new-rules.html.

Du, Biyu. "The Bilingual Trial: Access to Interpreting, Communication, and Participation in Chinese Criminal Courts." The University of Hong Kong, 2016.

Duchêne, Alexandre, and Monica Heller, eds. *Language in Late Capitalism: Pride and Profit*. New York: Routledge, 2012.

Dunbar, Robert. "Minority Language Rights in International Law", *International and Comparative Law Quarterly* 50, No. 1, (January 2001): 90–120.

Durant, Alan, and Janny H. C. Leung. *Language and Law: A Resource Book for Students*. Milton Park, Abingdon, UK; New York: Routledge, 2016.

Dwyer, John P. "The Pathology of Symbolic Legislation." *Ecology Law Quarterly* 17, no. 2 (1990): 233–316. https://doi.org/10.15779/Z388J9K.

Eades, Diana. "A Case of Communicative Clash: Aboriginal English and the Legal System." In *Language in the Law*, edited by John Gibbons, 234–64. London; New York: Longman, 1994.

Eades, Diana. "Legal Recognition of Cultural Differences in Communication: The Case of Robyn Kina." *Language & Communication*, Language, Society and the Law, 16, no. 3 (July 1, 1996): 215–27. https://doi.org/10.1016/0271-5309(96)00011-0.

Eades, Diana. “Participation of Second Language and Second Dialect Speakers in the Legal System.” *Annual Review of Applied Linguistics* 23 (March 2003): 113–33. https://doi.org/10.1017/S0267190503000229.

Edelman, Lauren B. “Legality and the Endogeneity of Law.” In *Legality and Community: On the Intellectual Legacy of Philip Selznick*, edited by Robert A. Kagan, Martin Krygier, and Kenneth Winston, 187–202. Lanham, MD: Rowman & Littlefield, 2002.

Edelman, Lauren B. *Working Law: Courts, Corporations, and Symbolic Civil Rights*. Chicago: University of Chicago Press, 2016.

Edelman, Lauren B., Sally Riggs Fuller, and Iona Mara-Drita. “Diversity Rhetoric and the Managerialization of Law.” *American Journal of Sociology* 106, no. 6 (2001): 1589–1641. https://doi.org/10.1086/321303.

Edmiston, Jake. “Judge Declares Mistrial after Court Fails to Find More than Two French-Speaking Jurors for Sexual Touching Trial.” *National Post*, August 14, 2013, sec. News. http://news.nationalpost.com/news/canada/judge-declares-mistrial-after-court-fails-to-find-more-than-two-french-speaking-jurors-for-sexual-touching-trial.

Ekin Association v. France, Application No. 39288/98, July 17, 2001.

Elder, Miriam. “Ukrainians Protest against Russian Language Law.” *The Guardian*, July 4, 2012, sec. World news. https://www.theguardian.com/world/2012/jul/04/ukrainians-protest-russian-language-law.

Els, T. J. M. van. “The European Union, Its Institutions and Its Languages: Some Language Political Observations.” *Current Issues in Language Planning* 2, no. 4 (December 1, 2001): 311–60. https://doi.org/10.1080/14664200108668030.

Ely, John. *Democracy and Distrust*. Cambridge, MA: Harvard University Press, 1980.

Endicott, Timothy A. O. “Linguistic Indeterminacy.” *Oxford Journal of Legal Studies* 16, no. 4 (1996): 667–97.

“English Is Now Official Language of Burundi.” *IWACU English News*, September 17, 2014. http://www.iwacu-burundi.org/englishnews/english-is-now-official-language-of-burundi/.

“Equatorial Guinea Adds Portuguese as the Country’s Third Official Language.” *PR Newswire*, October 14, 2011. http://www.prnewswire.com/news-releases/equatorial-guinea-adds-portuguese-as-the-countrys-third-official-language-131882808.html.

Erich Stauder v. City of Ulm, Case 26/69 [1969], ECR 419.

Erla María Sveinbjörnsdóttir v. The Government of Iceland, Case E-9/97, December 10, 1998.

Eskridge, William N., and John Ferejohn. “Super-Statutes.” *Duke Law Journal* 50, no. 5 (2001): 1215–76.

Eskridge, William N., Philip P. Frickey, and Elizabeth Garrett. *Legislation and Statutory Interpretation*. New York, NY: Foundation Press, 2006.

“EU Parliament Recommends Making Turkish 25th Official Language.” *France 24*, April 19, 2016. http://www.france24.com/en/20160419-eu-parliament-turkish-25th-official-language-cyprus-anastasiades.

European Commission Directorate-General for Translation. *Lawmaking in the EU Multilingual Environment*. Studies on Translation and Multilingualism. Luxembourg: Publications Office of the European Union, 2010.

European Commission v. Grand Duchy of Luxembourg, C-526/08 [2010], ECR I-6151.

European Commission v. French Republic [2010], Case C-492/08.

European Parliament. “Multilingualism in the European Parliament.” Accessed March 13, 2017. http://www.europarl.europa.eu/aboutparliament/en/20150201PVL00013.

European Parliament. “Never Lost in Translation.” Press Service, October 1, 2008.

Evans, Roderick. “Bilingual Juries?” The Centre for Welsh Legal Affairs’ Seventh Annual Lecture, November 25, 2006.

Fallon, John. “State Stops Probe into Judge’s Irish Language Skills: Independent.Ie.” *The Irish Independent*, April 9, 2008, sec. News. http://www.independent.ie/irish-news/state-stops-probe-into-judges-irish-language-skills-26436302.html.

Fanon, Frantz. *The Wretched of the Earth*. New York: Grove Press, 1965.

Farina, Cynthia R. “Statutory Interpretation and the Balance of Power in the Administrative State.” *Colombia Law Review* 89, no. 3 (April 1989): 452–528.

Farrow, Trevor C. W., Diana Lowe, Martha E. Simmons, Bradley Albrecht, and Heather Manweiller. “Addressing the Needs of Self-Represented Litigants in the Canadian Justice System.” A White Paper Prepared for the Association of Canadian Court Administrators, 2012.

Ferguson, C. A. “Diglossia.” *Word* 15 (1959): 325–40.

Fettes, Mark. “Life on the Edge: Canada’s Aboriginal Languages under Official Bilingualism.” In *Language and Politics in the United States and Canada*, edited by Thomas Ricento and Barbara Burnaby, 117–49. Mahwah, NJ: Lawrence Erlbaum Associates, 1998.

Fish, Stanley. “Boutique Multiculturalism, or Why Liberals Are Incapable of Thinking about Hate Speech.” *Critical Inquiry* 23, no. 2 (1997): 378–95.

Fishman, Joshua A. “Bilingualism with and without Diglossia; Diglossia with and without Bilingualism.” *The Journal of Social Issues* 23, no. 2 (1967): 29–38.

Fishman, Joshua A. “National Languages and Languages of Wider Communication in the Developing Nations.” In *Language in Sociocultural Change*, 191–223. Stanford, CA: Stanford University Press, 1972.

Fishman, Joshua A. “Societal Multilingualism: Stable and Transitional.” In *Language in Sociocultural Change*, 135–61. 1968. Reprint, Stanford, CA: Stanford University Press, 1972.

Fishman, Joshua A. “The Status and Prospects of Bilingualism in the United States.” *The Modern Language Journal* 49, no. 3 (March 1965): 143. https://doi.org/10.2307/322757.

Fleiner, Thomas. “Recent Developments of Swiss Federalism.” *Publius* 32, no. 2 (2002): 97–123.

Fonden Marselisborg Lystbådehavn v. Skatteministeriet, Case C-428/02 [2005], ECR I-1527.

Foster & Elam v. Neilson, 27 U.S. (2 Pet.) 253 (1829).

Fraser, Graham. “Protecting Language Rights: Overview of the Commissioner’s Interventions in the Courts 2006–2016.” Office of the Commissioner Official Languages, 2016.

Fuller, Janet. “Hearing between the Lines: Style Switching in a Courtroom Setting.” *Pragmatics* 3, no. 1 (December 21, 2009): 29–43.

Fuller, Lon Luvois. *Legal Fictions*. Stanford, CA: Stanford University Press, 1967.

Furbee, N. Louanna, and Lori A. Stanley. “A Collaborative Model for Preparing Indigenous Curators of a Heritage Language.” *International Journal of the Sociology of Language* 154 (2002): 113–28.

Gal, Susan, and Kathryn A. Woolard. “Constructing Languages and Publics: Authority and Representation.” *Pragmatics* 5, no. 2 (1995): 129–38.

Gambaro, Antonio. "Interpretation of Multilingual Legislative Texts." *Electronic Journal of Comparative Law* 11, no. 3 (2007): 1–20.

"Gambia to Drop English as 'Colonial Relic.'" *Al Jazeera*, March 14, 2014. http://www.aljazeera.com/news/africa/2014/03/gambia-drop-english-as-colonial-relic-201431314181473 4996.html.

Gardbaum, Stephen. "The 'Horizontal Effect' of Constitutional Rights." *Michigan Law Review* 102, no. 3 (2003): 387–459. https://doi.org/10.2307/3595366.

Gateraruke, Raymond. "Overview of Rwandan Legislative Process." *The Loophole: Journal of the Commonwealth Association of Legislative Counsel*, no. 1 (2012): 35–41.

Gavison, Ruth. "What Belongs in a Constitution?" *Constitutional Political Economy* 13, no. 1 (March 1, 2002): 89–105. https://doi.org/10.1023/A:1013691208701.

Gazzola, Michele. "Managing Multilingualism in the European Union: Language Policy Evaluation for the European Parliament." *Language Policy* 5 (November 1, 2006): 393–417. https://doi.org/10.1007/s10993-006-9032-5.

Geeraerts, Dirk. "Cultural Models of Linguistic Standardization." In *Cognitive Models in Language and Thought: Ideology, Metaphors and Meanings*, edited by Rene Dirven, Roslyn Frank, and Martin Putz, Reprint edition, 25–68. Berlin: Mouton de Gruyter, 2012.

Gellner, Ernest. *Nations and Nationalism*. Ithaca, NY: Cornell University Press, 1983.

"Georgia Begins Universal English Classes: Al Jazeera English." *Al Jazeera*, September 26, 2010. http://www.aljazeera.com/video/europe/2010/09/201092614516312607.html.

Ghosh, Palash. "Sacre Bleu! After More Than 120 Years of French Domination, Gabon Adopts English as Official Language." *International Business Times*, October 12, 2012. http://www.ibtimes.com/sacre-bleu-after-more-120-years-french-domination-gabon-adopts-english-official-language-845629.

Gibbons, John. *Forensic Linguistics: An Introduction to Language in the Justice System*. Malden, MA: Wiley-Blackwell, 2008.

Goldsmith, Rosie. "BBC News: South Sudan Adopts the Language of Shakespeare." October 8, 2011. http://www.bbc.co.uk/news/magazine-15216524.

Goldstein, Alyosha, ed. *Formations of United States Colonialism*. Durham, NC: Duke University Press Books, 2014.

Government of Canada, Department of Justice. "Access to Justice in Both Official Languages Support Fund." Accessed March 13, 2017. http://www.justice.gc.ca/eng/fund-fina/jsp-sjp/ol-lo/index.html.

Government of Canada, Department of Justice. "Contraventions Act Fund for Implementation of Language Obligations Evaluation." Accessed March 13, 2017. http://www.justice.gc.ca/eng/rp-pr/cp-pm/eval/rep-rap/12/loe-ole/p2.html.

Government of Canada, Privy Council Office. "Guide to Making Federal Acts and Regulations: Part 2: Making Acts: 2.3 Preparation and Cabinet Approval of Bills." Accessed February 26, 2017. http://www.pco.gc.ca/index.asp?doc=legislation/chap2.3-eng.htm&lang=eng&page=information&sub=publications.

Grammond, Sébastien, and Mark Power. "Should Supreme Court Judges Be Required to Be Bilingual?" *Special Series on the Federal Dimensions of Reforming the Supreme Court of Canada*, 2011, 49.

Grin, François. "Economic Considerations in Language Policy." In *An Introduction to Language Policy: Theory and Method*, edited by Thomas Ricento, 77–94. New York: John Wiley & Sons, 2006.

Guay, Marie-Claude. "The Yin and the Yang of Drafting in Two Languages: From Finesse to Faux Pas: A Canadian Perspective." *The Loophole: Journal of the Commonwealth Association of Legislative Counsel*, no. 1 (2012): 7–20.

Guesdon v. France, Communication No. 219/1986, U.N. Doc. CCPR/C/39/D/219/1986 (1990).

Gupit, Fortunato, and Daniel T. Martinez. *A Guide to Philippine Legal Materials*. Manila: Rex Book Store, 1993.

Gusfield, Joseph R. "Moral Passage: The Symbolic Process in Public Designations of Deviance." *Social Problems* 15, no. 2 (1967): 175–88. https://doi.org/10.2307/799511.

H., A. "Canada's Airports: Beware the Language Police." *The Economist*, August 16, 2012. http://www.economist.com/blogs/gulliver/2012/08/canadas-airports.

Hailsham of Saint Marylebone. "Use of Welsh in Courts in Wales." Hansard, House of Lords, Vol 343, cc532-40, June 12, 1973.

Hale, Sandra Beatriz. *The Discourse of Court Interpreting: Discourse Practices of the Law, the Witness, and the Interpreter*. Amsterdam: John Benjamins Publishing, 2004.

Hale, Sir Matthew. "Reflections by the Lord Chief Justice Hale on Mr. Hobbs His Dialogue of the Law." In *A History of English Law (7th Edn) Volume 1*, edited by Sir William Holdsworth, 505. London: Methuen, Sweet & Maxwell, 1956.

Hall, Marc. "EU Parliament Makes Cuts to Translation Budget." *EURACTIV.Com*, November 22, 2012. http://www.euractiv.com/section/languages-culture/news/eu-parliament-makes-cuts-to-translation-budget/.

Hans, Valerie P., and Neil Vidmar. "Jurors and Juries." In *The Blackwell Companion to Law and Society*, edited by Austin Sarat, 195–211. Malden, MA: Blackwell, 2004.

Hardy, Jean. "The Interpretation of Plurilingual Treaties by International Courts and Tribunals." *British Year Book of International Law* 37 (1961): 72–155.

Harrison, Selig. "Leadership and Language Policy in India." In *Leadership and Political Institutions in India*, edited by Richard Park and Irene Tinker, 151–65. Princeton, NJ: Princeton University Press, 1959.

Hathaway, Oona A. "Between Power and Principle: An Integrated Theory of International Law." *The University of Chicago Law Review* 72 (2005): 469–536.

Hathaway, Oona A., and Harold Hongju Koh. *Foundations of International Law and Politics*. New York: Foundation Press, 2004.

Hatim, Basil. "The Translation of Style: Linguistic Markedness and Textual Evaluativeness." *Journal of Applied Linguistics* 1, no. 3 (2004): 229–46.

Head, Randolph C. "A Plurilingual Family in the Sixteenth Century: Language Use and Linguistic Consciousness in the Salis Family Correspondence, 1580–1610." *The Sixteenth Century Journal* 26, no. 3 (1995): 577–93. https://doi.org/10.2307/2543140.

Hébert, Chantal. "Madeleine Meilleur's Appointment Fails the Non-Partisan Smell Test." *The Star*, May 24, 2017. https://www.thestar.com/news/canada/2017/05/24/madeleine-meilleurs-appointment-fails-the-non-partisan-smell-test-hbert.html.

Heffer, Chris, Frances Rock, and John Conley. *Legal-Lay Communication: Textual Travels in the Law*. New York: Oxford University Press, 2013.

Heller, Monica. *Paths to Post-Nationalism: A Critical Ethnography of Language and Identity*. New York: Oxford University Press, 2011.

Heller, Monica. "The Commodification of Language." *Annual Review of Anthropology* 39, no. 1 (2010): 101–14. https://doi.org/10.1146/annurev.anthro.012809.104951.

Helmut Müller GmbH v. Bundesanstalt für Immobilienaufgaben [2010], Case C-451/08.

Hernandez v. New York, 500 U.S. 352 (1991).

Hidalgo, M., ed. *Mexican Indigenous Languages at the Dawn of the Twenty-First Century*. Berlin: Mouton de Gruyter, 2006.

HKSAR v. Law San Ching and Others, HCMA 98/2002.

HKSAR v. Tam Yuk Ha [1997], 2 HKC 531.

Hobsbawm, E. J. *Nations and Nationalism since 1780: Programme, Myth, Reality*. Cambridge: Cambridge University Press, 1990.

Hoffmann, Charlotte. "Monolingualism, Bilingualism, Cultural Pluralism and National Identity: Twenty Years of Language Planning in Contemporary Spain." *Current Issues In Language and Society* 2, no. 1 (April 1, 1995): 59–90. https://doi.org/10.1080/13520529509615435.

Hohfeld, Wesley Newcomb. "Fundamental Legal Conceptions as Applied in Judicial Reasoning." *The Yale Law Journal* 26, no. 8 (1917): 710–770.

Holmes, Oliver Wendell, Jr. "The Path of the Law." *Harvard Law Review* 10, no. 8 (1897): 457–78.

Hornberger, Nancy H. "Frameworks and Models in Language Policy and Planning." In *An Introduction to Language Policy: Theory and Method*, edited by Thomas Ricento, 24–41. New York: John Wiley & Sons, 2006.

Hornberger, Nancy H. "Multilingual Language Policies and the Continua of Biliteracy: An Ecological Approach." *Language Policy* 1, no. 1 (2002): 27–51.

"House of Commons Debates, 30th Parliament, 3rd Session: Volume 6." June 23, 1978. http://parl.canadiana.ca.

Hudon, Marie-Ève. "Bilingualism in the Federal Courts." Legal and Social Affairs Division Parliamentary, Information and Research Service, 2016.

Hudon, Marie-Ève. "The Role of the Courts in the Recognition of Language Rights." Legal and Legislative Affairs Division, Parliamentary Information and Research Service, Canada, 2013. http://www.lop.parl.gc.ca/Content/LOP/ResearchPublications/2011-68-e.htm.

Hutton, Christopher. *Language, Meaning and the Law*. 1st edition. Edinburgh: Edinburgh University Press, 2009.

Hutton, Christopher. *Word Meaning and Legal Interpretation: An Introductory Guide*. Houndmills, UK; New York: Palgrave, 2014.

Hutton, Christopher. *Linguistics and the Third Reich: Mother-Tongue Fascism, Race and the Science of Language*. London; New York: Routledge, 1999.

Huws, Catrin Fflur. "(Language + Law)2 = ?" In *Current Legal Issues*, Volume 15: *Law and Language*, edited by Michael Freeman and Fiona Smith, 400–416. Oxford: Oxford University Press, 2013.

Huws, Meri. Letter from Welsh Language Commissioner to the First Minister. "Welsh Language Commissioner's Budget 2016–17." Letter from Welsh Language Commissioner to the First Minister, January 27, 2016.

Illich, Ivan. *Shadow Work*. London; New York: Marion Boyars, 1981.

In re the Administration of Justice (Language) Act (Ireland) 1737 [2009], NIQB 66.

Inglehart, Ronald, F., and Margaret Woodward. "Language Conflicts and Political Community." *Comparative Studies in Society and History* 10, no. 1 (1967): 27–45.

"Irish Protest as 'Rusty' Minister Joe McHugh Books Course." *BBC News*, July 16, 2014, sec. Europe. http://www.bbc.com/news/world-europe-28327755.

Irvine, Judith T., and Susan Gal. "Language Ideology and Linguistic Differentiation." In *Regimes of Language: Ideologies, Polities, and Identities*, edited by Paul V. Kroskrity, 35–84. Santa Fe, NM: School for Advanced Research Press, 2000.

Irvine, Judith T., and Susan Gal. "Language Ideology and Linguistic Differentiation." In *Regimes of Language: Ideologies, Polities, and Identities.*, edited by P. V. Kroskrity, 35–84. Santa Fe, NM: School of American Research Press, 2000.

Isop v. Austria, Application No. 808/60, March 8, 1962.

Ito, Hiroshi. "With Spanish, Guaraní Lives: A Sociolinguistic Analysis of Bilingual Education in Paraguay." *Multilingual Education* 2, no. 6 (2012): 1–11.

Jacob, Marc. *Precedents and Case-Based Reasoning in the European Court of Justice: Unfinished Business*. New York: Cambridge University Press, 2014.

J.G.A. Diergaardt et al. v. Namibia, Communication No. 760/1997, CCPR/C/69/D/760/1997.

Jhering, Rudolf von. *Law as a Means to an End*. Boston: Boston Book Company, 1913.

Jhering, Rudolf von. *The Struggle for Law*. Translated by John J. Lalor. 2nd edition. Union, NJ: The Lawbook Exchange, 2006.

Jochelson, Richard, Michelle I. Bertrand, R. C. L. Lindsay, Andrew M. Smith, Michael Ventola, and Natalie Kalmet. "Revisiting Representativeness in the Manitoban Criminal Jury." *Manitoba Law Journal* 37, no. 2 (2015): 365–98.

Jørgensen, Jens Normann. "Language and Languages in European Ideology, Political Documents and Real Life." In *Linguistic Diversity and European Democracy*, edited by Anne Lise Kjær and Silvia Adamo, 208–20. Surrey, England; Burlington, VT: Ashgate, 2011.

Judt, Tony, and Denis Lacorne, eds. *Language, Nation, and State: Identity Politics in a Multilingual Age*. London: Palgrave Macmillan, 2004.

Kachru, Barj B. "World Englishes: Approaches, Issues and Resources." *Language Teaching* 25, no. 1 (January 1992): 1–14.

Kalra, Aditya, and Shyamantha Asokan. "Indian PM's Push for Hindi Struggles to Translate in Some States." *Chicago Tribune*, June 19, 2014. http://articles.chicagotribune.com/2014-06-19/news/sns-rt-us-india-language-20140619_1_hindi-indian-pm-language.

Kaplan, Robert B. *Language Planning in the Asia Pacific: Hong Kong, Timor-Leste and Sri Lanka*. New York: Routledge, 2013.

Kaufman, Marc. "Jefferson Changed 'Subjects' to 'Citizens' in Declaration of Independence." *The Washington Post*, July 3, 2010, sec. Nation. http://www.washingtonpost.com/wp-dyn/content/article/2010/07/02/AR2010070205525.html.

Kay, Barbara. "Of Course Justin Trudeau Wants Bilingual Judges: He's the Product of Bilingual Privilege." *National Post*, July 28, 2015, sec. Comment. http://news.nationalpost.com/full-comment/barbara-kay-of-course-justin-trudeau-wants-bilingual-judges-hes-the-product-of-bilingual-privilege.

Kennedy, Duncan. "The Critique of Rights in Critical Legal Studies." In *Left Legalism/Left Critique*, edited by Janet Halley and Wendy Brown, 178–228. Durham, NC: Duke University Press, 2002.

Khan, M. Ilyas. "Uncommon Tongue: Pakistan's Confusing Move to Urdu." *BBC News*, September 12, 2015, sec. Asia. http://www.bbc.com/news/world-asia-34215293.

Kibbee, Douglas A. *Language and the Law*. Cambridge: Cambridge University Press, 2016.

Kibbee, Douglas A. "Language Policy and Linguistic Theory." In *Languages in a Globalising World*, edited by Jacques Maurais and Michael A. Morris, 47–57. Cambridge: Cambridge University Press, 2003.

Kimble, Joseph. "Plain English: A Charter for Clear Writing." *Thomas M. Cooley Law Review* 9, no. 1 (1992): 1–58.

Kirin-Amgen v. Hoechst [2004], UKHL 46.

Kirk, Robert. "Indeterminacy of Translation." In *The Cambridge Companion to Quine*, edited by Roger F. Gibson, 151–80. Cambridge: Cambridge University Press, 2004.

Kjær, Anne Lise, and Silvia Adamo, eds. *Linguistic Diversity and European Democracy*. Surrey, England; Burlington, VT: Ashgate, 2011.

Kjær, Anne Lise, and Silvia Adamo. "Linguistic Diversity and European Democracy: Introduction and Overview." In *Linguistic Diversity and European Democracy*, edited by Anne Lise Kjær and Silvia Adamo, 1–15. Surrey, England; Burlington, VT: Ashgate, 2011.

Klimas, Tadas, and Jurate Vaiciukaite. "Interpretation of European Union Multilingual Law." *International Journal of Baltic Law* 3 (June 1, 2005): 1–13.

Kloss, Heinz "Language Rights of Immigrant Groups." *International Migration Review* 5, no. 2 (Summer 1971): 250–68.

Koster, Cees. "The Translator in between Texts: On the Textual Presence of the Translator as an Issue in the Methodology of Comparative Translation Description." In *Translation Studies: Perspectives on an Emerging Discipline*, edited by Alessandra Riccardi, 24–37. Cambridge: Cambridge University Press, 2002.

Kraus, Peter A. *A Union of Diversity: Language, Identity and Polity-Building in Europe*. Cambridge: Cambridge University Press, 2008.

Kraus, Peter A. "Neither United nor Diverse? The Language Issue and Political Legitimation in the European Union." In *Linguistic Diversity and European Democracy*, edited by Anne Lise Kjær and Silvia Adamo, 17–33. Surrey, England; Burlington, VT: Ashgate, 2011.

Krauss, Michael. "The World's Languages in Crisis." *Language* 68, no. 1 (1992): 4–10.

Kress, Kenneth J. "Legal Indeterminacy." In *Philosophy of Law and Legal Theory: An Anthology*, edited by Dennis Patterson, 1st edition, 253–91. Malden, MA: Wiley-Blackwell, 2003.

Kroskrity, Paul V. "Regimenting Languages: Language Ideological Perspectives." In *Regimes of Language: Ideologies, Polities, and Identities*, edited by Paul V. Kroskrity, 1–34. Santa Fe, NM: School for Advanced Research Press, 2000.

Kubota, Ryuko, and Angel Lin. "Race and TESOL: Introduction to Concepts and Theories." *TESOL Quarterly* 40, no. 3 (2006): 471–93. https://doi.org/10.2307/40264540.

Kulyk, Volodymyr. "Language Identity, Linguistic Diversity and Political Cleavages: Evidence from Ukraine." *Nations and Nationalism* 17, no. 3 (2011): 627–648.

Kulyk, Volodymyr. "Language Policy in Ukraine: What People Want the State to Do." *East European Politics and Societies* 27, no. 2 (May 1, 2013): 280–307. https://doi.org/10.1177/0888325412474684.

Kymlicka, Will. *Multicultural Citizenship*. Oxford; New York: Oxford University Press, 1995.

Kymlicka, Will. *Politics in the Vernacular: Nationalism, Multiculturalism, and Citizenship*. Oxford; New York: Oxford University Press, 2001.

Kymlicka, Will, and Alan Patten, eds. *Language Rights and Political Theory*. Reprint, Oxford: Oxford University Press, 2007.

Laitin, David D. *Politics, Language, and Thought: The Somali Experience*. Chicago: University of Chicago Press, 1977.

Lalonde v. Ontario, 2001 CanLII 21164 (ON CA).

Landheer, Bart. *On the Sociology of International Law and International Society*. Dordrecht: Springer, 1966.

Lane, Edwin. "After Gaddafi, Libya's Amazigh Demand Recognition." *BBC News*, December 23, 2011, sec. Africa. http://www.bbc.com/news/world-africa-16289543.

Lavigne v. Canada [2002], 2 SCR 773.

Law, David S., and Versteeg, Mila, "Sham Constitutions." *California Law Review* 101, no. 4 (August 2013): 863–952.

Lawson, Guy. "Trudeau's Canada, Again." *The New York Times*, December 8, 2015. https://www.nytimes.com/2015/12/13/magazine/trudeaus-canada-again.html.

LeBlanc v. York Catholic District School Board [2002], O.J. No. 4640.

Lecomte, Lucie. "Official Languages or National Languages? Canada's Decision." Library of Parliament: Background Papers, February 6, 2015. http://www.lop.parl.gc.ca/Content/LOP/ResearchPublications/2014-81-e.html?cat=government.

Lee, Kuan Yew. "Speech Given at the Launch of the English Language Institute of Singapore (ELIS)." September 6, 2011.

Leow, Rachel. *Taming Babel: Language in the Making of Malaysia*. Cambridge: Cambridge University Press, 2016.

Leung, Ester S. M. "Interpreting for the Minority, Interpreting for the Power." In *Dimensions of Forensic Linguistics*, edited by John Gibbons and M. Teresa Turell, 197–211. Amsterdam: John Benjamins, 2008.

Leung, Janny H. C. "Cross-Jurisdiction Appropriation of the Equal Authenticity Principle." *The Journal of Legal Pluralism and Unofficial Law* 45, no. 2 (July 2013): 209–26. https://doi.org/10.1080/07329113.2013.772463.

Leung, Janny H. C. "Ideology and Political Meaning in Legal Translation." In *Meaning and Power in the Language of Law*, edited by Janny H. C. Leung and Alan Durant, 236–55. Cambridge: Cambridge University Press, 2018.

Leung, Janny H. C. "Language Rights." In *Handbook of Communication in the Legal Sphere*, edited by Jacqueline Visconti, 54–82. Boston; Berlin: DeGruyter, 2018.

Leung, Janny H. C. "Lay Litigation Behaviour in Postcolonial Hong Kong Courtrooms." *Language and Law / Linguagem e Direito* 2, no. 1 (2015): 32–52.

Leung, Janny H. C. "Negotiating Language Status in Multilingual Jurisdictions: Rhetoric and Reality." *Semiotica* 209 (November 4, 2016): 371–96.

Leung, Janny H. C. "Statutory Interpretation in Multilingual Jurisdictions: Typology and Trends." *Journal of Multilingual and Multicultural Development* 33, no. 5 (August 1, 2012): 481–95. https://doi.org/10.1080/01434632.2012.680462.

Leung, Janny H. C. "The Object of Fidelity in Translating Multilingual Legislation." *Semiotica* 2014, no. 201 (2014): 223–38. https://doi.org/10.1515/sem-2014-0026.

Leung, Janny H. C. "Translation Equivalence as a Legal Fiction." In *The Ashgate Handbook of Legal Translation*, edited by Le Cheng, King Kui Sin, and Anne Wagner, 57–69. London: Routledge, 2014.

Levert, Lionel A. "The Cohabitation of Bilingualism and Bijuralism in Federal Legislation in Canada: Myth or Reality?" Harmonization and Dissonance: Language and Law in Canada and Europe, May 7, 1999. http://www.justice.gc.ca/eng/rp-pr/csj-sjc/harmonization/hfl-hlf/b1-f1/bf1e.html.

Leybold-Johnson, Isobel. "Controversy Rages over Standardised Romansh." *SWI Swissinfo.Ch*, August 6, 2006. http://www.swissinfo.ch/eng/controversy-rages-over-standardised-romansh/41074.

Lis, Jonathan. "Israeli Ministers Greenlight Nation-State Bill: Arabic Isn't an Official State Language." *Haaretz*, May 7, 2017. http://www.haaretz.com/israel-news/1.787689.

Liu, Amy H. *Standardizing Diversity: The Political Economy of Language Regimes*. Philadelphia: University of Pennsylvania Press, 2015.

Llewellyn, Karl N. "Some Realism about Realism: Responding to Dean Pound." *Harvard Law Review* 44, no. 8 (1931): 1222–64. https://doi.org/10.2307/1332182.

Lötscher, Andreas. "Multilingual Law Drafting in Switzerland." In *Formal Linguistics and the Law*, edited by G. Grewendorf and M. Rathert, 371–400. Berlin; New York: Mouton deGruyter, 2009.

Lourens v. President of South Africa and Others [2010], ZAGPPHC 19; 2013 (1) SA 499 (GNP).

Lucini, Doris. "Romansh Row Inspires Strong Language." *SWI Swissinfo.Ch*, October 6, 2004. http://www.swissinfo.ch/eng/romansh-row-inspires-strong-language/4132548.

Luxembourg: Office for Official Publications of the EC. "Joint Practical Guide of the European Parliament, the Council and the Commission for Persons Involved in the Drafting of European Union Legislation (2nd Ed.)." 2013.

Maatschap M.J.M. Linthorst, K.G.P. Pouwels en J. Scheren c.s. v. Inspecteur der Belastingdienst/Ondernemingen Roermond [1997], Case C-167/95.

Mac Cárthaigh, Dáithí. "Interpretation and Construction of Bilingual Laws: A Canadian Lamp to Light the Way?" *Judicial Studies Institute Journal* 2 (2007): 211–28.

Mac Giolla Chríost, Diarmait. *The Welsh Language Commissioner in Context: Roles, Methods and Relationships*. Cardiff: University of Wales Press, 2016.

Macalister, John. "Language Policies, Language Planning and Linguistic Landscapes in Timor-Leste." *Language Problems and Language Planning* 36, no. 1 (January 1, 2012): 25–45. https://doi.org/10.1075/lplp.36.1.02mac.

Macaulay, Thomas B. "Minute on Education in India [1835]." In *Politics and Empire in Victorian Britain: A Reader*, edited by Antoinette Burton, 18–20. New York: Palgrave, 2001.

MacCárthaigh v. Éire [1999], 1 IR 186.

MacDonald, Roderick A. "Legal Bilingualism." *McGill Law Journal* 42 (1997): 119.

MacDonald v. City of Montreal, 1 S.C.R. 460 (1986).

Maceda, Teresita Gimenez. "The Filipino National Language: Discourse on Power." In *Papers from the Seventh Annual Meeting of the Southeast Asian Linguistics Society*, edited by Karen L. Adams, Thomas John Hudak, and F. K. Lehman, 90–108. Tempe: Arizona State University, Program for Southeast Asian Studies, 2003.

Macfarlane, Julie. "The National Self-Represented Litigants Project: Identifying and Meeting the Needs of Self-Represented Litigants." Convocation: Treasurer's Advisory Group on Access to Justice (TAG) Working Group Report, May 2013.

Mahoney, James. *Colonialism and Postcolonial Development: Spanish America in Comparative Perspective*. Cambridge Studies in Comparative Politics. New York: Cambridge University Press, 2010.

Malcolmson, John, and Gayla Reid. "British Columbia Court Self-Help Information Centre." Final Evaluation Report, August 2006.

"Mandate and Roles." Accessed March 13, 2017. http://www.officiallanguages.gc.ca/en/aboutus/mandate.

Mandela, Nelson. "Don't Silence Mother Tongues." *Sunday Times*, April 25, 2004, sec. Editorial.

Mangahas, Mahar. "Social Climate: Survey on Access to Court Justice." *Inquirer.Net*, July 5, 2008.

Manning, John F. "Textualism and Legislative Intent." *Virginia Law Review* 91 (2005): 419–50.

Marácz, László. "Multilingualism in the Transleithanian Part of the Austro-Hungarian Empire (1867–1918): Policy and Practice." *Jezikoslovlje* 13, no. 2 (2012): 269–98.

Markovits, Daniel. *Snowball Inequality: Meritocracy and the Crisis of Capitalism*. Harvard University Press, forthcoming.

Mar-Molinero, Clare. *The Politics of Language in the Spanish-Speaking World: From Colonisation to Globalisation*. London; New York: Routledge, 2000.

Marten, L., and N. C. Kula. "Zambia: One Zambia, One Nation, Many Languages." In *Language and National Identity in Africa*, edited by A. Simpson, 291–313. Oxford: Oxford University Press, 2007.

Martin, Isabel Pefianco. "Expanding the Role of Philippine Languages in the Legal System: The Dim Prospects." *Perspectives in the Arts and Humanities Asia* 2, no. 1 (March 29, 2012). https://doi.org/10.13185/121.

Mattila, Heikki E. S. *Comparative Legal Linguistics: Language of Law, Latin and Modern Lingua Francas*. Aldershot, UK: Ashgate Publishing, 2013.

May, Stephen. "Contesting Hegemonic and Monolithic Constructions of Language Rights 'Discourse.'" *Journal of Multicultural Discourses* 7, no. 1 (March 1, 2012): 21–27. https://doi.org/10.1080/17447143.2012.660944.

May, Stephen. *Language and Minority Rights: Ethnicity, Nationalism and the Politics of Language*. New York: Routledge, 2012.

May, Stephen. "Language Policy and Minority Rights." In *An Introduction to Language Policy: Theory and Method*, edited by Thomas Ricento, 255–72. New York: John Wiley & Sons, 2006.

McAuliffe, Karen. "Enlargement at the European Court of Justice: Law, Language and Translation." *European Law Journal* 14, no. 6 (November 1, 2008): 806–18. https://doi.org/10.1111/j.1468-0386.2008.00442.x.

McAuliffe, Karen. "Language and Law in the European Union: The Multilingual Jurisprudence of the ECJ." In *The Oxford Handbook of Language and Law*, edited by Peter M. Tiersma and Lawrence M. Solan, 200–216. Oxford: Oxford University Press, 2012.

McGee, Harry. "Experts Say Constitutional Changes Should Look at Subtlety of Irish Translation." *The Irish Times*, February 21, 2015, sec. News. http://www.irishtimes.com/news/politics/experts-say-constitutional-changes-should-look-at-subtlety-of-irish-translation-1.2111749.

McGreal, Chris. "Why Rwanda Said Adieu to French." *The Guardian*, January 16, 2009, sec. Education. http://www.theguardian.com/education/2009/jan/16/rwanda-english-genocide.

McRae, Kenneth Douglas. *Conflict and Compromise in Multilingual Societies: Switzerland*. Waterloo, ON; Wilfrid Laurier University Press, 1983.

McRae, Kenneth Douglas, Mika Helander, and Sari Luoma. *Conflict and Compromise in Multilingual Societies: Finland*. Waterloo, ON: Wilfrid Laurier University Press, 1997.

Mellinkoff, David. *The Language of the Law*. Eugene, OR: Wipf & Stock, 1963.

Merry, Sally Engle. "Colonial and Postcolonial Law." In *The Blackwell Companion to Law and Society*, edited by Austin Sarat, 569–88. London: Blackwell, 2004.

Merry, Sally Engle. "Legal Pluralism." *Law and Society Review* 22, no. 5 (1988): 869–96.

Milroy, James, and Lesley Milroy. *Authority in Language: Investigating Standard English*. 3rd edition. London; New York: Routledge, 1999.

Ministry for Foreign Affairs. "The Fourth Periodic Report of Finland on the Application of the European Charter for Regional or Minority Languages." Unit for Human Rights Courts and Conventions (OIK-40), 2010.

Ministry of Home Affairs. "Notes on Demands for Grants 2015–2016." Demand No. 53, n.d. http://www.indiabudget.nic.in/ub2015-16/eb/sbe53.pdf.

Mkhwanazi, Siyabonga. "Language Board Blew R100m." *IOL*, March 4, 2015, sec. News. http://www.iol.co.za/news/politics/language-board-blew-r100m-1827057.

Modino, Abigail A. "Creation of Sentro Ng Batas Sa Wika Sought." Press release, House of Representatives, Republic of the Philippines, August 12, 2010. http://www.congress.gov.ph/press/details.php?pressid=4346.

Moore, David Chioni. "Is the Post- in Postcolonial the Post- in Post-Soviet? Toward a Global Postcolonial Critique." *PMLA* 116, no. 1 (2001): 111–28.

Moore, Sally Falk. "Law and Anthropology." *Biennial Review of Anthropology* 6 (1969): 252–300.

Moussu, Lucie, and Enric Llurda. "Non-Native English-Speaking English Language Teachers: History and Research." *Language Teaching* 41, no. 3 (2008): 315–48. https://doi.org/10.1017/S0261444808005028.

Mowbray, Jacqueline. *Linguistic Justice: International Law and Language Policy*. Oxford; New York: Oxford University Press, 2012.

Mthethwa v. De Bruin NO & Another, 1998(3) BCLR 336(N).

Mufwene, Salikoko S. "Colonization, Globalization, and the Future of Languages in the Twenty-First Century." *International Journal on Multicultural Societies* 4, no. 2 (2002): 162–93.

Myers-Scotton, Carol. *Duelling Languages: Grammatical Structure in Codeswitching*. Oxford: Oxford University Press, 1993.

Myers-Scotton, Carol. "The Matrix Language Frame Model: Developments and Responses." In *Codeswitching Worldwide II*, edited by Rodolfo Jacobson, 23–58. Berlin; New York: Mouton de Gruyter, 2001.

Na Coimisinéirí Ioncaim v. An Coimisinéir Teanga [2015], IEHC 110.

Nahir, Moshe. "Language Planning Goals: A Classification." *Language Problems and Language Planning* 8, no. 3 (January 1, 1984): 294–327. https://doi.org/10.1075/lplp.8.3.03nah.

National Joint Council. "Bilingualism Bonus Directive." Accessed March 13, 2017. http://www.njc-cnm.gc.ca/directive/d1/en.

"National Report Submitted in Accordance with Paragraph 15 (a) of the Annex to Human Rights Council Resolution 5/1: Kiribati." UN General Assembly, 2010.

"New Zealand Sovereignty: 1857, 1907, 1947, or 1987?" Parliamentary Library, August 28, 2007.

Ng, Kwai Hang. "Legal Translation and the Problem of Heteroglossia." In *Comparative Law: Engaging Translation*, edited by Simone Glanert, 49–66. Milton Park, Abingdon, UK; New York: Routledge, 2014.

Ng, Kwai Hang. *The Common Law in Two Voices: Language, Law, and the Postcolonial Dilemma in Hong Kong*. Stanford, CA: Stanford University Press, 2009.

Ni Dhrisceoil, Verona. "Language Conflict in Northern Ireland: Revisiting the Irish Language Rights Debate." *Public Law* 4 (October 2013): 693–701.

Nickson, Robert Andrew. "Governance and the Revitalisation of the Guaraní Language in Paraguay." *Latin American Research Review* 44, no. 3 (2009): 3–26.

"N.W.T. Proposes Creating List of French-Speaking Jurors." *CBC News*, February 3, 2015. http://www.cbc.ca/news/canada/north/n-w-t-proposes-creating-list-of-french-speaking-jurors-1.2942577.

Nzanze, Vastina. "Challenges of Drafting Laws in One Language and Translating Them: Rwanda's Experience." *The Loophole: Journal of the Commonwealth Association of Legislative Counsel*, no. 1 (2012): 42–53.

Ó Beoláin v. Fahy [2001], 2 IR 279.

Ó Caollaí, Éanna. "Kenny Criticised for Comments about Appointment of Minister for Gaeltacht." *The Irish Times*, July 27, 2015. http://www.irishtimes.com/news/politics/kenny-criticised-for-comments-about-appointment-of-minister-for-gaeltacht-1.2297843.

Ó Conaire v. MacGruairc [2010], 3 IR 30.

Ó Cuirreáin, Seán. "Translation of Speaking Notes at the Houses of the Oireachtas Joint Committee on Public Service Oversight and Petitions." December 4, 2013. https://www.coimisineir.ie/userfiles/files/SpeakingnotesAnCoimisineirTeanga04122013.pdf.

Ó Domhnaill, Rónán. "Translation of Speaking Notes at the Houses of the Oireachtas Sub-Committee on the 20 Year Strategy for the Irish Language and Related Matters." May 27, 2014.

Ó Maicín v. Éire [2010], IEHC 179.

Ó Monacháin v. An Taoiseach [1986], ILRM 660.

Ó Murchú v. An Taoiseach & chuid eile [2010], IESC 26.

O'Barr, William M. *Linguistic Evidence: Language, Power, and Strategy in the Courtroom*. New York: Academic Press, 1982.

Odendahl, Kerstin, and Jan Scheffler. "The EU Principle of Integral Multilingualism: On the Road Towards Expansion or Restriction?" In *Language Rights Revisited: The Challenge of Global Migration and Communication*, edited by Dagmar Richter, Ingo Richter, Reetta Toivanen, and Iryna Ulasiuk, 97–111. Oisterwijk; Berlin: Wolf Legal Publishers; Berliner Wissenschafts-Verlag, 2012.

Office of Hawaiian Affairs v. Department of Education, 951 F. Supp. 1484 (D. Haw. 1996).

Office of the Court Administrator. "Pilot-Testing the Use of Filipino in Trial Court Proceedings." 2009. http://oca.judiciary.gov.ph/?page_id=175.

Office of the United Nations High Commissioner for Human Rights. "Report on the Human Rights Situation in Ukraine 16 August to 15 November 2016." n.d.

Office of the United Nations High Commissioner for Human Rights. "Report on the Human Rights Situation in Ukraine 16 February to 15 May 2015." n.d.

Ontario (Attorney General) v. Fleet Rent-A-Car Ltd. [2002], O.J. No. 4693, 2002 CarswellOnt 428629, C.P.C. (5th) 315.

Opeibi, Tunde Olusola. "Investing the Language Situation in Africa." In *The Oxford Handbook of Language and Law*, edited by Peter M. Tiersma and Lawrence M. Solan, 272–84. Oxford: Oxford University Press, 2012.

"Orban: Multilingualism 'Cost of Democracy' in EU." *EURACTIV.Com*, November 13, 2008. http://www.euractiv.com/section/languages-culture/interview/orban-multilingualism-cost-of-democracy-in-eu/.

Ortis, Margaux. "SC: Use of Filipino Language in Courts 'Positive.'" *Philippine Daily Inquirer*, July 1, 2008.

Ostrower, Alexander. *Language, Law, and Diplomacy: A Study of Linguistic Diversity in Official International Relations and International Law*. Philadlephia: University of Pennsylvania Press, 1965.

"P. Rico Senate Declares Spanish over English as First Official Language." *Agencia EFE*, September 4, 2015. http://www.efe.com/efe/english/life/p-rico-senate-declares-spanish-over-english-as-first-official-language/50000263-2704154.

Palmer, Vernon Valentine. *Mixed Jurisdictions Worldwide: The Third Legal Family (Second Edition)*. Cambridge: Cambridge University Press, 2014.

"Parliamentary Debates." Dáil Éireann Debate Vol. 833 No. 2, Written Answers Nos. 68–74, March 5, 2014. http://oireachtasdebates.oireachtas.ie/debates%20authoring/DebatesWebPack.nsf/takes/dail2014030500076#N8.

Parry, R. Gwynedd. "'An Important Obligation of Citizenship': Language, Citizenship and Jury Service." *Legal Studies* 27, no. 2 (June 1, 2007): 188–215. https://doi.org/10.1111/j.1748-121X.2007.00048.x.

Patten, Alan. "Who Should Have Official Language Rights?" In *Languages, Constitutionalism and Minorities*, edited by André Braën, Pierre Foucher, and Yves Le Bouthillier, 235–48. Markham, ON: LexisNexis Butterworths, 2006.

Patten, Alan, and Will Kymlicka. "Introduction: Language Rights and Political Theory: Context, Issues, and Approaches." In *Language Rights and Political Theory*, edited by Will Kymlicka and Alan Patten. 2003. Reprint, Oxford: Oxford University Press, 2007.

Paunio, Elina. *Legal Certainty in Multilingual EU Law: Language, Discourse and Reasoning at the European Court of Justice*. Burlington, VT: Ashgate, 2013.

Pavlenko, Aneta. "Multilingualism in Post-Soviet Countries: Language Revival, Language Removal, and Sociolinguistic Theory." *International Journal of Bilingual Education and Bilingualism* 11, no. 3–4 (2008): 275–314.

Pavlenko, Aneta. "Multilingualism in Post-Soviet Successor States." *Language and Linguistics Compass* 7, no. 4 (April 1, 2013): 262–71. https://doi.org/10.1111/lnc3.12024.

Paz, Moria. "The Failed Promise of Language Rights: A Critique of the International Language Rights Regime," *Harvard International Law Journal* 54, No. 1 (2013): 157–218.

Pennycook, Alastair. *English and the Discourses of Colonialism*. London: Routledge, 2002.

Pennycook, Alastair. "Language, Ideology and Hindsight: Lessons from Colonial Language Policies." In *Ideology, Politics, and Language Policies: Focus on English*, edited by Thomas Ricento, 49–65. Amsterdam: John Benjamins, 2000.

Perdue, Peter C. *China Marches West: The Qing Conquest of Central Eurasia*. Reprint edition. Cambridge, MA; London: Belknap Press, 2010.

Phillipson, Robert. *Linguistic Imperialism*. Oxford: Oxford University Press, 1992.

Plotnikoff, Joyce, and Richard Woolfson. *A Study of the Services Provided under the Otton Project to Litigants in Person at the Citizens Advice Bureau at the Royal Courts of Justice*. Great Britain, Lord Chancellor's Department, Research Programme, 1998.

Pool, Jonathan. "Optimal Language Regimes for the European Union." *International Journal of the Sociology of Language* 121 (1996): 159–79.

Pool, Jonathan. "The Official Language Problem." *The American Political Science Review* 85, no. 2 (1991): 495–514. https://doi.org/10.2307/1963171.

Poon, Wai Yee Emily. "The Cultural Transfer in Legal Translation." *International Journal for the Semiotics of Law* 18, no. 3–4 (December 1, 2005): 307–23. https://doi.org/10.1007/s11196-005-9004-7.

Pound, Roscoe. "The Need of a Sociological Jurisprudence." *The Green Bag* 19, no. 10 (1907): 607–15.

Powell, Richard. "Bilingual Courtrooms: In the Interests of Justice?" In *Dimensions of Forensic Linguistics*, edited by J. Gibbons and M. Teresa Turell, 131–59. Amsterdam: John Benjamins, 2008.

Powell, Richard. "English in Southeast Asian Law." In *English in Southeast Asia: Features, Policy and Language in Use*, edited by Ee Ling Low and Azirah Hashim, 241–66. Amsterdam: John Benjamins, 2012.

Powell, Richard. "Vernacularising the Law: Malaysia's Bilingual Policy as a Model for Postcolonial Common Law Systems." Melbourne Graduate School of Education, 2014. http://minerva-access.unimelb.edu.au/handle/11343/51109.

Powell, Richard, and Azirah Hashim. "Language Disadvantage in Malaysian Litigation and Arbitration." *World Englishes* 30, no. 1 (2011): 92–105.

Pozzo, Barbara. "Multilingualism, Legal Terminology and the Problems of Harmonising European Private Law." In *Multilingualism and the Harmonisation of European Law*, edited by Barbara Pozzo and Valentina Jacometti, 3–19. Dordrecht: Kluwer Law International, 2006.

Pozzo, Barbara, and Valentina Jacometti, eds. *Multilingualism and the Harmonisation of European Law*. Dordrecht: Kluwer Law International, 2006.

Privy Council Office. *Report of the Royal Commission on Bilingualism and Biculturalism. General Introduction*, Book 1: The Official Languages, 1967.

Pupavac, Vanessa. *Language Rights: From Free Speech to Linguistic Governance*. Basingstoke, Hampshire; New York, NY: Palgrave Macmillan, 2012.

Putter, Ad, and Keith Busby. "Introduction: Medieval Francophonia." In *Medieval Multilingualism: The Francophone World and Its Neighbours*, edited by Christopher Kleinhenz and Keith Busby, 1–14. Turnhout: Brepols, 2010. https://doi.org/10.1484/M.TCNE-EB.6.09070802050003050208030703.

Quebec (Revenue) v. Caisse populaire Desjardins de Montmagny, 2009 SCC 49 [2009], 3 SCR 286.

R. v. Beaulac, 1 S.C.R. 768 (1999).

R. v. Caron, 2014 ABCA 71.

R v. Dubois [1935], S.C.R. 378.

R v. Klippert [1967], S.C.R. 822.

R. v. Lamirande, 2002 MBCA 41.

R. v. Mac [2002], 1 S.C.R. 856.

R. v. Munkonda, 2015 ONCA 309.

R. v. Sarrazin [2005], 196 O.A.C. 224 (CA).

R. v. Simard (Ont. Ct. (Gen. Div.)) [1994], O.J. No. 1769.

R. v. Stadnick [2001], Q.J. No. 5226 (Que. S.C.).

R. v. Teerhuis-Moar, 2007 MBQB 165.

Raborife, Mpho. "Mthethwa Dissolves Pan South African Language Board." *News24*, January 13, 2016. http://www.news24.com/SouthAfrica/News/mthethwa-dissolves-pan-south-african-language-board-20160113.

Rafael, Vicente L. "Taglish, or the Phantom Power of the Lingua Franca." In *Philippine English: Linguistic and Literary*, edited by M. A. Lourdes S. Bautista and Kingsley Bolton. Hong Kong: Hong Kong University Press, 2008.

Rahman, Tariq. "Language Ideology, Identity and the Commodification of Language in the Call Centers of Pakistan." *Language in Society* 38, no. 2 (April 2009): 233–58. https://doi.org/10.1017/S0047404509090344.

Rahman, Tariq. "Urdu as the Language of Education in British India." *Pakistan Journal of History and Culture* 32, no. 2 (2011): 1–40.

Rampton, Ben. "Displacing the 'Native Speaker': Expertise, Affiliation and Inheritance." In *The Language, Ethnicity and Race Reader*, edited by Roxy Harris and Ben Rampton, 107–11. London; New York: Routledge, 2003.

Rañosa-Madrunio, Marilu. "Power and Control in Philippine Courtroom Discourse." *International Journal of Legal English* 2, no. 1 (2014): 4–30.

Rappa, Antonio L., and Lionel Hock An Wee. *Language Policy and Modernity in Southeast Asia: Malaysia, the Philippines, Singapore, and Thailand*. New York: Springer, 2006.

Rawls, John. *Justice as Fairness: A Restatement*. Edited by Erin Kelly. Cambridge, MA; London: The Belknap Press of Harvard University Press, 2001.

Re Cheng Kai Nam [2002], 2 HKLRD 39.

Re Manitoba Language Rights [1985], 1 S.C.R. 721.

Reid, Scott. *Lament for a Notion: The Life and Death of Canada's Bilingual Dream*. Vancouver: Arsenal Pulp Press, 1993.

Reilly, Gavan. "Investigation Finds Only 1 of 9 Officers in Gaeltacht Garda Station Spoke Irish." *TheJournal.Ie*, April 24, 2012. http://www.thejournal.ie/only-1-of-9-officers-in-gaeltacht-garda-station-spoke-irish-report-427481-Apr2012/.

Reisman, William Michael, and Aaron M. Schreiber. *Jurisprudence: Understanding and Shaping Law: Cases, Readings, Commentary*. New Haven, CT: New Haven Press, 1987.

Richland, Justin B. "Jurisdiction: Grounding Law in Language." *Annual Review of Anthropology* 42, no. 1 (October 21, 2013): 209–26. https://doi.org/10.1146/annurev-anthro-092412-155526.

Richter, Dagmar. "The Model Character of Swiss Language Law." In *Linguistic Diversity and European Democracy*, edited by Anne Lise Kjær and Silvia Adamo, 189–205. Surrey, England; Burlington, VT: Ashgate, 2011.

Romero, Simon. "A Language Thrives in Its Caribbean Home." *The New York Times*, July 4, 2010. http://www.nytimes.com/2010/07/05/world/americas/05curacao.html.

Rosenfeld, Michel. "Constitution-Making, Identity Building, and Peaceful Transition to Democracy: Theoretical Reflections Inspired by the Spanish Example." *Cardozo Law Review* 19 (1998): 1891.

Rubin, Joan. *National Bilingualism in Paraguay*. The Hague: Mouton, 1968.

Rubio-Marín, Ruth. "Language Rights: Exploring the Competing Rationales." In *Language Rights and Political Theory*, edited by Will Kymlicka and Alan Patten, 52–79. 2003. Reprint, Oxford: Oxford University Press, 2007.

Rutherford, Adrian. "Irish Language Act: Stormont Business Would Be Translated and Courts Heard in Irish." *Belfast Telegraph*, February 10, 2015. http://www.belfasttelegraph.co.uk/news/politics/irish-language-act-stormont-business-would-be-translated-and-courts-heard-in-irish-30980190.html.

"Rwanda Moves to Make Swahili Its Fourth Official Language." *Africanews*, February 10, 2017. http://www.africanews.com/2017/02/10/rwanda-moves-to-make-swahili-its-fourth-official-language/.

S. v. Macebo Damoyi (24441, A210/02, 44/02) [2003], ZAWCHC 65.

S. v. Matomela, 1998(3) BCLR 339 (Ck).

Sacco, Rodolfo. "Language and Law." In *Ordinary Language and Legal Language*, edited by Barbara Pozzo, 1–22. Milan: Giuffrè, 2005.

Safran, William. "Introduction: The Political Aspects of Language." *Nationalism and Ethnic Politics* 10, no. 1 (January 1, 2004): 1–14. https://doi.org/10.1080/13537110490450746.

Sage-Fuller, Bénédicte, Ferdinand Prinz sur Lippe, and Seán Ó Conaill. "Law and Language(s) at the Heart of the European Project: Educating Different Kinds of Lawyers." In *Current Legal Issues*, Volume 15: *Law and Language*, edited by Michael Freeman and Fiona Smith, 493–512. Oxford: Oxford University Press, 2013.

Sahrawi Arab Democratic Republic. "Periodic Report of the Sahrawi Arab Democratic Republic to the African Commission on Human and Peoples Rights Containing All the Outstanding Reports in Accordance with Article 62 of the Charter." 2011. http://www.achpr.org/files/sessions/55th/state-reports/2nd-2002-2012/periodic_report_sahrawi_eng.pdf.

Šarčević, Susan. "Challenges to the Legal Translator." In *The Oxford Handbook of Language and Law*, edited by Peter M. Tiersma and Lawrence M. Solan, 187–99. Oxford University Press, 2012.

Šarčević, Susan. *Language and Culture in EU Law: Multidisciplinary Perspectives*. London: Routledge, 2015.

Šarčević, Susan. "Legal Translation and Translation Theory: A Receiver-Oriented Approach." *Genéve 2000: Actes*, 2000. http://www.tradulex.com/Actes2000/sarcevic.pdf.

Šarčević, Susan. "Multilingualism: The Challenge of Enlargement." *Perspectives* 9, no. 4 (January 1, 2001): 313–24. https://doi.org/10.1080/0907676X.2001.9961427.

Šarčević, Susan. *New Approach to Legal Translation*. Dordrecht: Kluwer Law International, 1997.

Schane, Sanford. *Language and the Law*. London; New York: Continuum, 2006.

Schwarz, Solomon M. "Revising the History of Russian Colonialism." *Foreign Affairs* 30, no. 3 (1952): 488–93.

Sellars, Kirsten. "Imperfect Justice at Nuremberg and Tokyo." *European Journal of International Law* 21, no. 4 (November 1, 2010): 1085–1102.

Shelton, Dinah. "Reconcilable Differences: The Interpretation of Multilingual Treaties." *Hastings International and Comparative Law Review* 20 (1997): 611–38.

Shoemaker, Matthew. "Bilingualism and Bijuralism at the Supreme Court of Canada." *Canadian Parliamentary Review* 35, no. 2 (2012): 30–35.

Sibayan, Bonifacio P. "The Intellectualization of Filipino." *International Journal of the Sociology of Language* 88, no. 1 (1991): 69–82. https://doi.org/10.1515/ijsl.1991.88.69.

Sidiropoulos and others v. Greece, Application No. 26695/95, July 10, 1998.

Silverstein, Michael. "Language Structure and Linguistic Ideology." In *The Elements: A Parasession on Linguistic Units and Levels*, edited by Paul R. Clyne, William F. Hanks, and Carol L. Hofbauer, 193–247. Chicago: Chicago Linguistic Society, 1979.

Skoma-Lux sro v. Celní ředitelství Olomouc, Case C-161/06 [2007], ECR I-10841.

Skutnabb-Kangas, Tove. *Linguistic Genocide in Education—or Worldwide Diversity and Human Rights?* London: Routledge, 2000.

Smith, Michael Peter, and Luis Eduardo Guarnizo. *Transnationalism from Below*. New Brunswick, NJ: Transaction Publishers, 1998.

Sociale Verzekeringsbank v. Van der Vecht, Case 19/67 [1967], ECR 345.

Société des Acadiens v. Association of Parents, 1 S.C.R. 549 (1986).

Sökefeld, Martin. "From Colonialism to Postcolonial Colonialism: Changing Modes of Domination in the Northern Areas of Pakistan." *The Journal of Asian Studies* 64, no. 4 (2005): 939–73.

Solan, Lawrence M. *The Language of Statutes: Laws and Their Interpretation*. Chicago: University of Chicago Press, 2010.

Solan, Lawrence M. "Multilingualism and Morality in Statutory Interpretation." *Language and Law / Linguagem e Direito* 1, no. 1 (2014): 5–21.

Solan, Lawrence M. "The Interpretation of Multilingual Statutes by the European Court of Justice." *Brooklyn Journal of International Law* 34 (2009): 277.

Song, Jae Jung. "English as an Official Language in South Korea: Global English or Social Malady?" *Language Problems and Language Planning* 35, no. 1 (2011): 35–55. https://doi.org/10.1075/lplp.35.1.03son.

Spivak, Gayatri Chakravorty. "Subaltern Studies: Deconstructing Historiography." In *The Spivak Reader: Selected Works of Gayatri Chakravorty Spivak*, edited by D. Landry and G. MacLean, 203–36. London; New York: Routledge, 1996.

Spivak, Gayatri Chakravorty. *The Post-Colonial Critic: Interviews, Strategies, Dialogues*. London; New York: Routledge, 1990.

Spooner, Lysander. *Essay on the Trial by Jury*. Boston: John P. Jewett, 1852.

Srl CILFIT and Lanificio di Gavardo SpA v. Ministry of Health (Case 283/81) ECLI:EU:C:1982:335 [1982], ECR 3415, October 6, 1982.

"Standing Committee on Justice and Human Rights: Evidence." Number 014, 2nd Session, 41st Parliament, House of Commons, Canada, March 4, 2014.

State v. Rasabout, 2015 UT 72.

"Statutory Review of Part XVII of the Criminal Code." The Standing Committee on Justice and Human Rights, House of Commons, 41st Parliament, Second Session, April 2014.

Stavenhagen, Rodolfo. *The Ethnic Question: Conflicts, Development, and Human Rights*. Tokyo: United Nations University Press, 1990.

Stephens, Mamari, and M Boyce. "The Struggle for Civic Space between a Minority Legal Language and a Dominant Legal Language: The Case of Māori and English." In *Legal Lexicography: A Comparative Perspective*, edited by Máirtín Mac Aodha, 289–319. Surrey, England; Burlington, VT: Ashgate, 2014.

Stern, David. "Ukrainians Polarised over Language Law." *BBC News*, July 5, 2012, sec. Europe. http://www.bbc.com/news/world-europe-18725849.

Stockford v. R. [2009], Q.J. No. 8369.

"Strategy for the National Languages of Finland: Government Resolution." Prime Minister's Office Publications, July 2012.

Strydom, Hennie. "Obstacles in the Way of a Multilingual South African State." In *Law, Language and the Multilingual State*, edited by Claudine Brohy, Theodorus du Plessis, Joseph-G. Turi, and José Woehrling, 31–44. Bloemfontein: SUN MeDIA, 2012.

"Studies on Translation and Multilingualism." Language and Translation in International Law and EU Law. European Commission, 2012.

Sullivan, Ruth, and Elmer A. Driedger. *Driedger on the Construction of Statutes*. 3rd edition. Markham, ON: Butterworths, 1994.

Sumitomo Chemical, Joined Cases T-22/02 and T-23/02 [2005], ECR II-04065.

Sunstein, Cass R. "On the Expressive Function of Law Special Reports." *East European Constitutional Review* 5 (1996): 66–72.

Szporluk, Roman. "The Imperial Legacy and the Soviet Nationalities." In *The Nationalities Factor in Soviet Politics and Society*, edited by Lubomyr Hajda and Mark R. Beissinger, 1–23. Boulder, CO: Westview Press, 1990.

T. P. "The Language Holding Malays, Tamils and Chinese Together." *The Economist*, January 28, 2011. http://www.economist.com/blogs/johnson/2011/01/singapore.

Tabory, Mala. *Multilingualism in International Law and Institutions*. Alphen aan den Rijn, the Netherlands; Rockville, MD: Sijthoff & Noordhoff, 1980.

Tagupa v. Odo, 843 F.Supp. 630 (D. Haw. 1994).

Tali, Hjh Masmahirah Hj Mohd. "Courtroom Discourse: A Case Study of the Linguistic Strategies in Brunei Courtrooms." In *The Use and Status of Language in Brunei Darussalam: A Kingdom of Unexpected Linguistic Diversity*, edited by Noor Azam Haji-Othman, James McLellan, and David Deterding, 135–63. Singapore: Springer, 2016.

Tannen, Deborah. "The Relativity of Linguistic Strategies: Rethinking Power and Solidarity in Gender and Dominance." In *The New Sociolinguistics Reader*, edited by Nikolas Coupland and Adam Jaworski, 168–86. Basingstoke, UK: Palgrave Macmillan, 2009.

Taylor, Charles. *Multiculturalism and the "Politics of Recognition."* Princeton, NJ: Princeton University Press, 1992.

Taylor-Leech, Kerry. "Language and Identity in East Timor." *Language Problems & Language Planning* 32, no. 2 (June 1, 2008): 153–80. https://doi.org/10.1075/lplp.32.1.04tay.

The Canadian Bar Association. "Institutional Bilingualism at Supreme Court of Canada." 2010.

The Catholic Diocese of Hong Kong Also Known as the Bishop of the Roman Catholic Church in Hong Kong Incorporation v. Secretary for Justice, FACV No. 1 of 2011.

The Commissioner of Rating & Valuation v. Chan Ho-Chin Colin, LDMR 48/2000.

The Queen v. Tam Yuk Ha [1996], MA No. 933.

Thekiso, Elma. "A Sociolinguistic Study of Communication Processes in a Court of Law in Gaborone, Botswana." PhD thesis, University of Warwick, 2001.

Thomas, Mr. Justice, Judge Roderick Evans, Winston Roddick, Nerys Arch, Gwyn Griffiths, and Catrin Huws. "Bilingual Lawmaking and Justice: A Report on the Lessons for Wales from the Canadian Experience of Bilingualism." Office of the Counsel General, April 4, 2006.

Thompson, Roger M. *Filipino English and Taglish: Language Switching from Multiple Perspectives*. Amsterdam; Philadelphia: John Benjamins, 2003.

Tierney, Stephen. *Constitutional Law and National Pluralism*. Oxford; New York: Oxford University Press, 2006.

Tierney, Stephen. "Reflections on the Evolution of Language Rights." In *Languages, Constitutionalism and Minorities*, edited by André Braën, Pierre Foucher, and Yves Le Bouthillier, 3–27. Markham, ON: LexisNexis Butterworths, 2006.

Tiersma, Peter M. "A History of the Languages of the Law." In *The Oxford Handbook of Language and Law*, edited by Peter M. Tiersma and Lawrence M. Solan, 13–26. Oxford: Oxford University Press, 2012.

Tiersma, Peter M. *Legal Language*. Chicago: University of Chicago Press, 1999.

Tolbert, Kathryn. "English Could Become Japan's Official Second Language." *The Guardian*, February 23, 2000, sec. Education. https://www.theguardian.com/education/2000/feb/23/tefl1.

Tosi, Arturo, ed. *Crossing Barriers and Bridging Cultures: The Challenges of Multilingual Translation for the European Union*. Buffalo, NY: Multilingual Matters, 2003.

Trudeau, Pierre Elliott. "The New Treason of the Intellectuals." In *Federalism and the French Canadians*, 151–81. Toronto: Macmillan, 1968.

Tryon, Darrell T., ed. *Comparative Austronesian Dictionary, An Introduction to Austronesian Studies*. Berlin; Boston: De Gruyter Mouton, 1994. https://doi.org/10.1515/9783110884012.

Tushnet, Mark. "An Essay on Rights." *Texas Law Review* 62, no. 8 (1984): 1363–1403.

Tushnet, Mark, and Larry Yackle. "Symbolic Statutes and Real Laws: The Pathologies of the Antiterrorism and Effective Death Penalty Act and the Prison Litigation Reform Act." *Duke Law Journal* 47, no. 1 (1997): 1–86.

United States v. Percheman, 32 US (7 Pet.) 51 (1833).

United States – Sunset Reviews of Anti-Dumping Measures on Oil Country Tubular Goods from Argentina, WT/DS268/AB/R, WTO Appellate Body Report, December 17, 2004.

Utah v. Rasabout, 356 P.3d 1258 (Utah 2015).

Vaillancourt, François, and Oliver Coche. "Official Language Policies at the Federal Level in Canada: Costs and Benefits in 2006." Fraser Institute, Studies in Language Policy, May 2009.

Vaillancourt, François, Oliver Coche, Marc Antoine Cadieux, and Jamie Lee Ronson. "Official Language Policies of the Canadian Provinces: Costs and Benefits in 2006." Fraser Institute, Studies in Language Policy, January 2012.

Van Klink, Bart. "Symbolic Legislation: An Essentially Political Concept." In *Symbolic Legislation Theory and Developments in Biolaw*, edited by Bart Van Klink, Britta Van Beers, and Lonneke Poort, 19–35. Legisprudence Library. Cham: Springer, 2016.

Van Parijs, Philippe. "Linguistic Justice." *Politics, Philosophy & Economics* 1, no. 1 (February 1, 2002): 59–74. https://doi.org/10.1177/1470594X02001001003.

Van Parijs, Philippe. *Linguistic Justice for Europe and for the World*. Oxford; New York: Oxford University Press, 2011.

Varennes, Fernand de. "International and Comparative Perspectives in the Use of Official Languages: Models and Approaches for South Africa." South Africa: South African Language Council Afrikaanse Taalraad, 2012.

Varennes, Fernand de. "Language as a Right in International Law: Limits and Potentials." In *Language Rights Revisited: The Challenge of Global Migration and Communication*, edited by Dagmar Richter, Ingo Richter, Reetta Toivanen, and Iryna Ulasiuk, 41–61. Oisterwijk; Berlin: Wolf Legal Publishers; Berliner Wissenschafts-Verlag, 2012.

Varennes, Fernand de. "The Existing Rights of Minorities in International Law." In *Language, a Right and a Resource: Approaching Linguistic Human Rights*, edited by Miklós Kontra, Robert Phillipson, Tove Skutnabb-Kangas, and Tibor Várady, 117–46. Budapest; New York: Central European University Press, 1999.

Venuti, Lawrence. *The Scandals of Translation: Towards an Ethics of Difference*. London: Routledge, 1998.

Veracini, Lorenzo. "Settler Colonialism and Decolonisation." *Borderlands* 6, no. 2 (2007). http://ro.uow.edu.au/lhapapers/1337/.

Wade, Robert Hunter. "The Ukraine Crisis Is Not What It Seems." *Le Monde Diplomatique (English Edition)*, 2015. https://mondediplo.com/outsidein/the-ukraine-crisis-is-not-what-it-seems.

Wai-yee, Emily Poon. "The Pitfalls of Linguistic Equivalence: The Challenge for Legal Translation." *Target. International Journal of Translation Studies* 14, no. 1 (January 1, 2002): 75–106. https://doi.org/10.1075/target.14.1.04poo.

Wallace, Mike. "Statutory Review of Part XVII of the Criminal Code: Report of the Standing Committee on Justice and Human Rights." House of Commons, Canada, April 2014.

Ward, Roger K. "The French Language in Louisiana Law and Legal Education: A Requiem." *Louisiana Law Review* 57, no. 4 (1997): 1283–1324.

Weinreich, Max. "Der YIVO Un Die Problemen Fun Undzer Zayt [The Yiddish Scientific Institute and the Problems of Our Time]." *Yivo-Bleter* 25 (1945): 3–18.

Weinstock, Daniel M. "The Antinomy of Language Policy." In *Language Rights and Political Theory*, edited by Will Kymlicka and Alan Patten, 250–70. Reprint, Oxford: Oxford University Press, 2007.

Welsh Language Commissioner. "Estimate for the Financial Year 2015–16." 2014.

Williams, Colin Haslehurst. "In Defence of Language Rights: Language Commissioners in Canada, Ireland and Wales." In *Law, Language and the Multilingual State*, edited by Claudine Brohy, Theodorus du Plessis, Joseph-G. Turi, and José Woehrling, 45–69. Bloemfontein: SUN MeDIA, 2013.

Williams, Colin Haslehurst. "Perfidious Hope: The Legislative Turn in Official Minority Language Regimes." *Regional & Federal Studies* 23, no. 1 (March 1, 2013): 101–22. https://doi.org/10.1080/13597566.2012.754353.

Williams, Colin Haslehurst. "The Role of Para-Governmental Institutions in Language Planning." In *Languages, Constitutionalism and Minorities*, edited by André Braën, Pierre Foucher, and Yves Le Bouthillier, 137–59. Markham, ON: LexisNexis Butterworths, 2006.

Williams v. Cowell [2000], 1 WLR 187.

Wimmer, Andreas, and Yuval Feinstein. "The Rise of the Nation-State across the World, 1816 to 2001." *American Sociological Review* 75, no. 5 (October 1, 2010): 764–90. https://doi.org/10.1177/0003122410382639.

Witte, Bruno de. "Language Rights: The Interaction between Domestic and European Development." In *Linguistic Diversity and European Democracy*, edited by Anne Lise Kjær and Silvia Adamo, 167–88. Surrey, England; Burlington, VT: Ashgate, 2011.

Woelk, Jens, Francesco Palermo, and Joseph Marko. *Tolerance Through Law: Self Governance and Group Rights in South Tyrol*. Boston: Martinus Nijhoff, 2008.

Wolff, Leon. "Legal Translation." In *The Oxford Handbook of Translation Studies*, edited by Kirsten Malmkjær and Kevin Windle, 228–42. Oxford: Oxford University Press, 2011.

Wong, Alia. "De-Stigmatizing Hawaii's Creole Language." *The Atlantic*, November 20, 2015. https://www.theatlantic.com/education/archive/2015/11/hawaiian-pidgin-recognized/416883/.

Wood, Philip R. *The Fall of the Priests and the Rise of the Lawyers*. Oxford; Portland, OR: Hart, 2016.

Wren, Christopher S. "Canada's Bilingual Adventure: Pardon My French." *The New York Times*, October 14, 1986, sec. World. https://www.nytimes.com/1986/10/14/world/canada-s-bilingual-adventure-pardon-my-french.html.

Wright, Sue. *Language Policy and Language Planning: From Nationalism to Globalisation*. London: Springer, 2016.

Yazar and others v. Turkey, Application No. 22723/93, April 9, 2002.

Yen, Tony. "Bi-Lingual Drafting in Hong Kong." *The Loophole (Journal of the Commonwealth Association of Legislative Counsel)*, no. 2 (August 2010): 65–69.

Yeung, Matthew W. L., and Janny H. C. Leung. "An Empirical Study of Lay Comprehension of Chinese Legal Reference Texts in Hong Kong." *International Journal of Speech Language and the Law* 22, no. 1 (May 11, 2015): 79–110. https://doi.org/10.1558/ijsll.v22i1.17224.

Yeung, Matthew W. L. and Janny H. C. Leung (forthcoming). "I Have No Idea What They Were Talking About: Miscommunication between Unrepresented Litigants and Legal Professionals."

Young Loan Arbitration [1980], 59 ILR 494.

Young, Michael. "Down with Meritocracy." *The Guardian*, June 29, 2001, sec. Politics. https://www.theguardian.com/politics/2001/jun/29/comment.

Zhiping, Liang. "Explicating Law: A Comparative Perspective of Chinese and Western Legal Culture." *Journal of Chinese Law* 3 (1989): 55.

INDEX